# Economic Geography

Economic geographers study and attempt to explain the spatial configuration of economic activities, including the production of goods and services, their transfer from one economic agent to another and their transformation into utility by consumers. The spatial configuration, which includes both the pattern of activities on the map and the relationships between activities occurring in different places, is the outcome of a vast number of distinct but interrelated decisions made by firms, households, governments and a variety of other private and public institutions. The goal of this book is to provide the student with a rigorous introduction to a diverse but logically consistent set of analytical models of the spatial decisions and interactions that drive the evolution of the economic landscape.

The book begins by explaining fundamental concepts that are critical to all topics in economic geography: the friction of distance, agglomeration, spatial interaction, market mechanisms, natural resources and production technologies. The following sections cover major areas of inquiry including multiregional economies, location theory, markets for space and systems of cities. The final section synthesizes and builds on these topics to address two trends that provide particular challenges to economic geographers today: globalization and the emergence of the knowledge economy.

This book is distinct from some other contemporary economic geography texts that eschew the presentation of models in favor of more empirical and institutional approaches. It is also distinct from earlier texts that stressed the outcomes of model development, often with a high degree of geometric complexity. Here models are developed from initial assumptions via simple graphical formats and basic algebra so as to expose the fundamental logic behind their results. In all cases, examples of real-world spatial economic phenomena are included to illustrate both the utility and limitations of models in economic geography.

**William P. Anderson** is Ontario Research Chair in Cross-Border Transportation Policy, University of Windsor, Canada.

# Economic Geography

William P. Anderson

Routledge
Taylor & Francis Group

LONDON AND NEW YORK

First published 2012
by Routledge
2 Park Square, Milton Park, Abingdon, Oxon OX14 4RN

Simultaneously published in the USA and Canada
by Routledge
711 Third Avenue, New York, NY 10017

*Routledge is an imprint of the Taylor & Francis Group, an informa business*

*British Library Cataloguing in Publication Data*
A catalogue record for this book is available from the British Library

*Library of Congress Cataloging in Publication Data*
Anderson, William P. (William Peter), 1954–
    Economic geography / William P. Anderson.
        p. cm.
    1. Economic geography. 2. Space in economics. 3. Regional economics.
    I. Title.
    HF1025.A549 2012
    330.9—dc23                                        2011049395

ISBN: (hbk) 978–0–415–70120–4
ISBN: (pbk) 978–0–415–70121–1
ISBN: (ebk) 978–0–203–11498–8

Typeset in Times New Roman
by Keystroke, Station Road, Codsall, Wolverhampton

Printed and bound in Great Britain by the MPG Books Group

**For Laksh**

# Contents

# Illustrations

**Figures**

## Maps

## Tables

# Preface

I have taught courses in economic geography at a variety of levels over the past three decades and have never found a textbook to meet my needs. Unlike some contemporary economic geographers, I see great utility in the use of formal models in the teaching and practice of economic geography. From a teaching perspective, it is not so much the outcomes of models that are of value as the thinking process that leads to their development. I therefore think it is better to develop a simple model from first principles than to present the geometrically elaborate outcomes of more complicated models. My goal is to provide the student with a set of logically consistent economic mechanisms that can help explain the locations of economic activities and the relationships between activities located in different places.

While there are many excellent textbooks on economic geography, none really fits my pedagogical approach. Some recent textbooks leave out formal models entirely. Those that include models often do so only briefly as background to more empirical and institutional approaches. Earlier textbooks that featured models generally focused on the complex spatial systems they predict rather than on their underlying logic.

I have often told my students that they will never look out the window of a plane and see hexagons on the ground. Spatial patterns in the real world are far messier (and far more interesting) than the stylized results of spatial models. But I believe that understanding the economic forces that give rise to hierarchies and to the spatial dispersion of some things and the spatial agglomeration of others can help students understand and interpret real patterns. I have written this book in the hope that there are other instructors of economic geography who share my general perspective.

The overall structure of the book and the sequence of presentation in most of the chapters derive from an introductory course in economic geography that I taught at Boston University between 1998 and 2008. I have tried to keep the mathematics at a basic level. Those topics that require calculus or anything else beyond algebra have been separated into appendices. The level of mathematics and the complexity of graphical presentation is perhaps more typical of undergraduate economics courses than of geography courses, but I have found over the years that geography students can handle it with little trouble.

I hope the approach I have taken in this book is not seen as a refutation of the valuable work that has been done by those who follow the "cultural turn" in economic geography. But I couldn't disagree more with my colleagues who suggest that the modeling approach has little practical utility. My own work these days is almost exclusively in policy research, but I call on the analytical framework conveyed in this book constantly. My highest aspiration is to convey to a new generation of students an approach to making sense of economic geography that has served me well for many years.

This book is dedicated to Professor T.R. Lakshmanan, who is known to the world as "Laksh." As my teacher, mentor, collaborator and friend for over 30 years, he is the person most responsible for my fascination with economic geography.

# Acknowledgments

This book was written over a period during which I moved from Boston University to the University of Windsor in Canada and I am grateful for the support of both institutions. At Boston, Laura Guild was a great help in the early stages of writing. I am especially grateful to Charles Burke, my research associate at Windsor, who read and commented on the entire text and contributed to every phase of producing the final manuscript.

Rob Langham, Senior Editor at Routledge, initially suggested that I write this book, and provided great support and encouragement over what turned out to be a much longer period than either of us anticipated. Also at Routledge I want to thank Editorial Assistant Simon Holt for his seemingly endless patience and courtesy over the final stages of production.

# Part I
# Fundamental concepts

# 1 Introduction

Economic geographers study and attempt to explain the spatial configuration of economic activities. Economic activities include all human actions that do one of three things: (1) produce goods and services, (2) transfer goods and services from one economic agent to another, and (3) transform goods and services into utility through acts of consumption. All of these activities must take place somewhere – but where? Why does a firm elect to locate its factory in a particular country, region, locality and site? Why is a retail outlet located on a main street, along a highway or in an enclosed mall? Why does a household choose to reside and consume in a particular city, suburb or rural county? These are the questions that economic geographers seek to answer.

The answers to these questions depend on the decisions of a large number of interacting economic agents – firms, households, governments, and various private and public institutions. Each agent's choice depends on choices that have already been made, or are anticipated, by other agents. Furthermore, all decision making is influenced and constrained by the spatial distribution of environmental resources such as minerals, climate, landforms, vegetation and natural transportation corridors.

If it sounds complicated, it is. The role of the economic geographer, however, is to perceive order in all this complexity, to untangle webs of interrelated decision making and to elicit some basic principles that drive the evolution of the economic landscape. One way to do this is by building models, which attempt to abstract away from superfluous details and incidental interactions in order to focus on the main driving forces of the spatial economy. One must be careful though, complexity may in itself have implications for the evolutions of spatial patterns. Excessive abstraction may preclude an understanding of such implications.

Ultimately, the method of economic geography as it is described in this book is to use models to generate hypotheses that can then be tested against empirical observation. This, in essence, is the scientific method.[1] In order to generate hypotheses, one must ask rather specific questions. Before we can define such questions, we must ask a rather broad question that must be clearly answered before any analysis in economic geography may go forward. The question is *what do we mean by space?*

### Discrete and continuous space

We may envision space as being either discrete or continuous. Discrete space defines a finite set of non-overlapping spatial units that make up a larger study area. They may be called regions, zones, tracts or whatever the analyst wishes. Each unit has a boundary that encloses a known area, but no further geographical detail is assigned to it. We consider the variation in income across regions, but not variations within regions. We may attempt to predict flows of people, goods or money among zones, but we are not concerned with the flows among points within a zone.

In all but a very few cases, there will be no natural division of space into units.[2] Thus, the first step in any analysis based in discrete space is the division of the study area by a set of boundaries which the analyst must provide. How can we avoid making boundaries that are either arbitrary or subjective? The traditional approach of geographers has been to define either of two types of regions: *formal regions* and *functional regions*. A formal region is defined as enclosing an area that is relatively homogeneous in one or a few characteristics. For example, the American Corn Belt is a formal region because it defines an area within which a relatively homogeneous type of agriculture – cultivation of corn and soybeans to feed to swine or cattle – is practiced. Anyone familiar with American agriculture has a rough idea where the Corn Belt is, but a geographer seeks to draw a boundary to determine where it is and where it isn't. This may be done by including all areas in which the majority of farms are planted mostly in corn and soybeans. The most common formal regions are political jurisdictions such as nations, provinces, states, counties, municipalities, etc. All points within such regions are homogeneous in the sense that they are under the control of a common government.

In Figure 1.1a, we have a map of symbols representing different types of economic activities occurring at different points in space. The different symbols might represent different types of farms (grain, orchard, dairy), different classes of land users (residential, commercial, industrial) or households of different economic class (low income, middle income, high income). In Figure 1.1b, a geographer has superimposed a set of boundaries to define three regions – each with a dominant symbol – on the map.

Functional regions are defined not in terms of homogeneity but rather in terms of *spatial interaction*. Spatial interaction, which is one of the most critical concepts in economic geography, refers to the movement of people, goods, money or information from one place to another. A functional region is defined such that spatial interaction occurs more intensely within its borders than across them. The most common type of functional region is the metropolitan area. A metropolitan area may include a dense, low-income inner city neighborhood and a low-density, high-income suburb, along with many places that lie somewhere in between. Thus, if anything, metropolitan areas are noteworthy for their heterogeneity. Spatial interaction in the forms of commuting flows, shopping trips, deliveries of goods, phone calls and many more, however, define the metropolitan area as a functional whole. (Box 1 explains how metropolitan area boundaries used in the U.S. census are drawn based on commuting flows.)

---

*Box 1* **Defining functional regions: Metropolitan Statistical Areas in the United States**

When we make reference to a city, we may be referring to two very different entities. The first is a legally defined territory within boundaries called "city limits" and under the authority of a mayor and city council. Geographers usually call this the "political city." Referring to the definitions in chapter 1, this is an example of a formal region. The second is a geographically broader concept that includes the political city and surrounding communities that make up a politically and socially integrated urban region. Geographers refer to this as the "metropolitan area." Since the level of integration can be measured via various forms of spatial interaction, the metropolitan area is a functional region.

Sometimes our meaning is clear from the context. If we speak about the mayor of Detroit, we are referring to the political city. But if we speak about the Detroit automotive production complex, we are referring to facilities scattered across a broad urban field and mostly outside Detroit's city limits, so we mean the Detroit metropolitan area. We can generally make our meaning clear by referring to the "City of Detroit" and "Metro Detroit." Also, some cities have local names to refer to the metropolitan area, such as Greater Boston, Chicagoland, the GTA (Greater Toronto Area) or the Bay Area (San Francisco, Oakland and surrounding communities.)

Economic geographers, economists, market researchers and transportation analysts generally agree that the metropolitan area is a more useful spatial definition on which to measure things like employment, production and industrial composition. Therefore, they would like to see demographic and economic data reported at the metropolitan level, rather than just for political jurisdictions. In order for statistical agencies to provide information in that form, however, they must first draw lines on the map to determine exactly which places, peoples and things are located in a particular metropolitan area and which are not.

The U.S. government has been collecting and publishing data at the metropolitan level for about 60 years. For this purpose, it has defined 366 Metropolitan Statistical Areas (MSAs) ranging in size from just under 19 million for the New York–Northern New Jersey–Long Island MSA to just over 50,000 for the Carson City, Nevada MSA. Delineation of the MSAs is a major task not only because there are so many of them but also because their boundaries need to be readjusted over time to allow for the spread of the urban field around most cities ever further into the periphery.

The U.S. Office of Management and Budget (2000) sets the rules for defining MSAs. They start from two basic geographical entities: urbanized areas and counties. An urbanized area is some geographic entity (usually a political city) defined by the U.S. Census Bureau as having an identifiable center, an overall population density above 1,000 per square mile and a population of over 50,000. Only where an urbanized area is present is an MSA defined. Counties, of which there are more than 3,000 in the U.S., are the building blocks from which MSAs are assembled. The county in which the urbanized area is located is designated as the central county. In line with our definition of a functional region, additional counties are then added to the MSA on the basis of a key measure of spatial interaction: commuting patterns. The rule is that a county is included if it is contiguous to (that means touching) the central county or any other county in the MSA and if either 25 percent of its outbound commuting trips end in the central county or 25 percent of its inbound commuting trips originate in the central county (it is usually the former). If the county has a better than 25 percent commuting link with the central counties of two different MSAs it is assigned to the one with the stronger link. Minor variations on these rules are permitted to take account of unusual local circumstances, but the idea is to keep definition as consistent as possible across all 366 MSAs. The assignment of counties to MSAs is revised after every decennial census.

Map B1.1 shows the Chicago–Naperville–Joliet MSA. With a population of over 9 million it includes 14 counties that spill across state lines to include parts of Illinois, Indiana and Wisconsin. Cook County, which includes the City of Chicago, has more than half the total MSA population. As the map shows, when the U.S. government first defined a metropolitan area around Chicago in 1950, it included only six counties: five in Illinois and one in Indiana. Given the rule for defining the composition of MSAs, this implies that people now typically commute much longer distances to jobs in Cook County than they did in the past.

Figure 1.2a shows a set of arrows that represent daily commuting flows. The arrows begin at the residential area of commute trip origins and end at the location of the workplace destinations. In Figure 1.2b, a geographer has defined a functional region based on the commuting flows. While some flows cross the border of this region, the great majority of flows that begin within the region also end within it.

Three types of analyses can be done using discrete space. The first addresses variations in the values of one or more variables across spatial units. From a purely descriptive perspective, it might be enough to display such spatial differentiation on a map. We may go a step further and try to explain the variations by relating the value of one variable measured for each spatial unit to one or more variables measured for the same units. For example, we may be able to explain energy use per household in each U.S. state in terms of climate variables and socioeconomic variables, both of which vary across states as well.

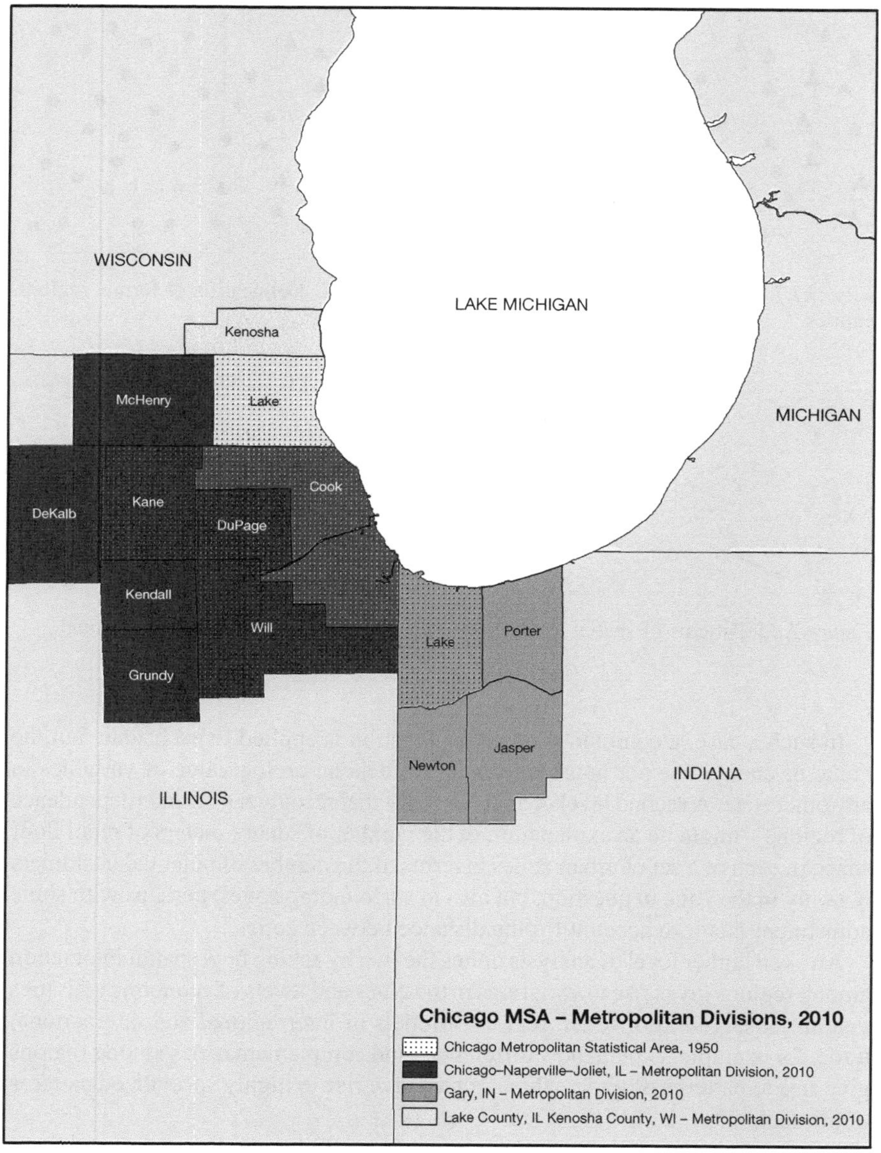

WISCONSIN

Kenosha

LAKE MICHIGAN

MICHIGAN

McHenry    Lake

Cook

DeKalb    Kane

DuPage

Kendall

Will    Lake    Porter

Grundy

Newton    Jasper

INDIANA

ILLINOIS

**Chicago MSA – Metropolitan Divisions, 2010**

Chicago Metropolitan Statistical Area, 1950

Chicago–Naperville–Joliet, IL – Metropolitan Division, 2010

Gary, IN – Metropolitan Division, 2010

Lake County, IL Kenosha County, WI – Metropolitan Division, 2010

*Map B1.1*  Chicago Metropolitan Statistical Area 1950, 2010

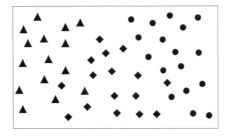

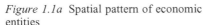

*Figure 1.1a* Spatial pattern of economic entities

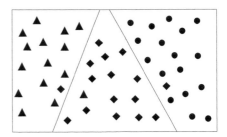

*Figure 1.1b* Delineation of formal regions

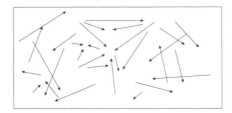

*Figure 1.2a* Patterns of spatial interaction

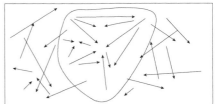

*Figure 1.2b* Delineation of functional region

In such a case, a common form of explanation is applied to each state, but the value of energy use per household does not depend on the value of variables in any other state. A second level of analysis – one that recognizes the interdependence of regions – might be an explanation of the number of square meters of retail floor space in each of a set of urban zones in terms of the number of potential customers not only in the zone in question, but also in surrounding zones, perhaps with some adjustment factor to account for the distance between zones.

An even higher level of analysis unites the two by asking how spatial interaction among regions gives rise to variations in the types and levels of economic activities that are observed in different regions. Models of interregional and international trade, for example, explain how differences and complementarities among regions give rise to patterns of trade, which in turn give rise to highly specialized patterns of production.

Continuous space is defined as comprising an infinite number of points that, of themselves, consume no space. This is the standard definition of space from geometry. Most of the models in this book will represent economic phenomena occurring in two-dimensional space – that is, in map space. In two-dimensional space each point is represented by a pair of coordinates $(x, y)$. On occasion, we will use the concept of one-dimensional space, whereby all economic phenomena occur on a straight line, as a useful simplification.

There are three types of analyses that can be conducted in continuous space: those dealing with the location of a point, those dealing with patterns of points, and those dealing with the division of space into subspaces.

One classic point location model deals with a manufacturing firm's decision over where to locate a single factory, given that it already knows the locations of its input sources and of the markets to which it must deliver its outputs. Weber's Triangle[3] (shown in Figure 1.3a) depicts a firm that must choose its best possible location P within a triangle defined by the location of the market C and of two material inputs M1 and M2. As we will see, each corner of the triangle exerts a locational pull on P. The strengths of these pulls depend on the relative transportation costs of inputs and outputs.

Analysis of point patterns is a more complicated business because we have to consider more than one economic agent whose decisions are interrelated. At a preliminary level of analysis, we can suppose either that each agent is attracted to other agents, meaning that he prefers a location close to someone else's location, or that each agent is repelled by other agents, meaning that he prefers the location that is as far as possible from other agents. Even these simple notions will tell us something about pattern. If each agent's location is represented as a point in two-dimensional space (Figure 1.4), then a clustered pattern will emerge if agents attract one another and a dispersed pattern will emerge if they repel one another. Of course, the agents may be completely indifferent to one another, in which case a random pattern is most likely.

We have already considered one case of the division of space: the methods of regionalization shown in Figures 1.1 and 1.2. Here, dividing space allows us to move from a reality of continuous space to a simpler depiction of reality in discrete space. More interesting cases of the division of space occur when we think of the economic agent not as a point in space but as a consumer of space. For example, we use up space in the process of feeding ourselves. The production of food takes up space (a farm plot), as does its transportation to market (a road or rail corridor), as does its sale to households (supermarket lot), as does its consumption (a residential lot). Manufacturing, retail, recreational activities, public utilities and all other providers or consumers of goods and services need to use space. In general,

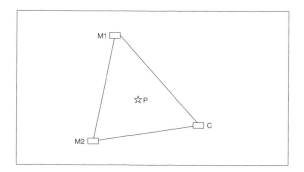

*Figure 1.3a*
Weber's Triangle

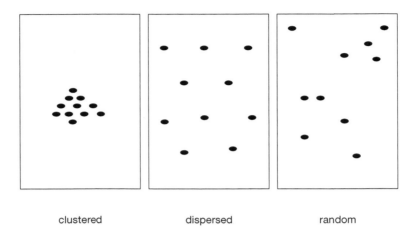

clustered                    dispersed                    random

*Figure 1.4* Point patterns

they need *exclusive* use of space, which means that any unit of space will ultimately be controlled by a single user or class of user. In a market economy, therefore, there is a market for space which, within institutional constraints, decides who gets to use what space.

The allocations of this market can be seen in the division of land in a metropolitan area into residential, industrial and commercial uses, or in the division of agricultural land into fruit and vegetable farming, grain farming and pastures. Not all markets are perfect, however, and markets for space are especially prone to failure when the occupation of a unit of space by one user has a negative impact on the use of an adjacent unit by a different user. For example, the market may allocate to a piggery a plot of land that is adjacent to a health spa. Such market failure may justify public sector land-use control. But the power of the public sector to exert such control does not diminish, but rather enhances, the need to understand the market forces that are at play.

## Economics and economic geography

At this point, the reader might wonder whether economic geography is anything more or less than the extension of economic theory into the spatial dimension. Is there a difference between an economic geographer and a spatial economist?

The short answer is that there is a great deal of overlap and complementarity between the work of economists and economic geographers, but there are important differences in emphasis and general orientation. One important difference that merits discussion at the outset of this book is that, while economists are generally satisfied developing models in an abstract, homogeneous space, geographers are ultimately interested in how economic processes play out in *differentiated space*.

Modern economists use simplifying assumptions to create an idealized world in which economic relationships can be seen more clearly. In the case of spatial economic models, this generally means an initial assumption that space is undifferentiated. Movement in all directions is equally costly and there are no variations in costs or productivity arising strictly from the characteristics of the point in space at which an activity occurs. This approach has been used to develop powerful models of how economic agents interact in space,[4] many of which will be described in this book.

The priorities and strategies of the economic geographer, however, are somewhat different. Ultimately the economic geographer would like to look at a map of economic activity at a regional, continental or global scale and try to explain how it came to look the way it does. To the geographer, it is never enough to explain how things would look in an ideal world. Such an explanation might be a useful step toward understanding real patterns, but the geographer must bear in mind that space is never homogeneous. Traveling a mile in one direction will generally have completely different implications from traveling a mile in another direction. Economic geography, therefore, deals with differentiated space.[5]

The importance of differentiated space derives in large part from the geographer's interest in the natural environment. Any locational decision must recognize the spatial variations in natural conditions that may affect the success of an economic enterprise. Choosing a location 100 miles to the north may mean a colder climate, while 100 miles south may mean a warmer climate. Moving west may lead to an arid plain, while moving east may lead to steamy lowland. Elements of natural environments provide natural corridors for and barriers to spatial interaction. No one could hope to explain the spatial pattern of economic activity in North America or Continental Europe without first knowing the locations of the coasts, mountain ranges and the courses of major rivers.

For a simple illustration let us return to Weber's Triangle. In Figure 1.3b, we have shown that the point of consumption C lies at the confluence of two rivers A and B. The source of the first input M1 lies along the course of river A, while the source of the second M2 lies along the course of river B. Suppose now that we are considering a society where there are two transportation options: cheap transportation along waterways and slow and costly transportation along poor roads. (This was in fact the situation in the U.S. and the U.K. before the introduction of the railroads.) The cost of traveling between M1 and M2 may be ten times as high as traveling the same distance between M1 and C. The likely location of the firm is now very different from the initial case because virtually any point on the line segments M1–C and C–M2 will be superior to points in the interior of the triangle. This simple model illustrates an important principle of economic geography: natural transportation corridors tend to concentrate industrial activities within narrow spatial bands.

*Figure 1.3b*
Weber's Triangle

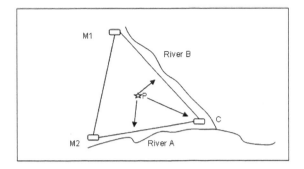

The notion of differentiated space derives not only from the natural environment, but also from the relative inertia of location decisions that have been made in the past. Location decisions by firms or households generally require substantial capital investments that are immobile once they are put in place. A household must have a house, a retailer must have a store, a manufacturer must have a factory, etc. Once a household is established at a particular location it cannot move its house. If the household moves on to another place some other household will take its old house in the original location. The same is true for firms. Thus, with the exception of pioneers in a new land, the locational options of households and firms are affected by locational choices made in the past.

Also, there is a variety of immobile capital investments known as *infrastructure* that is used collectively by households and firms in a particular locale. Infrastructure includes roads, water and sewage systems, electricity distribution systems, airports and many more. Institutions such as schools, museums, parks and business organizations also confer benefits collectively to all in their general vicinity. Once major infrastructural and institutional investments have been made in a particular place, that place becomes more attractive for firms and households that are making location decisions. In short, space is differentiated not only by variability in the physical environment but also by patterns of economic activity that have been set down in the past.

There is another more subtle way that space is differentiated by the history of human activity. This form of differentiation arises not from physical investments but rather from a long history of human interaction that results in the creation of a peculiar local culture. Geographers refer to this as the *sense of place*. While the genesis and dynamics of this phenomenon are the business of cultural geographers, economic geographers must be concerned with it because it affects spatial decision making. A household or firm contemplating a move over a relatively long distance must give up its sense of place. This is an intangible cost that must be weighed against economic benefits expected from the move. Similarly, when a firm or household moves into a new area it must adopt the peculiar local culture, with all the attendant costs and benefits.

What implications does the recognition of differentiated space have for the way economic geographers look at the world? Most importantly, it implies that the economic landscape must be seen to evolve over time. Just as an organism evolves through marginal changes in its structure, the economic landscape evolves through processes of redistribution and growth occurring over an existing pattern. Just as a change in climate may accelerate the pace of natural evolution a new technology or change in social structure may accelerate the evolution of the economic landscape, resulting in dramatic change over relatively short periods of time.

The key point is that spatial economic processes never occur on a clean slate, as is often the case for the static equilibrium models of economic theory. This does not mean that such models are not useful for the study of economic geography – in fact, much of this book will be devoted to such models – but rather that they are never sufficient to achieve the goals of economic geography.

## Site and situation

The essence of how economic geographers seek to explain spatial patterns is captured in the simple conceptual framework of site and situation attributes. This framework does not constitute a formal mathematical model in its own right. It is not capable of making specific predictions of the location of a particular economic activity, nor does it provide any quantitative measure for assessing the relative advantage of different locations. It does, however, offer a way to organize and compare the various drivers of economic location. It therefore serves as a useful starting point for the analysis of any spatial economic phenomenon.

We start by defining site and situation attributes. Site attributes are characteristics of a specific location that affect its suitability for a particular economic activity and that can be compared across potential locations. These include characteristics of the natural environment but may also include local economic factors, such as the existence of port infrastructure or electricity supply. Situation attributes refer to the accessibility of a location to the location of other economic activities or resources with which the economic activity in question will need to interact. (We can think of situation attributes as the "access to" attributes.)

Consider the case of an aspiring agriculturalist who wants to choose a location at which to rent or purchase land to start a farm. What does she have to consider in making this choice? Naturally, it is important that the location has fertile soil on level terrain, that it has adequate rainfall and a sufficiently long growing season. These are all site attributes. If the farmer only considers site attributes, however, she may choose a remote location that is only appropriate for subsistence farming. If she is to sell her produce she must have access to a market. She must also have reasonably good access to suppliers of seed, fertilizer and agricultural machinery. If she is to hire labor during the harvest period she may benefit from locating within commuting range of a population center from which she can hire temporary workers. These "access to" attributes are situation attributes. The success of the farm will ultimately depend about equally on the site and situation attributes of its location.

Site and situation attributes are not necessarily independent. Consider a location on the banks of a large river. Imagine that the site has an appropriate place for construction of marine facilities and that it is set on sufficiently high land to protect it from periodic flooding. These site attributes favor the development of a market town where goods can be trans-shipped from land to water transportation. However, the success of such a market town depends upon whether it has a sufficiently productive hinterland producing agricultural or other goods for shipment, and whether the river leads on to any important markets. Thus, the right situation attributes are necessary for the site attributes to be of any value.

In a market economy, site and situation attributes interact in another important way. One of the most important site attributes to be considered for the location of any firm or household is the price (or rent) of land. For example, a farmer may be better off with land of only moderate fertility if it is available at a much lower price than land of high fertility. As we will see in chapters 17–19, the price of land at a particular location depends in large part on its accessibility to other desirable locations. Thus, an attractive situation attribute (good accessibility) may be offset by an unattractive site attribute (land price) through the mechanism of land markets.

## Organization of the book

This book is organized into six parts. Part I introduces a number of fundamental concepts that are essential to analysis in economic geography. These include the friction of distance, agglomeration, markets, spatial interaction, networks, and environmental resources.

Part II is devoted to analysis of discrete space. A key theme here will be the notion of comparative advantage which can be applied to interregional and international trade. Models of trade based in agglomeration concepts will also be covered, as will migration and growth in a multiregional economy.

Part III deals with the location choices of firms and households in continuous space. In addition to addressing the location choice of a single agent, we also consider strategic location whereby location decisions of two or more agents interact.

Part IV introduces models of markets for space. These models were first developed to explain agricultural pattern but have since been extended to explain urban land-use patterns. Insights from these models are applied to case studies of modern real estate markets.

Part V broadens the scope to analyze the spatial pattern of cities at the national or continental scale. Abstract *central place* models that describe hierarchies of cities with nested market areas are introduced. We then consider what happens when we move from an abstract world to a more complex world of differentiated space.

Finally, Part VI recasts economic geography in the emerging global information economy. As the production of physical goods becomes less important relative to the production of information goods, it is reasonable to ask whether concepts from economic geography that focus on the friction of distance and the transportation of goods are still relevant. The answer is that these concepts are still relevant, but many spatial processes that are of increasing importance – global information networks, global personal transportation, trade in services and many more – provide a challenge for economic geography in the twenty-first century.

# 2    The friction of distance

Distance is the amount of separation between two things in space. Overcoming distance is one of the most important of all human tasks. All activities require being in a particular place at a particular time. Different activities must be done in different places. Since we all do a variety of things every day, we are constantly engaged in overcoming distance. To the extent that the need to overcome distance places limits on what we can achieve within any time interval, our economic productivity, level of social interaction and even our ability to enjoy leisure hours are all retarded to some degree by the friction of distance.

People can overcome distance in three ways. The first two involve transportation. They can move from the place where they are to the place where they want to be, or they can have something physically moved from the place where it is to the place where they are. These two options involve personal and freight transportation respectively. For certain types of activities, however, it may not be necessary to move anything but information. Sharing a conversation on the phone, placing a business order via the Internet or watching a remote sporting event via satellite television are all examples of human activities that occur across distance and depend on communication services. Transportation and communication are both friction-reducing technologies.

## Transportation costs

We turn first to transportation. Economic geographers have traditionally expressed the friction of distance in terms of the monetary cost of transportation. There are many examples in this book. The location choice of a household or a firm will depend on how spatially varying transportation costs affect their levels of utility and profit respectively. The amount of trade that occurs between two countries will depend in part on how much the cost of transportation offsets any potential benefits from trade. Spatial patterns of agriculture depend in part on differences in transportation costs across commodities. Thus, nothing is more fundamental in economic geography than an understanding of transportation costs.

It is generally true that transportation costs increase with distance. The farther a person or good has to travel, the more it will cost. But the relationship is not necessarily simple. It does not necessarily cost twice as much to move 2 miles as

1 mile, and it does not necessarily cost the same to move a mile south as to move a mile east. There are even circumstances where it may cost less to go a long distance than a short distance. For example, plane tickets from New York to Los Angeles often cost less than tickets between, say, Buffalo and Omaha. (The structure of infrastructure networks also affects the relationship between straight-line distance and transportation costs. See the Appendix at the end of this chapter.)

The cost of most trips has two components: terminal cost and line-haul cost. Terminal cost covers transportation services that occur at the beginning or end of a trip. These include loading or unloading goods, luggage or passengers; institutional costs such as customs and taxes; and the rental on the space the vehicle occupies while not moving. The critical thing about the terminal cost is that it is charged on a per trip basis.

Line-haul cost is charged on a per-mile basis. It includes the cost of fuels, labor and physical depreciation of the vehicle. Since the cost of each trip includes both terminal and line-haul cost, the schedule of costs for trips of different distances appears as in Figure 2.1. Note that, because of the fixed terminal cost, the cost per mile is lower for long trips than for short ones. Thus, it costs less than twice as much to make a trip that is twice as long.

Various modes of transportation are available and they differ in terms of the relative values of terminal and line-haul costs. For example, it may be possible to ship a consignment of freight by road (truck), rail or water. Which will have the lowest cost? As Figure 2.2 indicates, the answer may depend on the length of the trip. Road transport generally has a low terminal cost, but because of its lower energy efficiency and greater labor intensity it has a higher line-haul cost than rail or water. As the hypothetical figure shows, road transport would be cheapest over a short distance, but rail would be cheaper for intermediate trips. Because of its high terminal and low line-haul costs, water transport would be cheapest over the longest distances. As Figure 2.3 shows, we can think of the lower envelope of the

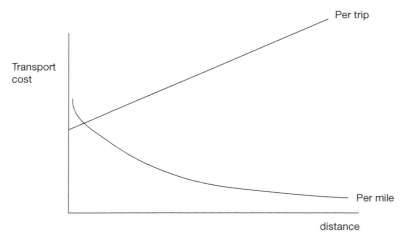

*Figure 2.1* Transportation cost per trip and per mile

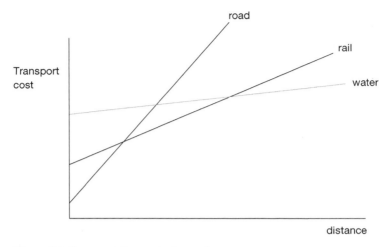

*Figure 2.2* Transportation costs for modes

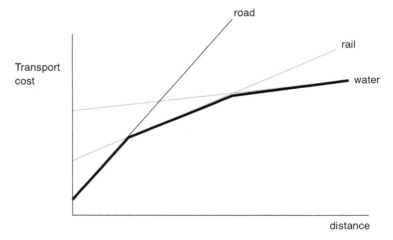

*Figure 2.3* Effective transport cost

modal transport costs as an effective overall transport cost schedule. It is clear that, even if each mode has a constant line-haul rate, the effective transport costs are increasing at a decreasing rate with distance.

   Naturally, factors other than cost may affect the choice of mode. Road transportation is more flexible, both in terms of the scope of points in space that it can serve and in terms of the range of load sizes that can be accommodated efficiently. Water transportation is sometimes unavailable. Also, the costs portrayed in Figures 2.1 to 2.3 are the costs to the providers of transportation services and, for various reasons that we will discuss later, the price paid by the consumer does not always

*Table 2.1* Average length of haul for U.S. domestic
freight shipments by mode, 2001

| Mode | Miles |
| --- | --- |
| Truck | 485 |
| Class 1 rail | 859 |
| Internal water | 476 |
| Coastwise water | 1,228 |

*Source*: Bureau of Transportation Statistics (2006: Table 1–35).
*Note*: Class 1 rail includes only rail carriers with annual revenue
in excess of $250 million.

reflect that cost. However, as Table 2.1 shows, it is generally true that road transport
is used for shorter shipments than rail and coastal water is used for very long
shipments. (Internal water, which includes canals and navigable rivers, has a shorter
average distance because of the limited extent of its network.)

What about air freight? Terminal costs for air freight are as high as or higher
than for water, rail or truck and line-haul costs are *much* higher. So there is no
distance over which air freight transportation is cheapest. Yet the proportion of
total freight – both domestic and international – that goes by air is increasing every
year (as shown in Table 2.2.). The reason, of course, is clear. Some goods are
shipped by air for the same reason that some people travel by air: because it is faster.

For many types of freight, the best solution is to move the goods part of the
way by one mode and part by another. This practice, which is called *intermodal
transportation*, is explored in Box 2.

*Table 2.2* Value and share of air freight in total U.S. domestic shipments

| Year | Value of shipments (billions of dollars) | Share of total (%) |
| --- | --- | --- |
| 1993 | 139 | 2.4 |
| 2002 | 265 | 3.1 |

*Source*: Bureau of Transportation Statistics (2006: Table 1–52).

## *Box 2* Containerization and intermodal freight transportation

Figure 2.2 shows that rail and water transportation are cheaper than trucking
for relatively long-distance shipments. But what if the goods have to be
delivered someplace where ships and trains cannot go? In fact, there are
relatively few situations where something can be moved all the way from
origin to destination on a train or ship. (Examples include the shipment of
coal on a rail line extending directly from the mine mouth to an electric

generating station and the shipment of crude oil by ship from an offshore production facility to a tidewater refinery.) Most of the time, goods must be transferred from a train or a ship to a truck for final delivery. In other words, most shipments are *intermodal*.

We define intermodal freight transportation as the practice of combining two or more modes to deliver goods from origin to destination. To give an example, consider how a pair of socks made in China finds its way to the aisles of your local Wal-Mart or other retailer. For this example, suppose you are located somewhere in the American Midwest. The socks were produced in a factory that is probably located in a coastal Chinese city. They are shipped by truck from the factory to a port where they are loaded onto a ship bound for a North American Pacific port such as Long Beach, Los Angeles, Seattle or Vancouver. Because they are still a long way from their final destination, it would be more economical to move them by train than by truck, but your Wal-Mart is not connected to a rail line. The solution is to move them by rail to somewhere close to their final destination and then transfer them to a truck for final delivery. In fact, they don't reach their ultimate destination until you buy them and transport them by car from the store to your house. Once they reach your house they can get on to your feet.

The problem with this process is that a new set of terminal costs are incurred at every point of transfer between modes. It may be cheaper to move goods from California to Illinois by train than by truck, but aren't the savings nullified by the cost of unloading the goods from a rail car and reloading them into a truck trailer? The key to making intermodal transportation economically viable is to reduce the cost of intermodal transfers, which has been accomplished over the past 50 years by means of *containerization*. Up until the 1950s, ships arriving at docks had to be unloaded by attaching ropes or cables to palettes of crates and hauling them out of the ship's hold. (You can get an idea of how this worked by watching the classic movie *On the Waterfront* starring Marlon Brando.) Then the goods go into warehouses, from which they are eventually loaded onto trains or trucks.

A man in the freight business named Malcolm McLean had a simple but brilliant idea. Why not pack all goods into large steel boxes, about the size of a truck trailer or a box car, before they are put on the ship. These boxes – called containers – ride on the deck of the ship rather than down in the hold. When they arrive at a port they are lifted by a giant crane from the deck and dropped directly onto a specially designed rail car or truck trailer and moved immediately on to their destination. All of the handling at the port, which once involved teams of stevedores, is handled by a single skilled crane operator. Containerization saves time as well as money because goods don't dwell in dockside warehouses. Not only has containerization revolutionized the marine, rail and road shipping industries, it also opened the door for globalized production by radically cutting the cost of shipping goods over very long distances. It also proves that not all economic innovations are "high tech" since it was easily implemented using existing technologies. The social costs of implementation were great, however, as many thousands of dock workers were made redundant. (Read *The Box* by Marc Levinson, 2005, for a fascinating history of the containerization revolution.)

To return to our example, an entire container load of the Chinese socks may not be needed at a single store. So containers are unpacked at distribution centers that are usually located at the end of the rail component of the trip. There, container loads are broken down and loaded onto trucks destined for individual stores. Given the volume of goods moving in containers globally, clusters of giant distribution centers have grown up at locations where rail lines come together with major highways such as the huge CenterPoint Intermodal Center on over 6,000 acres in Joliet, Illinois near Chicago. Despite being located thousands of miles from any ocean, this "inland port" serves as a gateway for global goods to the American heartland.

## Transportation and time

For both personal transportation and freight transportation, choices depend not only on cost but also on the speed of movement. For passengers, the decision whether to take a trip or not, where to go among a number of potential destinations and what mode of transportation to use will depend in part on how long the trip will take. Many people find all forms of travel arduous, so the less time spent traveling the better. Even for those who don't mind travel, time is a finite resource and any time spent traveling is time that cannot be spent doing something else: working, exercising, watching television, sleeping or whatever. So, other things being equal, most people prefer a brief trip to one that takes a long time. Time does not have a single intrinsic value. For example, some people may be more willing to spend time in their cars than on a bus. Those people may choose to drive rather than take the bus, even if the time involved is the same and the cost is greater for the car. (Of course, there are also those who would rather spend time on the bus where they can read or sleep – things that are not advisable while driving.)

At first, it might seem that speed is less important for freight transportation than it is for personal transportation. After all, a ton of coal doesn't suffer from the rigors of travel and a consignment of textiles doesn't have anything else that it would prefer to be doing with its time. But speed can be very important for freight because the value of some goods declines rapidly with time. An obvious example is a perishable commodity such as tomatoes or fish. The faster it can be moved to the market, the more it will be worth. Another example is a good that involves time-sensitive information. If a copy of the *New York Times* were shipped to London by sea, it would be worthless by the time it arrived, so it must be shipped by air.

Even something that is non-perishable or does not include time-sensitive information may have greater value if it can be transported quickly. Suppose a machine in a factory in Texas breaks down and the part needed to repair it can only be found in Chicago. Since the company that owns the machine is losing money for every hour it is out of service, it will be willing to pay a high premium to get the part delivered in a matter of hours rather than days.

Besides speed, we can define another important attribute of transportation that involves time. *Timeliness* is the ability of a transportation service to get the person or good where it needs to be when it needs to be there. Consider your commute to work or school. You need to plan your trip so you will not be late, but at the same time you do not want to be too early. If your mode of transportation is undependable – a highway with intermittent traffic jams, a bus that doesn't keep to schedule, a bicycle that gets flat tires – you will be forced to act conservatively and arrive too early on good travel days in order to avoid arriving too late on bad days. You would much prefer a timely mode of travel – that is one that gets you to work in the same amount of time every day. (In statistical language, we can measure the speed of your commute as inversely related to the average travel time and the timeliness as inversely related to the variance of the travel time.)

Timeliness can be just as important for freight. For example, an auto assembly plant may take delivery of hundreds of different components provided by dozens of different suppliers. If any component runs out, the entire assembly line may be shut down. If deliveries are not timely, the plant must maintain large inventories just in case components don't arrive on time. In recent years, most auto producers have adopted a *just-in-time* inventory system, whereby suppliers are required to deliver the components to the assembly plant within narrow time windows – in other words, just in time to go into the assembly line. This economizes on warehouse space and on inventory carrying costs (interest and insurance) but puts much greater burdens on suppliers to use timely transportation services. This system isn't limited to manufacturers. Mass retailers like Wal-Mart have discovered that they can increase profits by using as much of their floor space for sales as possible, which means using as little as possible for storerooms. In order to reduce the need for storage space, these retailers require suppliers to deliver consumer goods just in time to replenish stock on the sales floor. Again, timely transportation is the key ingredient.

To sum up, we would all like to overcome distance in ways that are cheap, fast and timely. But in general, transportation that is fast, timely or both is not cheap. Thus, a variety of personal and freight transportation options are offered in the market to serve the needs of those with different preferences or requirements in terms of economy, speed and timeliness. As an example, Table 2.3 gives prices that were quoted by UPS to deliver a 5 lb package from Los Angeles to Boston.[1] Here all shipments to be delivered within two days are by air, while shipments to be delivered in three or four days use ground shipment. If you send a package tonight, it costs nearly ten times as much to have it delivered first thing tomorrow morning as to have it delivered in four days. As an indication of the value of timeliness, UPS believes some of its customers would be willing to pay over 50 percent more to receive the package at 8 AM than at 10:30 AM!

*Table 2.3* Delivery cost for a 5 lb package shipped from
Los Angeles to Boston via UPS (September, 2006)

| Delivery time | Cost |
| --- | --- |
| Next day, 8 AM | $89.27 |
| Next day, 10:30 AM | $55.93 |
| Next day, 3 PM | $51.36 |
| Second day, 10:30 AM | $29.25 |
| Second day, 5 PM | $25.74 |
| Third day, 5 PM | $21.18 |
| Fourth day, 5 PM | $9.74 |

## Communication and the information economy

Communication is another way of overcoming distance. Just about every human activity involves some sort of movement in space. Sometimes it is the movements of molecules and sometimes it is the movements of bytes. Moving molecules – that is, stuff with mass – is the business of transportation. Moving bytes – the building blocks of digital information – is the business of electronic communications. It was only with the introduction of the telegraph and telephone that the movement of information beyond shouting distance was divorced from moving some physical stuff such as a letter or a book. During the twentieth century, the range of technologies available for overcoming distance via communications expanded, while the costs plummeted. At the same time, the cost and difficulty of communications became increasingly disconnected from distance. The most important information format at the dawn of the twenty-first century, the Internet, is almost completely insensitive to distance. It is as cheap and easy, and for all practical purposes as fast, to send email to the other side of the world as to the next county. At least for the type of communication that can be achieved via the Internet, the friction of distance is approaching zero.

Not only has communication gotten cheaper and faster, but the scope of information transfer has expanded. Very limited information can be conveyed in a phone call. The Internet allows words, pictures and databases to be transferred from place to place almost instantaneously, and permits people to interact in either an asynchronous or real-time environment. This makes possible forms of intense and productive interaction across space such as telecommuting, global interactive design and outsourcing of information inputs – all without moving people or goods.

At the same time there has been a complementary transformation from a materials-based economy to an *information economy*. The information economy can be described in a simple phrase: "more information and less stuff." When you buy a bag of charcoal a substantial proportion of the cost you pay is attributable to the materials that went into it: wood to make the charcoal, paper for the bag, etc. (Other cost components include the costs of processing, transportation, marketing and the retailer's markup.) When you buy a processed food product – let's say a box of Cheerios – the proportion of materials in total costs is lower than for charcoal, but still substantial. By contrast, when you buy a cell phone, a digital camera or a compact GPS unit, the cost of the materials used to make the unit is a minuscule proportion of the total cost. The lion's share of cost comes under the heading of information: research and development, design, manufacturing technology and so on.

This does not just apply to high-tech gadgets. The value of a genetically engineered seed, a new pharmaceutical or this year's golf clubs derives mostly from the information embodied in them. And, of course, an ever increasing proportion of our incomes is spent not on goods but on services, many of which have almost purely information value. Accordingly, the proportionate share of stuff in the value of GDP is decreasing and the share of information is increasing.

We have two trends here which, taken together, might have startling implications. The first is that the scope of communications has expanded, while its cost has been divorced from distance and the second is that information, which is moved by communications, accounts for an ever greater share of economic product than does stuff, which is moved by transportation. To some, the confluence of these two trends has a clear implication: the friction of distance is not very important any more (Cairncross, 2001), not only because movement of information can be achieved better and more cheaply but because much movement of people and goods is becoming unnecessary.

The problem with this argument is that it doesn't fit the facts. People and goods are moving around more rather than less. In the U.S., the average person traveled 47 miles per day in 2002 as compared with 42 miles per day in 1990.[2] Table 2.4 examines trends in the movement of freight measured in terms of total tons shipped (in millions) and ton-miles shipped (in billions). Both grew from 1993 to 2002, but ton-miles grew faster. This is because the average distance a ton of freight was shipped grew from 250 miles in 1993 to 269 miles in 2002. The decreased importance of "stuff" in the economy is evident from the fact that the rate of growth in tons shipped was more than 50 percent less than the rate of growth in gross domestic product (GDP). Because goods were shipped longer distances, however, growth in ton-miles, which is a better indicator of transportation activities, almost kept pace with growth in GDP.

Clearly, communications and the information economy have done little to diminish the importance of transportation. To understand why, we need to look harder at how communications and transportation relate to one another.

*Table 2.4* Trends in freight tons, ton-miles and GDP, 1993–2002

|  | *1993* | *1997* | *2002* | *% growth 1993–2002* |
|---|---|---|---|---|
| Freight tons (millions) | 9,689 | 11,090 | 11,668 | 20 |
| Freight ton-miles (billions) | 2,421 | 2,661 | 3,138 | 30 |
| GDP (billions of 2000 $) | 7,532 | 8,703 | 10,048 | 33 |

*Source*: Bureau of Transportation Statistics (2006: Table 1–52); Survey of Current Business (April, 2006: Table C1).

## Transportation and communications

If we view transportation and communications as substitutes by virtue of their common ability to reduce the friction of distance, we might reasonably expect the role of transportation to be declining these days. This perspective is a little too simple, however, because it fails to recognize that transportation and communications are in some ways mutually reinforcing (Mokhtarian, 1990). In the case where an email attachment takes the place of a letter, or a conference call eliminates the need for a business trip, communications may be said to substitute for transportation. But these are interactions where only information is exchanged. In fact, an exchange of information is necessary before an exchange of goods can occur. As people communicate over longer distances, shipments of goods over longer distances are likely to follow. Also, much of the increased volume of information exchanged in the economy is embodied in goods. Notebook computers, designer dresses and genetically engineered seeds are all examples of goods in which information or knowledge accounts for a much greater share of value than material inputs. While the ratio of mass to value for such goods is low, they require transportation services of a higher quality because they may be fragile or time sensitive.

Better communication is necessary for timely transportation. Just-in-time inventory systems are only possible if producers are in constant and effective communication with their input suppliers. Communications technologies that permit tracking of goods and remote sensing of vehicle locations, etc. help achieve levels of time reliability that would have been unthinkable even a decade ago. But such a system may require more expenditure on transportation services per unit of input or output because goods are shipped in smaller batches and reliability must be extremely high. Thus, transportation and communications technologies and infrastructure are mutually reinforcing in the field of logistics.

Even for the pure exchange of information, communications technologies cannot provide a perfect substitute for transportation. For those exchanges that involve highly complex information, or that seek to transform information into knowledge via intellectual interaction, face-to-face meetings are irreplaceable. A business interaction that starts with a single contact over the Internet may blossom into a major collaboration between firms in different countries. This collaboration will eventually require face-to-face communication. Thus, to the extent that the Internet spawns more international contacts, it ultimately increases the demand for international air travel. (The relationship between transportation and communications is explored further in chapter 26.)

## Friction, efficiency and the environment

Technological and institutional advances in transportation and communications have made it easier to overcome the friction of distance now than at any time in human history. Some people question whether this is necessarily a good thing. In particular, too much mobility may have a negative impact on the environment. For example, the widespread use of cars for transportation and of communications technologies that makes it possible to keep in touch over ever longer distances have contributed to a general reduction in the density of human settlement and economic activity. Lower density implies longer distances for most trips, more use of energy for transportation and consequently more air pollution (Anderson *et al.*, 1996).

Such environmental costs must be weighed against some important benefits. First, overcoming the friction of distance effectively expands our range of options. We can choose among more places to shop, a broader range of recreational facilities and a broader range of job opportunities. At a broader geographical scale, cheap freight and personal transportation along with global communications networks make it possible to reap the economic gains from international trade, which will be addressed in Part II. In weighing the costs and benefits of mobility, however, it is important to remember that some of the costs are external costs (such as the costs of pollution and congestion) that are not reflected in out-of-pocket payments. As we will discuss in chapter 6, where external costs are high, we cannot always rely on the market to solve our problems.

## Appendix: Transportation networks and accessibility

All modes of transportation include two types of physical elements: vehicles and infrastructure. The infrastructure includes facilities for docking, unloading, etc. called terminal infrastructure and paths or guideways along which vehicles move, such as roads or tracks, which are sometimes called linear infrastructure. (Even though airplanes do not move on physical guideways, they are directed by air traffic control to stay within designated paths, which constitute a kind of virtual linear infrastructure.) The combination of terminal and linear infrastructure elements creates transportation networks.

We can define a network in more general terms. Define the points at which trips begin and end (corresponding to terminal infrastructure) as nodes and the paths along which travel occurs (corresponding to linear infrastructure) as links.[3] Figure A2.1 represents a simple network where seven nodes are connected by six links. This network is completely connected in the sense that it is possible to get from any node to any other node by moving along the links.

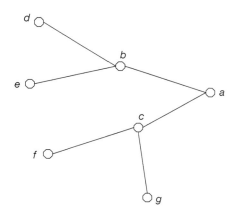

*Figure A2.1* A branching network

This is a particular type of network called a branching network. It is the network that provides complete connectivity to a set of nodes with the minimum possible number of links. If the number of nodes is *n*, a branching network connects all nodes (directly or indirectly) using *n-1* links. The particular configuration represents an "all roads lead to Rome" type network, where node *a* is Rome. (In network terminology, *a* is the "root" node.) Figure A2.1 is not the only way a branching network can be set up to connect these seven nodes. Verify for yourself that it is possible to create a network using only six links whereby "all roads lead to *g*."

The problem with branching networks is that points that are close together "as the crow flies" may be far apart on the network. Assume that the length of each link on the network is 1. Nodes *e* and *f* are separated by a distance 4 because to get from *e* to *f* you have to travel first to *b*, then to *a*, then *c* and finally *f*. The only way to make this distance shorter is to add links to the network. Figure A2.2 shows how the addition of a single link can reduce the distance between *e* and *f* from 4 to 1. Because the number of links is greater than *n-1*, this is no longer a branching network. Any network with *n* or more links is called a circuit network, because it is possible to travel in a circuit. In this case you can travel *e, b, a, c, f, e*. Adding the link also reduces some other distances. For example, the distance from *d* to *f* is reduced from 4 to 3.

Most transportation networks begin as branching networks because the first priority of the public or private agencies that build them is generally to get all points connected. Over time, more links can be added to reduce the average distance between nodes. For example, we can add an additional three links to Figure A2.2 to create a network shown in Figure A2.3, where the maximum distance between any pair of nodes is reduced from 4 to 3 and the average distance is reduced from 2.29 to 1.95. (Verify for yourself that you can add even more links and make the average distance even smaller.)

Networks take on different structures depending largely upon the relative value of user costs and builder costs. The network in Figure A2.2 reduces average costs from the user's perspective, but it will be much more costly to build. Networks with high costs for link construction tend to remain as branching networks. For example,

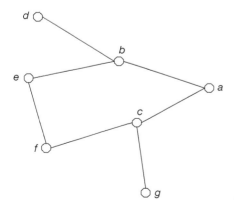

*Figure A2.2*  A circuit network

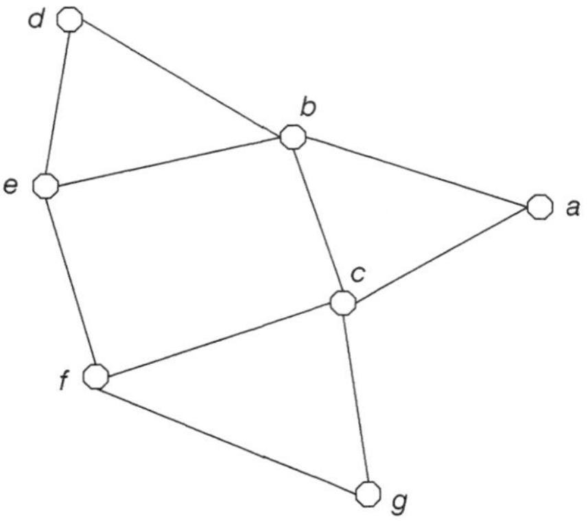

*Figure A2.3* Addition of more links

urban subways are very expensive to build because of the need to either tunnel or excavate trenches for their construction. Therefore, they tend to remain as branching networks or to have relatively few circuits. Bus networks, which have relatively low cost of adding links because they use existing roads, are generally much more highly connected.

In general, adding links to a network improves the *accessibility* of all nodes. We define accessibility as the ease of reaching desirable locations from a particular point in space. Economic geographers often compare the accessibility of points in space by calculating an indicator variable as follows:

$$A_i = \sum_{j \neq i} \frac{W_j}{d_{ij}}$$

This measure $A$ of the accessibility at some point $i$ is calculated by summing over all places that can be reached from $i$ a ratio of a weight $W_j$, which is some measure of the desirability or attractiveness of place $j$ to $d_{ij}$, which is the distance between $i$ and $j$.[4] The basic idea is that the contribution of each potential destination to accessibility is proportional to its attractiveness, but inversely proportional to how far away it is. Being close to attractive destinations gives a point high accessibility. (Note: The value of $A$ has no intrinsic meaning – it is only used to make comparisons.)

We can now use this accessibility measure to help understand the difference between our three hypothetical networks. To keep matters simple, assume that every node on the network is equally attractive, $W = 1$ for all nodes. Looking at the network in Figure A2.1, we would measure the accessibility of node $a$ as follows:

$$A_a = \frac{1}{d_{ab}} + \frac{1}{d_{ac}} + \frac{1}{d_{ad}} + \frac{1}{d_{ae}} + \frac{1}{d_{af}} + \frac{1}{d_{ag}}$$

$$= \frac{1}{1} + \frac{1}{1} + \frac{1}{2} + \frac{1}{2} + \frac{1}{2} + \frac{1}{2} = 4$$

Table A2.1 shows the value of the accessibility measure for each node under each of the three network structures. In the branching network (Figure A2.1) accessibility is much higher at nodes $a$, $b$ and $c$ than at the peripheral nodes $d$, $e$, $f$ and $g$. (Note that $b$ and $c$ have slightly higher accessibility than $a$, which is "Rome" in this branching network, because they are more centrally located.)

The addition of a single link in Figure A2.2 has a big effect on accessibility of two nodes, $e$ and $f$, but also improves the accessibility of all nodes except $a$. The most highly connected network (Figure A2.3) makes the accessibility of nodes $e$ and $f$ higher than the accessibility of $a$. So the ranking of the nodes in terms of accessibility actually changes with addition of links to the network. (See if you can reproduce some of these accessibility measures to make sure you understand how the calculations work.)

*Table A2.1* Accessibility in three networks

| Node | Figure A2.1 | Figure A2.2 | Figure A2.3 |
|---|---|---|---|
| a | 4.00 | 4.00 | 4.00 |
| b | 4.17 | 4.33 | 5.00 |
| c | 4.17 | 4.33 | 5.00 |
| d | 2.83 | 2.92 | 3.83 |
| e | 2.83 | 3.83 | 4.50 |
| f | 2.83 | 3.83 | 4.50 |
| g | 2.83 | 2.92 | 3.83 |
| average | 3.38 | 3.74 | 4.38 |

# 3   Agglomeration

Perhaps the most pervasive historical trend in the spatial configuration of human activity is the gradual transformation from dispersed to concentrated distributions. Early people were hunters and gatherers. They moved around over vast territories, following herds and harvesting natural vegetation that grew at low densities and at different places in different seasons. It took a lot of space to support a relatively small number of people, so population densities were low.

The agricultural revolution allowed people to produce much more food per hectare and to control the movement of the animals that provided their meat and dairy. Thus, they were less mobile (except, perhaps, for those who moved seasonally their flocks) and lived at higher population densities, often sleeping and eating in compact communities. Eventually, different communities of people specialized in the production of different types of food and so market towns grew as centers of exchange. (The fact that people need and love variety in what they consume was a powerful influence even then.)

Over the centuries, the proportion of people concentrated in towns and cities increased. This was not a monotonic trend – rather it came in fits and starts. For example, it accelerated in Roman times and waned at the start of the Middle Ages. By the beginning of the nineteenth century, however, the process of *urbanization* (by which a predominantly rural population becomes predominantly urban) proceeded at a spectacular rate, especially in the richest countries. While this process may appear to be more or less complete in, say, the U.S. or the U.K., it continues today at an unprecedented rate in places like Africa and China. (The process of urbanization is considered in much greater detail in chapter 20.)

*Agglomeration*, defined as the concentration of people and their activities in space, is the topic of this chapter. It stands to reason that if agglomeration has increased through time – despite efforts on the part of some governments to prevent it – people must derive some benefits from living and working in close proximity. These benefits may be social, cultural, military or economic in nature. While all these types of benefits are interrelated, in this book we are most concerned with the economic advantages of spatial concentration, which are called *agglomeration economies*.

## Agglomeration economies and scale economies

Intuitively, the notion of agglomeration economies would seem to have something to do with the notion of *scale economies*, defined as the economic advantage of producing a good or service at a large scale. In fact, a discussion of scale economies is a good place to begin a discussion of agglomeration economies.

Scale economies – or, more precisely, the mechanisms that underlie scale economies – can be divided into two categories: internal scale economies and external scale economies. Internal scale economies are the economic advantages of an increasing rate of output of a single production unit (firm, farm, factory, etc.). In economics, these are generally represented by the inverse relationship between the per unit (average) cost of production and the scale of production (output), as shown in Figure 3.1.

What causes internal scale economies? There are actually a number of possible mechanisms, some of which are listed in Table 3.1. The first and most famous of these explanations is the *division of labor*. This idea was first suggested by Adam Smith (1776) in the eighteenth century, using the example of the manufacture of pins. In those days, a lot of manufacturing was done via the "putting out" system, whereby an entrepreneur would purchase the materials necessary to produce some good and then put them out to individual households for production. In the case of pins, the entrepreneur would purchase metal wire and packing materials and distribute them to households. After a few days or weeks he would return to the household and expect to be presented with finished pins neatly packaged in little boxes of 100. This would require that a person in the household execute a number of different labor tasks associated with the production of pins: drawing the metal, sharpening the point, attaching the head, packing the pins, etc. Smith pointed out that this could be done more efficiently via the *factory system*, whereby a number of people would be gathered under one roof to produce pins. Smith described how, by assigning each of these people a single labor task (drawing wire, sharpening points, attaching heads, etc.), many more pins could be produced with the same input of labor hours.

What does this have to do with scale economies? In essence, this example illustrates the economic advantage of the large production unit (the pin factory)

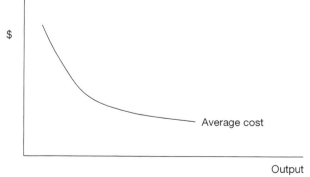

*Figure 3.1* Internal scale economies

over a smaller one (the household). Also, in order to institute the factory system, the entrepreneur would need to produce pins at a sufficiently high rate to keep all the workers busy. More than a century later, Henry Ford's assembly line was to be the ultimate expression of Adam Smith's pin factory.

Capital indivisibility is another explanation for internal scale economy. Consider a farmer who works his land using horse-drawn implements. The size of his farm is the maximum acreage that he and his horse can disc, plow and harvest in the time available. Now someone tries to sell him a tractor (an indivisible piece of capital). The farmer realizes that he can achieve all the farm tasks with the tractor in one-fourth of the time it would take to achieve the same tasks with his horse. But this is little use to him because the value of his produce is not high enough to cover the cost of the tractor. But what if he had a bigger farm? With the tractor he could work four times as much land in the time available and finish the year with a higher income, even after deducting the cost of the tractor. So he buys up the farms of his three neighbors. One big farmer with a tractor is more efficient than four small farmers with their horses: another example of internal scale economy.

We can think of the cost of the tractor as an example of a high fixed cost. In general, economic activities with high fixed costs have scale economies because, as the scale of production increases, the fixed cost is spread over more units of output, so average costs decline. (The alert reader will see the analogy with the terminal costs of transportation described in chapter 2.) Fixed costs do not have to involve capital. Consider the production of software. Most of the costs in producing a new program are in research and development. Once the program is complete, the marginal cost of copying and distributing the code is very low. Is it any wonder that Microsoft is more profitable than its smaller competitors?

For reasons that are better explained by an engineer than a geographer, there are some forms of production that simply are not efficient at small scale. In the rendering of iron from ore, for example, thermal efficiency, whereby iron is extracted with an efficiently small amount of fuel input, can only be achieved in very large blast furnaces. In the aftermath of the Chinese revolution, Mao Tse Tung hoped to achieve industrialization without urbanization. (People living in cities did not fit with his communist ideology.) He decreed that thousands of small blast furnaces be scattered across the rural landscape. Practical Chinese industrial planners soon discovered the gross inefficiency of this approach.

For many goods, one of the keys to profitability is producing just enough to meet an uncertain pattern of demand. Shoes are good example. No consumer will buy

*Table 3.1* Mechanisms underlying internal scale economies

| Mechanism | Example |
| --- | --- |
| Division of labor | Adam Smith's pin factory |
| Indivisible capital | Mechanized agriculture |
| Research and development | Software |
| Thermal efficiency | Iron and steel |
| Statistical scale economies | Shoes |

a pair of shoes that don't fit properly. Thus, the manufacturer must produce a variety of sizes. (Think of it – to include half sizes from 6 to 12 and to cover B, C, D and E widths requires 44 separate sizes!) Since shoes are a fashion item, those that are not sold at the end of the season are wasted or must be sold at a heavy discount. Thus, to make a profit the shoe manufacturer must correctly anticipate the distribution of demand across sizes.

Shoe producers have a pretty good idea of the distribution of foot sizes in the population of potential customers. In general we can think of the customers who come shopping for a particular brand of shoes as a sample from that population. Statistical theory tells us that the larger the sample, the more closely it will conform to the population distribution. Thus, a larger producer finishes the season with a smaller proportion of shoes unsold and a smaller proportion of potential customers disappointed. This phenomenon, known as statistical scale economies, applies in a surprisingly broad range of industries. (Consider a large airline that can offer flights at more times and to more places than a small competitor.)

Internal scale economies are related to agglomeration economies in the sense that if production is at a larger scale it will be concentrated at fewer points in the landscape. In Figure 3.2, the diamonds represent factories that produce a good for distribution to a number of small towns, represented by white circles. On the left side of the figure, there is one large factory to serve all the towns, while on the right side each town has its own factory. Scale economies will naturally favor the former. However, this figure also illustrates one of the most critical themes in economic geography: the trade-off between internal scale economies and transportation costs. If transportation costs are so high as to offset any scale economies gained by concentrating all production in one factory, the more dispersed distribution of production may actually be more efficient. (We'll explore this trade-off further in chapter 14.)

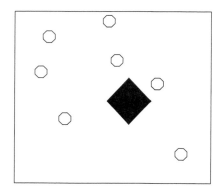

Minimum production cost

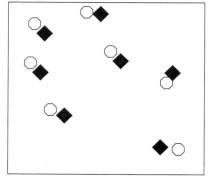

Minimum transportation cost

◯ town          ◆ factory

*Figure 3.2* Trade-off between internal scale economy and transport cost

External scale economies are economic advantages that arise from the size of an industry or group of firms, rather than from the scale of any single firm. Often, external economies of scale are spatial in nature, meaning that firms benefit from the combined scale of production in a group of firms that are clustered in space. Figure 3.3 should help illustrate the difference between internal and external scale economies in a spatial context. In the central pane of the figure there are nine production units distributed in a dispersed spatial pattern. In the left pane, all nine have been combined into a single unit, thus benefiting from internal scale economies. In the right pane, the nine have been clustered together, but not combined. If external scale economies are available in this particular industry, this clustered pattern of production should be more efficient than the dispersed pattern. In essence, external scale economies occur because each firm benefits from the close proximity of the other firms. Thus, spatially defined external scale economies constitute a class of agglomeration economies.

## Classes and causes of agglomeration economies

A number of different classes of agglomeration economies have been suggested over the years. The two basic classes are urbanization economies and localization economies.[1] *Urbanization economies* arise from benefits that accrue to a broad diversity of firms and households concentrated in an urban area, while *localization economies* are benefits that accrue exclusively to firms in the same or similar industries that are located in proximity.

An urbanization economy may arise for a variety of reasons, some of which are rather concrete in nature, while others have more to do with complex and dynamic social relations. One of the concrete reasons is the fact that certain types of infrastructure can be most efficiently provided for large clusters. To give an example to which we can all relate, consider what happens when you flush your toilet. If you live in a town or city, it probably is connected to a network of sewer pipes that lead (one hopes) to a waste treatment plant. If you live in a rural area, however, your toilet probably drains into a septic system on your property that you have had

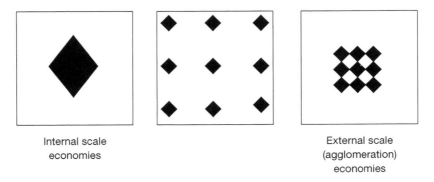

Internal scale
economies

External scale
(agglomeration)
economies

*Figure 3.3* Scale economies in space

to install and maintain yourself. Why the difference? It is not economically feasible to build a network of sewer pipes to serve a small number of highly dispersed households in a rural area, while it is much more economical to build such a network to serve a large number of households located close together. Water and sewage systems are a classic example of the type of infrastructure benefits that comprise urbanization economies.

Other examples of infrastructure include an airport, a rail terminus and a port. None of these things can pay its way unless there is a large concentration of economic activity in the vicinity. In short, there are a variety of infrastructure services that are only available to spatial concentrations because they would be prohibitively expensive to provide for a dispersed population. These economies apply to both firms and households because both can benefit from infrastructure services.

A subset of urbanization economies called *juxtaposition economies* are more specific in terms of whom they benefit. Manufacturing and service firms purchase a variety of inputs from other firms. For example, Figure 3.4 illustrates how an automotive assembly plant receives inputs from other firms that make glass, electronics, fabricated metal products, etc. (This figure is grossly simplified for illustration – an actual assembly plant has scores of inputs from other plants.) Goods must be transported between the input plants and the assembly plant and from the plant to the market. By clustering all these plants together in a location that is relatively close to the market, transportation costs are reduced. This cluster of plants is called a *spatial industrial complex* and it comes about in order to exploit juxtaposition economies. In this way, agglomeration benefits accrue to a group of firms that are diverse yet highly interconnected.

For reasons that have to do less with production technology and more with culture, urbanization economies may arise from the very fact that big places tend to be more diverse than small places. Jane Jacobs (1969) pointed out that the very diversity of large cities spawns a culture of innovation and rapid adoption of new technologies and institutions that is conducive to higher productivity. More recently

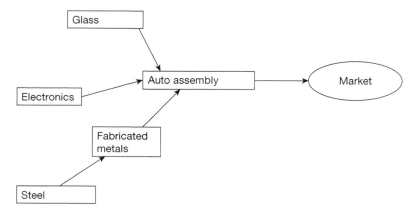

*Figure 3.4* Spatial industrial complex

Florida and Gates (2001) have argued that the general atmosphere of tolerance found in large, diverse cities – as indicated by such cultural factors as artistic communities and even gay populations – are highly conducive to economic vitality. As we will discuss further in chapter 21, big cities offer a greater variety of goods and services for people to buy with the incomes they earn. Since people love variety, this is another form of urbanization economy.

*Localization economies* arise when firms in the same general industry cluster together.[2] At first consideration, this may seem counterintuitive. Wouldn't a firm prefer to locate as far as possible from its competitors? Yet we see examples of such clusters all over the world: automobiles in Detroit; steel in Pittsburgh; microelectronics in Silicon Valley; movies in Hollywood and Bombay; biotechnology in Cambridge MA and Uppsala, Sweden; knitwear in north-central Italy, etc. (Porter, 1990).

How do firms benefit from this type of clustering? One common reason is that the industry in question involves very specific and rare labor skills. This is especially true of high-tech industries such as microelectronics and biotechnology. New entrants in the market naturally go to the place where the labor is already available. Furthermore, skilled people who wish to work in the industry are drawn to these same places where the industry is well established. So a specialized labor market emerges which benefits both firms and employees.

Industries that cluster are frequently very information intensive. We might use an example from the information technology industry, but instead let's consider the fashion industry that is concentrated in New York, Paris and Milan. Firms in this industry need to know what the hottest trends are and what their competitors will be introducing for the coming season. That sort of information is "in the air" in these fashion capitals, so it's "be there or be square."

Another example is the presence of highly specialized producer services that cater to a specific industry. For example, a cluster of steel plants may be served by a number of engineering firms who repair and maintain steel-making equipment. Movie clusters are served by specialized agents and lawyers who draw up contracts involving studios, actors, unions and distributors. In such cases there is a close link between internal and external scale economies. The firms that produce those services achieve internal scale economies by locating in areas where they will have lots of customers – and the savings from internal scale economies are passed on, at least in part, to the customers.

The basis of some forms of localization economy may be more sociological in nature. For example, Saxenian (1994) has shown that a culture of innovation and free exchange of information accounts for much of the success of Silicon Valley. (Other places that had the technological skills, but not the innovative culture, did not do so well.) Some industries, especially those based in highly risky enterprises, develop a community of players who provide a comfortable level of trust to those making major investments in endeavors whose futures are uncertain. Since these communities are generally concentrated in space, they produce another type of localization economy. (We return to this theme in chapter 26.) Whatever the reasons, it is important to recognize that the advantages that lead to localization may not be permanent. Saxenian showed that, while the cluster of the computer hardware industry has persisted in Silicon Valley, a similar cluster eventually collapsed in Route 128 region around Boston. Box 3 explains how an extraordinary localization of tire production in Akron, Ohio lasted for over 50 years but declined in the 1970s and 1980s.

---

### *Box 3* Akron, Ohio: the rise and decline of an industrial cluster

Automobile manufacturers almost never make their own tires. Rather, they buy them from a small number of specialized tire producers. While a car may run for 200,000 miles or more before it is scrapped, even the best tires won't last more than about 50,000 miles. Thus, the market for tires has two components: sales to the automotive OEMs (original equipment manufacturers) and sales to the general public as replacements. The first part of the market is concentrated at automotive assembly plants, while the second is broadly dispersed. The meteoric growth of North American automobile sales in the middle of the twentieth century led to a corresponding growth in tire sales. One might expect that tire production would either have been aligned with automotive production, which implies that it would be concentrated in Detroit, Michigan, or it would have been dispersed to all regions of the country with substantial replacement market demand. Instead, tire production became highly concentrated in the medium-sized city of Akron, Ohio.

As is often the case with industrial clusters, it was a decision by a single firm that started Akron's rise to dominance in the tire industry. In 1871, B.F. Goodrich was enticed by local businessmen to move his tire-manufacturing business from New York to Akron. At that time, the market for tires was limited to bicycles and carts. Goodrich eventually came up with a pneumatic tire design that became the standard for the nascent automobile industry. In the first two decades of the century over 250 firms entered the market for automobile and truck tires, but a rapid shakeout soon followed. By the 1930s, the market was dominated by four big companies: B.F. Goodrich, Goodyear, Firestone and U.S. Rubber (later Uniroyal). All but the last of these had their headquarters and most of their production capacity in or around Akron. It has been estimated that by 1935 about 60 percent of all the tires manufactured in the United States came from Akron (Sobel, 1954), a level of localization that has seldom been seen in any industry.

Why so much concentration, and why Akron? There were plenty of other industrial cities closer to Detroit, which is almost 200 miles away from Akron. In those days, the replacement tire market would have been much greater on the East Coast than around Ohio. Donald Sull (2003) provides an explanation based on the development and spatial concentration of technological expertise. While tires may seem like a rather boring industry today, it was one of the most technologically dynamic industries at the beginning of the twentieth century. Within a few years, improvements in design increased the average durability of tires from 500 miles to 10,000. At the same time, scale economies and improved production methods led to prices that, by the 1930s, were only a fraction of what they had been in 1910. (When you think of it, this combination of skyrocketing productivity and plummeting costs is reminiscent of the personal computer industry in the 1990s.) These improvements were not achieved via a single transformative technological innovation but rather through a large number of more marginal innovations in product design and manufacturing technique.

According to Sull, executives working for the three giant Akron-based tire producers formed a close-knit community who lived in the same neighborhood, belonged to the same clubs and supported common political and charitable causes. Their technological ideas were not closely guarded secrets but rather were implemented quite openly. Whenever one company came up with an innovation the other two would quickly adopt it and build upon it. The result was that the Akron producers stayed far ahead of competitors from other cities by implicitly pooling the fruits of their research and development. Some other researchers doubt whether the exchange of information was quite so voluntary, arguing that technical competence passed from one firm to another through the mechanism of employees of one company moving to new companies and bringing their expertise with them (Buenstorf and Klepper, 2009). Either way, it appears to be an advantage in technological competence rather than any inherent cost advantage that helped Akron emerge as America's "rubber capital."

With the rapid growth of car ownership and the westward shift of the American population in the 1950s and 1960s, the major producers found it advantageous to add production in locations in the south and west, but the industry was still controlled from headquarters located in Akron. The introduction of the radial tire by the French manufacturer Michelin seems to have triggered the end of Akron's dominance. Perhaps because they had so much invested in the old bias-ply technology, and perhaps because they dreaded the sales implications of radial tires that lasted for 50,000 rather than 20,000 miles, the Akron firms were slow to acknowledge the superiority of the new technology. Ultimately, it was the decision in 1972 by the Detroit OEMs to equip new cars only with radial tires that forced them to change course. The tardy changeover to the new technology and the reluctance to retire redundant production capacity led to hard financial straits from which only one of the three Akron tire producers survived as an independent corporation.

One might argue that Akron's tire industry was a victim of its own success. Because the local business model had worked so well for so long, it was difficult to adjust to changes in the broader economic and technological environment (Sull, 2003). It may have been especially difficult for Akron's producers to believe that someone from as far away as France had a better idea of how to make tires. To some extent, the potential for this type of decline exists in all dominant industrial clusters.

A word of caution is in order here. A clustering of a particular activity in space does not necessarily imply the existence of a localization economy as described above. Consider a typical gold rush, such as the ones that occurred in California, the Yukon, the Amazon and many other places over the years. At the peak of the rush, we will find a lot of gold miners clustered in space. Does this mean they somehow benefit from each other's presence? Certainly not – most of them would prefer to have it all to themselves. They are where they are because that's where the gold is. A good economic geographer always considers the possibility that some force other than mutual attraction causes firms in the same industry to cluster.

Forces other than mutual attraction are known collectively as *natural advantage*. Concentration of food processing industries in agricultural regions, paper and cardboard industries in areas of forest resources and petrochemical industries near oil and gas fields are all examples of natural advantage rather than localization economies. Location at natural harbors or along inland waterways for industries such as cement that need cheap water transportation also falls into this category. Natural advantage and localization economy are not mutually exclusive, however. For example, petrochemical industries may still benefit from pools of skilled labor or providers of specialized services, even though these factors were not the initial impetus for locating in a particular place.

## Empirical evidence of agglomeration economies

In a society where people and firms are free to locate where they wish, the very fact of urbanization is evidence of agglomeration economies. Since rents are generally higher in big cities, people would not live in them and firms would not locate in them if there were not a substantial economic advantage. The concentration of certain industries in certain cities, if it cannot be explained by natural advantage, is evidence of localization economy.

These general trends tell us that agglomeration economies are real, but they don't tell us much about what types are most important or what factors cause them. In the past 20 years or so, there have been many statistical studies that try to see how important agglomerations are and what mechanisms drive them. Most of these studies involve statistical methods that are outside the scope of this book. Some of them are still contentious (different studies reach different conclusions) and they are nearly all based on data from North America, Japan or Europe, so their conclusions may not apply everywhere. With those qualifications in mind, here are some of the most interesting conclusions:[3]

- A large number of studies conducted over many years indicate that, as the size of a city increases, the productivity of economic activities in that city also increases. Estimates vary, but most studies indicated that doubling the size of a city increases its overall productivity by between 3 and 8 percent.
- Productivity can also be shown to increase with density. One study concluded that, if the economic activity concentrated in New York City were evenly spread across the counties of New York State, productivity would decline (Ciccone and Hall, 1996).

- Not only size, but also diversity, confers benefits leading to more rapid growth in more diverse cities.
- While nominal wages rise with city size, real wages (adjusted for the cost of living) fall with city size (Tabuchi and Yoshida, 2000). This suggests that people are willing to accept lower real wages in order to enjoy the consumption advantages – the greater variety of goods and services – of living in large cities.
- Natural advantage plays an important role in explaining spatial concentration with industry groups. More than half of concentration, however, is due to localization economies.
- In the absence of natural advantage, those industries with high research and development expenditure, highly skilled labor requirements and strong links to universities are the most concentrated.

## Is agglomeration always good?

Most of what has been said in this chapter runs contrary to a common perception that big cities are evil, corrupt and inefficient, while small towns and rural areas are wholesome, honest and rational. Much of this perception arises from social problems such as drug addiction and political corruption that are outside the scope of this book. (The fact that they are outside our scope does not, of course, make them any less real.) But there are other things – including congestion and pollution – that are within our scope and which appear to get worse as cities get bigger.

Congestion arises because the movement of goods and people increases beyond the optimal capacity of the infrastructure such as roads and rails that are designed to carry them. As this capacity is exceeded, the speed of movement is reduced, sometimes almost to a stand-still. Congestion is a general and complex phenomenon, about which there will be much more in chapter 6. For the moment we can observe that congestion most often occurs when a large amount of flow converges on relatively compact areas. Examples are shopping malls, sports stadiums on game days and the downtown areas of large cities. It would be a mistake to think that congestion is purely the outcome of spatial concentration. Poor network design, a lack of coordination among vehicles and excessive reliance on space-consuming transport modes such as automobiles all exacerbate the problem of congestion. Still, by and large, agglomeration and congestion go together, with the largest cities generally suffering the worst congestion.

Pollution is generally perceived not in terms of the total volume of effluents released to that atmosphere, but in terms of the concentration of those pollutants in the air we breathe. Most economic activities create some air pollution. It is not necessarily true that people living in cities generate more air pollution on a per capita basis. In fact, they often produce less because, when compared to people living at low densities, they travel shorter distances and use less energy to heat or cool their smaller homes. But, because people and firms are closer together, the pollutants are discharged into a smaller volume of air, leading to higher concentrations. Differences in industry mix, automobile use and local meteorological conditions can lead to different levels of pollutions, even across cities of the same size. Still, by and large, agglomeration and pollutant concentrations go together, with the largest cities generally suffering the worst air quality.

So, as cities get bigger, some things – such as productivity and variety – improve, while others – such as pollution and congestion – get worse. Figure 3.5 is a hypothetical view of how these effects might net out. Here agglomeration benefits increase with city size, but at a decreasing rate. The costs of agglomeration increase at a constant rate. At some point $s*$, therefore, the costs catch up with the benefits. Beyond $s*$, increasing city size makes everyone worse off.

When does big become too big? Is there any evidence that cities in the world have reached or exceeded their optimal sizes? Some recent research suggests that in the developing world there are quite a few cases where a single dominant city (also called a *primate city* – see chapter 20) grows to be inefficiently large.[4] There are a couple of reasons why this may happen. Highly centralized (and perhaps even corrupt) regimes tend to use their political power to concentrate all economic activities into a single city where they can be more easily controlled by the political elite. In other cases, the development of transportation infrastructure is neglected, so that entrepreneurs have no choice but to locate in the capital because all other cities are so poorly connected. The result is cities that are so massively congested that normal commerce is retarded and so polluted that the health of residents is severely impaired.

What about the biggest cities in free market economies? If we assume that the sizes of these cities are driven by economic rather than political forces, the fact that big cities continue to grow suggests that they have not yet reached the point where the costs of agglomeration exceeds the benefits. It is worth noting, however, that in a lot of cases the growth of the largest cities has slowed down. The data in Table 3.2 show that, between 1990 and 2004, the populations of the three largest metropolitan areas in the U.S. grew more slowly than the overall population. This is not because the process of urbanization was slowing down – the urban share

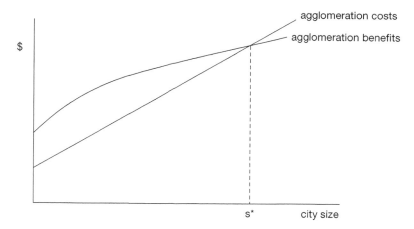

*Figure 3.5* Costs and benefits of agglomeration

*Table 3.2* Population in millions of U.S. and three largest metropolitan areas, 1990–2004

|  | *1990* | *2004* | *% growth* |
|---|---|---|---|
| United States | 248,791 | 293,657 | 18.0% |
| New York–Northern New Jersey–Long Island, NY–NJ–PA | 16,846 | 18,710 | 11.1% |
| Los Angeles–Long Beach–Santa Ana, CA | 11,274 | 12,925 | 14.7% |
| Chicago–Naperville–Joliet, IL–IN–WI | 8,182 | 9,392 | 14.8% |

of the U.S. population increased from 75 percent to 79 percent over the same period. Rather, these numbers indicate that other, smaller cities grew more rapidly. What do we take from this? One interpretation is that, while there are still agglomeration economies to be reaped in the largest cities, there are greater agglomeration economies in smaller cities. Thus, this is evidence that the net agglomeration benefits (benefits minus costs) are declining in city size.

## Dispersion within concentrations

This chapter began by saying that concentration in space is a pervasive trend in human history. Yet residents of most metropolitan areas in North America and much of Europe can look around and see that things are getting more spread out rather than more concentrated. People are moving from flats to suburban houses on large lots. Firms are moving from compact urban centers to sprawling industrial parks along peripheral highways. Even institutions such as hospitals and colleges are locating further from the city center and adopting more space-consuming layouts.

There seems to be a contradiction here, but it is really a question of geographic scale. At a broad scale, where cities appear as points on the map, population is getting more concentrated as more people live in the urban points and relatively fewer live in the intervening spaces. At a more local scale, where the city is an area on the map with a rural fringe around it, the settlement pattern is becoming more dispersed. The process of *urban sprawl* – at first an American pattern, but increasingly a global trend – results in cities that take more space as people live and work at lower densities. This process, which is largely but not exclusively the outcome of widespread car ownership, will be addressed in chapters 18 and 19.

# 4 Markets

A market can be a place where people come together for the exchange of goods and services. Such "place" markets include agricultural market towns, Middle Eastern bazaars, country flea markets and the New York Stock Exchange. The common characteristic of these markets is that they bring large numbers of buyers and sellers together in space for the purpose of exchange. Not all markets have discrete locations, however. For example, the "job market" may span an entire metropolitan area. The oil market spans the globe. These markets are better described as institutions – by which we mean sets of rules and arrangements that put buyers and sellers in contact with one another – than as places. Defined broadly, markets comprise large numbers of buyers and sellers and whatever physical and institutional facilities are needed to make it easy for them to exchange goods and services.

Imagine a world without markets. At some early stage of human development, people probably lived as small family groups who consumed only those things that they produced for themselves through hunting, scavenging, gathering and agriculture. Naturally, this sort of arrangement was not very efficient because everything had to be produced at such a small scale. Also, the range of goods and services that people could consume was limited by the skills and assets of the group and by the natural resources of the territory it controlled. Farmers only got to eat plants, while hunters only got to eat meat.

Eventually, these small groups must have realized that they could benefit from exchanging goods with one another. For example, a small farming group might exchange grain for meat provided by a hunting group. This gave both groups a more balanced diet and helped satisfy the love of variety, which is a great human motivator. But now suppose the hunting group wants grain but the farming group does not want meat. It wants fish. The farmers might then approach a small group of fishermen and offer grain for fish. But suppose the fishermen don't want grain. They want meat. Sooner or later, everyone would figure out that, if they keep interacting in pairs, no one will be able to make a satisfactory trade. But, if they all meet in the same place, they should be able to swap things around until every group gets what it wants – the hunters get grain, the farmers get fish and the fishermen get meat. This, then, is the beginning of a market.

Of course, as the number of traders and the number of goods in the market increases, the swapping around gets more complicated. Suppose you come to market with grain hoping to exchange it for wine. Unless you are lucky enough to run into a wine producer who happens to want grain, you are likely to have to make several intermediate swaps to finally get the wine. This requires a lot of effort and there is always the danger that you will never get your hands on anything that the wine producer will accept – so you end up with goods you don't even want. Things would be much easier if there were a single commodity that everyone would trade for. Suppose that silver were such a commodity. You could exchange your grain for silver with the certain knowledge that anyone you meet with wine to trade will accept silver for it. If silver is commonly accepted as the universal commodity of trade, it becomes what we call money.

Even in this simple example you can see that, in order to function, a market needs a set of rules and arrangements, including an agreed-upon location and the designation of a single commodity as money. But what about the question of how much silver (money) is required in exchange for a given quantity of wine, wheat, meat, fish or whatever? Should that value (known as the price) be part of the rules and arrangements that are predetermined before the market gets started? Throughout the history of exchange, various types of authorities (there is usually a king or a high priest around) have attempted to set prices in the market at some level that they think is appropriate. But it is not necessary, nor in general is it wise, to set prices. So long as there are sufficient numbers of buyers and sellers of a particular good, the market price will find its best possible level through the normal mechanisms of exchange. (What we mean by "best" is explained below.) How that happens is the main topic of this chapter.

## Theory of the market

Even a simple market has a few prerequisites. It needs to have a sufficiently large number of both buyers and sellers so that some sort of competition occurs. Buyers compete by bidding against one another for a desired good. Suppose you wish to buy wheat. Another buyer is willing to buy all the wheat in the market for a price of 1.[1] In order to get any wheat you may need to offer a price of 1.1. Thus, buyers competing against one another tend to drive the price up. On the other hand, suppose a new seller comes into the market and finds that a seller that was already there is providing wheat to all the sellers at a price of 1. If he is to sell any wheat at all, he may have to offer his wheat at a price of 0.9. Thus, sellers competing against one another tend to drive the price down.

Another prerequisite for a working market is a set of rules and arrangement. Some of these (location of the market, commodity accepted as money) we have already mentioned. Another important prerequisite is a definition of property rights. In order to buy and sell, it must be clear who owns a particular good at a particular moment. There must be laws of exchange and protection against theft and fraud. Here some sort of government authority needs to be involved.

Once the prerequisites are met, the processes of competition should give rise to a single *market price* for each good on offer. The market price is defined as that price at which demand is met and the market clears. Demand is met if there is no one in the market who is willing to buy the good at the market price but is unable to get it and the market clears when there is no one in the market who is willing to sell at the market price but cannot find a buyer. A simple explanation of how this price gets determined is provided by the intersection of supply and demand functions as illustrated in Figure 4.1.

Here there are two functions that represent the relationship between the price and the quantity bought or sold in the market. The demand function, which is marked D, is a downward sloping function that defines how much all of the buyers in the market will demand (purchase) at a particular price. If the price goes up, they demand less. The supply function is an upward sloping function that defines how much all the producers of the good in the market will supply (offer for sale) at a particular price.[2] The intersection of these two lines defines the price P* at which the quantity demanded and the quantity supplied are identical: Q*. Returning to our definition of the market price, it is evident that demand is met and the market clears.

Figure 4.1 indicates that a market price exists. But how do the actions of multiple buyers and sellers bring that price about? In other words, how does the market find the market price? The best way to explain this is to see what happens if we arbitrarily set the price to some value other than the market price. But, before we get to that, we need to ask two more fundamental questions: Why does the demand function slope down? *and* Why does the supply function slope up?

There are two ways to explain why the demand function slopes down. They both start from a realization that the market demand function in Figure 4.1 is an aggregate demand function, so it represents the sum of the individual demand functions of a large number of potential buyers, each defining the amount an individual buys at a given price. Suppose first that all those potential buyers have the same individual demand function. If the market function is downward sloping then all the individual functions must be downward sloping as well. This means that each person buys less of a good as the price goes up. There are two reasons why this will happen. First, a buyer typically distributes the money she has available across a number of different goods. If the price of one good goes up, she might buy less of that good and more of a different good that fills a similar need. For

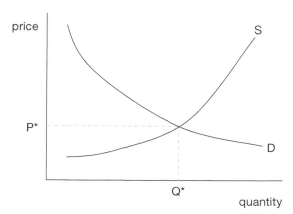

*Figure 4.1* Market price determination

example, if the price of coffee goes up but the price of tea stays the same, she might buy less coffee and more tea. This is called the *substitution effect* and it comes into play when the price of a good goes up relative to the price of other similar goods. But even if relative prices stay the same – that is, prices of all goods rise and fall at the same rate – the individual will buy less as prices rise. We assume each person has a fixed income to distribute across all the available goods. If the prices of all goods go up, the cost of living goes up and therefore she must buy a little less of everything. This *income effect* is another reason that individual demand functions slope down and thereby another reason why the market demand function slopes down.

We can also explain the downward slope of the market demand function without assuming that individuals have downward sloping demand functions. We can assume instead that every person has a maximum price in mind for every good. If the market price is below that price, he will buy some predefined quantity of the good but if it is above that price he will not buy the good at all.[3] Different people have different maximum prices. You have a high maximum price either because you are rich or because you have a strong liking for the good in question (or perhaps both). Given a distribution of maximum prices across the population, if the market price is high there will be only a few buyers, so the level of demand is low. Every time the price goes down it drops below the maximum prices of a few more people, so more buyers enter the market and the demand goes up. When the price goes up, potential buyers are priced out of the market and demand goes down. For this reason the market demand function slopes downward.

Why does the market supply function slope upward? Again, the market function is an aggregation of individual supply functions. If all individual functions slope upward the market function will do so as well. But why do individual supply functions slope upward? To understand this, bear in mind that no producer of any good will provide that good for the market if the price she receives is lower than her marginal cost of production, which is defined as the cost of producing an additional unit of the good. In many types of production, that marginal cost increases with the amount produced. For example, suppose you have a farm, you already have all your land in cultivation and you are producing 10,000 bushels of wheat per season. To increase output, you would need to make some additional expenditure on things like fertilizer or machinery that allow you to increase the yield of your land. So, as you increase output, your marginal cost of production is rising. This means you would require a higher price per bushel to produce 11,000 bushels of wheat than to produce 10,000 – in other words, your supply function is upward sloping.

We do not have to assume that individual supply functions are upward sloping to get an upward sloping market supply function. Simply assume that each producer has a constant marginal cost and that she will not offer goods for sale unless the market price is equal to or greater than that cost. In other words, each producer has a minimum price, below which she will not offer goods in the market. This minimum varies across producers because of differences in resources or skills. For example, wheat farmers with the most fertile soil will have the lowest marginal costs, so they will have lower minimum prices. At a low price, only these low-cost farmers will provide wheat to the market. As the market price rises, farmers with inferior soil are able to enter the market. Thus, the market supply function is upward sloping.

Now we can turn to the question of how the market price is determined. For the purpose of this explanation, assume the first rationale for the slopes of both the demand and supply functions. That is, assume that each buyer has a downward sloping demand function and each producer has an upward sloping supply function. Looking at Figure 4.2, imagine that the price is arbitrarily set to some level P''. By seeing where the horizontal line drawn from the vertical axis at the level P'' intersects the supply and demand function, we can see that the market will not clear because suppliers will bring a greater quantity to market than potential buyers will demand at that price. This is, in fact, the situation that often occurs when some government authority attempts to set an artificially high price. In order to maintain that price, the government has to buy up all the excess supply in the market and put it in storage.

In the absence of government intervention, the market will correct itself. Producers who are unable to sell their goods will simply scale back their production. Assuming they eliminate their most expensive production first, they will reduce their marginal costs to be equal to some price at which buyers will demand exactly the amount that they supply. At this market price P* the market will clear.

Now suppose that the price is somehow arbitrarily set to some value P' below the market price. At this price, the amount that buyers demand will be much higher than the amount producers supply. This condition of excess demand is what occurs when a government sets artificially low prices as did many of the socialist economies of the late twentieth century. At the artificially low price, demand is not met. This explains the chronic scarcity of goods in those socialist economies. In the absence of government interference, buyers will bid the price up to a level where supply and demand meet.

The forces of supply and demand tend to resist deviations from the market price. This does not mean, however, that the market price will not change over time.

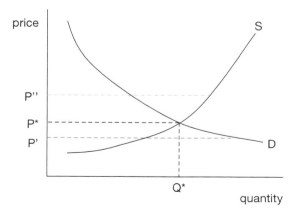

*Figure 4.2* Why does market price prevail?

Forces that are exogenous to the market can shift the demand and supply functions and thereby change the price. For example, suppose there is an increase in the disposable income of the potential buyers in the market. This could occur due to a number of exogenous changes, such as an increase in the price of some export commodity or a reduction in taxes. An increase in disposable income would mean that buyers would demand more of every good at any given price. Thus, the market demand function would shift to the right, as shown in Figure 4.3. The result would be that both the price and quantity of each good in the market would increase.

Another way that an exogenous change can influence the market is when the price of some imported commodity increases. The classic example here would be an increase in the price of petroleum. Since petroleum is used as a source of energy in the production of most goods, the marginal cost of production would increase generally. Recalling that the supply function reflects the marginal cost of production, the increase in the petroleum price would produce a leftward shift in the supply function, as each producer would be willing to offer less for sale at any given price. This is shown in Figure 4.4. The result is that the market price would increase, while the quantity supplied and demanded would decrease.

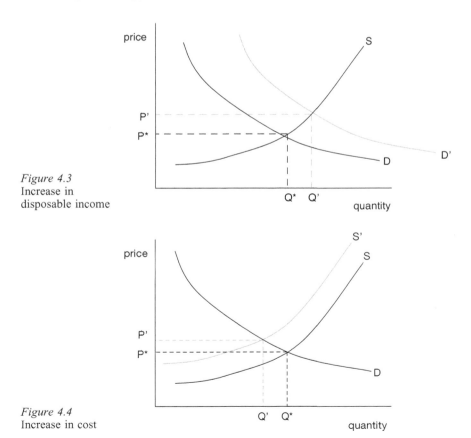

*Figure 4.3*
Increase in
disposable income

*Figure 4.4*
Increase in cost

## Imperfect competition

Market price determination as it is described above assumes that there are large numbers of both sellers and buyers in the market. Because sellers compete with one another to put downward pressure on prices while buyers compete with one another to put upward pressure on prices, this type of market is called perfectly competitive. In some real-world contexts, however, the number of sellers in the market is quite small. The extreme case of only one seller is called monopoly. Monopolies come about either in cases of extremely high fixed costs, such that it is only feasible for one firm to operate in the market. Electric utilities sometimes are monopolies because the cost of establishing a transmission grid is so high that a second firm cannot enter the market. Monopolies also exist for institutional reasons. Throughout history, governments have granted monopolies to certain firms, either to encourage the production of some good or service that would otherwise not be profitable, to prevent what has been called "ruinous competition"[4] or to reward firms that are politically well connected.

In a perfectly competitive market, each firm produces a relatively small share of market output, so no single firm can influence the price much by its actions. A monopolist, by contrast, realizes that its choice of how much output to produce affects the price it receives in the market. Because the demand function is downward sloping, if the monopolist wants to produce more output, it must accept a lower price to dispose of it. Because all output sells at a single price and each additional unit of output reduces that price, when you produce one more unit, you get less revenue for each of the units you already produced. For example, suppose the monopolist produces 10 units and, based on the demand function, it can get $1 for each unit. If it produces an 11th unit, the price goes down from $1 to $.95. What is the addition to total revenue? First, we have to take account of the 95 cents it gets for the 11th unit. But, because all output must sell for the same price, it will receive 5 cents less for the first 10 units than it would have if it had not produced the 11th unit. So the net effect – which we call the marginal revenue – is only 45 cents. Marginal revenue decreases with the level of output, because the more units you produce, the greater is the second, negative, component of marginal revenue. Should the firm produce the 11th unit? The answer is simple, if the marginal revenue is greater than the cost of production, the firm will lose money by producing an extra unit. So the monopolists' rule is to produce output up to that level where the marginal revenue is equal to the marginal cost.

This is illustrated graphically in Figure 4.5. Note that the marginal revenue function lies below the demand function, so the supply function (the marginal cost function of the firm) has its intersection with the marginal revenue function at a lower level of output than its intersection with the demand function. This means that under monopoly, less is produced and consumed than under perfect competition. Since the price must be consistent with the value of the demand function for that lower level of output, the monopoly price is higher than the price determined in a perfectly competitive market. (The Appendix to this chapter gives a mathematical derivation of how price and quantity are determined under monopoly.)

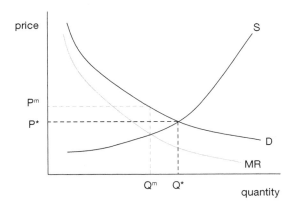

*Figure 4.5* Market price
determination under monopoly

You can now see why, from a policy perspective, monopoly is viewed as a bad thing. People get to consume less and have to pay a higher price.

Monopoly is an extreme case. A more common kind of market structure is oligopoly, which means there are only a few firms in the market. If there are only two or three firms, there is a strong incentive for them to collude by agreeing to produce collectively the same output that a monopoly would produce. There are more complex forms of market behaviors in oligopoly, but in general it is true that, if there are too few producers in the market to create an environment of perfect competition, production is constrained and the price is elevated.

The description of markets above assumes implicitly that goods that each seller brings to the market are perfectly interchangeable – that is, the perfect competition and monopoly models describe markets for commodities. In this book, we make a distinction between commodities and differentiated goods. As the name applies, differentiated goods are a little bit different, depending upon who makes them. A Chevrolet is not a perfect substitute for a Toyota. Dresses from different design houses have very different looks. Each manufacturer of fishing rods stresses unique features of its rods that differentiate them from all others. Thus, the simple market models described above do not do a very good job describing the markets for cars, designer dresses or fishing rods.

A general framework for describing the markets for differentiated goods, which goes by the paradoxical name "monopolistic competition," is of growing importance in both economics and economic geography. The growing importance of monopolistic competition in economic theory is explained by the fact that, while the standard market models were developed at a time when people spent most of their incomes on commodities, today people spend most of their incomes on differentiated goods. From the perspective of economic geography, the monopolistic competition model has some extremely important results. For example, it tells us that, as the aggregate demand in a market grows, so does the diversity of differentiated goods on offer. (The alert reader will see some parallels with the relationship between diversity and agglomeration economy discussed in the preceding chapter.)

# Markets in space

The theory of markets in microeconomics is generally presented without any specific reference to location and space. Buyers and sellers are all assumed to be in the same location, or else they live in a world of free transportation so that goods can be exchanged over space without cost. Economic geographers and spatial economists bring space out of the background to see how the locations of buyers and sellers affect the functioning of the market. There are numerous ways, many of which are introduced throughout the course of this book. We introduce a couple here for the sake of illustration.

First, consider how space comes into the supply function of an agricultural market, which is located at a particular point on a map.[5] We have already said that the supply function reflects the marginal cost of producers of the crop in question. Since crop production takes up space, however, the farmers must be dispersed around the market: some close by and some in more remote locations. In addition to their production costs, farmers have transportation costs that are higher the further they are from the market. How will this affect the aggregate supply function?

Assume there is no variation in fertility and all farmers have access to the same technology, so each farmer has the same simple linear supply function illustrated in Figure 4.6 reflecting his marginal cost of production. Here there is a minimum price $P_0$, below which the farmer produces nothing. Marginal cost is increasing at a constant rate, so the supply function above $P_0$ is an upward sloping straight line.

To keep things simple, assume that there are just three farmers called A, B and C. In Figure 4.7, the horizontal axis on the left side represents distance from the market (measuring from right to left) and quantity produced on the right side (measuring from left to right). For each farmer, there is a straight line indicating per unit transportation costs at varying distances from the farm. The only relevant value here is the cost of transporting a unit of output to the market, which we define as $t_A < t_B < t_C$. Since the supply function in Figure 4.6 reflects production costs only, each farmer's supply function at the market is shifted by their transportation cost, so farmer A sells in the market at a minimum price $P_0 + t_A$ and so on for B and C. The aggregate supply function is defined by adding the output provided across the three farmers at each price. The function is "kinky" because different farmers enter the markets at different prices.

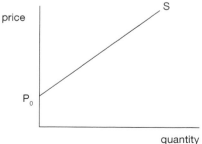

*Figure 4.6* Linear supply function

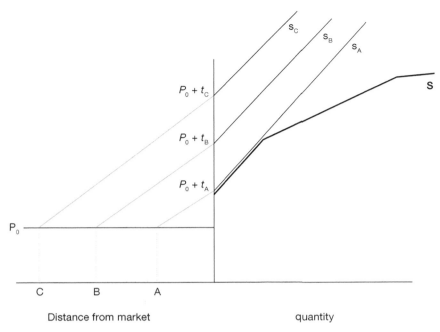

*Figure 4.7* Spatial supply function

This simple example illustrates a couple of interesting things. First, when transportation costs come into play, the shape of the aggregate supply function may be different from the shapes of the individual supply function, even if all farmers have the same marginal costs. The individual supply functions are linear (increasing at a constant rate), while the aggregate function is increasing at a decreasing rate. Second, shifts in demand that lead to increases in the market price will lead to agricultural activity spreading onto ever more remote land – an important principle of agricultural geography. (If you are not sure why this is so, add a demand function to Figure 4.7, then see what happens as you shift it to the right.)

The underlying assumptions that give rise to the perfectly competitive market model become increasingly unrealistic when space and location are considered. For example, a market may have a large number of sellers, but, if they are dispersed and if transportation costs are high, each may function as a spatial monopolist. Take producers of construction aggregates (sand and gravel) as an example. There are hundreds of producers in the United States, but because these commodities are so expensive to transport many of those producers may enjoy virtual spatial monopolies. As Figure 4.5 shows, the monopoly price $P^m$ is greater than the perfectly competitive price $P^*$. A producer located in a remote area will be able to enforce the higher monopoly price so long as the transportation costs to import aggregates from the closest competitive market is greater than the difference between the monopoly price and the competitive price.

In an oligopolistic market, space can be used as a convenient basis for collusion. An excellent example is provided by the way that organized crime, until recently, managed commercial waste haulage in the New York metropolitan area. By assigning locations to each haulage firm and enforcing the rule that no firm poaches on another's territory, each firm had a virtual spatial monopoly (see Box 4 for a full explanation).

---

### *Box 4* **Spatial collusion in the New York refuse industry**

In New York City, household garbage is collected by the sanitation department, but private firms ranging from corner grocery stores to managers of financial district skyscrapers must pay private haulers known as "carting firms" to collect their refuse. Starting in the 1950s, private garbage collection became dominated by a cartel that suppressed competition to such an extent that firms in New York paid hundreds of millions more per year than comparable firms in other cities. Naturally, such anti-competitive arrangements are against the law, but the cartel was controlled by an organization that had no compunction about breaking laws. Private refuse collection in New York City was the exclusive domain of the Mafia. (The details of the Mafia's garbage racket were made public after a brave New York City police detective went undercover and became accepted as a cartel member; see Cowan and Century, 2002.)

Many more sophisticated and subtle organizations have engaged in spatial collusion in the past, but the Mafia's scheme was so blatant and universal that it provides a textbook explanation of how to earn excessive profits by granting spatial monopolies. The scheme was based in a system of "property rights" whereby every one of the thousands of locations requiring refuse pickup was "owned" by a single collection firm. Who owned what was determined by a central organization masquerading as a legitimate industry association but actually comprising high-level Mafiosi. Not all carting firms were owned by gangsters, but they all knew that to avoid severe consequences they must play by the Mafia's rules. For small customers, neighborhoods were assigned to specific firms and no one was to poach on them. Larger customers put the service up to bid, but a charade was organized whereby several firms would bid slightly higher prices than the predetermined "owner." Any carting firm that tried to operate outside the cartel was eventually confronted with two choices: join the cartel or be driven out of business in a ruthless, and sometimes deadly, manner.

We are all charmed by Mafia stories. The racket had its own distinctive language. Joining the cartel was known as "renting a room" and firms that tried to operate outside the cartel's rules were called "outlaws." Unusually stubborn and ruthless gangsters were called "Barese" after the Italian town of Bari, where the entire population was reputed to be "Barese." The story is full of people with interesting names like "Joey Surprise," "Cockeye" Ratteni and "Sal Skates." Throughout its history, the number-one rule of the cartel was "Don't upset the apple cart." But the consequences of this criminal enterprise are less amusing. Many honest businessmen had to quit the industry, suffer the humiliation of carrying on as Mafia puppets, or – worse yet – suffer violent consequences. Tragically, innocent employees such as truck drivers were often attacked in order to send a message to their bosses.

The economic consequences were not much better. It has been estimated that refuse collection services throughout the City were subject to a "Mafia tax" of about 40 percent with a total value of $600,000 (Cowan and Century, 2002: 15). This tax contributed significantly to the notoriously high cost of doing business in New York City. As evidence of an extreme case of overcharging, when a legitimate national refuse firm tried to enter the New York market in the 1990s, it quoted a monthly price of $5,000 to collect refuse from a high-rise building that had been paying $94,000 per month to a cartel member (Cowan and Century, 2002: 230). This case provides a vivid example of the magnitude of excess profits to be gained through spatial collusion and the economic damage imposed by such behavior. Clearly, when we assume "perfect competition" in our theories and models, we are assuming a lot!

The existence of New York's Mafia-led garbage cartel was an open secret for almost 40 years. Numerous investigations by various levels of government – including the U.S. Congress – failed to bring it down, largely because no one involved was willing to face the possible retribution that would result from testifying against the Mafia bosses. Finally, in 1995, indictments were handed down against all of the major players and most of the carting firms involved. Based largely on evidence provided by Detective Rick Cowan, who posed as a cartel member obtaining hours of incriminating recordings, the bosses were given long prison sentences and the New York garbage racket was finally destroyed.

## Markets for space

In addition to markets in space, we will be considering markets *for* space. Since most economic activities take up space, payment for the exclusive use of land, whether by purchase or rental, is a major component of costs for most firms and households. Markets for land are peculiar because supply is generally constrained. There is an old saying that the value of land always increases "because they ain't making any more of it." Still, fortunes have been lost by investing in land at the wrong time and the wrong place.

Variations in the price of land have two bases, which arise from the notion of site and situation. Land has site attributes such as soil quality, slope, elevation and climate. Two plots of land adjacent to one another can have very different prices if one is in a fertile valley bottom while the other is on an eroded hillside. Situation attributes (the "access to" attributes) tend to lead to land prices that vary more systematically over the map.

As in any market, potential buyers influence the price by bidding against one another for the same land. Land markets, however, generally have different categories of buyers who have very different preferences because they want to use the land in different ways. These heterogeneous buyers influence not only the spatial patterns of land prices but also the patterns of land uses. This is illustrated in Figure 4.8, which shows the prices that two different types of farmers – vegetable farmers and wheat farmers – would be willing to pay for an acre of land at different distances from a market town.

Vegetable farmers can yield produce of higher value from each acre of land, so close to the market they are willing to pay more for the land. As we move further away from the market, however, transportation costs become a greater concern. Because they are perishable, vegetables are more expensive to transport than is wheat. Thus, the price vegetable farmers will pay to use the land declines more rapidly with distance from the market than the price wheat farmers will pay. Beyond some distance $d^*$, the wheat farmers would outbid the vegetable farmers for available land. Thus, we expect to see vegetables grown close to the market and wheat grown farther away.

This simple example captures the logic behind an approach to modeling markets for land which we will consider in much greater detail in chapters 17 and 18. As we shall see, the same basic logic that explains spatial patterns of agricultural land can also be applied to spatial patterns of urban land.

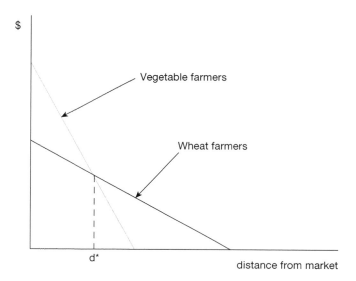

*Figure 4.8* Willingness to pay per acre of land

## Appendix: Price determination in a monopoly

Because there is only one supplying firm in a monopoly, it is possible to derive the monopoly price as the outcome of that firm's desire to maximize profit. The monopolist does not "set" the price directly, but rather chooses a level of output that will produce the profit-maximizing price. Thus, we have an optimization problem where the objective function is profit and the activity variable is the firm's level of output.

A fundamental assumption of the monopoly model is that the firm is aware of the market demand function. Ultimately, it is the demand function that sets the price. The monopolist firm chooses a level of output and the demand function determines the price that will clear the market of that much output.

We define $P(Q)$ as the demand function, where $P$ is the market clearing price and $Q$ is the output of the monopolist. (This is actually an inverse demand function – in the basic demand function the quantity demanded is a function of the price.) The downward sloping nature of the demand function is assured by the assumption that $dP(Q)/dQ < 0$. The profit of the monopolist firm is defined as the difference between cost and revenue. Define $C(Q)$ as the cost of producing $Q$. As usual, marginal cost is assumed to be increasing: $dC(Q)/d(Q) > 0$. Indicating profit as $\Pi$ we have:

$$\Pi(Q) = P(Q)Q - C(Q)$$

To find the value of $Q$ that maximizes $\Pi$ we set the derivative to zero:

$$\frac{d\Pi(Q)}{dQ} = P(Q) + \frac{dP(Q)}{dQ}Q - \frac{dC(Q)}{dQ} = 0$$

Rearranging terms:

$$P(Q) + \frac{dP(Q)}{dQ}Q = \frac{dC(Q)}{dQ} \tag{A4.1}$$

The left-hand side of equation A4.1 is marginal revenue (remember that the second term on the left-hand side is negative) and the right-hand side is marginal cost, which is the supply function for any value of $Q$. Thus, equation A4.1 gives us the same rule of price and output determination in monopoly as the one represented in Figure 4.5.

# 5   Spatial interaction

Spatial interaction is defined as the movement of people, goods, information or money between two points in space. Commuting, shopping, migration, international trade, foreign direct investment, phone calls, Internet transactions and tourism are all forms of spatial interaction. Observing, explaining and predicting spatial interaction are among the most important tasks of the economic geographer.

Given the diverse nature of the many forms of human activity that fall under this heading, one might think that no common analytical framework could possibly apply to all forms of spatial interaction. But geographers have discovered that certain common principles and processes characterize most, if not all, forms of spatial interaction.

## Three bases of spatial interaction

To understand spatial interaction we must first ask why we see higher levels of interaction between some pairs of places than between others. Why, for example, are there more airline trips between Boston and Washington D.C. than between Seattle and Denver? Why is there more migration from Lebanon to Canada than from Kuwait to Mexico? Why do more tourists from Minnesota than from Arizona visit Florida in the winter? As you read this, you are probably coming up with reasonable answers to each of these questions, but you are considering them independently and the answers are very specific to the individual questions. In the 1950s, a geographer named Edward Ullman (1956) suggested that all such questions can be addressed within a common framework.

According to Ullman, there are three bases of spatial interaction: complementarity, transferability and intervening opportunities. We will consider each in turn, but first a few definitions. We define all forms of spatial interaction as flowing from one place to another place. These places can be any standard spatial unit – cities, counties, states, provinces or whatever. They can be as broad as continents (as in trade between Asia and Europe) or as precise as individual addresses (as in mail sent between 63 Pleasant Street and 112 Walnut Avenue). Hereafter, we refer to the "from" place as the *origin* and the "to" place as the *destination.* We will measure spatial interaction as a magnitude of flow of people, goods, information or money from an origin to a destination.

*Complementarity* of the origin and destination means that there is some rationale for spatial interaction to occur between them. In most cases, complementarity implies that the origin and the destination derive mutual benefit from spatial interaction.[1] A classic example of complementary regions is where one produces food, while the other produces agricultural implements. The first region cannot produce any food without the implements and the second cannot produce the implements without food for production workers. Our notion of complementarity is very broad here and is best illustrated by a few examples, as provided in Table 5.1. For each example, we propose two indicators: an indicator of the origin's ability to *generate* spatial interaction and an indicator of the destination's ability to *attract* spatial interaction.

Suppose daily commuting is the type of spatial interaction we wish to study. The city is divided into a mutually exclusive set of zones and we measure the number of commuters who travel between pairs of zones on a typical morning. How would we define pairs of zones that are complementary? Generally, there is no single measure to define complementarity; rather, we need to measure something at the origin and something else at the destination. In this case, a good origin indicator might be the employed population of each zone and a good destination indicator might be the number of jobs located in each zone. Other things being equal, we would expect the largest flows to occur between origins with lots of employed population and destinations with lots of jobs.

A couple of important things arise from this example. First, in most cities residences and workplaces are rather segregated, so if you make the zones small enough they will tend to fall into the categories of predominantly residential and predominantly employment zones. We do not expect to see much commuting between pairs of residential zones or between pairs of employment zones, but rather between residential and employment zones. In this case, opposites attract. Or, to put it more generally, spatial interaction arises out of spatial differentiation. A second point is that spatial interaction flows are not necessarily symmetric. We would expect to see a substantial flow of morning commuters from residential to employment zones, but not from employment to residential zones. (Commuting has a peculiar property, however, in that we would observe a set of afternoon flows that are symmetric with the morning flows.)

The second type of spatial interaction on Table 5.1 is migration. Migration researchers often speak in terms of push factors (things that make you want to move away from a place) and pull factors (things that make you want to move to a place).

*Table 5.1* Indicators of complementarity

| Type of interaction | Origin | Destination |
|---|---|---|
| Commuting | Employed population | Number of jobs |
| Migration | Unemployed population | Vacant jobs |
| Trade in steel | Steel production | Output of industries that use steel |
| Phone calls | Population | Population |

From an economic perspective, unemployment is a push factor and the number of vacant jobs are a pull factor. The two together constitute complementarity. (The economics of labor migration is taken up in chapter 9.)

The trade of a commodity like steel naturally must have its origin in a place where steel is produced and its destination in a place where there is a demand for steel. The spatial pattern of steel production is easy to observe, but the pattern of potential demand is more difficult. It can generally be indicated by the level of output in industries such as automobile manufacturing and commercial construction, both of which are huge consumers of steel.

The number of phone calls between places qualifies as a form of spatial interaction because it is a movement of information. The reasons for phone calls are so diverse that only very general indicators of complementarity are possible. Perhaps the most general is population. The more people there are in both origin and destination, the greater is the potential for phone calls. This is an unusual case because the largest number of calls can be expected to occur between an origin and a destination that are similar, rather than different, in the sense that they both have large populations. Also, in this case, unlike the previous three mentioned, we can expect the spatial interaction flows to be roughly symmetric.

The second basis of spatial interaction is *transferability*, defined as the ease of movement of people, goods, information or money. Ullman (1956) originally defined this basis simply as distance, assuming that distance is a good inverse indicator of the ease of movement. As noted in chapter 2, however, distance is not a perfect indicator. Costs of movement may not be directly proportional to distance and, in some cases, such as communication over the Internet, costs may be independent of distance. It is therefore better to be more flexible in the way we define transferability. Table 5.2 proposes some indicators of transferability for the four types of spatial interaction we have already considered. (Note that unlike complementarity, which required separate indicators for origin and destination, these indicators are defined for each origin–destination pair.)

Transferability affects commuting flows in the sense that people choose their residential locations so as to have relatively easy commutes to their jobs. (Or they may choose their jobs to be easy to reach from their residences.) In an economic sense, the cost of travel such as bus fares, the cost of gasoline and parking charges are possible inverse measures of transferability. (The $1/x$ indicates an inverse measure. If the cost is low, transferability is high.) There has been a great deal of research on commuting, however, and most studies find that time rather than cost

*Table 5.2* Indicators of transferability

| Type of interaction | Indicators of transferability |
| --- | --- |
| Commuting | Travel cost in time or money ($1/x$) |
| Migration | Cost ($1/x$), common language, lagged migration |
| Trade in steel | Freight cost ($1/x$), tariffs ($1/x$), common standards |
| Phone calls | Cost ($1/x$), common language |

is the controlling factor in commuting decisions. This is a case where distance would provide only an imprecise measure of transferability. Due to the irregular pattern of congestion bottlenecks, commuting time in some cities is only roughly correlated with distance.

For migrants, the cost of physically moving (plane fares, the cost of moving trucks) may only be a small element of transferability. That cost may be high, but it need only be paid once. There is a more important social cost associated with adapting to an unfamiliar environment. Factors that mitigate this social cost increase transferability. For example, international migrants will find it easier to adapt in a country where their native language is spoken. Research has shown that migrants find it much easier to adapt in a destination where people with roots in their origin region have already settled. Thus, lagged migration flows are often a good indicator of transferability.

For trade in steel freight costs are a critical inverse indicator of transferability. If the steel is to move across international borders, tariffs are also important. Different countries may have different standards for steel in terms of carbon content and general quality. A common set of standards in the origin and destination therefore aids transferability.

Since phone communication requires that both participants speak the same language, we would expect to have more calls between London and New York than between Paris and New York, so a common language is an indicator of transferability. Cost is also an important inverse indicator. Costs of long-distance telephone calls have plummeted in recent years due to better technologies and institutional changes like deregulation. At the same time, the link between cost and distance has become more tenuous. With Internet telephony, cost is divorced from distance.

To understand the third basis for spatial interaction, *intervening opportunities*, let's start with an example, which is illustrated in Figures 5.1 and 5.2. Suppose there are a number of people living in a residential area. Some distance away there is a shopping mall. We would expect to observe a number of shopping trips from the residential area to the mall. In this simple example we can assume that distance is an inverse measure of transferability. The distance from the residential area to the mall is represented by the length of the arrow in Figure 5.1 and the volume of trips is represented by the thickness of the arrow. Now imagine that a new mall (B) opens as shown in Figure 5.2. Now there will be some trips to that mall as well. Because mall B is closer than the original mall A, the number of trips to mall A declines significantly. (If malls A and B were perfect substitutes, the trips to mall A would all disappear, but, because malls generally differ in terms of the mix of shops and services, some shoppers would still make trips to the more distant mall.)

The key point here is that both the complementarity and the transferability between the residential area and mall A are unchanged between Figures 5.1 and 5.2. But in Figure 5.2 the spatial interaction between them is lower because of the introduction of mall B, which constitutes an intervening opportunity.

We can define an intervening opportunity for a particular destination as an alternative destination with the similar or greater complementarity for a particular origin, but with superior transferability. In practice, we need to expand the scope

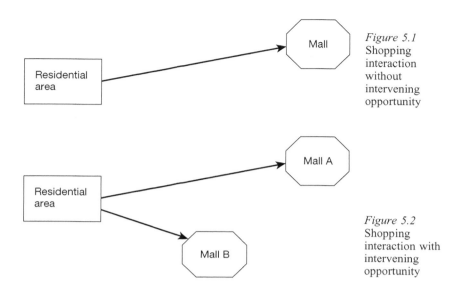

*Figure 5.1* Shopping interaction without intervening opportunity

*Figure 5.2* Shopping interaction with intervening opportunity

of this definition to include all alternative destinations. If, for example, mall B were more distant rather than closer, it is likely that it would still have some negative impact on the number of shopping trips to mall A, so long as the two were not perfect substitutes. In essence, the idea of intervening opportunities is that alternative destinations compete to attract the spatial interactions generated by each origin.

The implication of intervening opportunities as a basis of spatial interactions is quite important. It means that we cannot expect to understand what drives the level of spatial interaction between two places (origin and destination) without also considering the characteristics of one or more other places (alternative destinations). Thus, spatial interaction should not be addressed on a pairwise basis, but rather on a system-wide basis. The danger in ignoring intervening opportunities in planning for spatial interaction is illustrated by the case of Montreal's Mirabel Airport, in Box 5.

---

### *Box 5* Montreal's Mirabel Airport: an object lesson on intervening opportunities

"Build it and they will come" is a popular cliché applied to airport construction. The demand for air transportation has exploded all over the world in recent decades. In most high-income countries, however, it is very difficult to accommodate the growing need for new airport runways and gates because of local objections to noise pollution. So, in those rare cases where it is possible to build a new airport in the vicinity of a major metropolitan area, planners expect little problem with insufficient demand. Yet the case of Montreal's Mirabel Airport demonstrates that even an airport will not be successful if it is located in the wrong place.

With a metropolitan population of over 3.5 million, Montreal is the second largest city in Canada and the seventh largest in North America. From the 1940s, Montreal's rapidly growing domestic and international air travel was served through Dorval Airport (now called Pierre Elliott Trudeau Airport), which is located less than 20 km from downtown Montreal. In the 1960s, Canada's federal government decided that Dorval could not support air traffic growth indefinitely and a new airport was needed. After the usual political wrangling, a site was chosen in St. Scholastique, which is about 60 km to the northwest of downtown. One reason for choosing such a remote site was that the government was able to expropriate a huge area of land around the site, providing a sound buffer and possible location for airport-related industrial development. The new Montreal-Mirabel International Airport opened in 1975, in time for the 1976 Montreal Olympics. It was designed to serve up to 20 million passengers per year. Yet it never saw more than about 3 million passengers per year, and today it has been relegated to the status of a cargo-only airport, with regularly scheduled passenger services having ceased in 2004.

What went wrong? A number of market factors worked against Mirabel Airport. Up to the 1970s, Montreal had been the hub for Canada's international flights to Europe. But a new generation of airplanes that could travel farther without refueling made it possible for airlines to route most flights through the larger, but more distant, city of Toronto. Also, the sovereignty movement in Montreal's home province of Quebec created political uncertainty that may have retarded economic growth in the 1980s and 1990s. As a result, official projections of air travel demand in Montreal proved too high. But the choice of Mirabel's location certainly contributed to its failure.

Even by North American standards, the location of an airport 60 km from downtown is unusual. Denver International Airport (DIA), which is noteworthy for its remote location, is only 40 km from downtown Denver. Furthermore, Denver's earlier airport, which was much closer to downtown, was closed upon the opening of DIA in 1995. By contrast, the more convenient Dorval Airport remained in service, providing an *intervening opportunity* for air travelers in the Montreal region. At first, all international flights were required to use Mirabel, leaving Dorval with only domestic flights. But this provided frequent travelers with the stark comparison of the convenience of traveling 20 minutes to Dorval as compared with at least 50 minutes to Mirabel. A high-speed rail connection that had been envisioned between downtown Montreal and Mirabel Airport fell victim to budget cuts, so travelers were left with a choice between a long drive and a slow bus. The dissatisfaction of the traveling public led to pressure to reopen Dorval to international flights, which finally happened in the 1990s. More recently, Dorval has been expanded to accommodate 20 million passengers per year, making Mirabel Airport completely redundant as far as passenger flights are concerned.

You can have some sympathy for the planners of Mirabel Airport, who had to deal with political interference and the problem of noise pollution. Perhaps if the intervening opportunity had been eliminated by shutting down Dorval Airport completely, Mirabel would be a busy passenger airport today. But the inconvenience to travelers might have detracted from Montreal's position as a center of international commerce. Much as attempts by governments to defy market forces and manipulate prices often lead to undesirable outcomes, the case of Mirabel Airport demonstrates that attempts by government to defy the forces that drive spatial interaction are apt to end in failure.

## The gravity analog

Another way of thinking about spatial interaction is by analog to the gravitational force in physics, which is defined as the mutual attraction between objects with mass which makes them tend to accelerate toward one another. The strength of gravity increases with the mass of the objects in question and decreases with their separation in space. Thus, the gravitational force between objects of great mass that are close together is large relative to the force between objects of lesser mass that are farther apart. More specifically, the gravitational force $F$ of two objects (indexed as 1 and 2) with masses $m_1$ and $m_2$ separated by a distance $d_{12}$ is defined by the equation

$$F_{12} = \frac{\gamma\, m_1 m_2}{d_{12}^{\,2}} \tag{5.1}$$

where $\gamma$ is called the gravitational constant.

As early as the nineteenth century, scholars began to notice an analogy between the force of gravity and human behaviors that come under the heading of spatial interaction. For example, in studying the phenomenon of migration from rural villages to cities, Ravenstein (1889) observed that migrants were about equally likely to move to relatively small cities close to their home villages as to larger cities that were farther away. This general phenomenon is illustrated in Figure 5.3, where the rectangles on the left represent rural villages, the octagons on the right represent cities, the length of the arrow represents distance and the width of the arrow represents the volume of migration. In the first two cases we see about the same volume of migration to a small city that is nearby as to a large city that

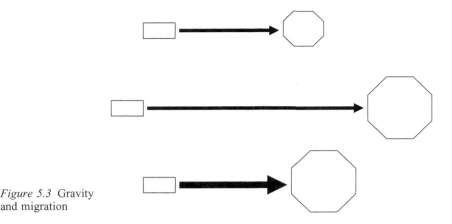

*Figure 5.3* Gravity
and migration

is more distant. Thus, in migration, as in gravity, the negative impact of distance
can be offset by the positive impact of mass (represented as city size.) As the third
example illustrates, the largest migrations occur to large cities that are nearby.

By the early part of the twentieth century, geographers and other social scientists
began to put this analogy into practice, devising "gravity models" to predict the
level of interactions between places along the following basic specification

$$I_{12} = \kappa \frac{P_1 P_2}{d^2} \tag{5.2}$$

Here $I_{12}$ is some form of spatial interaction, $P$ is the population of each place and
$\kappa$ is an empirical constant. Unlike the gravitational constant $\gamma$ in equation 5.1, which
remains the same at all places and all times, $\kappa$ must be determined separately from
observed data for each context in which the model is applied. (How this is done is
the subject of the Appendix to this chapter.)

This basic formulation was applied in a number of contexts, for the first time
making it possible not only to observe but also to predict levels of migration, intercity travel and other thing. But its utility as a model of spatial interaction is limited.
We can think of the model as having two predictive components: $P_1 P_2$ which
represents complementarity and $1/d_{12}^2$ which represents transferability. We know
from our earlier discussions that population is a good indicator for complementarity
in only a limited range of contexts. Also, this specification implies that spatial interaction (like gravitational force) is symmetric, which is not true in most cases. We also
know that distance is a good inverse indicator for transferability only in limited
contexts. Also, there is no reason to believe that interaction is inversely proportional
to the $d^2$ just because that is true in the case of gravity. Why not $\sqrt{d}$ or simply $d$?

What was needed was a more generalized type of spatial interaction model –
one less closely wedded to physical gravity. But, before introducing this model, a
word about notation. Throughout this book, whenever we write down expressions

involving spatial interaction, we index the origin as $i$ and the destination as $j$. If there are M possible origins, $i$ can represent any origin 1, 2 . . . M and, if there are N possible destinations, $j$ can represent any destination 1, 2 . . . N. With this in mind, we write our generalized gravity model as follows:

$$I_{ij} = \kappa \, \frac{V_i W_j}{c_{ij}^\beta} \qquad (5.3)$$

In this equation, $V_i$ is some measure of the ability of the origin $i$ to generate spatial interaction, $W_j$ is some measure of the ability of the destination $j$ to attract spatial interaction and $c_{ij}$ is some generalized cost of interaction, which serves as an inverse measure of transferability. This cost is raised to the power $\beta$, which can vary according to the context and must be estimated based on observed data.[2] (See Appendix to this chapter.) The advantage of this generalized gravity model is that it can be customized to suit any form of spatial interaction. The second and third columns of Table 5.1 provide variables that can be used for $V_i$ and $W_j$ respectively and Table 5.2 provides variables that can be used for $c_{ij}$.

The gravity model has played an important role in the history of economic geography. It provided a stepping stone from descriptive to quantitative research. It is still in broad use today, especially in urban transportation research. As the model is specified here, it has serious shortcomings. The alert reader will already have noted that it does not fulfill Ullman's framework because it has no way of representing intervening opportunities. But a slightly more complex version of the model does (see Haynes and Fotheringham, 1984). Other model extensions have been developed to enforce constraints on the amount of spatial interaction that can be generated by or attracted by a particular place.[3] The more the model is developed, the less recognizable are its roots in physics. The gravity model, in its various specifications, is useful because it makes good economic sense[4] and not because there is any cosmic homomorphism between human spatial interaction and the gravitational attraction between objects in space.

## Appendix: Calibrating gravity models

The gravity equation from physics (equation 5.1) includes a physical constant $\gamma$ that has been measured with great precision over the years and which applies in all places and all times. If you want to determine the gravitational force between two planets, and you have accurate measurements of their masses and the distances between them, the gravitational constant can always be relied upon.

The same is not true of the constant $\kappa$ in the gravity model (equation 5.2). In a sense, this is not a constant at all, because it may take different values for different types of spatial interaction in different places and times. It can never be expected to give a precise measure of the spatial interaction in question. The best way to think of $\kappa$ is as an empirical parameter that is used to provide the best possible prediction of a particular type of spatial interaction in a particular space–time context. But how do we find out the value of $\kappa$?

The process of estimating the values of unknown parameters in a gravity model is called calibration. It starts with measuring the values of both the endogenous variable $I_{ij}$ and the exogenous variables $P_i$, $P_j$ and $d_{ij}$ for a sample of observations – each observation being an *ij* pair. For example, we might contact the airlines to determine the number of passengers who fly between a sample of city pairs for which we also know the populations and the intercity distances. We can then plot the measure of spatial interaction against the left-hand side of equation 5.2, as shown in Figure A5.1.

We can see that there is an upward slope in the plot, to which we fit a straight line using least squares regression. The slope of the line gives us the value of $\kappa$. We could then use our calibrated gravity model to make estimates of the airline passengers between city pairs that are not in our sample.

The generalized gravity model (equation 5.3) gives us greater flexibility and will generally allow us to make more accurate estimates of spatial interaction flows. But it has two unknown parameters to estimate, $\kappa$ and $\beta$, instead of one. With a little manipulation, however, we can get it into a linear form that will allow us to estimate both parameters by least squares regression. Rearranging terms gives us

$$\frac{I_{ij}}{V_i W_j} = \frac{\kappa}{c_{ij}^{\beta}}$$

We then take logarithms to get

$$\log \left( \frac{I_{ij}}{V_i W_j} \right) = \log \kappa - \beta \log c_{ij}$$

which we can plot as shown in Figure A5.2.

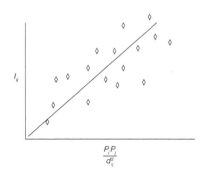

*Figure A5.1* Estimating the value of parameter $\kappa$

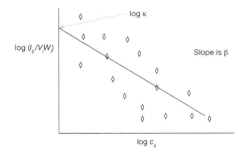

*Figure A5.2* Estimating the values of $\kappa$ and $\beta$

# 6   Resources and the environment

Economic activities interact with the natural environment in two ways. First, resources are withdrawn from the environment to provide food; material inputs for manufacturing and construction; and fuels that provide energy. Second, all economic activities produce some sort of waste products which, unless they are recycled for use in other economic activities, are discharged into the environment, usually with deleterious effect.

Why must we be concerned with the impacts of human activity on the natural environment? That question can be answered from three perspectives. The first is purely pragmatic. We rely on products from nature for our sustenance and as inputs to our production processes. If we exhaust the supply of inputs, our economies can no longer expand. If we exhaust the supply of food, we all starve. The second perspective is aesthetic. People derive utility from the environment in its natural state. If we no longer have unspoiled areas, we cannot derive utility from hiking, camping, fishing, hunting or more generally observing and experiencing the beauty of nature. The third is an ethically grounded concern that people do not have the right to destroy nature. Even a plant or an insect that we hardly ever see has an "existence value."

Which of these perspectives we adopt will influence our idea of how a society ought to address environmental issues. For example, what should be our policy toward a natural forest? From the first perspective, it would seem best to manage the forest so that it yields the largest possible flow of wood products, even if it means tampering with the ecology by eliminating species without any practical value to us. From the second, it would seem best to refrain from cutting wood and to keep the ecosystem intact, but to provide roads and other facilities that help people see and enjoy the forest. The third perspective would lead us to make no alteration to the forest at all and to forbid any human incursions that might damage any species – even those that we cannot see.

It is beyond the scope of this book to argue the relative merits of these three points of view. It is, however, important to acknowledge them. Economists and economic geographers are best at addressing environmental issues from the first perspective. To a more limited extent, it is possible to address the second perspective, as in measuring the trade-off between preserving a landscape to promote tourism and transforming it to support manufacturing. The realm of existence values is *terra incognito* for the economic sciences.

## Resources and population

Resources are stocks of goods and services upon which people can draw to support their economic activities. Natural resources are those stocks that exist in nature, including land, water, forests, minerals, fish, mammals and clean air. Natural resources can be used as sources of material and energy inputs, but they can also be used as sinks for the disposal of the wastes generated by human activity.

It is useful to make a distinction between renewable and non-renewable resources. Renewable resources are those that "grow back" or otherwise renew themselves. Forests are renewable in the sense that trees that are cut can be replaced with new trees that grow over a number of years. A fishery is a renewable resource in the sense that fish that are removed can be replaced by natural reproduction. Of course, these resources can be destroyed by excessively high rates of withdrawal or by discharging wastes (pollutants) that interfere with their natural processes. Deforestation in Africa, the destruction of the North American bison herds and the collapse of fisheries around the world attest to the vulnerability of renewable resources. In the face of increasing demands for withdrawals, renewable resources have to be managed to stay viable in the long run. Management can lead to the creation of environments that are completely different than those that occur naturally. Agriculture is essentially the outcome of intensive management of renewable plant resources.

Non-renewable resources are available in limited quantities. Mineral resources in general are non-renewable. This is a critical point because most of our energy is derived from a few mineral resources: petroleum, natural gas and coal.

The natural resource base is finite, yet the number of people drawing upon it continues to expand. The population grows because more people are born every year than die. Thus, we can examine the dynamics of population growth by looking at the relative trends of birth rates and death rates. The birth rate (BR) is defined as the number of live births per 1,000 population, while the death rate (DR) is defined as the number of deaths per 1,000 population. The rate of natural increase (RNI), which is the rate at which the population of a place grows in the absence of in or out migration, is defined as:

$$RNI = \frac{BR - DR}{10}$$

(The reason for the 10 in the denominator is that BR and DR are, by convention, expressed per 1,000 population, while RNI is expressed as percent.) The rate of natural increase tends to shift over time because of changes in the relative values of birth and death rates. Most countries in the world have gone through, or are going through, a period of rapid population growth called the *demographic transition*, which is illustrated in Figure 6.1. This transition occurs as a country goes from a period of relatively low economic development, during which both birth and death rates are high, to a period of affluence, during which both birth and death rates are low. The jump in the rate of natural increase occurs because death rates drop more rapidly than birth rates.

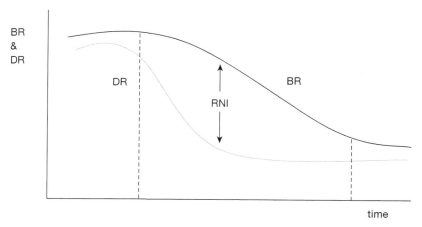

BR
&
DR

DR

RNI

BR

time

*Figure 6.1* The demographic transition

The simplest explanation for why this happens is that death rates are affected by technological changes, which can be applied quite rapidly, while birth rates are more dependent on cultural changes that are adopted by the population over a much longer period of time. Death rates can be reduced by the application of advanced medical technology and improved sanitation. These things are expensive, but if the money is available they can happen rather quickly. Reductions in the birth rate involve such things as an increased participation by women in the workforce and in some cases acceptance of contraceptive methods. These things depend on changes in popular beliefs and attitudes that may take a generation or more to occur.

Table 6.1 shows the variations in the birth and death rates across countries at different levels of economic development. Since the countries are listed in order of per capita income, it is easy to see the tendency for low-income countries to have higher birth rates. The highest birth rate is in Somalia, a country so disrupted by civil war that no economic data are available, and the second highest is for Burkina Faso, one of the poorest countries in the world. Only the very poorest countries have extraordinarily high death rates. For example, Zimbabwe, with its high birth and death rate and a reasonably low rate of natural increase, has yet to enter the rapid growth stage of the demographic transition. Some developing countries, such as Egypt and Mexico, have lower death rates than the affluent countries. This can be attributed to the fact that their populations contain very high proportions of children. Japan, Austria and Denmark, which are affluent, highly urbanized and have aging populations, have little or no natural increase. The Russian Federation is an anomalous case where the population is actually contracting due to the surplus of deaths over births.

The values at the bottom of the table for the entire world and for low-, medium- and high-income countries confirm the relationship between income and natural increase.

*Table 6.1* Demographic and economic indicators, 2003

| Country | Population (millions) | Per capita income (US$) | Birth rate | Death rate | RNI |
|---|---|---|---|---|---|
| United States | 290.8 | 37,870 | 14 | 9 | 0.50 |
| Japan | 127.6 | 34,180 | 9 | 8 | 0.10 |
| Denmark | 10.2 | 33,570 | 12 | 11 | 0.10 |
| Austria | 8.2 | 26,810 | 10 | 10 | 0.00 |
| France | 59.8 | 24,730 | 13 | 9 | 0.40 |
| South Korea | 47.9 | 12,030 | 12 | 7 | 0.50 |
| Czech Republic | 10.2 | 7,150 | 9 | 11 | − 0.20 |
| Mexico | 102.3 | 6,230 | 19 | 5 | 1.40 |
| Malaysia | 24.8 | 3,880 | 21 | 5 | 1.60 |
| Argentina | 36.8 | 3,810 | 18 | 8 | 1.00 |
| Russian Federation | 143.4 | 2,610 | 10 | 15 | − 0.50 |
| Iran | 66.4 | 2,010 | 18 | 6 | 1.20 |
| Egypt | 67.6 | 1,390 | 24 | 6 | 1.80 |
| Canada | 1,288.4 | 1,100 | 15 | 8 | 0.70 |
| Philippines | 81.5 | 1,080 | 26 | 6 | 2.00 |
| India | 1,064.4 | 540 | 24 | 8 | 1.60 |
| Haiti | 8.4 | 400 | 32 | 14 | 1.80 |
| Zimbabwe | 13.1 | 380 | 29 | 22 | 0.70 |
| Nigeria | 136.5 | 350 | 43 | 18 | 2.50 |
| Burkina Faso | 12.1 | 300 | 43 | 19 | 2.40 |
| Somalia | 9.6 | unknown | 50 | 18 | 3.20 |
| World | 6,272.6 | 5,510 | 21 | 9 | 1.20 |
| Low Income | 2,311.9 | 440 | 30 | 11 | 1.90 |
| Middle Income | 2,988.6 | 1,930 | 17 | 8 | 0.90 |
| High Income | 972.1 | 28,600 | 12 | 9 | 0.30 |

*Source*: World Bank (2006).

Withdrawals of both renewable and non-renewable resources grow over time not only because the population keeps growing but also because economic development generally leads to increasing resource use on a per capita basis. Since non-renewable resources are finite and since renewable resources can support only limited withdrawals, it would seem evident that the processes of population and economic growth are subject to some limit. The nineteenth-century economist Thomas Malthus was one of the first to come to this conclusion. He said that the nature of population is to grow at an exponential rate, while the available resources can expand, at best, at a linear rate. His grim assessment was that population growth would quickly lead to widespread famine and economic collapse.

While the twentieth century witnessed famines costing millions of lives, these were relatively brief and localized. Why didn't the collapse of the resource base that Malthus predicted come about? The main reason is that rapid technological progress made it possible to increase agricultural yields and extend cultivation onto land that had previously been deemed non-arable. Other, more recent studies that extended Malthusian logic to predict dire resource shortages by the end of the twentieth century also turned out to be wrong (Meadows, 1974). What these studies missed was the effect of the market in the face of resource scarcity. As any particular resource becomes scarce, its market price goes up. (Remember what happens when you shift back the supply curve.) With a higher market price there are incentives both to develop technologies that use resources more efficiently and to search for new supplies. Still, we have seen the collapse of some once-bountiful resource bases, such as the North Atlantic cod fishery, so the Malthusian resource collapse is a real possibility (see Box 6).

---

### *Box 6* The collapse of the Newfoundland cod fishery

The cod fish found off the shores of New England and Atlantic Canada constitute one of the most important nutritional resources in the history of the western world. In fact, cod was one of the first resources that attracted Europeans to North America, with fishermen from as far away as Spain plying the waters of the northwest Atlantic by the sixteenth century. Not only were the cod plentiful, but they could be salted and transported thousands of miles without spoiling. Thus, cod from the icy northern waters became a staple of diets in Spain, Portugal and even Italy.

One of the richest cod stocks lies in the Grand Banks off the eastern shores of the Canadian province of Newfoundland. Cod fishing became by far the most important economic activity in that remote province, although locals were joined by international fishermen who exploited the resource without even touching North American shores. By the second half of the twentieth century, giant factory ships from as far away as East Asia could be found fishing within a hundred miles of Newfoundland's shores. (For a history of the cod fishery, see Kurlansky, 1998.)

Since the fish were in international waters, there was no way to regulate fishing. Thus, the "tragedy of the commons" played out over the course of the twentieth century. It has been estimated that cod catches off Newfoundland, which had been around 100,000 tons per year in 1900, had skyrocketed to 800,000 by 1970.[i] Not only were boats from ever more countries entering the fishery, but boats with great hold capacity, large nets with fine mesh and sophisticated equipment for locating fish were all being used. As with any reproducing population, there came a point where the number of fish removed was too great to sustain high rates of reproduction, and the size of the fish stock dwindled.

In order to protect coastal fish stocks, countries around the world began to institute 200-mile offshore zones in which they claimed control over fish stocks. Canada declared the right to exclude foreign boats from its 200-mile zone (which included all but a small portion of the Grand Banks) in 1977. Many observers believed that the cod stocks were now safe. To address the common resource problem, Canada instituted a system of regulation whereby fisherman ranging from operators of small inshore trawlers to large Canadian-owned fishing corporations were issued quotas. The idea was to set the quotas so as to optimize the fishing catch without degrading the resource – this is essentially the high point of the curve in Figure 6.2.

Unfortunately, the regulatory regime proved ineffective. There is much debate over what went wrong. A number of practices such as "high-grading," whereby low-quality fish are dumped so that only the best fish count toward the quota, meant that some fishermen killed more fish than they brought to market. Also, while the intention was that the quota be set on the best available science, there was little information on which to determine a safe fish take and politics often interfered in the process. Still, some argue that the regulatory system would have been more successful if fishermen and fishing communities had more input into its design (Charles, 1997).

By 1990, the fish take began to collapse and it was clear that the cod stock was on the brink of disappearing. In 1992, the Canadian government took the extreme step of declaring a moratorium on fishing in most of the waters off eastern Newfoundland. The economic impact on Newfoundland was devastating. Not only were fishermen laid idle, but also fish-processing plants were shut down and the economic decline spread to nearly all provincial industries. The moratorium was originally supposed to be for a period of two years, after which it was hoped the fish stocks would rebound. Because this never happened, the moratorium was never lifted and only very limited fishing has been allowed for almost 20 years. While Newfoundland has diversified into other economic sectors, including an offshore oil industry, the centuries-old culture that developed around fishing as a way of life may never fully revive.

## Note

i   Millennium Ecosystem Assessment, http://maps.grida.no/go/graphic/collapse-of-atlantic-cod-stocks-off-the-east-coast-of-newfoundland-in-1992 (accessed September 19, 2011).

## The problem of common resources

The collapse of the fisheries can be attributed not only to increasing population pressure, but also to the general problem of over-exploitation of common resources. A common resource is one that can be used without restriction by as many people as wish to take advantage of it. In the absence of effective regulation, the fish in the ocean are an example of a common resource. Another example is the common pasture, which was a fixture of medieval communities and which existed as late as the nineteenth century in North America. (Boston's Common is now a park, but it was originally a common pasture, where any citizen could graze livestock.) There are other examples of common resources that most of us can relate to. The public road network, in the absence of toll charges, is a common resource that most of us use. Prior to pollution regulations, both water bodies and the atmosphere were common resources that producers were allowed to use as sinks for the disposal of their wastes.

The nature of common resources is that they tend to be used at inefficiently high levels. To understand why, we can turn to the example that Garrett Hardin used in his classic paper "The Tragedy of the Commons." Imagine that there is a common pasture on which a large population of people is allowed to graze its livestock. The livestock is being reared to provide some product, which could be meat, wool or milk. For our purposes, suppose that the animals are cows and the product is milk and that, within limits, the more grass a cow eats the more milk it produces. The more cows on the pasture, the less grass each can eat. Therefore, the curve in Figure 6.2, which represents the milk produced as a function of the number of cows on the pasture, increases at a decreasing rate. The pasture is a renewable resource, but if it is overused its ability to regenerate itself declines. Thus, beyond some point, the total milk produced may be decreasing for the number of cows because of a decreasing amount of grass available. There is no aggregate gain achieved by placing more than $n^*$ cows on the pasture. Yet on a common pasture it can easily happen.

Suppose you are the owner of cow number $n+1$. If you bring your cow to the common pasture, it will produce some milk. If you do not, it will produce no milk and will have to be destroyed. It is therefore economically rational for you to bring your cow to the pasture. What you don't know about – or, if you do know, you don't care about – is that the degradation of the resource due to the addition of your cow will cause each of the $n$ cows that were already on the pasture to produce slightly less milk. The aggregate of all those small reductions in milk production is greater than the milk you are getting from your cow. Putting your cow on the pasture makes you better off, but it makes "the economy" worse off.

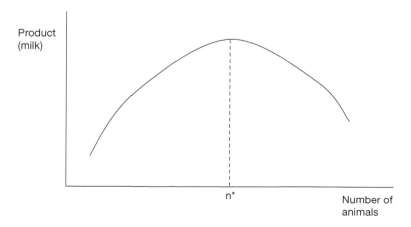

*Figure 6.2* "Tragedy of the commons"

A situation like this, where the economic incentives of an individual run counter to the aggregate well-being, is called a market failure. This is a bit of a misnomer, because there is really no market to fail here. There is no supply function for access to the common resource because it is provided as a free good.

The common pasture may seem an arcane thing to worry about, but a very similar argument applies to the use of a public highway. Suppose there is a commuter road with an entrance at one end and an exit some miles away at the other end. We can think of movement, measured as car-miles per hour, as the output of the highway. As more cars attempt to enter the highway, the number of cars increases but their speed decreases. So movement is increasing with the number of cars, but at a decreasing rate. Beyond a certain number of cars, congestion gets so bad that the relationship between the number of cars and the output of movement turns negative. Thus, Figure 6.2 could just as easily apply to a highway as to a common pasture.

Now think about it. Suppose you need to get to your home, which is at the end of that highway, and there is no alternative road. You may realize that by entering the highway you will add to the congestion, so much so that the movement you achieve is less than the aggregate reduction in movement you cause to all the other cars. Are you likely to say "I choose not to go home tonight because it would not be socially efficient"?

## Externalities and environmental policy

We define an externality as an effect that the actions of one economic agent (whether a producer or a consumer) has on another agent in the absence of any payment of compensation. A classic example is the case of two businesses located along a river: a paper mill and laundry. The paper mill is upstream. When the paper mill discharges waste products into the river, it dirties the water that the laundry uses to wash linens. Thus, the action of the paper mill has a negative effect on the laundry. If no compensation is paid, this is an example of a negative externality. The addition of a cow and the addition of a car in the examples described above are both cases of negative externalities.

The applications of this concept to environmental issues generally focuses on negative externalities, but positive externalities are equally possible. Suppose you own a small tavern along a highway. Now suppose a big developer comes along and builds a football stadium in the lot adjoining your property. The increased traffic of thirsty fans will increase your business, but you are under no compulsion to make any compensation to the developer for this windfall. This is a positive externality for you, but that does not guarantee that it has a positive net effect on society. Perhaps the stadium moved from an earlier downtown location. Its relocation will result in a negative externality for downtown taverns.

A note on terminology is in order here. The terms *positive externality* and *external economy* can be used interchangeably. In fact, we have already seen positive externalities in the form of agglomeration economies as described in chapter 3. The term *negative externality* can be used interchangeably with *external diseconomy*.

Interactions between people and the environment give rise to a lot of negative externalities, whereby aggregate well-being is reduced by a few individuals acting in their own best interests. How are the rights of society to be defended against the actions of some individuals? The natural answer is that the public sector must intervene. Environmental regulation is essentially an effort on the part of government to mitigate the effects of negative externalities.

Some may dispute whether government regulation is necessary. Inefficient outcomes arise not so much from the failure of a market as from the absence of a market, as access to resources is provided as a free good. The answer therefore is to create a proper market by placing the resource in the hands of private individuals, who will ensure that it is not misused. For example, if the pasture represented in Figure 6.2 were in private hands, the owner would never allow more than $n$ cows to graze on it. Thus, privatization of common resources is a possible solution to the problem of negative externalities.

Proponents of this view point to the fact that the ultimate solution to the problem of common pastures was the "enclosure movement" in England and elsewhere in Europe, beginning from about the sixteenth century. Enclosure meant that common pastures were fenced off, usually subdivided and reserved for the exclusive use of a single farmer. The problem with enclosure is that, while it may have led to greater efficiency (historians still argue about this), it had negative distributional consequences, as landless peasants were deprived of their livings.[1]

Even if it were desirable to privatize environmental resources, it would not be practical in many cases. How would we privatize the Mississippi River, the Mediterranean Sea or the entire atmosphere? Nevertheless, the notion of private ownership of common resources may provide some useful guidance in policy formulation. In the regulation of air pollution, for example, we know that too much pollution will be emitted but we also know that the elimination of all pollution is neither technologically feasible nor economically desirable. The government has to limit the amount of pollutants released into the atmosphere, but to what level? Imagining that the atmosphere was a privately owned resource and determining how much pollution would be allowed (and how much the owner would charge polluters for the privilege of polluting) can provide at least a useful benchmark.

At this point, however, it is important to refer back to our three perspectives on the environment. Such calculations are consistent with the first (pragmatic) perspective and might even embrace the second (aesthetic) perspective, so long as the utility derived from the beauty of nature could be reduced to economic terms. The notion of private ownership of environmental resources is inimical to the third (existence value) perspective, however.

## Space, time and the environment

Economic geographers have been especially active in environmental research for a couple of reasons. The first is that the relationship between human activities is one of the central themes in the discipline of geography. The second is that most negative externalities are of a spatial nature. Returning to the example of the paper mill and the laundry, there would be no negative externality if the two firms were on different rivers or, for that matter, if the laundry were upstream from the paper mill. The existence and magnitude of both negative and positive externalities generally depend on the location of two economic agents relative to one another.

A farmer's field that is richly spread with fresh manure may not be an environmental problem at all, so long as it is sufficiently remote. If it is located on the edge of a suburban development or if it drains into a public water supply, however, it creates a negative externality of the first order. Thus, environmental regulations often restrict not how much of an offending activity may take place, but rather where it may take place. The rationale for zoning regulations and other place-specific restrictions is that they are designed to reduce negative externalities whose effects diminish with distance from the source activity.

Just as positive externalities (agglomeration economies) tend to draw people together, negative externalities often encourage dispersion. By living at low density, you reduce your possible exposure to negative externalities caused by your neighbor's activities: pollution, noise, crime, offensive colors of exterior house paint, etc. Of course, you also lose out on positive externalities, but you can offset this somewhat by using the mobility afforded by car ownership to interact only with people of your own choosing. There is, however, an enigma here. By trying to create a more desirable environment for yourself, you may be contributing to a general degradation of the larger environment. Figure 6.3 illustrates the positive feedback circuit of urban sprawl. In an attempt to avoid pollution, people move away from the center of the metropolitan area. The lifestyle that low-density living entails, with its high levels of automobile use and energy-intensive houses, leads to more pollution, which in turn reinforces the desire to move to ever more remote locations.

Consideration of environmental resources brings up questions not only of what to do at any point in time, but also of how to assign certain activities over an indefinite time horizon. This is especially true with respect to non-renewable resources and to renewable resources whose future potential can be diminished by overuse in the present. As we have already noted, most environmental resources are not private property, so society as a whole, usually represented by its governments, must decide how best to use them. But just as it can be argued that these resources are not the exclusive property of any individual who is alive today, it can also be argued that they are no more the collective property of people who are

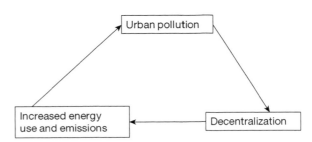

*Figure 6.3*
Pollution and sprawl

alive today than of people who will be alive in the future. This gives rise to unique issues of generational equity in making decisions about resource exploitation. The main notion of "sustainable development" is that society must make decisions with the rights and needs of future generations in mind.

It is a general economic principle that people would rather have something of value today than at some time in the future. For example, if you had a choice between receiving $1,000 today or receiving $1,000 next year, you would always choose to receive it today. The reason is simple. You could take the money you receive today, put it in the bank and earn interest on it. If the interest rate were 10 percent, you would have $1,100 dollars at the end of the year. So asking whether you would prefer to have $1,000 today or next year is equivalent to asking whether you would prefer to have $1,000 or $1,100 next year. The answer is obvious.

The method of comparing the values of things received at different points in times is called discounting and it is described more technically in the Appendix to this chapter. The relevance of discounting to questions of resource depletion is that economic rationality leads people to try to exploit a resource as quickly as possible. For example, if you have an oil reservoir, you are better off getting the oil out and turned into cash as quickly as possible (unless you expect the price of oil to rise on the future). But this decision is based only on your own well-being (or, in the case of social ownership, on the well-being of the current generation). Discounting tends to work against the interests of future generations.

## Appendix: Discounting and the environment

The concept of net present value (NPV) allows us to compare the value of things of value received in the future to things received today. Let's say you are promised $1,000 one year from now. What is that promise worth today? Net present value is calculated as:

$$NPV = \frac{1000}{1 + r}$$

where $r$ is the interest rate. If the rate is 10 percent ($r = 0.1$), the NPV is $909.09. So we are indifferent between having that value today or $1,000 in a year. If the interest rate is only 5 percent, however, the NPV is $953.38. Essentially, what we are doing here is discounting the value received according to the time we have to wait and the interest rate – which is therefore called a discount rate. If we have to wait longer, the NPV will be smaller. If we are to receive $1,000 in two years, we would essentially have to take the NPV for one year and discount it again for the second year:

$$NPV(2) = \frac{\left(\dfrac{1000}{1 + r}\right)}{1 + r} = \frac{1000}{(1 + r)^2}$$

Now the NPV is $826.45 for 10 percent and $907.03 for 5 percent. In general, the net present value of some value $V$ we are going to receive in $t$ years is

$$NPV(t) = \frac{V}{(1 + r)^1}$$

We can also calculate the NPV of a flow of benefits we are going to receive in the future. For example, we might ask how much is $100 to be received at the end of each of the next five years. We would calculate the NPV as follows:

$$NPV = \frac{100}{1 + r} + \frac{100}{(1 + r)^2} + \frac{100}{(1 + r)^3} + \frac{100}{(1 + r)^4} + \frac{100}{(1 + r)^5} = \sum_{i=1}^{5} \frac{100}{(1 + r)^t}$$

With a 10 percent discount rate, this works out to $379.08. (See for yourself what the NPV is with a 5 percent discount rate.) If we received the entire $500 at the end of one year, the NPV is $454.54. Thus, the sooner we can get something that is coming to us, the better off we are.

NPV calculations are useful when we are considering making an investment now that yield benefits in the future. For example, suppose you are in the market for a new car and you have the option of purchasing the model of your choice with either a conventional engine or a hybrid engine. You plan to keep the car for ten years and you assume that the resale value at the end of the ten years will be the same for both the hybrid and conventional options. You have done some calculations and determined that, assuming the price of gasoline does not change, you will save $500 a year with the hybrid from reduced fuel purchases. Would you pay $5,000 for the hybrid option? Only if your discount rate is zero.

So what would you pay for the hybrid option? The answer is simply a matter of calculating the NPV of $500 per year over ten years. At a discount rate of 10 percent, the value is about $3,072. So, if the extra amount you have to pay to get the hybrid is less than $3,072, it makes sense to get it. If the discount rate is only 5 percent, you may be willing to pay a good deal more, about $3,860. Of course, this does not rule out the possibility that you would pay more out of a desire to improve the environment – NPV calculations generally don't take account of altruism. Also, the government may choose to subsidize the cost of the hybrid option in order to help capture external benefits from reduced fuel use.

It should not be hard to envision how this basic framework could be extended to a whole range of environmental issues. For example, we might use NPV to see whether it is worth making expenditure in energy-efficient technologies and infrastructure now to avoid environmental costs arising from climate change in the future. But, in this case, the benefits (defined as avoided costs) will tend to increase with time, so they will be much higher in 100 years than in five years. The problem here is that discounting will tend to make those benefits virtually irrelevant to the decision problem. For example, $(1 + r)^{100}$ is equal to 13,781. So $1 million of avoided environmental costs in 100 years would be worth only $72.56 today![2] Clearly, the goals of sustainable development and intergenerational equity call for alternative ways of valuing future environmental costs and benefits.

# 7  The production technology

Economic activities are of two general types: production activities and consumption activities. Production refers to the transformation of productive inputs into the output of a good or a service. Consumption refers to the process of using goods and services to create *utility*, which is defined as a general level of satisfaction. Firms purchase productive inputs and transform them into goods and services. Households purchase goods and services and transform them into utility. (The reason a good is called "good" is that you can increase your utility by consuming it.) In this chapter, we focus on production, with a particular emphasis on how inputs are transformed into goods and services. We also illustrate that the same logic that applies to the firm's production choices can apply to a household's consumption choices.

Not all goods and services that are produced by firms are consumed by households. Sometimes goods produced by one firm are purchased by another to use either as an intermediate good (a material input that is not a raw material) or as a capital good (a fixed asset). Services may also be provided for other firms rather than for households, in which case they are called producer services.

Both goods and services have value, as evidenced by the fact that people will pay for them. The distinction is that goods are things with mass and services are not. Sometimes, the distinction is obvious: a tomato is a good, a haircut is a service (you cannot bring a haircut home in a paper bag). For some other things the distinction becomes less clear – if you buy software on a disk it seems like a good, but if you download it from the Internet it seems more like a service. Neither goods nor services can be created from nothing – they require productive inputs.[1] The tomato requires land, the labor of farm workers, seed, fertilizer, farm equipment and transportation to market. We can also think of adequate rainfall and sunshine as inputs. The haircut requires the labor of the barber, scissors and other implements, various toiletries, space within a building for the barber to work and the energy and equipment needed to keep that space comfortable (that is, for heating and air conditioning).

## Productive inputs

Given the endless variety of inputs that go into the production of goods and services, it is useful to define some categories. We define eight categories of productive inputs: labor, capital services, public infrastructure services, producer services, energy, materials, land and environmental services. Each region has stocks from which these inputs can be drawn. These stocks are generally called "resources" or "endowments." For some inputs, the firm can draw on stocks in other regions – such inputs are called "tradeables." Most input stocks are privately owned, so the firm must pay a price for inputs. Inputs from publicly owned stocks may be paid for indirectly through taxation or directly through user fees. We now turn to a brief discussion of each of our eight categories of inputs.

1   Labor inputs have two aspects: simple energy and skills. A person whose job it is to move bags of sand from one part of a construction site to another provides little more than simple energy. The same work could be done by a trained animal or by a machine using diesel oil to provide energy. Most jobs involve a great deal of skill, which is embodied in the individual worker. A research scientist or a computer programmer provides very little simple energy, but draws heavily on skills. When we talk about labor resources, we use two terms that correspond roughly to this energy/skills dichotomy. The "labor force" refers to the stock of people available to work, while "human capital" stock refers to the skills embodied in labor. In modern economies, human capital defines a more important resource, but the labor force is an easier stock to measure.

2   Capital services are provided by fixed assets such as buildings, machinery and vehicles that are owned by the firms. We make a distinction between capital service and capital stock because production does not directly consume part of the stock. However, most stocks "depreciate" which means that their abilities to provide services decline as more and more services are consumed in production. The type and level of capital services available in a region depends on the regional stock, which means that the current endowment depends on investments made in previous periods. (Hence the link between "capital" and "human capital," because the latter depends on investments made in education and training in earlier periods.)

3   Public infrastructure services are provided by fixed assets that belong to the public sector, rather than to the firm itself. Highways are a notable category of public infrastructure without which very few firms could do business. In a market economy, public infrastructure exists because there are certain types of capital that many firms or households need for their production and consumption activities, but which no individual firm or household can efficiently provide for itself.

4   Producer services are things that do not have mass that the firm purchases from other firms because they are needed in the production process. Examples are the services of cleaners, auditors, consulting engineers, data processing firms, plumbers, advertising agencies and many more. Most producer services could feasibly be provided "in house" using the firm's own labor and capital, but are more efficiently provided by firms who gain scale economies by specializing in a narrow range of services and providing them to a large number of customers.

5    Energy refers to the fuels and electricity that are consumed by capital stocks in the provision of capital services. This category is distinct from the energy provided by labor. When the mover of bags of sand described above is replaced by a machine, a combination of capital and energy are substituted for labor. Energy is one of the tradeable inputs. Some regions may be rich in stocks of energy such as oil and coal, much of which will be shipped to other regions rather than used by economic activities within the region. Electricity is a special case because it is generated via a capital-intensive process using a fossil fuel, nuclear fuel or energy from wind and the movement of water. Like other forms of energy, however, it is tradeable via transmission lines.

6    Material inputs are used principally in the production of goods. Manufacturing firms produce goods that have mass and material inputs provide the mass in those goods. They are of two general categories: raw materials which are taken "directly from nature" (agricultural produce, timber, minerals, fish, etc.) and intermediate goods, which are the outputs of another manufacturing firm. For example, a steel maker transforms iron ore (a raw material) to produce steel which is used as an intermediate good by other manufacturing firms that produce cars, appliances and so on. Material inputs are tradeable, but, since transportation is expensive, they are generally cheapest in their regions of origin.

7    Land, like labor, is an input with two aspects. The first is simply space. All economic activities take up space, but some are more space intensive than others. For example, a corporate law office in a high-rise building uses only a tiny amount of land, first because it is relatively compact and second because it is sharing the space on the ground (land) with offices on all the other floors. A supermarket may generate the same amount of revenue as the law office, but it takes up more land. A farm that generates the same amount of revenue will take up even more land. Regions with very little land are generally not well suited to space-intensive economic activities. The second aspect of land has to do with the quality of soils and the terrain. Most types of agriculture are most productive in rich soils on level terrain.

8    Environmental services include clean air, clean water, favorable climate and other inputs that are taken from the environment either freely or at very low cost. Beautiful scenery and healthy populations of flora and fauna are environmental services that are essential inputs to tourist activities. As we saw in chapter 6, the fact that environmental services are generally free goods often leads to overuse and to the degradation of environmental resources. Thus, the public sector often regulates these resources.

Figure 7.1 is a graphical representation of how these different categories of inputs fit into a production process for a good. At the far right, there are a number of supplier firms that provide three categories of inputs: material, energy and producer services. These are delivered to the firm using public transportation infrastructure, thus the designation "PI" on the links connecting supplier firms to the producing firm. Capital and labor are shown inside the block representing the firm. This is

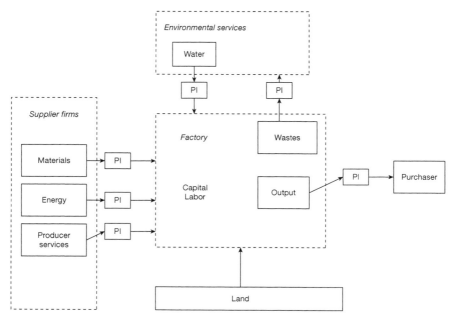

*Figure 7.1* Inputs into a production process for a good

because they are relatively permanent inputs that are carried over from one production cycle to the next. We can think of the firm's function as taking inputs from other firms and from the environment and creating output whose value is greater than the combined value of the inputs. Capital and labor are the inputs that "add value" to the other inputs in the production process.[2] At the top of the figure is a block of environmental resources that provide environmental services. One shown here is water, which is withdrawn from the environment, while the other is waste disposal which involves transferring some undesirable byproduct to the environment. In both cases, some public infrastructure may be used, such as water management and distribution systems and sewer infrastructure for disposal of liquid wastes. (How water fits here depends on its use. If water is used for cooling, processing and waste disposal, it is an environmental service. Sometimes, however, it is used as a material input – as in the case of soft drinks or beer.)

At the bottom of the figure is land, in this case the land occupied by the production facilities. Finally, output is transferred to the purchaser, which may be another firm if the output is an intermediate or capital good, or a household if it is a consumer good. In either case, some services from public infrastructure will be required.

There is a further resource that varies across regions but does not provide productive inputs in the conventional sense. Entrepreneurship is the ability to create new activities and to adjust existing activities to a changing economic environment.

Entrepreneurs are people, but their contribution is distinct from labor. Instead of producing goods and services, entrepreneurs make the investments and related decisions that make such production happen, directing resources to the most profitable activities and taking the risks that are necessary for innovation and economic growth. A wealth of entrepreneurship may account for superior economic performance in a region relative to other regions with similar endowments of productive resources.

## The production technology

"Technology" is a word with many meanings. In a broad sense, it refers to the application of scientific knowledge to create means of production and consumption that are cheaper, faster and better. In economics, technology refers to the quantitative relationship between amounts of inputs and amounts of outputs. We can define a list of inputs that are needed for the production of a particular good or service. Knowledge of the production technology tells us how much of each input is required to produce a given quantity of output.

One way to think of the production technology is as a recipe. A recipe for a cake would specify the amount of all ingredients (flour, eggs, sugar), the capital services required (mixer, oven), the labor required as defined by cooking activities, and so on. A similar recipe might tell us how much ore, scrap and coal and what types of labor and capital services are required to produce a ton of steel. The analogy to a cooking recipe is not perfect, however, because recipes generally do not express two important characteristics of production technologies: returns to scale and input substitution.

Before explaining these two characteristics, we need to define a basic functional relationship used to describe production technologies: the production function. Imagine a firm that produces a single good. Define the amount of that good produced by the firm over some time interval (a month, a year) as $q$. In order to produce that much output, the firm must purchase specific quantities of inputs, represented by $x$. Referring to the numbers above, $x_1$ is the quantity of labor, $x_2$ is the quantity of capital service and so on. These quantities will be measured in different units, as appropriate to the type of input. Labor is generally measured in terms of person-hours. Since the quantity of capital services used depends on the magnitude of the capital stock, the value of the capital stock is generally used as a proxy measure of capital services. The production function is defined as follows:

$$q = f(x_1, x_2, x_3, x_4, x_5, x_6, x_7, x_8)$$

The notation $f(\ )$ represents some mathematical expression in which the terms in the parentheses are variables. For our purposes, we do not need to present the exact form, but simply note that the value of $q$ is positively related to all the $x$ values. (The Appendix to this chapter introduces some simple specifications for the production function.) There are eight values of $x$ corresponding to our eight categories of inputs. In general, however, the number of inputs in a particular production technology may be less than eight (for example, some services don't require material inputs) or more than eight (most manufacturing processes require more than one material input). So it is more general to say the production technology requires some number $n$ inputs and write the production function as follows:

$$q = f(x_1, x_2, ..., x_n)$$

A couple of things are important to understand here. The first is that the production function is a quantitative relationship: $q$ and $x_1$ do not just "represent" output and labor, $q$ is a specific quantity of output and $x_1$ is a specific quantity of labor. The second is that the production function represents a *most efficient* relationship between inputs and outputs. If it is technologically feasible to produce a ton of steel with 10 hours of labor, it is also feasible to produce the same ton with 12 hours if the employees do not work efficiently. For any level of $q$ the values of $x$ are efficient in the sense that, if you reduce one of them while leaving the others constant, the value of $q$ will go down.

The production function gives us a way to formalize the concept of returns to scales. Recall from chapter 3 that scale economies are defined as the advantage of producing a good or service at large scale. (The terms *scale economy* and *increasing returns to scale* are equivalent.) This suggests that we can determine whether a production technology has increasing returns to scale through the relationship between inputs and outputs as expressed in the production function. Suppose we increase all the inputs in the production function by a constant positive factor $\lambda$. Increasing returns to scale means

$$\lambda q < f(\lambda x_1, \lambda x_2, ..., \lambda x_n)$$

For example, if $\lambda = 2$, doubling the quantity of each input more than doubles the quantity of output. The reason that this is called a "scale economy" is that, if the price of inputs remains constant, increasing the scale of production decreases the per unit cost of producing output. The production technology exhibits constant returns to scale if

$$\lambda q = f(\lambda x_1, \lambda x_2, ..., \lambda x_n)$$

and decreasing returns to scale is

$$\lambda q > f(\lambda x_1, \lambda x_2, ..., \lambda x_n).$$

Input substitution is the characteristic of production technologies that gives the firm some flexibility with regard to what combination of input they choose and, as we shall see, allows them to respond to changes in the relative prices of inputs.

The most frequently noted case of input substitution is the substitution of capital for labor. To consider a hypothetical example, imagine that you are in the business of taking whole logs and transforming them into firewood. (Note that in this example you will be adding value because a ton of firewood is worth more than a ton of logs.) You may have a choice between two production methods. The first is to set ten men with ten axes to cut up the logs. The second is to give two men chainsaws, with which they can cut up the same number of logs. Our proxy measure of capital services is the capital stock, measured as the value of the capital goods. Since two chainsaws have a greater value than ten axes, the first option is labor intensive and the second option is capital intensive. If you start with the first option but then switch to the second, you will be substituting capital for labor.

Since both methods produce the same output, how would you choose between them? Obviously you would choose the method with the lowest production cost. This will depend on the price of labor. If wages are very low, it may be cheaper to pay the ten workers and save the extra cost of the chainsaws. If wages are high, however, it is more likely that you will choose the more capital-intensive option.

The history of manufacturing in most countries reflects the fact that the cost of labor has been increasing relative to the cost of capital. And so, through time, production tends to become more capital intensive. Figure 7.2 shows indexes of capital stock and employment in U.S. manufacturing from 1960 to 2000. While employment was relatively flat over this period, capital stock grew rapidly, leading to more capital per worker. Growing capital intensity can also be observed in agriculture, as illustrated for the case of China in Box 7.

---

### *Box 7* Food production in China

From the 1960s to the first decade of the twenty-first century, China underwent an economic transformation from a rural society focused on traditional agricultural production to an ever more urban society that has become the world's manufacturing powerhouse. This transformation required the movement of hundreds of millions of people away from agricultural villages and into rapidly growing industrial cities. But, if all those people are no longer on the land producing food, how does China feed her enormous population?

Figure B7.1 provides a crude quantitative picture of what happened by tracking indexes of food production and agricultural labor force from 1961 to 2004. (An index defines a base year and then expresses a variable as the ratio of its value in a given year to the value in the base year. So the value of the output index at just above 3 in 1990 means that agricultural production in that year was three times as high as in 1961.) Over the period of transformation, food production somehow grew much faster than the number of people available to produce it. In fact, between 1990 and 2004, the number of agricultural workers basically remained constant, while the food they produced more than doubled.

How is this possible? We can explain it as the outcome of two concepts introduced in this chapter: input substitution and technological progress. In traditional economies, labor is fairly cheap, so labor-intensive production methods involving hand tools and a few draught animals are economical. As more workers move off the land, however, labor becomes scarcer and therefore more expensive. Thus, it makes sense to try to reduce agricultural labor requirements by using more labor-saving machinery. Nearly all industrialized societies go through a period of rapid capital for labor substitution as farm workers are attracted to cities by higher wages. As evidence of the speed of this process in China, it is estimated that there were about 6,000 mechanical harvesting machines in use during the early 1960s. This number increased by a factor of over 60 to more than 360,000 in 2003.[i] This type of machine can be operated by one or two people but do the work of more than a dozen. So less labor is needed to produce a given quantity of food.

The substitution of machines for human and animal labor does not tell the whole story. Over the period in question, technological progress means that, even on a farm where there has been no change in the levels of inputs, increases in agricultural yields would have increased. These are changes to the characteristics of inputs themselves that make seeds more likely to sprout, fertilizers more likely to increase yield, pesticides more effective, machines more reliable and efficient, and even improve the productivity of people by teaching them how to work more effectively. The sources of technological progress range from rural training sessions that teach workers not to waste water or energy to creation of biologically engineered seeds.

There are limits to both of these processes. Dependence on machines may reduce the quality of food and application of advanced fertilizers and pesticides may have negative environmental consequences. In the final

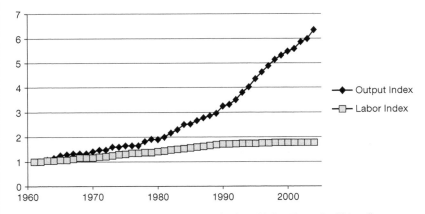

*Figure B7.1* Index of food output and agricultural labor force in China (base year 1961)

*Source*: Data adapted from World Resources Institute (n.d.) Earth Trends: The Environmental Information Portal.

analysis, as long as there is a limited amount of land available, all efforts to increase food production reach diminishing returns at some point. But the important point is that urbanization and industrialization would not be possible without input substitution and technological progress in agriculture.

## Note

[i] Same source as Figure B7.1.

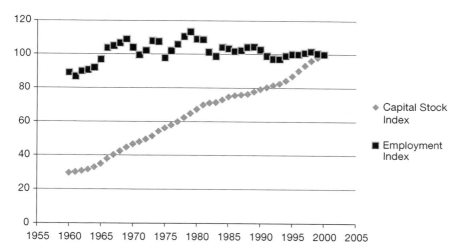

*Figure 7.2* Indexes of manufacturing capital stock and full-time equivalent employment in the U.S., 1960–2000 (2000 = 100)

*Source*: U.S. Bureau of Economic Analysis (n.d. a, n.d. b).

Capital and labor are not the only inputs for which substitution is possible. Sometimes there may be substitution between inputs in the same category, such as when iron ore and scrap are substituted in the production of steel, or when coal and residual oil are substituted in the generation of electricity. Capital may substitute for energy if new, more expensive equipment uses less fuel to do the same work. As we have already noted, labor often substitutes with producer services.

We can represent substitution between inputs in the production function as occurring when

$$q = f(x_1, x_2, ..., x_n) = f([x_1 + \Delta_1], [x_2 - \Delta_2], ..., x_1)$$

What this says is that you can decrease the level of input 2 by $\Delta_2$ and maintain the same level of output if you increase the level of input 1 by $\Delta_1$. The ratio $\Delta_1/\Delta_2$ is called the technical rate of substitution between inputs 1 and 2.

If the price of input 2 goes up relative to the price of input 1, the firm will want to substitute 1 for 2. But by how much? We can answer this question with the aid of a classic diagram from microeconomic theory. To present this diagram, we must assume that there are only two inputs in the production technology, which we call input 1 and input 2. (They need not be capital and labor.)

The curved line in Figure 7.3 is called an isoquant. The word *isoquant* means constant quantity, so each point on the isoquant is a combination of levels of inputs 1 and 2 that produce a constant quantity of output. So, for example, if the combination $(x_1, x_2)$ produces 100 units of output, then the combination $(x_1', x_2')$ also produces 100 units of output. The slope of the isoquant at any point is the negative value of the increase in 1 needed to substitute for a decrease in 2: that is, the technical rate of substitution $\Delta_1/\Delta_2$.

Suppose the firm wants to produce the level of output associated with the isoquant in Figure 7.3. How will it choose the point along the isoquant at which its production costs are minimized? First, define the cost of production as

$$C = p_1 x_1 + p_2 x_2$$

where $p_1$ and $p_2$ are the prices of inputs 1 and 2 respectively. Rearranging terms,

$$x_2 = \frac{C}{p_2} - \frac{p_1}{p_2} x_2$$

For a fixed value of $C$, we can graph this line in the same space of inputs 1 and 2 in which the isoquant is graphed. In Figure 7.4, any combination $(x_1, x_2)$ that lies on this *isocost line* can be purchased for the value $C$. The dotted lines represent isocost lines associated with different higher and lower values of $C$. Note that they all have different intercepts but the same slope.

The firm's problem of finding the values $(x_1{}^*, x_2{}^*)$ that minimize its production costs amounts to finding the point at which the isoquant intersects the lowest possible isocost line (Figure 7.5). This is the point where the technical rate of

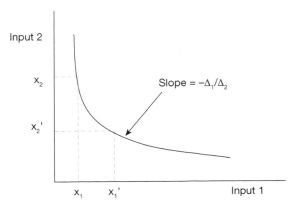

*Figure 7.3* Input substitution: the isoquant

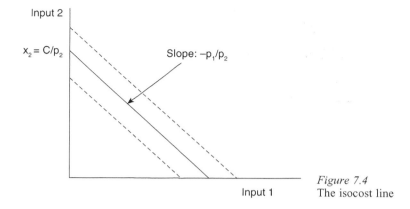

Figure 7.4
The isocost line

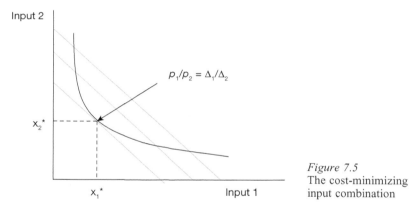

Figure 7.5
The cost-minimizing
input combination

substitution is equal to the price ratio, which is the rate at which the two goods exchange in the market.

We can take this graphical model a step further to see what happens if relative prices change. Suppose the price of input 2 increases while the price of input 1 remains the same. This has no effect on the isoquant, but it changes the slope of the isocost line. Since $P_2$ is in the denominator, the slope of the isocost line decreases as shown in Figure 7.6. The new optimal input combination $(x_1^{**}, x_2^{**})$ combines less of the good that has become relatively expensive $(x_1^{**} < x_2^{*})$ and more of the good that has become relatively inexpensive $(x_1^{**} > x_1^{*})$.

Not all production technologies admit the possibility of input substitution. For example, producing gunpowder requires precise proportions of three ingredients: carbon, sulfur and phosphate. The producer is not able to alter the proportions of these three in response to changes in their relative prices because deviations from the prescribed proportions may produce powder that will not go off. We call a production technology that does not allow input substitution a *fixed proportion production technology*. Even when substitution is possible in reality, it is often

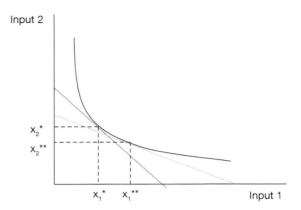

*Figure 7.6*
The effect of an increase in
the price of input 2

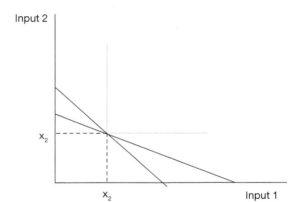

*Figure 7.7*
Isoquants for a fixed
proportion production
technology

useful to assume a fixed proportion production technology in order to keep the
development of a model simple.

Isoquants for a fixed proportion production technology are of the form shown
in Figure 7.7. Here we see that the best combination of inputs is the same for all
possible slopes of the isocost line.

## Technological progress

The production technology represents the set of all technologically feasible, efficient
input/output combinations available to the producing firm at a particular point in
time. The qualifying phrase "at a particular point in time" is necessary because
production technologies tend to change through time so as to make it possible to
produce a constant amount of output with smaller amounts of input. The change
in production technology over time is called "technological progress."

There are many concrete examples of technological progress. Improvements in
engine technology makes it possible to do the same amount of work with less fuel.

Improvements in extraction technologies make it possible to get the same amount of metal (iron, gold, copper, etc.) from less ore. Labor-saving devices make it possible to produce the same amount of any good or service with less labor input.

We can represent technological progress in the production function as follows:

$$q = a(t) f(x_1, x_2, ..., x_n)$$

Here $a$ is a positive function of time $t$, so, as time passes, the value of $q$ increases, even if the value of each input remains constant. We can represent technological progress in the isoquant diagram as shown in Figure 7.8. As time passes, the curve that defines the set of values for the two inputs that can produce a constant output $\bar{q}$ shifts closer to the origin.[3]

## The production technology and economic geography

The concept of the production technology will return many times in this book. Agglomeration economies, as described in chapter 3, are in part the outcome of increasing returns to scale in the production technology. Models of the multiregional economy presented in Part II (chapters 8–11) will all require some assumptions about production technologies – and, as we will see, different assumptions about scale economies and input substitution will have important implications.

For a variety of reasons, the prices of inputs tend to vary in space. Most material and energy inputs are produced at a point in space (a mine, factory, refinery, hydroelectric dam, etc.) and must be transported or (in the case of electricity) transmitted to the point of production. This means that the price of all such inputs has two components: the price of the good at its point of origin, called the "mill price," and the transportation or transmission cost. The price you pay depends on where you are. Labor costs vary significantly from place to place because labor markets are inherently spatial. It is not unusual for high unemployment and severe labor shortage to coexist in different parts of the same national economy, at least in the short run. The price of land is perhaps more spatially variable than the price of any other input.

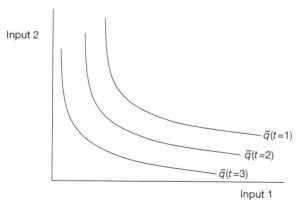

Figure 7.8 Technological progress and the isoquant

Economy geographers address the question of spatial variability in the prices of productive inputs in three ways:

1 Explaining spatial variability: Prices vary either because of transportation costs or because of the differences between regional markets for those inputs. We introduced the issues of transportation cost in chapter 2 and will return to them in Part III. We will pick up the issue of regional labor markets in chapter 9 and markets for land are the main topic of Part IV.
2 Explaining how spatial variability in input prices affects the way firms combine inputs: There are really two effects here. One is that firms at different points in space will choose to produce the goods and services whose technologies are most intensive in the inputs that are relatively cheap at their location. Firms in cheap labor regions will produce labor-intensive goods and services, and so on. The second is that, even in the production of the same good, firms in different places will choose different input combinations because the slope of their isocost lines are different. These issues are taken up in Part II.
3 Explaining how spatial variability in input prices affects the location choice of firms: Microeconomic theory generally assumes that the firm is a price taker, so input prices are exogenous to its behavior. If the firm is mobile, meaning it can choose its location, it actually has some control over the input prices it pays. If it thinks wages are too high, it can move to a place where they are lower. But such a move might also result in higher material or energy prices and might move it away from its main customers. All these issues are incorporated into the theory of location presented in Part III.

## Households, utility and consumption

Households[4] play a different role in the economy than do firms. While firms produce goods and services, households are the ultimate consumers of goods and services. Still, a very similar logic to that which is used above to describe the behavior of firms can be used to describe the behavior of households. The common thread between firms and households can be defined as follows: firms purchase inputs and use them to produce outputs, while households purchase goods and services and use them to produce utility.

The meaning of the word "utility" has been the topic of much debate, but for our purpose it is sufficient to define it as a measure of a household's level of material well-being. More specifically, it is the level of well-being that is achieved through the purchase of goods and services. Naturally, there is a more comprehensive notion of well-being that is affected by things that we cannot purchase: the love of family, the companionship of friends, religious faith, appreciation of great literature and a variety of other things that are outside the scope of the market.

Much like the production function of the firm, the household has a utility function

$$u = f(g_1, g_2, \dots, g_m)$$

Here utility is a function of $m$ goods and services. The household differs from the firm, however, in the sense that it has a fixed quantity of income $y$ to spend, which implies a budget constraint

$$y = g_1 p_1 + g_2 p_2 + \dots + g_m p_m$$

The household seeks to consume levels of goods and service in such a way as to maximize its utility, while at the same time staying within its budget constraint. Consider a household that consumes only two goods. If we assume that goods can substitute for one another in the utility function similar to the way inputs can substitute in production function, we can draw a line of equal utility in the space of the two inputs called the "indifference curve."

As shown in Figure 7.9, the household is indifferent between the combination of goods $(g_1, g_2)$ and $(g_1', g_2')$ because they both yield the same level of utility. A set of indifference curves can be drawn for different levels of utility, as shown in Figure 7.10, where $u < u' < u''$:

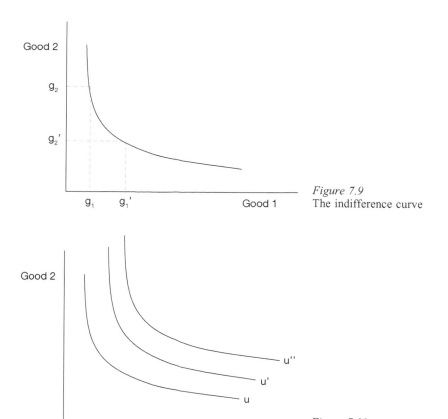

Figure 7.9
The indifference curve

Figure 7.10
A set of indifference curves

The household would like to be on the highest possible indifference curve, but must choose the level of goods to be consistent with the budget constraint $y = p_1 g_1 + p_2 g_2$. We can rearrange terms to yield an expression that can be graphed as a straight line in the space of the two goods, as shown in Figure 7.11.

The household can now maximize its utility by finding the point at which the highest possible indifference curve is tangent to the budget constraint.

## Appendix: Mathematical form of the production function

So far we have been content to leave the production function in a general form as

$$q = f(x_1, x_2, ..., x_n)$$

where the $f()$ represents some unspecified mathematical form. The purpose of this Appendix is to ask what that unspecified expression looks like. For simplicity, assume that there are only two inputs, so

$$q = f(x_1, x_2)$$

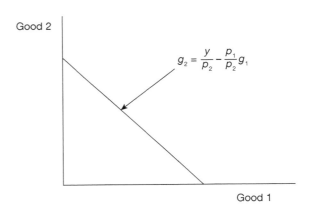

Figure 7.11
The budget constraint

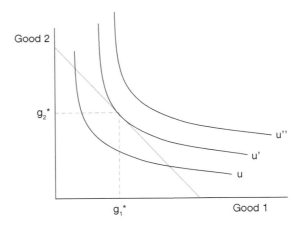

Figure 7.12
Optimal consumption for
the household

The simplest possible specification is a linear expression

$$q = a_1 x_1 + a_2 x_2$$

Linear expressions have a lot of attractions. They are easy to show graphically (you can verify for yourself that the isoquant for this production function would be a straight line). They are also amenable to statistical estimation. If we had several observations on output and input levels, we could estimate the values of $a_1$ and $a_2$ using linear regression.

Unfortunately, a linear expression just doesn't do the job. For one thing, it implies that you could produce some non-zero quantity of output using only one input. (Set the value of $x_1$ to zero. If $x_2$ is positive, $q$ is positive.) Also, if you hold the value of one input constant and add more of the other, you get the same increment of output no matter how much you add. Think about our example of cutting wood. If you hold capital constant (whether it is two chainsaws or ten axes) and keep adding more workers, the marginal addition to output ought to go down because each additional worker has progressively less capital to work with. This increment is called the marginal product of labor. If $x_1$ is labor, the marginal product is written

$$\frac{\partial q}{\partial x_1} = a_1$$

So it is independent of the level of any other input.

There is an important lesson here. Every mathematical specification for the production function (or any other functional relationships) has assumptions built into it. Generally, the simpler the mathematical form, the stronger is the implied assumption. Our linear production function implicitly assumes that we can eliminate any input and still produce output and that the marginal product of any input is independent of the value of any other input. Since these are unreasonable assumptions, the linear specification is not useful.

The trick in building a mathematical model is generally to find the simplest mathematical form that does not impose unreasonable assumptions. The following multiplicative form suits the purpose:

$$q = x_1^{\beta_1} x_2^{\beta_2}$$

In this expression, if you set $x_1$ or $x_2$ to zero, $q$ is equal to zero, so you need some of both inputs. Also, the marginal product of each input depends on the value of the other input:

$$\frac{\partial q}{\partial x_1} = \beta_1 x_1^{(\beta_1-1)} x_2^{\beta_2}$$

You can verify for yourself that, as long as $\beta_1 < 1$, the marginal product of input 1 will go down if you increase $x_1$ while holding $x_2$ constant. The values of the parameters in this production function also define returns to scale in the production technology: $\beta_1 + \beta_2 = 1$ indicates constant returns to scale, $\beta_1 + \beta_2 > 1$ indicates increasing returns to scale and $\beta_1 + \beta_2 < 1$ indicates decreasing returns. The multiplicative form is easily transformed to a linear form by taking logarithms.

$$\log q = \beta_1 \log x_1 + \beta_2 \log x_2$$

So linear regression methods can be used to estimate the values of $\beta_1$ and $\beta_2$.

This functional form can also be augmented with a term to incorporate the effect of technological progress:

$$q = a(t)x_1^{\beta_1}x_2^{\beta_2}$$

$da(t)/dt > 0$ implies that $q$ increases over time if inputs $x_1$ and $x_2$ are held constant.

The functional form described here still imposes some assumptions on input substitution. Varian (1992: ch. 12) explains these built-in assumptions and presents some more complicated forms that impose fewer restrictions on substitution.

# Part II
# The multiregional economy

# 8 Specialization and trade

This is the first of several chapters dealing with the spatial configuration of economic activity in a multiregional economy. Multiregional implies that some larger spatial unit is broken down into components called regions. We will be considering how these regions function and interact economically. Since we are not for the moment interested in spatial patterns occurring within regions, our analysis of the multi-regional economy is set in discrete space.

The first step in a multiregional analysis is to define a large spatial unit and the borders within it that define its regions. In applied analysis the large spatial unit is generally a country, but this need not be the case. We can just as easily define regions within, for example, the North American economy or even the world economy. Again, in applied work, the regions are usually political units such as states, provinces, counties, prefectures and so on. This is because the data needed for empirical analysis are usually only available at the level of such political divisions. Ideally, however, regions should be defined according to economic, rather than political differentiation. Recalling our definitions of formal and functional regions, each region might be internally homogeneous in terms of economic activity (agricultural regions, manufacturing regions, tourist regions) or internally bound together by patterns of spatial interaction (a metropolitan area, the hinterland of a port or river). The main point is that, for a set of multiregional borders to make economic sense, points within borders should be either more similar or more interrelated than points across borders.

It is fundamental to the notion of multiregional analysis in economic geography that the regions are somehow different from one another – recall that economic geographers usually start from a condition of spatial differentiation rather than of homogeneous space. The difference between regions implies that, for any economic activity you might name, some regions will be better suited than others. For wine making, regions with mild climates will be best suited; for smelting, regions with sources of metal ores and fuels will be best suited; and for trade, regions with natural harbors and navigable rivers will be best suited. These examples depend on differentiation across regions in terms of natural endowments. But, at any point in time, regions will also have different levels of resources that have been created by human activity in earlier periods. For example, due to public investment in earlier periods, some regions have the infrastructure resources that are needed for development of an industrial complex. Due to educational activities, some regions have the stock of skilled and creative people that are required for the most innovative and technologically advanced activities.

Because of these differences, economic forces will give rise to differences in the spatial pattern of economic activity – that is, to regional specialization. As each region becomes specialized, it makes good economic sense for people to exchange goods and services across regional borders – that is, to trade. The message of this chapter is that regional differentiation gives rise to specialization and trade within multiregional economies.

## Absolute advantage

Because of differences in resources, different regions are better at producing different things. Consider the simple example of a country that is divided into two regions, The Hills and The Plains. The people of this country produce and consume only two goods: bread and wine. The bread is produced from wheat, which grows best in The Plains with its rich soils and warm climate. Wine is produced from grapes, which grow best in The Hills where the climate is cooler and the soils are more acid. (To keep things simple, we assume that wheat and grapes are transformed into bread and wine respectively in the same region where they are grown.)

Either wheat or grapes can be grown in each region. In order to grow wheat in The Hills, however, it is necessary to terrace the land and apply fertilizers, both of which require a lot of labor. So wheat cultivation is more labor intensive in The Hills than it is in The Plains. To grow grapes in The Plains, it is necessary to build canopies to protect them from the sun during the hottest weather and apply acid supplements to the soil. Again, this makes grape cultivation in The Plains more labor intensive than it is in The Hills. We assume there is no shortage of land in either region, so the limiting production resource is labor: there are 100 workers in each region. Table 8.1 sums up our simple example. Note that the output of bread in loaves and wine in bottles per worker per day is used here as a measure of labor productivity, which is the inverse of labor intensity.

The question is now what is the most efficient way for the labor in these two regions to be distributed across production of wine and bread? Should workers in both regions produce both goods or should they specialize? Table 8.2a shows what happens if 50 percent of the workers in each region produce bread and the other 50 percent produce wine. Table 8.2b shows what happens if all the labor in The Plains produces bread and all the labor in The Hills produces wine.

*Table 8.1* Labor productivity in two regions

| Region | Output per worker per day | | Number of workers |
|---|---|---|---|
| | bread (loaves) | wine (bottles) | |
| The Plains | 100 | 15 | 100 |
| The Hills | 70 | 25 | 100 |

*Table 8.2a* Output of bread and wine

| Region | Workers | | Output | |
|---|---|---|---|---|
| | bread | wine | bread (loaves) | wine (bottles) |
| The Plains | 50 | 50 | 5,000 | 750 |
| The Hills | 50 | 50 | 3,500 | 1,250 |
| Total | 100 | 100 | 8,500 | 2,000 |

*Table 8.2b* Output of bread and wine

| Region | Workers | | Output | |
|---|---|---|---|---|
| | bread | wine | bread (loaves) | wine (bottles) |
| The Plains | 100 | 0 | 10,000 | 0 |
| The Hills | 0 | 100 | 0 | 2,500 |
| Total | 100 | 100 | 10,000 | 2,500 |

The result is simple. If all the labor in each region is dedicated to producing that good for which it is best suited, the aggregate amount of both bread and wine produced in the larger economy increases. Specialization yields an extra 1,500 loaves of bread and an extra 500 bottles of wine. This is fine from a production point of view, but what about the satisfaction of the consumers? It appears here that people in The Hills will have nothing but wine and people in The Plains will have nothing but bread. (This could lead to some dull dinner conversations in The Plains and some bad hangovers in The Hills.) The solution, of course, is that the two regions exchange bread for wine so that the workers in each region get to consume some of both. Thus, regional specialization and interregional trade go hand in hand.

Whenever there is trade in goods, however, there must be transportation. Imagine that, in our example, labor must be diverted from the production of bread and wine to the provision of transportation services in order to make trade possible. The more expensive (in terms of labor) it is to transport goods between the two regions, the smaller will be the incremental output due to specialization and trade. If transportation is sufficiently difficult, it may require so much labor that the aggregate outputs of wine and bread are lower under specialization than they would be under autarky. (Autarky is defined as a situation where production of each good in each region is just great enough to meet local demand.) Here is an important principle: the benefits of specialization and trade can be offset partially or completely by high transportation costs. Reductions in transportation costs, therefore, tend to promote specialization and trade.

In the situation described above, The Hills are said to have absolute advantage in the production of wine and The Plains are said to have absolute advantage in the production of bread. But what if The Plains had higher labor productivity in the production of both bread and wine? Would it ever make sense for the farmers in The Plains to specialize and trade with the farmers in The Hills if the former were more efficient in either kind of production? At some intuitive level, it may seem that the answer is "no," but the theory of comparative advantage demonstrates that the correct answer is "yes."

## Comparative advantage

The theory of comparative advantage is one of the greatest contributions of economic science. To better understand it, a bit of historical context is helpful. The idea of comparative advantage is most closely associated with a nineteenth-century economist named David Ricardo. Ricardo was not only an economist, but also a member of the British Parliament and a staunch opponent of legislation known as the Corn Laws, which were enacted in order to prevent the importation of foreign agricultural commodities to Britain. Proponents of the Corn Laws (principally the landed aristocracy) argued that British agriculture was the most efficient in the world, so no possible benefit could come from importing produce from less-efficient foreign producers. Ricardo begged to differ.

To explain his case, Ricardo began with a kind of parable, which is changed somewhat here to make more sense to modern readers. Suppose that in an isolated town there lived a doctor and a typist. The doctor needed medical reports and records typed up on a regular basis. Normally, she would contract this work out to the typist. This particular doctor, however, was also a very fast typist. In fact, she could type 80 words per minute, while the typist could only manage 60 words per minute. She asked herself, "Does it make any sense for me to contract out my typing when I can do it more efficiently myself?"

The correct answer is "yes" for the following reason. The doctor has a limited amount of time available in the day, so any time spent typing is time that cannot be spent providing medical services. Doing her own typing will have an *opportunity cost* equal to the value of the lost medical services. Assuming that medical services are worth more than typing services, it clearly makes no sense for the doctor to do her own typing. In this case, the doctor has absolute advantage in both medicine and typing, but the typist (whose opportunity cost is zero) has comparative advantage in typing.

In Ricardo's time, technological and institutional innovations that had been developed in England and Scotland gave Britain a huge productivity advantage in the rapidly growing manufacturing industries. Ricardo was willing to concede that British agriculture was at least as efficient as that of its trading partners. So Britain had absolute advantage in both agriculture and manufacturing. He argued, however, that agriculture had a very high opportunity cost for Britain because labor resources devoted to agriculture could not be used for manufacturing where they would produce goods of greater value. Thus, Britain's less advanced continental trading partners had comparative advantage in agriculture. By specializing in manufacturing and meeting its need for agricultural goods through imports, the British economy would be much better off. This simple but profound logic has been the basic argument against restrictions on international trade ever since Ricardo's day, but it applies equally well to explaining specialization and trade within multiregional economies.

Let's return to our original example and see if the notion of comparative advantage works. Table 8.3 presents a situation where The Plains has absolute advantage over The Hills in the production of both bread and wine. The advantage in wine is small, while the advantage in bread is very large.

Tables 8.4a and 8.4b compare the situation where both regions' labor forces are equally split between bread and wine with the situation of complete specialization. The results are not quite as clear cut as they were in the absolute advantage case. Specialization yields a lot more bread (1,500 loaves) but at the cost of a little less wine (50 bottles). This means that specialization produces a superior outcome only if 1,500 loaves of bread are worth more than 50 bottles of wine. This in itself tells us something interesting about comparative advantage. Under absolute advantage, specialization produces more of both goods, so you don't need to know the price of the two goods to know that specialization is superior. To identify a case of comparative advantage, however, you need to know the prices of the goods in question.

*Table 8.3* Labor productivity in two regions

| Region | Output per worker per day | | Number of workers |
| --- | --- | --- | --- |
| | bread (loaves) | wine (bottles) | |
| The Plains | 100 | 26 | 100 |
| The Hills | 70 | 25 | 100 |

*Table 8.4a* Output of bread and wine

| Region | Workers | | Output | |
| --- | --- | --- | --- | --- |
| | bread | wine | bread (loaves) | wine (bottles) |
| The Plains | 50 | 50 | 5,000 | 1,300 |
| The Hills | 50 | 50 | 3,500 | 1,250 |
| Total | 100 | 100 | 8,500 | 2,550 |

*Table 8.4b* Output of bread and wine

| Region | Workers | | Output | |
| --- | --- | --- | --- | --- |
| | bread | wine | bread (loaves) | wine (bottles) |
| The Plains | 100 | 0 | 10,000 | 0 |
| The Hills | 0 | 100 | 0 | 2,500 |
| Total | 100 | 100 | 10,000 | 2,500 |

To better understand the mechanisms that drive regions to specialization and to see how the prices of the goods come into play, we can construct a simple model based on the notion of a production possibility frontier (PPF). Figures 8.1a and 8.1b are the PPFs for The Plains and The Hills respectively. These lines define combinations of bread and wine that each region can produce given its supply of workers and its output per worker for each good. (The reason these lines are called "frontiers" is that they show the maximum achievable output combinations. Output combinations below the PPF can always be achieved by leaving some workers idle.) If we were to superimpose these two figures, we would see that the PPF of The Hills lies completely below the PPF of The Plains, indicating that the latter has absolute advantage in both goods. The slope of the PPF tells us how much wine must be foregone to get one more loaf of bread. It is determined by the values of

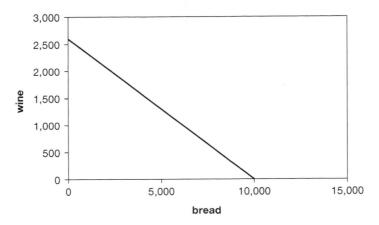

*Figure 8.1a* Production possibility curve: The Plains

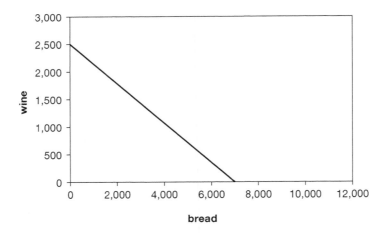

*Figure 8.1b* Production possibility curve: The Hills

the labor productivities of the two goods. In The Plains, workers produce 26 bottles of wine or 100 loaves of bread, so the slope is 26/100 = .26. This value is called the opportunity cost of bread. The opportunity cost is essentially a relative price of bread denominated in bottles of wine. If the people in The Plains want another loaf of bread they must give up .26 bottles of wine. For The Hills, the outputs per day are 25 for wine and 70 for bread so the opportunity cost (the slope of the PPF) is .357. This essentially means that bread is more expensive in The Hills than in The Plains. We can turn this around, however, and say that the opportunity cost of wine is 100/26 = 3.85 in The Plains and 70/25 = 2.80 in The Hills. So wine is more expensive in The Plains.

Interpreting the opportunity costs as relative prices allows us to answer our earlier question about whether 1,500 loaves of bread are worth more than 50 bottles of wine. Whether we use the relative price of bread in The Hills (.357 bottles of wine) or in The Plains (.26 bottles of wine), the answer is "yes." So The Hills has comparative advantage in wine. In general, the region with the lowest opportunity cost for a particular good has comparative advantage in that good. So The Plains has comparative advantage in bread.

Now suppose it is possible to ship bread and wine back and forth between the two regions. (To keep things simple, assume for the moment that transportation is costless.) First, consider what benefits this entails for the people in The Hills. Suppose that the workers in The Hills are evenly split between producing bread and producing wine. This means that the economy of The Hills is at point A on the PPC as shown in Figure 8.2, producing 3,500 loaves of bread and 1,250 bottles of wine. Now suppose that people in The Hills want to consume more bread. They can get more bread in two ways. The first is to shift labor resources from wine to bread, thus producing less of the former and more of the latter. This is represented by a movement from point A on the PPC to point B.

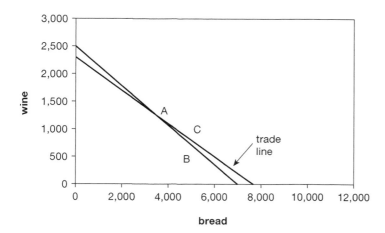

*Figure 8.2* PPC and the trade line

The second way to get more bread is to leave the distribution of labor resources as it is but to take some of the wine produced in The Hills and give it to people in The Plains in exchange for bread. Why would this make sense? By the first method, the relative price of bread is .357 bottles of wine, but in The Plains the price is only .26 bottles of wine. So the same amount of wine buys more bread in The Plains. Of course, people in The Plains would also want to get some benefit from trading with The Hills, so they would negotiate a trade price that lies between the before-trade prices of .26 and .357. Let's pick a round number and say that the trade price is .3.

To illustrate this, we draw another line in Figure 8.2 called the trade line. This line passes through point A and defines all the possible combinations of bread and wine that the people in The Hills can consume if they produce at point A and trade. Clearly, by trading some wine for bread, it is possible to reach a point C that has as much bread as point B and more wine. Thus, specialization and trade allows the people in the Hills to consume a combination of bread and wine that is *above* the production possibility frontier.

Since the people in The Hills can always get more bread by trading a bottle of wine to The Plains rather than by shifting labor from wine to bread, it makes sense for them to produce nothing but wine and to get all their bread through trading. This is the situation depicted in Figure 8.3. Production at point D allows consumption of bread and wine at all points along the new trade line, all of which lie above the PPF. (In reality, complete specialization is sometimes not possible because the PPF is not linear – we return to this in chapter 24.) Of course, the people in The Plains will similarly benefit by specializing in bread because, for them, the trade price of wine is less than its opportunity cost. (As an exercise, reproduce the graphs above to show how The Plains benefits from specialization and trade.)

Recall that we assumed transportation of the bread and wine between the two regions was costless. If we relax this assumption, the situation may change. For

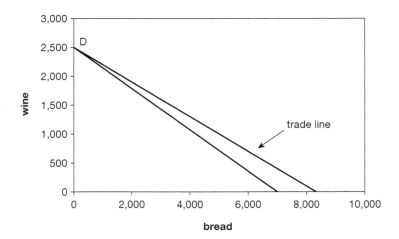

*Figure 8.3* PPF and the trade line with complete specialization

example, the relative price of bread in The Hills is .357 bottles of wine and the trade price is .3 bottles of wine. In order for the residents of The Hills to benefit from trade, the labor required for transportation must be less than the labor required to produce .057 bottles of wine. Transportation costs above that level will make trade infeasible. Here we observe a simple rule of interregional trade: people in region A will buy a particular good from another region B only if the cost advantage of B over A is greater than the cost of transportation from B to A. (Box 8 explores how not only transportation costs but also the innovation of refrigerated cargo shaped the trade in beef between the American Midwest and East Coast in the nineteenth century.)

---

### Box 8  The railroads and Chicago beef

The 1870s saw radical reductions in transportation costs between the American interior and East Coast cities such as Boston, New York and Philadelphia due to the construction of the major east–west rail lines. The railroads made it profitable to grow crops like wheat in previously inaccessible regions for shipment to eastern markets. The same applied to beef. It was much cheaper to raise beef in western grasslands than in the east, where land was more expensive and soils and terrain were often unfavorable for cattle rearing. Prior to the railroads, the comparative advantage of western cattle ranching was not sufficient to overcome the costs of either driving cattle across the Appalachian Mountains or shipping them down the Mississippi and up the East Coast. With the coming of the railroads, however, the cost of shipping live animals by rail was much lower than the cost advantage of western cattle ranching. So, eastern slaughter-houses quickly shifted from buying local-bred cattle to buying western cattle delivered by rail. Diners in New York restaurants probably never realized that their steaks had traveled over 1,000 miles – a distance that few people had ever traveled in those days.

Within a decade, a further innovation in rail transportation took this regional specialization in beef to another level. Since only about 40 percent of a steer's weight is made up of edible meat, it would be more economical to slaughter the steers at some western point and ship only the dressed beef to eastern markets. The problem was that the meat would spoil in transit. A group of Chicago-based beef packers – led by Gustavus Swift and Phillip Armour, whose names would become permanently associated with meat in America – found a way around this problem. They introduced the refrigerated box car, in which freshly dressed sides of beef from their Chicago slaughter-houses could be shipped east without spoiling. In those days, refrigeration amounted to filling an insulated car with beef and large blocks of ice cut from the Great Lakes during the winter and stored in insulated buildings. The ice might have to be replenished once or twice along the way, but it was still possible to get a beef roast into an East Coast oven more economically by transporting it on ice, rather than on the hoof.

The economic logic described in this chapter tells us that "Chicago Dressed Beef" should have supplanted beef from eastern slaughter-houses right away. But, as is often the case, reality was a bit more complicated. Swift and Armour's innovation implied the economic demise both of eastern meat packers and of firms that had been making handsome profits shipping live animals by rail. These interests used a number of tactics to try to undermine the Chicago packers. As it happened, some of the people with the most to lose also had financial interests in the railroads. They used their influence to institute a system whereby shippers had to pay a much higher rate for refrigerated car shipments than for live animal shipments, effectively nullifying the cost advantage of Chicago beef. They also waged a publicity campaign alleging (falsely) that Chicago beef was vile tasting and unhealthy, urging the public to boycott butcher shops that carried it.

In the end, market forces won out. Swift found a Canadian railroad that was willing to move its beef east at a fair price, and the public eventually discovered that high-quality beef from Chicago was better value. Chicago was to become the greatest center for meat packing in the world. (See Kujovich, 1970, for more on the history of Chicago dressed beef.) In this example, we see that reductions in transportation cost brought about by the creation of the railroads and the innovation of refrigerated cars led to regional specialization in two industries: cattle rearing and meat packing. Over the next century, advances in the technology of refrigerated shipping would have many more impacts on the spatial distribution of agriculture and food processing.

## Empirical evidence of regional specialization

Real multiregional economies are much more complicated than the one described above. They usually include more than two regions and there are hundreds if not thousands of goods and services produced and traded among them. Still, it is generally fairly easy to observe regional specialization by analyzing data on output or employment at the regional level.

Economic geographers often use a simple measure of regional specialization called the *location quotient*. Suppose we have a multiregional economy with $I$ industry groups and $R$ regions. Define $E_{ir}$ as the number of employees working in industry group $i$ in region $r$. We further define the national employment (summed across all regions) in industry group $i$ as $E_{iN}$. We calculate the location quotient for industry $i$ in region $r$ as follows:

$$Q_{ir} = \frac{\dfrac{E_{ir}}{\sum\limits_{i=1}^{I} E_{ir}}}{\dfrac{E_{iN}}{\sum\limits_{i=1}^{I} E_{ir}}}$$

To put this into words, the location quotient is the ratio of industry $i$'s share in the total employment of region $r$ to industry $i$'s share in the total employment of the entire multiregional economy. If the employees in all regions were distributed across industries in the same proportions, the value of the location quotient would be 1 for all industry–region combinations. If there is regional specialization, however, each region's employment will be more highly concentrated in that industry (or those industries) in which it specializes. So, if the location quotient is substantially greater than 1, there is evidence of regional concentration. (Of course, specialization in some industries implies that there are fewer employees available to work in some other industries. Those industries will have location quotients of less than 1.)

We can illustrate how the location quotient works by applying it to Canadian regional employment data (see Map 8.1). Canada is a wonderful example of a multiregional economy because it encompasses huge regional variations in agricultural potential; endowments of mineral, forest and fishery resources; and climate. (Believe it or not, there are large areas of Canada where it hardly ever snows.) The economic history of the four Atlantic Provinces (Newfoundland, Prince Edward Island, Nova Scotia and New Brunswick) is dominated by the North Atlantic cod fishery, although New Brunswick is also a major forestry area. Only Prince Edward Island, whose soils are especially well suited to growing potatoes, has been successful in agriculture. The Central Canadian provinces of Quebec and Ontario are culturally dissimilar (they speak French in Quebec and English in Ontario) but economically similar. These huge provinces are rich in mineral, forest, agricultural and hydroelectric resources. They are also rich in institutions, infrastructure and human capital, and have become Canada's industrial heartland. The vast prairie-land provinces of Manitoba and Saskatchewan are ideally suited for the cultivation of grain, which they export not only to the rest of Canada but around the globe. The western province of Alberta is one of the most petroleum-rich areas in the world – a fact that has triggered rapid economic growth over the past 50 years. Finally, in the Pacific coast province of British Columbia, the revenue generated by forest-based activities has been reinvested over the past century to create one of the most sophisticated and diversified regional economies in the world. Its mild climate and unparalleled scenery make it a magnet for tourists.

Table 8.5 provides employment data for Canada and its ten provinces.[1] These numbers give a good idea of the relative scale of economic activity in the ten provinces. More than 60 percent of total employment is concentrated in the Central Canadian provinces of Quebec and Ontario. It is quite difficult, however, to see

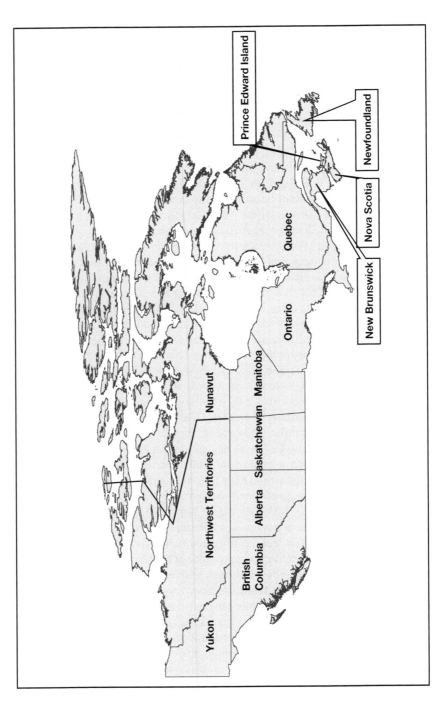

*Map 8.1* Provinces of Canada (2007)

patterns of specialization in Table 8.6 because it is not easy to tell whether regional variations in the employment within industry groups is due to differences in scale or differences in the distribution of employment across industries. Patterns of specialization are much easier to see in the location quotients, which are presented in Table 8.6.

All four of the Atlantic Provinces have high location quotients in the forestry, fishing, mining, oil and gas group. If our data were more detailed, we would probably see that it is fishing that accounts for this high value in Newfoundland, Prince Edward Island and Nova Scotia, but forestry in New Brunswick. Although these are relatively rural provinces, only Prince Edward Island has a high location quotient for agriculture (again those potatoes). That province also has a high location quotient for accommodation and food services. (Its sandy landscape and uncrowded beaches became known to the world through a series of children's novels about "Anne of Green Gables.")

The dominant roles of Quebec and Ontario in manufacturing are evident by the fact that only those two provinces have location quotients above 1 for that important sector. The highest location quotient in the table is for agriculture in Saskatchewan. This is offset by very low values for manufacturing and professional, scientific and technical services in that province. The second highest location quotient is for forestry, fishing, mining, oil and gas in Alberta – undoubtedly this high value is almost exclusively due to Alberta's oil and gas industry. Similar to Saskatchewan, the high value in a resource sector is offset by a low value in manufacturing. Unlike Saskatchewan, however, Alberta has a fairly high location quotient for professional, scientific and technical services, probably because the oil and gas industry is a major consumer of such services.

In Canadian history, British Columbia is generally associated with the forest industries. Thus, we might expect to see a high location quotient for forestry, fishing, mining, oil and gas in that province. In fact, the location quotient is only about .9. With the exception of manufacturing and accommodation and food services, most location quotients in British Columbia are close to 1. The fact that manufacturing is low indicates a predominance of service industries and the fact that accommodation and food services is high reflects the role of tourism. Although it has its roots in the forests, the economy of British Columbia has evolved into a highly diversified, service-oriented economy in the twenty-first century.

While Canada provides an excellent example of specialization, it is not fair to conclude that all the observed specialization is the outcome of interregional trade. International trade also plays a major role. A large proportion of Alberta's oil and gas, Saskatchewan's wheat and the manufactured goods of Ontario and Quebec is exported to other countries. Canada's international trade has distinct regional patterns, so interregional trade and international trade both contribute to create a high degree of regions specialization.

Table 8.5 Employment (by thousands) by industry in Canada and its provinces

| | Canada | Newfoundland | Prince Edward Island | Nova Scotia | New Brunswick | Quebec |
|---|---|---|---|---|---|---|
| All industries | 16,201.1 | 211.8 | 67.7 | 444.0 | 349.1 | 3,737.2 |
| Agriculture | 353.0 | 2.6 | 3.8 | 5.6 | 7.5 | 68.2 |
| Forestry, fishing, mining, oil and gas | 308.4 | 15.3 | 2.4 | 16.1 | 11.2 | 36.4 |
| Utilities | 130.0 | 2.6 | 0.4 | 2.6 | 3.5 | 33.3 |
| Construction | 1,031.1 | 13.1 | 4.8 | 27.9 | 18.0 | 189.3 |
| Manufacturing | 2,182.2 | 16.9 | 7.0 | 40.2 | 34.5 | 607.5 |
| Trade | 2,575.9 | 38.0 | 9.2 | 78.5 | 60.2 | 614.4 |
| Transportation and warehousing | 813.1 | 11.4 | 2.4 | 22.4 | 19.7 | 174.2 |
| Finance, insurance, real estate and leasing | 992.6 | 7.2 | 2.1 | 19.9 | 12.7 | 203.6 |
| Professional, scientific and technical services | 1,047.7 | 7.0 | 2.4 | 21.1 | 16.4 | 221.2 |
| Business, building and other support services | 676.4 | 7.6 | 2.9 | 25.9 | 21.1 | 144.8 |
| Educational services | 1,110.0 | 18.0 | 4.7 | 33.7 | 26.2 | 248.4 |
| Health care and social assistance | 1,745.5 | 28.8 | 7.9 | 55.7 | 47.5 | 452.1 |
| Information, culture and recreation | 725.3 | 5.7 | 2.9 | 15.2 | 12.5 | 163.3 |
| Accommodation and food services | 996.5 | 12.1 | 5.5 | 30.7 | 22.5 | 216.9 |
| Other services | 676.7 | 12.1 | 2.8 | 20.3 | 14.4 | 150.8 |
| Public administration | 836.6 | 13.5 | 6.5 | 28.2 | 20.9 | 212.5 |

| | Ontario | Manitoba | Saskatchewan | Alberta | British Columbia |
|---|---|---|---|---|---|
| All industries | 6,405.4 | 580.2 | 481.8 | 1,787.0 | 2,137.0 |
| Agriculture | 97.1 | 29.5 | 47.5 | 54.3 | 37.9 |
| Forestry, fishing, mining, oil and gas | 36.1 | 5.7 | 19.2 | 129.0 | 37.1 |
| Utilities | 49.9 | 7.2 | 4.8 | 14.5 | 11.2 |
| Construction | 392.9 | 28.1 | 26.2 | 163.4 | 168.8 |
| Manufacturing | 1,057.7 | 68.8 | 31.9 | 126.9 | 192.6 |
| Trade | 1,004.3 | 79.8 | 78.0 | 272.0 | 338.4 |
| Transportation and warehousing | 291.8 | 34.5 | 25.4 | 108.3 | 122.9 |
| Finance, insurance, real estate and leasing | 459.0 | 34.7 | 27.0 | 94.5 | 137.0 |
| Professional, scientific and technical services | 439.9 | 25.6 | 17.6 | 135.5 | 164.3 |
| Business, building and other support services | 289.9 | 19.3 | 13.5 | 58.7 | 90.5 |
| Educational services | 415.3 | 50.6 | 35.2 | 118.5 | 149.5 |
| Health care and social assistance | 624.0 | 72.6 | 58.2 | 181.6 | 220.2 |
| Information, culture and recreation | 299.5 | 25.6 | 20.6 | 70.0 | 107.0 |
| Accommodation and food services | 359.9 | 37.7 | 28.1 | 109.2 | 174.3 |
| Other services | 257.4 | 28.2 | 21.3 | 83.7 | 89.1 |
| Public administration | 330.8 | 32.4 | 27.5 | 67.0 | 96.2 |

Table 8.6 Location quotients for Canadian provinces

| | Newfoundland | Prince Edward Island | Nova Scotia | New Brunswick | Quebec |
|---|---|---|---|---|---|
| Agriculture | 0.563 | 2.576 | 0.579 | 0.986 | 0.838 |
| Forestry, fishing, mining, oil and gas | 3.795 | 1.862 | 1.905 | 1.685 | 0.512 |
| Utilities | 1.530 | 0.736 | 0.730 | 1.249 | 1.110 |
| Construction | 0.972 | 1.114 | 0.987 | 0.810 | 0.796 |
| Manufacturing | 0.592 | 0.768 | 0.672 | 0.734 | 1.207 |
| Trade | 1.128 | 0.855 | 1.112 | 1.085 | 1.034 |
| Transportation and warehousing | 1.072 | 0.706 | 1.005 | 1.124 | 0.929 |
| Finance, insurance, real estate and leasing | 0.555 | 0.506 | 0.732 | 0.594 | 0.889 |
| Professional, scientific and technical services | 0.511 | 0.548 | 0.735 | 0.726 | 0.915 |
| Business, building and other support services | 0.859 | 1.026 | 1.397 | 1.448 | 0.928 |
| Educational services | 1.240 | 1.013 | 1.108 | 1.095 | 0.970 |
| Health care and social assistance | 1.262 | 1.083 | 1.164 | 1.263 | 1.123 |
| Information, culture and recreation | 0.601 | 0.957 | 0.765 | 0.800 | 0.976 |
| Accommodation and food services | 0.929 | 1.321 | 1.124 | 1.048 | 0.944 |
| Other services | 1.368 | 0.990 | 1.095 | 0.988 | 0.966 |
| Public administration | 1.234 | 1.859 | 1.230 | 1.159 | 1.101 |

| | Ontario | Manitoba | Saskatchewan | Alberta | British Columbia |
|---|---|---|---|---|---|
| Agriculture | 0.696 | 2.334 | 4.525 | 1.395 | 0.814 |
| Forestry, fishing, mining, oil and gas | 0.296 | 0.516 | 2.093 | 3.792 | 0.912 |
| Utilities | 0.971 | 1.547 | 1.242 | 1.011 | 0.653 |
| Construction | 0.964 | 0.761 | 0.854 | 1.437 | 1.241 |
| Manufacturing | 1.226 | 0.880 | 0.492 | 0.527 | 0.669 |
| Trade | 0.986 | 0.865 | 1.018 | 0.957 | 0.996 |
| Transportation and warehousing | 0.908 | 1.185 | 1.050 | 1.208 | 1.146 |
| Finance, insurance, real estate and leasing | 1.170 | 0.976 | 0.915 | 0.863 | 1.046 |
| Professional, scientific and technical services | 1.062 | 0.682 | 0.565 | 1.173 | 1.189 |
| Business, building and other support services | 1.084 | 0.797 | 0.671 | 0.787 | 1.014 |
| Educational services | 0.946 | 1.273 | 1.066 | 0.968 | 1.021 |
| Health care and social assistance | 0.904 | 1.161 | 1.121 | 0.943 | 0.956 |
| Information, culture and recreation | 1.044 | 0.986 | 0.955 | 0.875 | 1.118 |
| Accommodation and food services | 0.913 | 1.056 | 0.948 | 0.993 | 1.326 |
| Other services | 0.962 | 1.164 | 1.058 | 1.121 | 0.998 |
| Public administration | 1.000 | 1.081 | 1.105 | 0.726 | 0.872 |

# 9    Interregional movements of labor and capital

In the last chapter, the productive resources of each region were treated as fixed endowments. Regions in this case interact solely through the exchange of goods and services. In reality, two critical resources, labor and capital, can move from one region to another. Although it is sometimes possible for a person to live in one region and work in another, interregional movement of labor usually takes place via the migration of population. Some forms of capital can also "migrate." For example, vehicles and some sorts of machinery can move from one region to another. Buildings and other types of infrastructure are spatially fixed, however. Most interregional movement of capital actually takes place via the more gradual process of interregional investment. Profits generated in one region are reinvested in a second region. Thus, as the capital stock in the first region depreciates, it grows in the second region. In this chapter, we explore the mechanisms that underlie such movements. What causes workers in one region to move and seek employment in another region? What makes a firm located in one region transfer its investments to another region?

## The migration of labor

For the moment, assume that regional capital stocks are fixed so that only labor is a mobile production input. What makes laborers move? Migration can occur for a variety of cultural and political reasons. In the case of retired people, migration is often in the direction of some regional amenity such as a warm climate. But most migration that occurs within a multiregional economy is economically motivated. People move because they perceive that they can be better off in another region. In some extreme cases, people find themselves unable to find any kind of employment in their home regions, so they must either migrate or go on public assistance (if it is available). More typically, people migrate because they think they can earn more income in another region.

Migration is a form of spatial interaction. Thus, the volume of migration between any two regions may be attributed to complementarity, transferability and intervening opportunities. If region B has a large supply of workers who are earning low wages and region A has a shortage of workers, resulting in high wages, regions A and B are complementary for labor migration. Note that, as in most cases, complementarity is not symmetric – we would expect to see workers moving from B to A but not from A to B. Transferability is inversely related to the cost of migration, which need not be a simple out-of-pocket cost. Cultural factors that make the transition difficult also reduce transferability. Finally, intervening opportunities exist if there are regions other than A that also offer jobs at high wages.

In what follows, we simplify things by assuming that all workers are perfectly transferable (that is, migration costs are zero) and that there are only two regions, so no intervening opportunities come into play. We also assume that labor is homogeneous, which implies that differences in wages reflect market conditions and not differences in the "quality" of labor across the two regions. It also implies that a worker from the regions with the lower wage can migrate to the other region and earn the same wage as the workers who are already there.

This may appear to leave us with a fairly simple problem – if the wage is higher in region A, everyone in region B has an incentive to migrate. Does that mean region B will be abandoned? The answer, of course, is "no," because the relative wages of A and B are not exogenous. There is a market for labor in each region. As more workers enter the market in A, the wage in A goes down. As more workers leave the market in B, the wage in B goes up.

The situation is represented in Figure 9.1. We assume that there is a perfect market for labor in each region. This assumption would be violated if, for example, there were a single employer (monopsonist) or a single labor union (monopolist) in one or both regions. We assume the regional labor demand function, which is the summation of the demand function of individual firms in the region, is the same in both A and B. Because of the larger number of workers in region B, however, the labor supply function lies further to the left in that region than it does in region A. Thus, the wage, which is the market price of labor, is higher in A. We would therefore expect some workers to migrate from B to A. But how many?

Figure 9.2 shows that the impact of migration is to shift the supply functions of both regions: $S_A$ shifts to the right and $S_B$ shifts to the left. The wage goes up in B

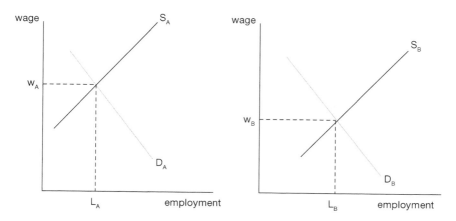

*Figure 9.1* Labor market with wage disparity

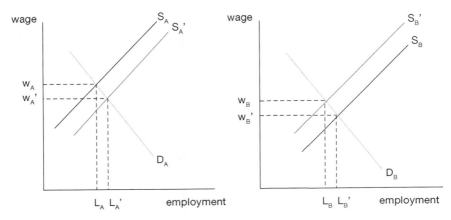

*Figure 9.2* Effect of worker migration

and down in A. Once sufficient migration has occurred to make the new wages equal ($w'_A = w'_B$) the incentive for any further migration disappears.

The outcome is a multiregional equilibrium in labor markets. In this idealized example, interregional migration causes interregional wage convergence. The amount of migration required to achieve this convergence depends on the initial difference in the wage and the steepness of the demand and supply curves. For example, if the demand curve is "flatter," as shown in Figure 9.3, it would take more migration (as indicated by large shifts in $L_A$ and $L_B$) to make the wages converge. A flatter demand curve simply means that buyers (in this case employers) are less responsive to small reductions in the price (in this case the wage).

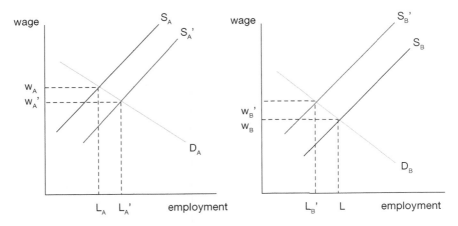

*Figure 9.3* Effect of worker migration, flatter demand

## Interregional capital movement

The tendency of the market to reduce equilibrium wage differences can also work through the mechanism of capital mobility. Assume for the moment that labor is immobile, but that capital can move between regions. Assume further that all other conditions that might influence the productivity of capital and labor – level of technology, infrastructure, access to market and so on – are the same in regions A and B. This means that a firm located in region A can make more profit by relocating its capital to region B, where the wage is lower. Since the regional demand function is an aggregate of individual firm demand functions in the regions, shifting firms (or, more precisely, their capital) from A to B results in a shift to the left of the demand function in A and a shift to the right of the demand function in B, as shown in Figure 9.4.

So, at least in this abstract, two-region economy, movements of capital and movements of labor (migration) have the same effect: convergence of wages. There is one important difference, however. When only labor moves, employment in the (initially) high-wage region expands at the expense of employment in the low-wage region. When only capital moves, the effect is opposite because in that case resources are shifted from the high-wage region to the low-wage region.

## Empirical evidence on wage convergence

The model suggests that wage differences across regions are only transitory phenomena. Is this really the case? To test the validity of the model described above, we must ask three empirical questions. First, do interregional wage differences stimulate migration from low- to high-wage regions? Second, do interregional wage differences decline over time? And, finally, can observed reductions in interregional wage differences be attributed to migration and interregional investment.

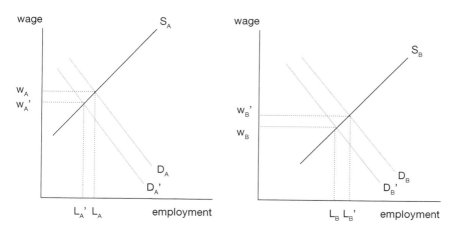

*Figure 9.4* Capital movement and wages

There is a wealth of empirical research to support the hypothesis that, other things being equal, people tend to move from low-wage regions to high-wage regions.[1] There is also some evidence that regional wages (or at least incomes) within developed countries tend to converge over time. But convergence is generally a slow process. A famous study by Barro and Sala-i-Martin (1991), for example, found that, during the twentieth century, incomes among U.S. states converged at a rate of only about 2 percent per year. (See Box 9 for a discussion of wage convergence in the U.S.)

---

### *Box 9*  **Regional wage convergence in the U.S.**

For much of its history, the U.S. multiregional economy showed a marked division between its northern and southern states in terms of wages and income. The north includes the major cities extending from Boston to Washington DC, as well as the manufacturing belt that extends westward through the Great Lakes region. The south includes those states that formed the Confederacy, which attempted to secede during the U.S. Civil War of the 1860s. While the north industrialized in the latter part of the nineteenth century, the south remained largely rural and agricultural, with an emphasis on cash crops like cotton and tobacco.

In the aftermath of the Civil War, the south had lost much of its infrastructure and wages plummeted to only about 40 percent of the northern level, as shown in Table B9.1. The economic condition of the south failed to improve much, with wages still well below 50 percent of northern levels in 1900, 35 years after the end of the war. This largely reflects the declining condition of agriculture relative to manufacturing industries. But gradually, throughout the twentieth century, the south caught up, with wages reaching 90 percent of northern wages by 1980 and remaining at least that high more recently. Thus, U.S. economic history provides a clear example of wage convergence, but it also shows that it can be a very slow process.

Interregional migration of labor surely played a role in this transformation. African Americans in particular migrated away from the south in very large numbers, shifting their demographic center of gravity from the rural south to the urban north during the middle decades of the twentieth century. But structural transformations were also important as southern labor shifted from agriculture into higher-wage manufacturing. The wages of those remaining in agriculture also increased as farming became more capital intensive (Caselli and Coleman, 2001). Both the growth of manufacturing in the south and the mechanization of agriculture were almost certainly made possible by the movement of capital from north to south in order to take advantage of lower wages. The magnitude of this flow is unknown, however, since there are no data available on interregional movements of capital.

*Table B9.1* South–North wage convergence in the U.S.

|                           | 1880 | 1900 | 1920 | 1940 | 1960 | 1980 |
|---------------------------|------|------|------|------|------|------|
| South–North Relative Wage | 0.41 | 0.44 | 0.59 | 0.60 | 0.78 | 0.90 |

Source: Caselli and Coleman (2001).

The third question is perhaps the most difficult to answer. Just because we see migration to regions with higher wages and we also see reductions in regional wage differences does not necessarily mean that the observed migration is the reason for the observed convergence. A host of other factors – including the workings of real estate markets, government subsidies and shifts in demand or technology that work against regions with established industrial bases – could just as easily account for the convergence. By careful statistical analysis, Barro and Sala-i-Martin found that no more than one-third of income convergence across U.S. states can be attributed to migration.

These results are instructive, because they are fairly typical of the way theoretical models relate to the real world. The process described in the theory appears to be real and reasonably important. However, the outcome predicted by the theory does not occur, at least not immediately, for a couple of reasons. The first is that most models are static, which means they don't tell us how long it will take for something to occur. A real economy is full of inertia, so changes may occur so slowly as to be difficult to observe. The second is that the world is more complicated than our model. While the processes the model describes are working, other processes are working as well. Some processes are mutually reinforcing, while others are mutually offsetting. This does not mean that theoretical models are not useful. In fact, without theoretical models to generate hypotheses about how elements of the economy interact, it would be nearly impossible to empirically disentangle the multiple processes at work in observed data.

## Persistence of wage differences

So why do interregional wage differences sometimes persist? When the results of a model do not conform to reality, the first place to look for an explanation is at the assumptions. Two assumptions in particular may deviate from reality: the assumptions that laborers are perfectly mobile and homogeneous.

Perfect mobility means that there is no cost to migrating from one region to another. Of course, there are the costs of transporting yourself and your belongings. In principle, these costs are an impediment to migration, because, if the extra wage income earned by migrating is less than the migration cost, you are better off staying home. In practice, however, such costs have relatively little effect because they are one-time costs, while the wage benefits will be earned over many years of employment. Not all migration costs are simple monetary costs, however. Migration often means separation from friends and family, abandoning cultural amenities and facing the uncertainties of an unknown environment. If a person is unwilling to move despite a significant wage difference, it may simply mean that, for that person, these non-monetary costs outweigh the income benefits. If enough potential migrants are in the same position, significant wage differences can persist.

Another possible explanation for the persistence of regional wage differences is that labor is not homogeneous. It is well known that workers vary according to their level of skills. For our discussion, not only the level but also the transferability of skills is an important factor. Transferable skills are those that a worker can carry to a new employer or a new region. Electricians, registered nurses, accountants, auto mechanics, engineers and chefs are all people with transferable skills. Fishermen, farmers, coal miners and workers in highly specialized industries such as steel production have skills that are relatively non-transferable. Consider two people, an electrician and a fisherman, who live and work in the low-wage Canadian province of Newfoundland. They are both highly skilled workers. The difference is that the electrician's skills are in demand in virtually any part of Canada. Not only are the fisherman's skills specific to an activity that is only present in a few regions, but they are also specific to the waters of Newfoundland. The electrician can leave Newfoundland and find work as an electrician in a higher-wage region such as Ontario. The fisherman, on the other hand, would have to abandon his skills and enter the labor force as an unskilled worker if he were to migrate to Ontario. Migration that leads to wage convergence is more likely to occur if the workers in the low-wage region have transferable skills.

Since the benefits of migration vary across the population of workers in any region, we say that migration is a "selective" process. This selectivity implies that migrants will not be typical of the regional labor force, but rather will be on average younger and have more transferable skills. It also means that the labor force in a region that has significant out-migration becomes, on average, older and with a higher proportion of non-transferable skills. This transformation may have a negative impact on the growth prospects of the region. For example, investors may not be able to take advantage of lower wages in a particular region if the labor force does not provide the skills necessary to make investments in new plant and equipment profitable. We return to this issue in chapter 10.

Heterogeneity in something as basic as workers' ages can affect the ability of migration to eliminate regional wage differences. We can think of the cost of migration – whether monetary or otherwise – as an investment that the worker makes in order to increase her lifetime earning potential. Imagine that a worker in a low-wage region earns $35,000 (or pounds, euros – whatever) annually in her home region and can earn $50,000 annually in another region. If she expects that earning difference to remain constant into the future, and if she expects to work for 20 years, the gross value of extra earnings is $300,000. From an investment perspective, however, she should calculate the net present value of the extra earnings. At a discount rate of 7 percent, the present value is $158,910. If she expects to work 30 years the present value of the same migration is $186,136, while if she only expects to work ten years it is only $105,354. The number of years she expects to work depends, in large part, on how old she is. The message, therefore, is clear: migration as an investment is worth more to younger people than to older people.[2] If the majority of workers in the low-wage region are so old that migration does not represent a good investment for them, wage convergence may not occur.

Another reason that migration may fail to bring out wage convergence is that institutional barriers tend to retard wage adjustments, especially if they are downward adjustments. When the wage remains constant despite a downward shift in demand, the result is generally unemployment. To illustrate this, Figure 9.5 shows what would happen in the high-income region if the wage remained at $w_A$ after the labor supply function shifted from $S_A$ to $S_{A^1}$ as in Figure 9.3. At that wage the amount of labor demanded would be unchanged at $L_{AD}$ (which is the same as it was before migration) while the supply would be $L_{AS}$. The excess supply of labor $(L_{AS} - L_{AD})$ would remain unemployed. This could play out in two ways. None of the new immigrants might find jobs, so they would return to their region of origin and the labor market in region A would go back to its initial state. Alternatively, some workers who were previously in A would lose their jobs to new migrants and become unemployed. In the first case, the labor migration process would be foiled completely. In the second case, it would lead to a smaller amount of wage convergence (since wages in B would still go up) but it would result in unemployment in region A.

It is a matter of some debate whether regional differences in wages should be viewed as a "problem" that needs to be addressed by public policy. A situation where some regions have chronically high levels of unemployment, however, is almost universally seen as a problem. We will return to the question of unemployment and regional policy in chapter 12.

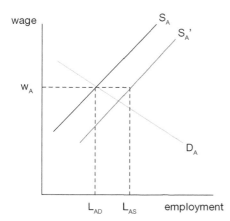

*Figure 9.5* Effect of worker migration with no wage adjustment

# 10 Polarization in the multiregional economy

So far, we have considered market mechanisms that are mutually beneficial to all regions. The theory of comparative advantage says that each region will maintain its role in the multiregional economy by specializing in those goods and services for which it has the lowest opportunity cost. Our simple model of interregional movements of capital and labor says that, in the long run, regional differences in wages will be eliminated by a process whereby productive inputs flow in the direction of those regions in which they are in short supply. The general picture is one of harmony and balance among the regions of the multiregional economy.

In reality, it is often the case that some regions thrive economically, while others languish. Sometimes regions decline because of economic changes that rob them of their comparative advantages. Examples include fishing regions in Atlantic Canada after the collapse of the Atlantic cod fisheries or coal-producing regions in the United Kingdom after the switch away from coal for electricity generation. In many affluent countries, agricultural regions and regions specializing in textiles and apparel have suffered relative economic decline because the market prices of their specialties, which are determined in global markets, declined relative to the prices of goods produced in other regions.

Even in the absence of such dramatic changes in economic circumstances, multiregional economies may experience a process of "polarization" by which human and capital resources flow in the direction of one or a few regions, leaving other regions worse off. The outcome is a multiregional economy with a core, comprised of one or more regions with high income, productivity and growth potential, and a periphery comprised of economically stagnant regions with low income, productivity and growth potential.

The core–periphery dichotomy is a common characteristic of multiregional economies. Well-known examples include Italy, with its affluent, urban north and its poor, rural south (see Box 10); Canada, whose central and western provinces have outpaced its Atlantic and prairie provinces; and Brazil, where meteoric growth in the south coincided with stagnation in the northeast. The process of polarization is starkly evident today in China, where the cities of the southeastern coast are growing at rates unparalleled in human history, while much of the rural interior is in economic decline. Even in the U.S., where most regions have enjoyed rapid economic growth, there are pockets of economic stagnation in the Appalachian region.[1]

## *Box 10* Il Mezzogiorno

The 1950s and 1960s have been called the period of Italy's "economic miracle." Rising from the destruction of World War II, and with the help of the Marshall Plan, Italy emerged as an industrial power on a par with neighboring states in western and northern Europe. But the miracle did not extend to all parts of Italy. Regions south of Rome, along with the islands of Sicily and Sardinia – known collectively as "Il Mezzogiorno" – remained largely rural and poor, with little industrialization and high levels of unemployment. In 2008, for example, these regions had per capita GDP at only about 66 percent of the Italian average, and not much more than 50 percent of the per capita GDP in Italy's industrial northwest.[i]

Mezzogiorno means mid-day, and refers to the relentless sunshine of the region. But the general connotation of the term as applied to southern Italy is one of poverty, backwardness and a general absence of economic vitality. How it got that way is a complex question with roots deep in European history. During the Italian Renaissance of the fourteenth through to the seventeenth century, when the city-states of central and northern Italy were hotbeds of artistic and economic innovation, the south – then known as the Kingdom of Naples – was intermittently ruled by the Spanish and French crowns, changing hands by means of frequent wars. The region remained overwhelmingly rural and semi-feudal, with tenant farmers serving absentee landlords, until the end of the eighteenth century. It was only integrated politically with the rest of Italy by the "Risorgimento" campaign of 1860, by which the entire Italian peninsula with its two large islands were united as the Kingdom of Italy. But political integration did not lead to economic integration, as Il Mezzogiorno remained the poor cousin of the Italian multiregional economy. The natural environment was also a problem. Much of the region is mountainous and suffers severe erosion due to overgrazing.

The long periods of foreign domination and the persistence of semi-feudal social structures left the region with poorly developed civil institutions such as courts, law enforcement and municipal government. Organized crime often filled this governance gap; the power of the Mafia remained an impediment to economic development up to the 1990s. By the early years of the twentieth century, Il Mezzogiorno started losing many of its most productive sons and daughters to emigration. Today, most of the people with Italian heritage in the U.S., Canada and Australia can trace their ancestry to southern Italy.

Land reform, which was instituted after the war, broke the grip of absentee landlords but also led to fragmentation into ever smaller farms that were unable to take advantage of capital-intensive farming innovations. By the 1960s, it was evident that some policy was needed to promote growth in the south. The Italian government created an agency called Cassa per il Mezzogiorno that tried to promote development by channeling 60 percent

of all government investment to the region. This included massive investments in government-controlled industries such as iron and steel. The
problem was that this influx of government capital did little to promote private
investment. Even those industrial firms that were created in the region tended
to source all their inputs from northern and central Italy, so the multiplier
effect described in chapter 10 was virtually absent.

By the 1980s, it was evident that the top-down approach to regional
economic development employed by Cassa per il Mezzogiorno had not
worked. In the 1990s, a new approach that favored improving the business
environment at the local level was tried. An element of this approach was
an increased law enforcement and justice effort which finally eliminated the
scourge of organized crime. (This was especially beneficial for the tourism
industry, which had long been dampened by travelers' fears of lawlessness.)
Also, local governments and civic institutions were given control over
economic development policy in the hopes of creating a more efficient and
competitive environment (Barca, 2001).

Despite almost 50 years of efforts, regional economic disparities have
not been eliminated in Italy. Recent studies show that firms in Il Mezzogiorno
are not as productive as their counterparts in central and northern Italy
(Erbetta and Petraglia, 2011). Until productivity improves, wages cannot
catch up so disparities must persist. Still, the elimination of organized crime
and the growth of local institutions are positive developments for the region.

### Note

[i]   Derived from Eurostat news release, reference STAT/11/28, "Regional GDP Per
Inhabitant in 2008," dated February 14, 2011.

Why does polarization occur? To answer this question, we start with the
proposition that history matters. Every multiregional economy has a history that
has influenced the distribution of economic activity and resources that we observe
in the present. Some places were favored by historical events, so they emerged as
core regions at an early stage of development. In most cases, the emergence of these
regions was based on superior site and situation attributes. Take, for example, the
regions that grew up around Montreal and New York and were well established as
the economic cores of the U.S. and of British North America by the early years of
the nineteenth century. Both had situation advantages of holding key locations on
major rivers: New York at the mount of the Hudson and Montreal at that point along
the St. Lawrence beyond which ocean vessels could not penetrate the Canadian
interior. Both also had an important site advantage: located on islands, they were
easily defended from attack. By the second half of the twentieth century, the
relevance of these site and situation attributes had declined because air power had

negated the defensive advantage of islands and the relative importance of water transportation in the U.S. and Canadian economies had declined. Yet the status of the metropolitan areas of New York and Montreal as economic core regions remained.

Some places are favored by history for reasons that have little to do with economic geography. Mexico City is the largest urban region in the western hemisphere and the undisputed core of the Mexican multiregional economy. Yet, from the perspective of economic geography, it is not very well situated. Far from the coasts and located in a high valley, it is not served by any navigable river. Because much of its area is a former lakebed, it has poor drainage and buildings suffer a great deal of damage from frequent earthquakes. The reasons for its location have more to do with history, politics and religion than with economics. Located on the site of modern Mexico City, Tenochtitlan was the ceremonial capital of the Aztecs, who controlled a vast empire from the fourteenth through the sixteenth century. When the Spanish conquered the Aztecs, they kept their capital on the same site, building their cathedral close to the ruins of the Aztec ceremonial monuments. This served notice to the diverse people of what is now central Mexico that they were assuming control of all the territories of their defeated predecessors. Once established, Mexico City became the economic core of the emerging Spanish/Indigenous society, despite the disadvantages of its location.

But why do those places that are established early on as economic core regions tend to persist in that role? Why don't other regions catch up with them over time by means of the economic mechanisms described in chapters 8 and 9? In some cases they do. For example, the American southeast, long regarded as the periphery of the U.S. economy, did substantial catching up in terms of growth and per capita income with the core regions of the northeast during the 1970s and 1980s. Whether the core–periphery dichotomy is preserved over time depends on the relative strength of forces leading to economic convergence and forces leading to economic polarization.

The Swedish economist Gunnar Myrdal coined the terms "spread effects" and "backwash effects" to refer to forces of convergence and polarization respectively.[2] He noted at the time that economic models tended to emphasize the spread effects and neglect the backwash effects. (While this criticism is still largely valid, new streams of modeling described in chapter 11 are seeking to redress the imbalance.)

In Table 10.1, three mechanisms of economic interaction among regions are considered: trade, migration and interregional investment. Each mechanism can give rise to both spread effects and backwash effects. In the case of trade, there is a spread effect because, even if peripheral regions have lower productivity (absolute disadvantage) in all goods and services, they can benefit from growth in the core region by producing goods for which they have comparative advantage. If the core region expands, the demand for those goods and services will expand as well. Thus, growth in the core causes growth in the periphery. In the long term, however, trade based on comparative advantage can have a polarizing effect because the pattern of interregional trade may lock the peripheral region into producing goods and services with low growth potential. Some goods are "income elastic." This means

*Table 10.1* Spread and backwash effects

| Economic process | Spread effect | Backwash effect |
|---|---|---|
| Trade | Even low-productivity regions can benefit from trade | Periphery "locked in" to income-inelastic activities |
| Migration | Out-migration from periphery increases regional wage | Migration is selective, so low-periphery loses young workers with transferable skills |
| Investment | Capital flows from core to periphery in search of lower wages | Outflows of savings from periphery in search of higher return in core |

that, as the average income of the population rises at a rate $r$, the demand for those goods rises at a rate that is greater than $r$. This happens because as your income rises you spend a larger proportion on things that are "luxuries" such as home electronics, sporting goods, vacation trips, art works and so on, and less on things that are "necessities" such as basic foodstuffs and clothing. Luxuries are income elastic, while necessities are income inelastic. In an economy where per capita incomes are growing, those regions (usually in the core) that specialize in income-elastic goods grow faster than those (usually in the periphery) that specialize in income-inelastic goods. This is why development agencies in peripheral regions often focus on tourism, which is an income-elastic activity.

The standard model described in chapter 9 says that migration acts to reduce regional differences in wages – thus, it is a mechanism for spread effects. But as we have already noted migration is selective, so it may retard the growth of the peripheral region by tapping off young people with transferable skills. Efforts by the governments of peripheral regions to upgrade their human capital by investing in education may be foiled because the transferable skills conferred by colleges and universities make it easier for young people to migrate to other regions.

Interregional investment, by which savings generated in one region are transferred to another, can act as a mechanism for increasing wages in a peripheral region. This was the case in the rapid growth of the southeastern states in the U.S. during the latter part of the twentieth century. Financial institutions acted to shift investment dollars away from the regions in which they had traditionally concentrated and toward regions in the periphery, in large part in order to take advantage of low wages. This process surely contributed to the convergence in wages across U.S. regions. A similar process can be seen at the global scale as foreign direct investment in Taiwan, South Korea and, more recently, China has contributed to rapid increase in their industrial wages.

But investment dollars can easily flow in the opposite direction. As we will see in chapter 26, the most rapidly growing industries in the affluent countries are information-intensive activities such as nanotechnology and biotechnology. These activities are far more dependent on the availability of highly skilled workers and an innovative milieu than on the cost of routine labor. The resources they need are found in greatest abundance in the core regions. Since these are the fastest-growing activities, they tend to attract a greater than proportional share of the investment dollars, including dollars generated by savings in peripheral regions.

## Self-reinforcing regional growth

Regions that gain an early advantage tend to preserve their core status because, under the right circumstances, regional growth is a self-reinforcing process.[3] Here "self-reinforcing" refers to a situation where any process, once it is given an initial impulse, tends to build on itself like a snowball rolling down a hill. There can be both good and bad examples of self-reinforcing processes. An example of a bad one is the self-reinforcing cycle of debt. A person borrows in order to consume beyond his current income. When the bill comes due he is unable to pay, so he borrows again to make the payment, thus increasing his debt. As this continues, the debt grows higher and higher and the process can only end in bankruptcy. We usually refer to such a negative self-reinforcing process as a "vicious cycle."

There are also "virtuous cycles" whereby a favorable process is self-reinforcing. If a person spends less than her income she can add the residual amount to savings. Because the savings yield interest her income in the next period is higher, so if once again she spends less than her total income she can add an even larger amount to savings. As the principal grows, the interest grows so the process expands over time, ending in an early retirement in a sunny climate.

The idea of agglomeration economies essentially describes a self-reinforcing process. Every time a new economic activity is added to the region, the regional economy becomes larger and thereby more efficient. This has the effect of attracting new firms to the region and making the firms that are already there more able to compete successfully in the broader economy. In the absence of all other considerations except agglomeration economies, the largest region in a multiregional economy has the most efficient firms and attracts all new firms. Every time the region grows at the expense of smaller regions, this advantage is reinforced. The end result of this virtuous cycle is that all economic activity ends up concentrating in a single region. (This is a virtual cycle from the perspective of the largest region, but a vicious cycle from the perspective of all other regions.) In reality, variation in resource endowments, increasing rents and wages, and agglomeration diseconomies such as congestion and pollution prevent complete concentration.

A variety of economic processes contribute to the phenomenon of self-reinforcing growth. Two important ones are multiplier effects and threshold effects. A multiplier effect occurs when an initial growth stimulus triggers additional growth. For example, the addition of a new firm may create 1,000 new jobs directly, but an additional 500 new jobs indirectly. In this case there is an employment multiplier of 1.5. A threshold effect occurs when a region grows large enough to support a broader variety of economic activities. As we will see, these two types of effects interact to make the process of regional growth self-reinforcing.

A simple illustration of the multiplier effect is provided by one of the oldest and most broadly applied models in regional economics: the economic base model.

Assume that every region has an economic base, defined as the set of industries that produce goods and services principally for sale to customers outside the region's borders. (For this reason, the economic base is sometimes called the "export base.") The economic base includes all those economic activities in which the region specializes, which in principle should be those activities in which the region has comparative advantage.[4] Activities in the economic base are called "basic" activities. There is also a set of "residentiary" activities that produce goods and services primarily for consumption within the region.[5] Assuming all economic activities fall into either the basic or residentiary category, we can define total income in the region as the sum of basic and residentiary income:

$$Y = Y_b + Y_r$$

A critical assumption of the economic base model is that there is a constant ratio between residentiary and basic income: $\vartheta = Y_r/Y_b$. The logic behind that assumption is that basic activities bring income into the region from outside, and therefore are the ultimate source of the money that is necessary to support residentiary activities. If basic activities grow, residentiary activities grow in the same proportion. Given this assumption, we can restate the regional income as follows:

$$Y = Y_b + \vartheta Y_b = (1 + \vartheta)Y_b$$

We can now use this expression to assess the effect of some event that increases basic income, such as the opening of a new factory, a sudden surge in demand for a good the region specializes in or the location of a national government facility in the region. If this event increases basic income by an amount $\Delta Y_b$, the effect on total income is

$$\Delta Y = (1 + \vartheta)\Delta Y_b$$

Thus, $(1 + \vartheta)$ is the income multiplier. We could just as easily define an employment multiplier by repeating the exercise above using employment instead of income. (The value of the multiplier might be different, however, if income per job differs between basic and residentiary activities.)

The economic base model explains how an initial growth impulse is multiplied in a region, but it does not, in itself, explain polarization. If the value of the multiplier $(1 + \vartheta)$ is the same in every region, then the growth impulse will have the same impact wherever it occurs. Empirical research has indicated, however, that the multiplier is higher in core regions than in peripheral regions.

To understand why this should be the case, consider two holders of basic sector jobs – one located in the New York City region and the other located in a small town in rural Iowa – and compare how they will spend their incomes. Both will spend a portion on rent, spend a portion at the local grocery store and deposit a portion in the local bank. Beyond these common things, the person in New York will spend a much larger proportion of his income within his region of residence because there are simply more opportunities to do so. For example, the New Yorker may buy clothing from a department store or specialty shop, while the Iowan may have to purchase his clothing from a mail-order retailer located in another state. The New Yorker can spend his money in exotic restaurants, at a museum or on a Broadway show. If the Iowan wants to enjoy such cultural amenities, he will have to travel outside his home region.

The purpose of this example is not to argue the relative merits of living in New York vs. Iowa – remember, the New Yorker must also contend with crime, pollution, congestion and high taxes. Rather, it is meant to illustrate that, in a core region, a larger proportion of basic income earned is used to support residentiary activities within the region than is the case for basic income earned in a peripheral region. Thus, the multiplier effect, which is higher in the core than in the periphery, promotes polarization.

The difference in multipliers between core and peripheral regions can be explained in terms of demand thresholds. Any economic activity has fixed costs and therefore requires a minimum level of demand to make it viable. From a spatial perspective, this means that any activity can be found only in those regions where there is sufficient population and income to meet its threshold. To define opposite ends of the spectrum, a convenience store selling bread, milk and a few other necessities requires only a small population to support it because it has relatively low fixed costs and because most members of the population will give it some business. It is therefore a low-threshold activity. An opera, which has huge fixed costs and which is supported by only a tiny proportion of any population, is a classic example of a high-threshold activity. This is why convenience stores are found in even the smallest communities, while operas are found in only the largest cities.

Multipliers are higher in core regions because they are large enough to have passed the thresholds for a wider variety of economic activities. Furthermore, this effect is self-reinforcing, because as the city grows it passes more thresholds and thus the multiplier increases further. (This means that in reality the ratio of residentiary to basic is not really constant, as the model assumes.)

The economic base model provides an incomplete picture of multiplier effects because it neglects the impacts of intermediate purchases. In addition to basic activities, which produce goods and services for export, and residentiary industries, which provide goods and services for consumption, there are many activities that provide intermediate goods and services as inputs to both basic and residentiary activities. Suppose automobile production is part of a region's economic base. The automobile assembly plant must purchase inputs of steel, glass, electronic equipment, tires and a long list of parts and components. If demand for automobiles grows, not only will the automotive industry grow but so will each industry that provides intermediate goods for automobile production.

If the firms that provide intermediate goods and services are located in the same region as the automobile producer, their growth should be included in a comprehensive multiplier. (Thresholds play a role again, for as a region grows it becomes more likely that intermediate inputs will be sourced locally.) Keeping track of all the flows of goods and services among firms may seem an impossible task, but the input–output model described in the Appendix to this chapter simplifies the calculation of multipliers that take account of intermediate purchases.

Figure 10.1 illustrates how agglomeration economies, multipliers and thresholds interact in a self-reinforcing process of regional growth. (For clarity, we refer to the economic base model multiplier as an "income multiplier" and the additional multiplier due to intermediate inputs as an "interindustry multiplier.") Here an exogenous impulse leads to an increase in the demand for the region's basic activities. Multiplier effects magnify this demand, contributing to a general expansion in the regional economy. As the economy expands, thresholds are achieved making the multiplier effects even larger. The growth of the economy leads to improved efficiency due to the various mechanisms that drive agglomeration economies. This makes the region's producers more competitive in broader markets and therefore leads to a further growth in demand for the region's basic activities.

These cycles of growth generally dampen out, so the initial impulse does not generate infinite growth. The important point is that the larger and more diversified the region is at the time of the initial impulse, the greater is the ultimate impact on regional growth.

Thresholds and multipliers are not the only mechanisms that give rise to self-reinforcing regional growth.[6] The following mechanisms are also important:

*   *Migration*: Higher productivity and more rapid growth attract migrants from other regions. As we have already discussed, migration is generally selective. Therefore, the higher the percentage of new migrants in the population, the higher is the percentage of young people with transferable skills.

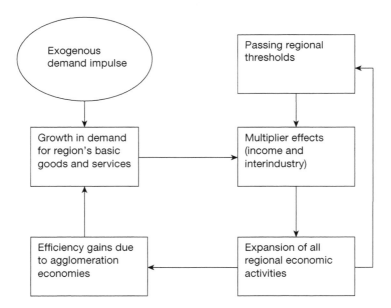

*Figure 10.1* Self-reinforcing regional growth

- *Infrastructure*: Just as there are thresholds for economic activities, there are thresholds for public infrastructure elements such as airports, subways and container ports. Also, a growing economy provides more money for expanding highways. These investments result in higher connectivity within the region and better accessibility to markets in the rest of the world.
- *External image*: The larger a place becomes, the more interest it engenders in the mass media. As markets become global, potential customers may favor firms in Tokyo, London or New York simply because they have heard a lot about those places and expect firms that are based in them to have greater capabilities than firms located in smaller regions.
- *Innovativeness*: As we will discuss in Part VI, economic success is increasingly based in the ability to generate technological and institutional innovations and transform them into marketable products. Much research has gone into explaining what regional factors are conducive to innovation. Large communities of people with specialized skills; the presence of universities and other research institutions; financial firms that are willing to make risky investments; and a generally open-minded and flexible social environment are all conducive to innovation. While some of these ingredients may be available in smaller regions, they are more likely to be found together in large economic regions.

## Appendix: Input–output multipliers

Input–output multipliers define the total increase in output across all industries that results from an exogenous increase in a single industry. For the purpose of illustration, imagine a hypothetical regional economy with four production sectors: tools, steel, lumber and agriculture. The tools industry produces things like hammers, axes, handsaws, hoes and plows, all of which are made of steel and wood. It is the major export industry of the region. All of the steel industry outputs are consumed as intermediate inputs by the tool industry. The lumber industry sells part of its output to the region's tool industry and exports the rest. The agricultural industry produces mostly food for households, but a small part of its output is leather, which is used to make handles and sheaths by the tool industry. Recognizing that steel, lumber and agriculture are all linked to the tools industry by intermediate purchases, we would like to calculate a multiplier that explains how an increase in the output of the tool industry translates into a larger increase in the output of all industries combined.

We begin with a set of regional economic accounts as shown in Table A10.1. These are called "input–output" accounts because they keep track of all inputs flowing into each industry and outputs flowing out of each industry. All the figures in the accounts are in currency terms (dollars, pounds, euros) over a time interval (usually a year) and input expenditures are found by reading down the columns, while output values are found by reading across the rows. For example, we can find the tool industry's expenditures on inputs by reading down the first column. Its intermediate goods purchases are as follows: 300 from steel, 200 from lumber and 20 from agriculture. It also purchases intermediate goods valued at 80 from outside the region. It pays 300 to labor and 100 to capital in the forms of profit dis-

Table A10.1 Input–output accounts for a hypothetical region

| Sales → Expenditures ↓ | Intermediate demand | | | | Total intermediate | Final demand | | Total final | Total output |
|---|---|---|---|---|---|---|---|---|---|
| | 1. Tools | 2. Steel | 3. Lumber | 4. Agriculture | | Households | Exports | | |
| 1. Tools | 0 | 100 | 100 | 100 | 300 | 50 | 650 | 700 | 1,000 |
| 2. Steel | 300 | 0 | 0 | 0 | 300 | 0 | 0 | 0 | 300 |
| 3. Lumber | 200 | 0 | 0 | 0 | 200 | 0 | 100 | 100 | 300 |
| 4. Agriculture | 20 | 0 | 0 | 100 | 120 | 300 | 0 | 300 | 420 |
| Labor | 300 | 100 | 100 | 100 | | 0 | | | |
| Imports | 80 | 50 | 50 | 70 | | 250 | | | |
| Capital | 100 | 50 | 50 | 50 | | 0 | | | |
| Total expenditure | 1,000 | 300 | 300 | 420 | | | | | 2,020 |

tribution, interest and depreciation expenses on capital equipment. Its expenditures on all inputs total 1,000.

By reading across the top row, we can see how the tools industry disposes of its output. Since steel, lumber and agriculture use tools in their production processes, it sells 100 to each of them. Thus, it has total intermediate sales of 300. Sales to final demand include 50 to households in the region (hammers, saws and so on for the home handyman) and 650 as exports. The export category may actually include intermediate sales to firms in other regions, but by convention we treat all sales outside the region as a component of final demand.[7] Note that the total sales and total input expenditures have the same value: 1,000. Input–output accounts always balance in this way. (The reader can verify that this is true for the other three industries.) In this set of accounts, the combined payment of all four industries to labor is equal to the total expenditure by households (both are valued at 600).[8]

It might seem curious that the agricultural industry sells intermediate inputs worth 100 to itself. This is often the case in input–output accounts because different types of activities are subsumed under each industry heading. For example, this could represent feed grains such as corn or alfalfa being sold to livestock farmers.

To go from our set of input–output accounts to an input–output model, we must make the crucial assumption that for each industry the ratio of intermediate inputs purchased from each other industry to total output is constant. For example, we see that, in order to produce an output of 1,000, the tools industry purchases 300 from steel. The ratio of steel input to tools output, which is .30, is assumed constant. This means that there are constant returns to scale and no input substitution in the production technology of the tools industry. Define $x_{ij}$ as the value of intermediate sales of goods from industry $i$ to industry $j$ and $x_i$ as the total output of industry $j$. For each industry pair we can define a technical coefficient

$$a_{ij} = x_{ij}/x_j$$

The total output of any industry $j$ can be defined by the following equation:

$$x_i = \sum_i a_{ij}x_i + y_i$$

where $y_j$ is total final demand for the output of industry $j$. Thus, an algebraic representation of the first four rows of Table A10.1 is provided by the following four equations:

$$a_{11}x_1 + a_{12}x_2 + a_{13}x_3 + a_{14}x_4 + y_1 = x_1$$
$$a_{21}x_1 + a_{22}x_2 + a_{23}x_3 + a_{24}x_4 + y_2 = x_2$$
$$a_{31}x_1 + a_{32}x_2 + a_{33}x_3 + a_{34}x_4 + y_3 = x_3$$
$$a_{41}x_1 + a_{42}x_2 + a_{43}x_3 + a_{44}x_4 + y_4 = x_4$$

This is a set of four linear equations in four unknowns, so it can be written in matrix notation as:

$$\mathbf{Ax} + \mathbf{y} = \mathbf{x} \tag{10.1}$$

Where:

$$A = \begin{bmatrix} a_{11}, a_{12}, a_{13}, a_{14} \\ a_{21}, a_{22}, a_{23}, a_{24} \\ a_{31}, a_{32}, a_{33}, a_{34} \\ a_{41}, a_{42}, a_{43}, a_{44} \end{bmatrix}$$

$$x = \begin{bmatrix} x_1 \\ x_2 \\ x_3 \\ x_4 \end{bmatrix}$$

$$y = \begin{bmatrix} y_1 \\ y_2 \\ y_3 \\ y_4 \end{bmatrix}$$

Using the data in Table A10.1, we can fill in the values as follows:

$$A = \begin{bmatrix} 0.000 & 0.333 & 0.333 & 0.238 \\ 0.300 & 0.000 & 0.000 & 0.000 \\ 0.200 & 0.000 & 0.000 & 0.000 \\ 0.020 & 0.000 & 0.000 & 0.238 \end{bmatrix}$$

$$x = \begin{bmatrix} 1000 \\ 300 \\ 300 \\ 420 \end{bmatrix}$$

$$y = \begin{bmatrix} 700 \\ 0 \\ 100 \\ 300 \end{bmatrix}$$

The reader can substitute these values into equation 10.1 to verify that they work. Now we would like to use this model to tell us the multiplier effect of an exogenous increase in the output of one industry – such as an increase in the exports of tools. Since exports is a component of final demand, we are looking for the relationship between an increase in $y$ on the level of $x$. We cannot do this directly with equation 10.1 because $x$ appears on both sides of the equality. However, we can rearrange equation 10.1 as follows:

$$x - Ax = y$$
$$(I - A)x = y$$

where **I** is an identity matrix of the same dimension as **A**. Defining an inverse matrix yields

$$x = (I - A)^{-1}y \tag{10.2}$$

$(I - A)^{-1}$ is a matrix of interindustry multipliers. Using the values of the elements of **A** from Table A10.1

$$A = \begin{bmatrix} 1.209 & 0.403 & 0.403 & 0.378 \\ 0.363 & 1.121 & 0.121 & 0.113 \\ 0.242 & 0.081 & 1.081 & 0.076 \\ 0.032 & 0.011 & 0.011 & 1.322 \end{bmatrix}$$

To understand how this matrix works, imagine that there is an exogenous increase in final demand for tools of 100, while the final demand for all other industries remains constant. Using the symbol Δ to indicate a change in the value of a variable, we have

$$\Delta y = \begin{bmatrix} 100 \\ 0 \\ 0 \\ 0 \end{bmatrix}$$

Since equation 10.2 is a linear expression, we can rewrite it as follows:

$$\Delta x = (I - A)^{-1}\Delta y$$

Using this expression, we arrive at a vector of changes in output in each industry in response to the increase in the final demand for tools:

$$\Delta x = \begin{bmatrix} 120.9 \\ 36.3 \\ 24.2 \\ 3.2 \end{bmatrix}$$

Note that total tools production increases by 120.9, while final demand increases by only 100. In order to produce more tools, it is necessary to consume more inputs from steel, lumber and agriculture. In order to provide these inputs, the other three industries must, in turn, consume more tools. So there is a direct (100) and indirect (20.9) increase in output. Because of these input requirements (and because the other three industries require inputs from each other) steel output increases by 36.3, lumber output increases by 24.2 and agricultural output increases by 3.2. The total output arising from the increase of 100 in the final demand for tools is 184.5, so the input–output multiplier is 1.845. (Note that you can obtain the multiplier for any industry by summing down its column in the $(I - A)^{-1}$ matrix.)

We can now use this simple example to see how the size and diversification of a regional economy affects its multipliers. Suppose that the economy of our region is not large enough to support its own steel industry, so the tools industry must import its steel input from other regions. We can represent this situation by changing the entry of 300, which represents the purchases of steel by the tools industry to 0 in Table A10.1. Since the tools industry would still need to purchase the steel from outside the region, the "imports" in the tools column would increase from 80 to 380. The new matrix of technical coefficients is now

$$
\hat{A} = \begin{bmatrix}
0.000 & 0.333 & 0.333 & 0.238 \\
0.000 & 0.000 & 0.000 & 0.000 \\
0.200 & 0.000 & 0.000 & 0.000 \\
0.020 & 0.000 & 0.000 & 0.238
\end{bmatrix}
$$

and

$$
(I - \hat{A})^{-1} = \begin{bmatrix}
1.079 & 0.360 & 0.360 & 0.337 \\
0.000 & 1.000 & 0.000 & 0.000 \\
0.216 & 0.072 & 1.072 & 0.067 \\
0.028 & 0.009 & 0.009 & 1.321
\end{bmatrix}
$$

The reader should verify that the resulting multiplier for the tools industry is now 1.323.

The point of this comparison is that larger regions, which tend to be more diversified and therefore have a greater internal flow of intermediate goods among industries, have higher multipliers. An exogenous impulse that increases the final demand for the goods of a larger region will therefore have a larger total economic impact.

The multipliers we have just calculated only capture the effect of interindustry purchases of intermediate goods. There is another important multiplier effect that they do not capture: the effect of increasing wage earnings on purchases by households. It is possible, however, to extend the input–output model to take account of such an effect. It is simply a matter of thinking of all the laborers in the region as comprising an industry that produces labor services and purchases consumer goods as inputs. As output expands, they produce more labor services and spend the extra wage revenue on more goods from the other industries in the region. (The mathematical details of such an extension can be found in Miller and Blair, 1985.)

# 11 Scale economies and imperfect competition in the multiregional economy

In the last chapter, we introduced a number of mechanisms that can lead to polarization, rather than convergence, in a multiregional economy. The reader may have noticed that the descriptions of these mechanisms were almost exclusively verbal and that there was a notable lack of mathematical expressions and graphics portraying specific functional relationships between variables. This reflects what was, until recently, the state of play in the analysis of multiregional economies: formal models could capture mechanisms leading to convergence, but not mechanisms leading to polarization.

In this chapter, we introduce a relatively new line of research that is able to capture polarization processes in a variety of formal models. The common thread among these models is that they use an alternative assumption about the structure of markets known as "monopolistic competition," which is explained below. This class of models has come to be known collectively as the "new economic geography" – an appellation that is unfortunate for a number of reasons. For one thing, nothing remains new for long, so we will have to think of something else to call it 20 years from now. Also, this is not the first, nor is it the only current, line of research to call itself the "new economic geography." In fact, there is a very active field of research based on postmodern social theory that has adopted the same name. Finally, the models in this class in no way should be seen as superseding the "old" economic geography, as they only address a limited set of questions, often in very limited ways. Nevertheless, since we must call it something, we will refer hereafter to the class of spatial economic models based in monopolistic competition as the "NEG" models.

The NEG model formulations all involve mathematics that are beyond the scope of this book, so the presentation that follows is somewhat pared down and does not capture the full general equilibrium rigor. (Readers who are proficient in mathematics may consult Fujita *et al.*, 1999 or Brakman *et al.*, 2001.) The goal of this chapter is to show how ideas about product differentiation and the love of variety – both important characteristics of the post-industrial economy – give rise to a powerful force for polarization in a two-region economy.

## Monopolistic competition

So far, we have considered two models of markets based in two different assumptions about competition. The first, perfect competition, assumes a market in which there are an arbitrarily large number of firms all producing the same homogeneous commodity. Because there are so many competitors, no individual firm has market power – that is, it cannot strategically affect the price of the commodity it is producing. Thus, every firm is a price taker – it seeks to maximize its profit based on a price over which it has no control. The second competitive assumption is monopoly, where there is only one firm (the monopolist) producing the commodity in question. The monopolist realizes that increasing its output causes the price to decline because of the downward sloping demand function. Therefore, it chooses its level of output in such a way as to produce the price that will maximize its profit. As explained in chapter 4, the monopolist produces less than would be produced under perfect competition, thereby keeping the price higher.

The NEG model is based on a third competitive assumption known by the seemingly self-contradictory name *monopolistic competition*. (A fourth assumption called "oligopoly" will appear in Part III.) Monopolistic competition differs from monopoly and perfect competition in two ways. First, it assumes that firms produce differentiated goods rather than a single commodity. Second, instead of predefining the number of firms in the market (arbitrarily large for perfect competition, one for monopoly), the number of firms is endogenous in a model of monopolistic competition.[1]

The best way to understand the difference between a commodity and differentiated goods is to look at it from the perspective of a consumer. If you are buying a certain grade of gasoline for your car, you are not much concerned about which firm provides it. You will simply choose the brand of gasoline that has the lowest price. Gasoline is a commodity.[2] When you are buying a particular class of car (compact, mid-size, full size, etc.), however, a whole range of factors other than price comes into your decision. You may prefer one brand of car over another because of its styling, its interior layout, its reputation for reliability, its warranty or whether your favorite athlete endorses it. A car is a differentiated good.

From the perspective of price competition, we can think about the difference in the following way. Suppose there is a perfectly competitive market for gasoline and that all the competitors in the market offer regular grade gasoline at $3.00. Now suppose one of the competitors attempts to increase its margin of profit by charging $3.10. The assumption in perfect competition is that it would sell no gasoline at that price because consumers would have no reason to pay more than $3.00.[3] Now suppose all the producers of cars offer their mid-size model at $25,000, and one firm decides to unilaterally increase its price to $26,000. No doubt its sales will fall, but they will not go to zero. There will be some consumers who value the unique features of that brand of car enough to pay the extra $1,000.

In light of this example, the term "monopolistic competition" should make a bit more sense. The automobile firm is a monopolist in the sense that no one else can produce exactly the same car.[4] Thus, Chevrolet has a monopoly on the production of Malibus, VW has a monopoly on the production of Rabbits and Toyota has a monopoly on the production of Corollas. Unlike the monopolist in a commodity market, however, the automobile firm is affected by its competitors. Malibus, Corollas and Rabbits are not perfect substitutes, but they are substitutes. If Toyota chooses to unilaterally increase the price of Corollas, it will lose some (but not all) sales to VW and Chevrolet. Also, if a new firm enters the market with its own mid-size car model (as, for example, when the Korean firm Hyundai entered the North American auto market), all producers are likely to lose some sales to the new competitor. The presence of differentiated goods in the economy has an important implication for international trade. In a world of commodities, we would expect each country to export goods for which it has comparative advantage and import goods for which it does not. But it is perfectly normal for a country to both export and import cars, which are differentiated goods. This leads to a phenomenon called intra-industry trade (see Box 11).

---

### *Box 11* Intra-industry trade

The classic model of comparative advantage was developed in a world where trade was dominated by commodities. Thus, in the example offered in chapter 2, where The Plains exports bread and The Hills exports wine, there is no consideration of product differentiation – bread is bread and wine is wine, irrespective of where it comes from. Even if goods are somewhat differentiated, the model is pretty good at explaining trade patterns between countries with significantly different endowments and capabilities, and therefore significant differences in comparative advantage. It worked quite well, for example, to explain why England exported manufactured goods to Portugal and Portugal exported wine to Britain in the nineteenth century. But, in the twentieth century, a very large share of the trade in the world tended to defy the logic of comparative advantage. For example, Canada and the United States – two countries with similar resource endowments, labor markets, levels of technology and access to capital – shared the largest bilateral trade relationship in the world. Similarly, with the creation of the Common Market (precursor to the European Union) trade between similarly endowed countries like France and Germany grew rapidly. The idea of comparative advantage focuses on the differences between trading partners, but much of the trade in the world was between similar partners. So there must be some other explanation.

Not only is there a great deal of trade between similar countries, but the trade is often in similar goods. For example, for many years, Canada's number-one category of exports to the U.S. was automotive vehicles and parts. At the same time, the number-one category of American exports to Canada was automotive vehicles and parts. In Europe the picture was much the same – not only were similar countries trading with one another, but they were all exporting and importing similar categories of goods.[i] This phenomenon, known as *intra-industry trade*, does not make sense within the logic of comparative advantage. But it makes sense in the real world when you consider two factors that are not included in the classic trade model: product differentiation and scale economies.

Consider the fact that the U.K. and Italy both export cars to one another. There is nothing surprising about this when you consider that the cars flowing in the two directions are not exactly the same good. Well-heeled Britons may appreciate the speed and elegance of a Ferrari, while some Italians may choose the brute power of a Range Rover. Even cars that are pretty similar, such as Fiat 500s and Mini Coopers, have sufficient differences in features and appeal to produce two-way trade in cars. Thus, in a world of differentiated goods there is nothing counter-intuitive about intra-industry trade.

One might reasonably ask why, if there is a significant demand for Fiat 500s in the U.K., and if the costs of production in the U.K. are roughly the same as the cost of production in Italy, these cars should not be produced in the U.K. The answer lies in scale economies. Each car model must be built on a separate production line, so it is more efficient to produce all the 500s that are to be consumed in Europe in a single plant in Turin, Italy. For more remote markets, it might make sense to build a new plant in order to save transportation costs. Thus, Fiat is currently gearing up to build 500s in a new Mexican plant to serve the North American market.

It is easy enough to come up with examples of intra-industry trade, but how important is this phenomenon in the world of global commerce? There is a standard measure called the Grubel-Lloyd index that we can use to measure this phenomenon. For a particular category of goods designated by $i$, define the exports from a country as $X_i$ and the imports to the same country as $M_i$. The Grubel Lloyd index is calculated as:

$$GL_i = 1 - \frac{|X_i - M_i|}{X_i + M_i}$$

Here's how this odd-looking equation works. If a country only exports category $i$ goods, then $X_i > 0$ while $M_i = 0$ so $GL_i = 0$, which means there is no intra-industry trade in this type of good. If the country only imports, then $X_i = 0$, $M_i > 0$ and again $GL_i = 0$. But if the amount exported is completely balanced by the amount imported so that $X_i = M_i$ then $GL_i = 1$, which indicates the maximum possible level of interindustry trade.

Figure B11.1 shows the result of an analysis by the World Bank, where weighted average values across countries and industry groups are used to show global trends in the Grubel Lloyd index.[ii] Separate values are calculated for primary goods (outputs from the agriculture, forestry, fishing and mineral sectors), final goods and intermediate goods. For all three categories, the index rises over the period from 1962 to 2006. Not surprisingly, the index is lowest for primary goods because all pure commodities are included in this category. Final goods are higher and rise much faster. Interestingly, intermediate goods (the manufactured goods that are exchanged among manufacturers) have the highest average value and show the greatest increase over the period. This reflects the increasing tendency for any final good to contain components from more than one country. An example of this is the North American automotive industry, where components flow among specialized plants in Mexico, the U.S. and Canada, so that every car includes parts from all three countries. A more global example is your laptop computer, which contains components sourced literally from around the world.

## Notes

[i] Economist Paul Krugman, one of the main developers of the NEG models, explores these trends and the theoretical approaches he took to address them in his Nobel lecture, which may be viewed at http://www.nobelprize.org/media player/index.php?id=1072 (accessed September 29, 2011).

[ii] Calculation of this index is sensitive to the level of industrial detail in the data. For example, if all manufacturing were treated as a single industry you would get a higher value than if it were broken down into various types. In the World Bank analysis, all economic activities were defined at the 3-digit Standard Industrial Trade Classification level. This is sufficiently detailed to distinguish, for example, automotive components from finished vehicles and finished cars from trucks, but not to distinguish sub-categories of components, cars and trucks.

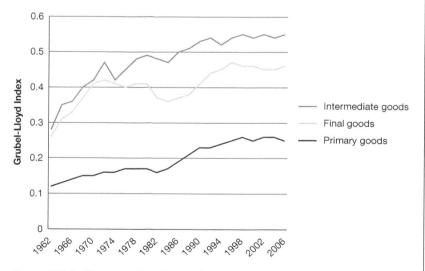

*Figure B11.1* Global trends in intra-industry trade

*Source*: World Bank (2009: 20).

One could argue that the modern economy is more closely in tune with the assumptions of monopolistic competition than with those of perfect competition. Think about how you spend your monthly income. How much of it goes for differentiated goods and services and how much for commodities? If you are like most people, most of your expenditures will be in the former category. If you try to put yourself in the position of a person who lived 100 years ago, however, you will realize that a larger proportion of income went to commodities such as basic foodstuffs; lighting and heating fuels; raw textiles; and basic services like water and sewage. Even housing had more of a commodity nature in those days as there were fewer residential options and people were less inclined to move away from the communities where they grew up. Both perfect competition and monopolistic competition are simplifying assumptions and therefore do not describe the real world accurately. The point is that, through time, the world has become less like perfect competition and more like monopolistic competition.

Monopolistic competition also has practical advantages over perfect competition as an underlying structure upon which to build a model of the multiregional economy. Recall that the basic result of a market model based on perfect competition is that the price of the commodity equals the marginal cost of producing it. If a firm has both fixed and marginal costs – which implies that it has increasing returns to scale – the average cost of production is always greater than the marginal cost. Thus, perfect competition is not a good basis for modeling industries with increasing returns to scale because, if the price of the commodity is less than the average cost of producing it, all firms lose money. The market model based on monopolistic competition, by contrast, is well suited to describing the behavior of firms with increasing returns to scale.[5]

The NEG model assumes that each firm's production cost has a fixed and per-unit (marginal) component. For example, suppose the only input is labor. A certain number of employees are necessary for things like administration and maintenance, irrespective of how much output the firm produces. Beyond that, a constant number of employees is needed per unit of output produced. This implies the average cost (AC) and marginal cost (MC) lines shown in Figure 11.1. The AC line, which takes account of both the fixed and per unit cost components, declines as the fixed cost is spread over more units. The MC line is flat because per unit costs are constant. Clearly, this is a case of increasing returns to scale because average costs decline with output.

Since we are treating the firm as a monopolist, it will produce a level of output $Q^*$ at which the marginal revenue is equal to the marginal cost (the reasoning behind this is explained in chapter 4). The margin of profit per unit is the difference between the values of P and AC at output level $Q^*$. (Notice that, if the perfect competition rule that P = MC prevailed, the firm would lose money because average cost is always higher than marginal cost.)

The difference between monopoly and monopolistic competition is that, in the latter, we assume that the position of the demand curve (D) and the marginal revenue curve (MR) that is derived from it is affected by other competitors in the market. The slope of the curve depends on how easily the firm's product substitutes with

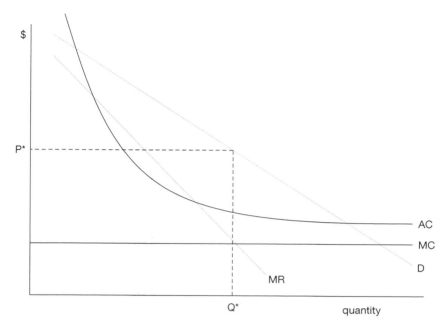

*Figure 11.1* Monopolist's price and output determination

other differentiated goods. If it is highly substitutable the slope is relatively flat, meaning that a small change in price results in a large change in demand. Furthermore, the level of the demand curve reflects the *number* of competitors in the market. Unlike classic monopoly, we assume here that new firms are free to enter the market. Any new firm will take some customers away from incumbent firms, so the demand curve shifts back as shown in Figure 11.2. In this case, the demand curve has shifted back so far that at the point where MC = MR, profits are reduced to zero because P = AC. In this diagram, the profits are literally squeezed as more firms enter the market.

The NEG model assumes that all the firms in the monopolistically competitive market have the same cost structure and face the same demand curve. Once a certain number of firms have entered the market, all firms' profits are reduced to zero. Once profits are zero, there is no incentive for any further firms to enter the market. Thus, the number of firms is determined in the model as the number necessary to reduce profits to zero. Furthermore, firm entry is the mechanism that gives rise to the monopolistic competition pricing rule: P = AC.

Naturally, the number of firms that can enter the market depends on the size of the market. This is because aggregate demand is higher in a large market, so the amount by which the entry of a single firm shifts the demand functions of other firms is small. A unique characteristic of the monopolistic competition market model is that it predicts that, as the size of an economy (defined in terms of

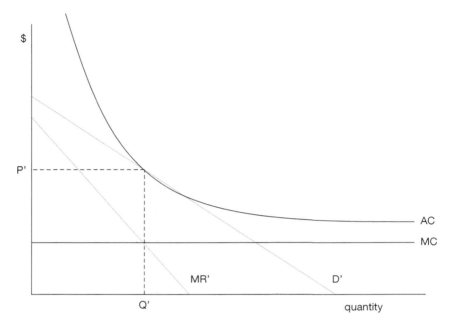

*Figure 11.2* Zero profit equilibrium in monopolistic competition

population or income) increases, the number, rather than the average size, of firms increases.

## Differentiated goods and the love of variety

Under the assumption of monopolistic competition, as an economy gets bigger, the number of differentiated goods on offer increases. This outcome has significant implications if we combine it with the assumption that people love variety, so utility is an increasing function of the number of goods. Under this assumption, even if a household's income remains fixed, it is better off if it can spend it on a wider variety of goods. As the economy becomes larger, the number of differentiated goods increases and the household becomes better off. As we will see, this "love of variety" assumption is critical to the NEG model.

We can defend this assumption in a couple of ways. First, it is easy to demonstrate that if utility of all goods is marginally declining – meaning that the more you have of a good, the less benefit you get from an additional unit of the good – people have higher utility if there are more goods to buy. To demonstrate this, consider the simple utility function

$$U = x_1^{.5} + x_2^{.5} + x_3^{.5} + x_4^{.5}$$

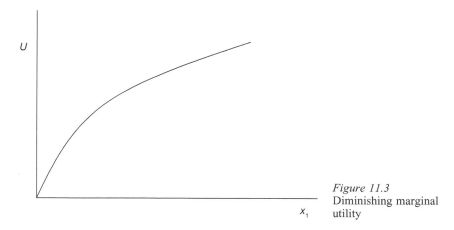

*Figure 11.3*
Diminishing marginal
utility

If we vary the value of one good, while holding the value of all other goods constant, we get a relationship as shown in Figure 11.3, where utility is increasing at a decreasing rate in $x_1$.

Now suppose a household has an income of 100 to spend and the price of each good is 1. You can verify numerically that the household reaches its highest possible utility by spreading its income evenly over the four goods, consuming 25 units of each and gaining a total utility of 20. If we now introduce another good, also with a price of 1, and define the utility function as:

$$U = x_1^{.5} + x_2^{.5} + x_3^{.5} + x_4^{.5} + x_5^{.5}$$

the household can take the same income of 100 and buy 20 units each of the five goods, yielding a utility of about 22.4. Thus, a greater variety of goods yields a higher level of utility for the same income.

The love of variety assumption can make sense even in the absence of the diminishing marginal utility assumption. Imagine that each household buys only one good, but that tastes vary across households. Each household has an ideal good in mind, and its utility is higher the closer the good it actually buys is to that ideal good. Clearly, the more goods there are to choose from, the closer each household is likely to get to its ideal good.

The love of variety has a powerful implication in a multiregional economy. If one region is larger than the others, it will produce more goods. In the absence of trade, people with the same income will be better off living in the largest region. Even if trade is possible, people in small regions will have to pay higher transport costs to consume the same variety of goods as people in the largest region. Given the opportunity, people will move to the largest region. Thus, the love of variety drives a mechanism for self-reinforcing growth in the multiregional economy. One of the goals of the NEG model is to shed light on that mechanism and how it interacts with other economic mechanisms.

## Two-sector, two-region economy

We can now apply the assumption of monopolistic competition to the setting of a two-sector, two-region model. Assume that the economy is made up of two broad sectors, which for convenience we will call agriculture and differentiated goods. Since agricultural goods are commodities, that part of the economy functions under the assumption of perfect competition, while the differentiated goods are produced and sold in a monopolistically competitive market.

Assume further that there are two regions in the economy. In each region there is an initial population of both agricultural and differentiated goods workers. We assume that workers cannot switch from one type of production to the other. Furthermore, while we assume that differentiated goods workers can migrate from one region to another, we assume that agricultural workers are unable to migrate. These assumptions may seem arbitrary, but, in fact, they capture some aspects of reality. Think of the agricultural workers as those without transferable skills. Because they have so much invested in the skills of farming, because those skills are specific to the place where they farm and because those skills have little or no value either in another region or another line of work, it is seldom to their economic advantage to change jobs or to migrate. In reality, such people are not *absolutely* immobile as they are presented here, but the assumption that they cannot move is probably more in tune with reality than the assumption that they are perfectly mobile.

Figure 11.4 portrays this basic situation. For regions 1 and 2 we have boxes whose sizes are proportional to the regional labor forces. The labor force is broken down into agricultural and differentiated components: $L_1 = L_{1a} + L_{1d}$ and $L_2 = L_{2a} + L_{2d}$. The part of each regional box representing the agricultural workers $(L_{1a}, L_{2a})$ is shaded to indicate that those workers are immobile.

In this model we assume that all production resources other than labor are either unimportant or equivalent across the two regions. In other words, there is no shortage of land, capital, natural resources or anything else that makes the productive potential of one region smaller than that of the other. Since labor is the only scarce resource, it would appear that region 1, with its larger agricultural workforce, will be the larger of the two regional economies. The initial sizes of the differentiated sectors, as determined by their labor forces, are the same $(L_{1d} = L_{2d})$.

This immediately raises the question of whether it is possible to have a situation where $L_{1a} > L_{2a}$ while $L_{1d} = L_{2d}$. Under monopolistic competition, the number of

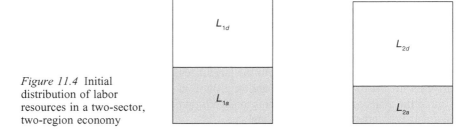

*Figure 11.4* Initial distribution of labor resources in a two-sector, two-region economy

differentiated goods increases with the size of the market, other things being equal. Since both agricultural and differentiated workers consume differentiated goods, the market is larger in region 1. But since labor is the only input in our model the same number of workers cannot produce more goods. How is this seeming inconsistency resolved?

You may already have guessed that both interregional migration and interregional trade have roles to play in answering this question. Let's start by considering the effect of migration. (For the moment, we will rule out the possibility of trade, so workers can consume only what is produced in their own region.) Since differentiated goods workers are able to migrate, there is an upward sloping supply function for this type of labor, as shown in Figure 11.5. Since demand is higher in region 1, $w_{1d} > w_{2d}$. Higher wages in region 1 induce differentiated goods workers from region 2 to migrate, resulting in $L_{1d} > L_{2d}$.

In a model based on perfect competition, migration would occur until the wage equalized across the two regions. In a model of monopolistic competition, however, there is another force at play. As $L_{1d}$ increases, the number of differentiated goods in region 1 also increases. (Remember, in this model a bigger market yields more firms, rather than bigger firms.) Even if the wage is the same in the two regions, workers are better off in region 1 because, with more goods on offer, their incomes yield greater utility. Furthermore, this is a self-reinforcing process. As more workers migrate from region 2 to region 1, the differential in the number of goods increases, inducing still more workers to migrate. As long as the increase in the real wage due to an increased number of differentiated goods outpaces the decrease in the nominal wage due to the increasing number of workers, migration will continue.

Were it not for the immobile agricultural workers in our model, there would be nothing to prevent this process from going on until all differentiated goods workers are located in region 1. Because immobile workers insure that there is always some demand for differentiated goods in region 2, however, the wage would rise in region 2 sufficiently to insure some differentiated goods workers remain.

Since this is an important mechanism, let's look at it more carefully. Define $n_1$ and $n_2$ as the number of firms (which is also the number of differentiated goods) in regions 1 and 2 respectively. Now define two types of wages: nominal wages

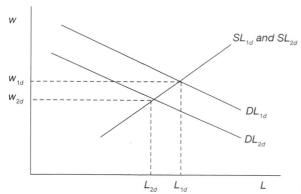

*Figure 11.5* Labor markets for differentiated goods sector with migration

$w_1$ and $w_2$, which are simply the amount of money received per hour worked in regions 1 and 2 respectively, and real wages $w_1$ and $w_2$. The term "real wage" is normally used for a wage that is adjusted for inflation, but in this case it is a wage adjusted for the difference in the number of goods. Define

$$W_1 = u\left(\frac{n_1}{n_2}\right)w_1$$

and $W_2 = w_2$. Here $u$ is a utility adjustment term defined as follows: $u > 1$ if $n_1/n_2 > 1$, $u = 1$ if $n_1/n_2 = 1$ and $u < 1$ if $n_1/n_2 < 1$. It represents the ratio of the utility that can be gained in region 1 (where there are $n_1$ goods) over the utility that can be gained in region 2 (where there are $n_2$ goods) if both regions have the same nominal wage. For example, recall in the earlier example that, with the same income it was possible to have 20 units of utility with four goods and 22.4 with five goods. In this case

$$u\left(\frac{5}{4}\right) = \left(\frac{22.4}{20}\right) = 1.12$$

If region 1 has five goods and region 2 has four, then a worker would be indifferent between earning a wage of 1 in region 1 and a wage of 1.12 in region 2. So workers are willing to migrate to the larger region even if the nominal wage is significantly lower there. As more and more workers migrate from region 2 to region 1, the market in 1 gets larger, inducing new firms to enter, while the market in 2 gets smaller, inducing firms to exit. The ratio $n_1/n_2$, therefore, becomes higher, so the gap between the real wages increases and the incentive to migrate is reinforced. This self-reinforcing process is represented in Figure 11.6.

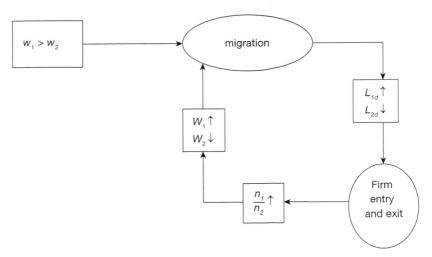

*Figure 11.6* Self-reinforcing interregional migration

As we have already noted, however, this process cannot continue until there are no differentiated goods workers left in region 2. The reason is that we have assumed already that all workers (including agricultural workers) spend a certain proportion of their incomes on differentiated goods. In the absence of trade, the agricultural workers who are fixed in region 2 will be willing to pay higher prices for differentiated goods, so differentiated goods firms will pay wages that are high enough to entice some differentiated goods workers to remain in region 2.

## Interregional trade and transportation costs

The example above is a bit contrived, because it assumes that migration between the regions is possible while trade is not. It is presented simply to introduce the mechanism by which migration and the love of variety act in favor of polarization. The obvious question is: what happens if we introduce the movement of goods between regions? As we will see, the impact of trade varies according to the level of transportation costs.

Assume first that transportation costs for both differentiated and agricultural goods are zero. In this case, any good produced in either region is available at the same price to all workers, irrespective of where they are located. So any worker is indifferent between living in the two regions and any distribution of workers across regions is equally advantageous. But, if you think about it, if there is no cost to the movement of goods or people between regions, there is really just one big region rather than two. So the case of zero transportation cost is meaningless in the context of regional analysis.

Now assume that differentiated goods can be transported between the regions with some transportation cost $t$. To keep things simple, we will assume that the transportation cost for agricultural goods is zero. If the price of a good produced in region 1 is $p$, someone living in region 2 would have to pay a delivered price $p + t$ to consume that good. If all differentiated goods have the same price $p$, then the average delivered prices for people living in regions 1 and 2 can be defined as follows:

$$p_1 = \frac{pn_1 + (p + t)n_2}{N}$$

$$p_2 = \frac{(p + t)n_1 + pn_2}{N}$$

where $N = n_1 + n_2$. The implication is that $p_2 > p_1$ if $n_1 > n_2$. If this is the case, the same wage buys more differentiated goods in region 1. In fact, we can easily define a new set of real wages as follows:

$$W_1 = \frac{P_2}{P_1} w_1$$

$$W_2 = w_2$$

This means that the self-reinforcing process of interregional migration that was described for the no-trade case (and which is illustrated in Figure 11.6) also occurs in the case with interregional trade. But there is an important difference. In the no-trade case, it was not possible for migration to continue until all differentiated goods workers had left region 2 because region 2's agricultural workers still demanded differentiated goods. With trade, those workers have access to differentiated goods produced in region 1. So long as the transportation cost does not become too high, agricultural workers in region 2 can buy all their differentiated goods from firms located in region 1. Thus, all of region 2's differentiated goods workers move to region 1 and complete polarization of differentiated goods production occurs.

If transportation costs are too high, complete polarization will not occur. To illustrate this with an extreme case, if transportation costs are infinitely high, trade is never economically feasible. Thus, the case with infinite transportation costs is equivalent to the no-trade case. To put this in more realistic terms, if the price of differentiated goods in region 1 is $p$, agricultural workers in region 2 must pay $p + t$ to consume them. This means that a differentiated goods firm located in region 2 could charge a price equivalent to $p + t$ and still remain competitive with firms from region 1. It also means that the nominal wage could be higher in region 2 than in region 1 ($w_2 > w_1$). If this gap becomes high enough, it can outweigh the advantages of moving to region 1, preventing complete polarization. This is an interesting result because it means that improvements in technology and infrastructure that reduce transportation costs tend to promote polarization in multiregional economies. The effect of reductions in transportation costs on the spatial concentration of economic activities is a theme to which we will return in Part III.

This non-technical introduction can only scratch the surface of the NEG modeling framework. Models have been extended in various directions to reveal various directions for looking at questions such as how transportation costs for agricultural goods affect the distribution of differentiated goods production (they tend to retard it) and how interregional and international trade affects regional productivity (it tends to increase it). The important point is that NEG models provide a formal framework that is flexible enough to explain both convergence and polarization in multiregional economies.

# 12 Unemployment and regional policy

The regional models we have considered thus far have dealt with regional differences in real and nominal wages; explanations for regional specialization and trade; and the drivers and outcomes of interregional migration. While these are important issues, they are not the most important issues in policy debates. Especially in the context of peripheral regions or regions undergoing major economic restructuring, government agencies, politicians and public interest groups are primarily concerned with a single issue: unemployment.

Despite this, economic analyses frequently either ignore the phenomenon of unemployment or brush it aside as either a short-term aberration or the outcome of political interference in free markets. Some models, such as the NEG models of the last chapter, assume that all regional economies are at full employment at all times, while others assume that all unemployment is voluntary.

Such offhand dismissals of unemployment as a permanent and problematic aspect of the economic landscape are not good enough. If economic geographers are to contribute to the formulation of policies that promote affluence and alleviate hardships, they must treat unemployment as an important research topic. In this chapter, we will examine the underlying mechanisms that result in unemployment and discuss policies that have been used in hopes of mitigating unemployment, especially in peripheral regions.

## Voluntary unemployment

Few economies are ever at full employment in the strictest sense. An upward sloping labor supply function, as shown in Figure 12.1, implies that there is almost always some voluntary unemployment. Here, a vertical line is drawn to represent the level of full employment – where every person capable of taking a job is working full time. The supply function is upward sloping to indicate that, at a wide range of wages, some people choose not to work, or choose only to work part time. Of course, not all people have that much flexibility, but a substantial portion of the workforce is made up of people whose decision whether to work or not depends on the financial inducement provided by the wage level. Such people include those who are financially able to retire, but might be induced to keep working a bit longer for sufficiently high wages; members of two-earner households for whom it may only make sense to work if the earnings exceed the cost of contracted child care,[1] and people who may choose not to work at certain times of the year in order to pursue leisure activities supported by wages either earned earlier or anticipated in the future.

The gap between full employment and equilibrium employment, shown as $L^{max} - L^*$ in Figure 12.1, is called voluntary unemployment. A related phenomenon is frictional unemployment, which includes all those who are temporarily out of work as they transition from one job to another. Neither voluntary unemployment nor frictional unemployment indicates poor economic performance. In fact, both may be characteristics of an affluent region where people are free to exercise employment options.

A sudden increase in voluntary unemployment, however, may indicate an economy in decline if it is the outcome of a shift downward in the labor demand function, as shown in Figure 12.2. Such a shift might be the outcome of a general decline in demand for the region's products due to declining terms of trade or competition from outside the region. As a result the wage drops from $w^*$ to $w^{**}$ and voluntary unemployment increases by $L^* - L^{**}$. It would not be strictly correct to say that those people "volunteered" to leave the workforce, but at least they had the option to remain working at a reduced wage.

## Involuntary unemployment and wage rigidity

Wage rigidity – sometimes called "sticky" wages – refers to a situation where the wage remains at its prior level despite an upward shift in the labor supply function or a downward shift in the labor demand function. We already considered the case of wage rigidity in response to an inflow of labor migration that shifts up the regional labor supply function (see Figure 9.5). A similar situation arises when wages remain

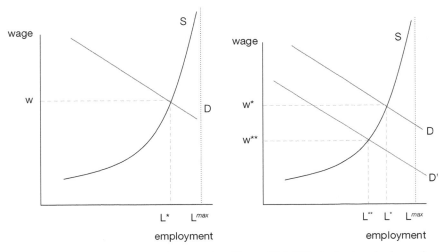

*Figure 12.1* Equilibrium employment and wage

*Figure 12.2* Effect of a drop in demand

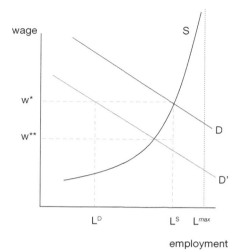

wage

S

w*

w**

D

D'

L$^D$    L$^S$   L$^{max}$

employment

*Figure 12.3* Drop in demand with "sticky" wages

fixed in response to a downward shift in demand as illustrated in Figure 12.3. Here the wage remains at $w^*$ despite the fact the amount of labor $L^D$ that is demanded at that wage is much lower than the amount $L^S$ that would be supplied at that wage. The resulting difference $L^S - L^D$ is involuntary unemployment.

What would prevent the wage from adjusting downward from $w^*$ to $w^{**}$ in response to the shift in the labor demand function? Common answers are minimum wage policies and transfer payments. If the minimum wage is $w^*$, workers cannot accept a lower wage even if they are willing to do so. The result of transfer payments may be that, below a certain wage, workers earn more by not working. Typically, however, these policies occur where there is a distribution of different wage levels paid based on skills and productivities. Since they affect only those workers who are at the very bottom of the distribution, their impacts on average wages may be small.

Another explanation is that wages are set via collective bargaining agreements and therefore employers cannot cut their wages or hire new workers below pre-vailing wages. If the workers make decisions as a group, rather than as individuals, it may be better for aggregate income if a few workers are laid off, while all others remain working at a higher wage than if all workers accept the lower wage. Union dues may even be used to compensate those workers who lose their jobs.

A failure of wages to adjust may also reflect the behavior of firms. Firms may choose not to reduce wages to their incumbent employees in response to changing labor market conditions because of the negative impact it could have on morale and productivity. Also, employees whose wages have been cut may be more likely to leave and accept jobs elsewhere (including migration to other regions), which would cause the firm to lose any investment it had in the training of workers.

One point of view sees unemployment as a problem that is easily solved. If workers exercise sufficient flexibility in their wage demands, no one need be unemployed. In practice, this is not so much an easy solution as a solution that is easily offered. Typically, workers are hard pressed to exercise flexibility in wage demands because they are unable to exercise flexibility in their expenditures. For example, a worker may not have the flexibility to reduce his mortgage payments or college tuition bills for his children just because his weekly paycheck has been reduced. Workers may be willing to risk unemployment because the outcomes of wage reductions appear equally catastrophic. This is not to say that greater flexibility would not lead to a more efficient economy, but that rigidities exist throughout the economy, not just in wages.

From a regional perspective, downward flexibility in wages tends to encourage out-migration. It is a matter of considerable dispute whether this is a good thing or a bad thing. Many analysts argue that out-migration is beneficial both to the migrants and to the workers who remain behind, because it promotes wage increases (Courchene, 1974). Still, as we have discussed earlier, such adjustments tend to occur very slowly and the selective nature of migration often taps off the most productive workers. Even if a good economic argument can be made for letting some regions decline, political realities obviate such a policy. Thus – rightly or wrongly – national governments in multiregional economies tend to adopt policies that retard out-migration from low-income regions.

## Regional policy

While unemployment can be a problem in even the most affluent parts of a multi-regional economy, it tends to be most endemic in two types of regions: peripheral regions and declining industrial regions. Peripheral regions often specialize in the production of resource-based commodities. Because such industries tend to be income inelastic,[2] experience declining terms of trade, have seen massive capital-for-labor substitution and, in some cases, have exhausted critical natural resources, labor demand is often in decline. Declining industrial regions are typically con-centrated in manufacturing industries with relatively low skills requirements, which are most vulnerable to foreign competition. Regional policy refers to public sector interventions designed to prevent such regions from falling behind the rest of the multiregional economy. While slow growth and low incomes are seen as problems, persistent regional disparities in unemployment are the main reason for regional policy (Armstrong and Taylor, 2000: 166).

Sometimes, regional policy amounts to nothing more than transfer payments to either workers or firms in the region that is experiencing high unemployment. Transfers to workers essentially provide an income to those people who are unemployed. Transfers to firms essentially provide a subsidy sufficient to make up the gap between the market wage and the prevailing "sticky" wage. In either case, the policy represents a permanent drain on government revenue, while doing nothing to address the underlying problem. Such policy is generally based on the expectation that the slump in labor demand is temporary and the problem will correct itself in a reasonably short time.

Since the downward shift in the labor demand function is often the outcome of long-term trends, transfers to individuals and firms may become permanent. Not only is this expensive, but it may also create a climate of dependency that is not conducive to the creation of human capital or to entrepreneurial activity. A more viable long-term regional policy is one that tries to shift the labor demand function in Figure 12.3 *D'* back up to *D*, so that the higher wage can be maintained without involuntary unemployment.

How do you shift the regional labor demand function up? To answer this question, we must first ask how the regional demand function is determined. Since it is an aggregate demand function, it represents the summation of individual demand functions for all the firms in the region. The individual firm's demand function in a competitive market reflects the rule that the wage is equal to the marginal revenue product ($w = MRP$). MRP is the amount of hourly output produced by the last hired worker (the marginal output) multiplied by the price of the firm's output. When a firm considers whether to hire another worker, it asks whether the revenue it will earn from hiring this worker is greater than the wages it will have to pay him. Because of diminishing returns, the revenue per person-hour declines as the firm hires more and more workers – this is the reason that the demand function is downward sloping. When it has declined so far that the revenue generated by the last person hired is exactly equal to the wage she is paid ($w = MRP$), the firm knows it cannot hire more workers without incurring a loss. (The formal derivation of this rule is presented in the Appendix to this chapter.)

With this in mind, the government can shift the regional labor demand function upward by instituting policies that do one or more of the following three things: increase the price of output, increase the marginal product of labor and increase the number of firms whose individual demand functions are aggregated into the regional demand function. In general, the government is not able to increase the price of output. So this leaves increasing the marginal product (or, more generally, increasing labor productivity) and increasing the number of firms. The following general strategies attempt to achieve one or both of those ends:

- *Location of government facilities.* Certain national government activities such as legislative bodies, central military command and the national bank must be located in the capital or other core regions. Other activities can be moved to peripheral areas without much loss in efficiency, especially given the communications technologies that are available today. These include facilities for the processing of tax returns, production of government publications, processing of old age pension checks and so on. Moving these activities into regions with high unemployment has the same effect on regional labor demand as does attracting new firms. However, this is a zero-sum game – one region's loss is another region's gain.
- *Investment in human capital.* Investments in education at all levels, vocational training, and subsidized internships and apprenticeships are all strategies to upgrade skills and thereby increase productivity. Such investments may also increase entrepreneurial skills, making it more likely that people in the region will start new businesses and shift existing firms into new, faster growth lines of business. Investments in human capital may, however, make workers more

mobile, especially if transferable skills are conferred. Thus, some of the benefits of such investments are lost to out-migration.

- *Investment in infrastructure.* Empirical studies have indicated that investments in major public infrastructure projects such as ports, airports, highways and so on contribute to the productivity of private firms.[3] Access to transport and other infrastructure is also an inducement for new firms to locate in the region. For these reasons, infrastructure investments often claim the lion's share of regional policy expenditures, especially in North America. (Based on the model introduced in chapter 11, investments that reduce transportation costs may actually have a negative effect on peripheral regions.)

- *Private investment incentives.* The government has a variety of means at its disposal to make it more attractive for private firms to make capital investment in one or more regions that are targeted by regional policy. Loans can be guaranteed by the government or financed directly by the government at a subsidized rate. Also, special tax rules, such as accelerated depreciation of capital for corporate income tax purposes, may apply only in the targeted region. Such a policy increases aggregate labor demand in two ways. First, it encourages the location of new firms in the region. Second, encouraging existing firms to make new capital investments can have a positive effect on the productivity of labor. (As shown in the Appendix to this chapter, the marginal product of labor increases with the amount of capital input per worker.)

Regional policy programs have been adopted in a variety of countries over the past 50 years. These include programs to assist lagging regions such as the Appalachian region in the U.S., the Atlantic Provinces in Canada and the northeast region of Brazil. The most extensive regional policy program, the "cohesion policy" of the European Union, is discussed in Box 12.

---

### *Box 12* Regional policy in the European Union

The European Union (EU) seeks to create an integrated economy encompassing 27 member countries with diverse histories, resource endowments and levels of economic development. Not surprisingly, there are huge economic disparities among the member states. For example, per capita income in Luxembourg is seven times higher than in Romania. Even within member countries there are regional disparities. For example, people in London are richer than people in Glasgow and people in Milan are better off than their countrymen in Naples. In order to ensure that the economic fruits of European integration are spread broadly, the EU has from its inception used policy instruments to help the poorer regions. As membership expanded to include a number of lower-income countries – first from the Mediterranean region and later from Eastern Europe – the problem of regional disparities grew and the role of regional policy expanded.[i]

The EU's regional policy comes under the heading of European Cohesion Policy because it seeks to draw the member states and their regions together in a common enterprise with broadly shared benefits. As is the case with most regional policy programs, the main instrument is money for investment in infrastructure such as transportation and electric power facilities. Additional funds are provided for training, development of local institutions and support for local businesses. In the 1960s and 1970s, regional policy funds were focused on mountainous and peripheral regions in the original six members, especially in southern Italy. Currently, 80 percent of funds are concentrated on regions where per capita income is less than 75 percent of the EU average, a designation that covers about a third of the EU population. These regions make up the entire territories of new member states in Eastern Europe as well as large swathes of Portugal, Spain and Greece. The remaining funds are reserved for pockets of slow growth within the more affluent member states and for cross-border regions. While funds for regional policy were originally modest, they are now about €50 billion annually, accounting for about one-third of the entire EU budget and exceeding even funds for agricultural support.[ii]

The focus of the EU on regional policy arises not only from the diversity of the member states but also from certain characteristics of European culture and lifestyle that are different from North America and other parts of the world. For one thing, Europeans have relatively low residential mobility. Faced with economic decline in their home regions, Americans tend to pack up and move to where the jobs are. Europeans are less inclined to do this, partly because of strong cultural attachments and partly because language differences make relocation more difficult. So the processes described in chapter 9 as leading to convergence in regional wages have limited effect. Also, Europeans are relatively unlikely to live in the megacities where a disproportionate share of economic growth has occurred in recent decades. Only 7 percent of the EU population is in cities of over 5 million, compared with 25 percent in the U.S. (Commission of the European Communities, 2008). Large-scale migration to a few megacities has generally been regarded as an undesirable outcome in Europe. So the alternative is to use regional policy to increase the productivity and well-being of people in their current locations. The goal of the policy is to make expenditures that increase the productivity of lagging regions so that they can become fully integrated into the European market economy, rather than to create permanent dependency on government transfers.

The need for regional policy also arises from the process of EU expansion. It is in the nature of economic integration across national borders to create winners and losers. The theory of international trade tells us that with the opening of trade each country should focus its resources on industries in which it has comparative advantage. This implies that other industries will be de-

ıbandoned. Since regions within countries tend to specialize,
ıt specialize in industries with comparative advantage will
that specialize in industries without comparative advantage
`, declining industrial regions are undesirable side effects
_˛ ıntegration. A goal of regional policy is to help these regions
ıııake the transition to new activities in which they can be more competitive.

Has European Cohesion Policy succeeded in eliminating regional economic
disparities? The evidence is mixed at best. Certainly, disparities still exist even
within affluent member countries, but one might argue that they would be
greater in the absence of the policy. Some would argue that there is a social
benefit to allowing people to remain in their home towns, even if they never
achieve the level of affluence available in the largest cities of Europe. On
the other hand, others argue that such a focus on regional policy has been
detrimental to the long-range economic prospects of the EU as a whole. A
policy that directs resources from those places that are most productive to
those that are least productive is likely to reduce aggregate productivity.
Furthermore, the general tendency of regional policy to retard the forces of
agglomeration that are so powerful all over the world today may work against
the competitiveness of Europe in the global economy. An approach to regional
policy that works to prevent underdevelopment – defined as the inability to
make productive use of regional resources – but does not necessarily promote
full convergence in regional fortunes is currently under discussion in the EU
(Farole, Rodriguez-Pose and Storper, 2011).

## Notes

[i]   A review of the history of regional policy, along with facts and figures about
regional disparities, may be found at http://ec.europa.eu/regional_policy/policy/
history/index_en.htm (accessed August 2011).

[ii]  An overview of current EU regional policy may be found at http://www.euractiv.
com/en/regional-policy/eu-cohesion-policy-2014-2020-linksdossier-501653
(accessed August 2011). A good discussion of recent debates around cohesion
policy is found in Begg (2010).

## Appendix: Demand for labor by individual firms

Consider a firm that produces output using just two inputs: capital (K) and labor
(L). We assume it has a constant returns to scale production technology defined by
the production function $Q = f(K, L)$. Its objective is to maximize profit:

$$\Pi = pQ - rK - wL = p.f(K, L) - rK - wL$$

where $p$ is the unit price of its output, $r$ is the rental cost of capital.[4] To find the
profit-maximizing solution, we take derivatives with respect to K and L

$$\frac{\partial \Pi}{\partial K} = p \, \frac{\partial f(K, L)}{\partial K} - r = 0$$

$$\frac{\partial \Pi}{\partial L} = p \, \frac{\partial f(K, L)}{\partial L} - w = 0$$

Rearranging terms:

$$r = p \, \frac{\partial f(K, L)}{\partial K}$$

$$w = p \, \frac{\partial f(K, L)}{\partial L}$$

These conditions say that, in order to maximize profit, the firm must purchase each input up to the point where price is equal to its marginal revenue product, defined as the marginal product times the price of output. As an illustrative example, consider the following constant returns Cobb-Douglas production function:

$$Q = K^\alpha L^{1-\alpha}$$

Using the results above, we define the wage as

$$w = p(1 - \alpha)K^\alpha L^{1-\alpha} = p(1 - \alpha)\left[\frac{K}{L}\right]^\alpha$$

This illustrates that the wage is a positive function of the capital/labor ratio.

# Part III
# Location theory

# 13  Transportation and location

This is the first of a series of chapters that deal with the location decisions of firms – a branch of economic geography known as "location theory." Here we begin a significant departure from the models presented in Part II by shifting our analysis from discrete space to continuous space. This means that, instead of a space comprising a finite set of regions, we consider a space of points, each of which can be defined by a set of $(x, y)$ coordinates. Since, at least in theory, an infinite number of such points exist, analysis in continuous space is more exacting. The advantage is that critical factors such as distance, transportation cost and travel time are "point-to-point" concepts and therefore are more realistically set in continuous space.

The spatial configuration of economic activities is the outcome of a great many individual location decisions. One of the most important questions that economic geographers ask is therefore: why does a firm choose to locate at a particular point in space? A variety of factors can influence the firm's location choice:

- *Transportation costs.* Each firm faces transportation costs associated with getting inputs to its production site and getting its goods and services to its customers. The firm can minimize these transportation costs by choosing the right location. As we will see, that "right" location may depend on a number of factors, including the relative cost of transporting inputs and outputs, the firm's scale of production and the relative price of inputs.
- *Taxes, land and utilities cost.* These costs vary significantly across space and they affect location choice to different degrees. Land-intensive activities (shopping malls, heavy industry) are especially sensitive to land costs, while electricity-intensive industries (aluminum, chemicals) are especially sensitive to utilities costs.
- *Access to cheap labor.* In most lines of business, labor is the single largest cost category. Thus, other things being equal, profits are substantially higher where local wages are low.
- *Access to skilled labor.* Especially in knowledge-intensive industries, it is not the cost so much as the quality of labor that affects the location choice.
- *Agglomeration economies.* There is a variety of reasons why a firm may benefit from locating close to other firms (see chapter 3). The underlying reasons for agglomeration vary from the need to use infrastructure elements such as

airports that are only found where there is a significant concentration of firms and households to the desire to poach labor from competing firms.
- *Competitive strategy*. Most firms have competitors: other firms that sell the same or similar products. In conventional economic theory, a firm competes principally by adjusting its price. Location theory demonstrates that a firm can also compete by means of its choice of location.
- *Personal experience and preferences*. One of the most enduring findings of empirical research is that start-up firms often locate near the homes of the entrepreneurs who found them. This may reflect personal idiosyncrasies, but it also reflects the fact that rational decision makers prefer a familiar environment.

We will address all these factors in the coming chapters. In this chapter, we will focus on the first category of factors: transportation costs. But first we need to define the context (or contexts) within which our location models will be set. Recall that a model is a simplified version of reality. We need to specify the simplified reality within which our firm must choose its location. To this end, we define three simplified realities, which we will call "locational contexts:"

- *Location on a line*: Here we assume that all economic activities take place on a straight line. The firm must choose its location as a point on that line. This is the simplest possible assumption, so it is generally a good place to start. While it is clearly divorced from reality, it is surprising how many of the insights from location theory can be captured by this context.
- *Location on a plane*: Here we assume that all economic activities take place on a two-dimensional plane. Each activity occurs at points defined by $x, y$ coordinates in this plane. The firm, therefore, seeks the ideal $x, y$ at which to locate.
- *Location on a network*: Here again all activities occur at points in a plane, but movement between points is limited to a set of network links representing transport infrastructure (roads, rails, canals, etc.). Since no economic activity can function in isolation from all others, potential locations are limited to points on the network.

We will address the role of transportation costs on the location decision in all three locational contexts. To keep things simple, however, some of the topics covered over the next few chapters will be limited to the "location-on-a-line" context.

## Weberian location models

To address the effect of transportation on location, we use a class of models that are known collectively as "Weberian" location theory,[1] after the German economist Alfred Weber whose 1909 book *Theory of the Location of Industries* got it started. The simplest Weberian model assumes that the locations of all input suppliers and markets are fixed and that the firm must choose a location that will minimize the sum of its inbound and outbound transportation costs.

On the surface, this type of location modeling seems highly abstract. But Weber was interested in some very practical questions. He had observed a major shift in the spatial pattern of manufacturing industries over the latter half of the nineteenth century. While at an earlier time German manufacturing had been concentrated in the great eastern urban centers of Berlin and Munich, the rapid industrial growth of the nineteenth century occurred mostly in what were previously smaller cities in northwest Germany – an industrial region known as "The Ruhr" after the river that flows through it. As we will see, the abstract model that Weber devised shed significant light on why this shift in the location of industries had happened.

Weberian models are best applied to a manufacturing firm which purchases physical quantities of raw materials, intermediate goods and fuels as inputs and produces some physical quantity of output. Some inputs, such as water, are assumed to be available anywhere and are therefore called *ubiquitous* inputs. Other inputs, called *localized* inputs, are only available at one or a few locations. The firm incurs two types of transportation costs: *assembly costs*, which are the cost of transporting localized inputs from their sources to the production site and *distribution costs*, which are the cost of transporting the finished output to the market. The objective of the firm is to find the location for the production site that minimizes total transportation costs (the sum of assembly and distribution cost).

## Location on a line

The best way to describe a model is to start by enumerating its assumptions. The simplest kind of Weberian location model assumes the following:

1   The firm uses one localized input available at a single point $S$ on a featureless plane and sells all of its output in a single market located at point $M$ on the same plane (see Figure 13.1).
2   The production technology of the firm yields constant return to scale and allows no input substitution.[2]
3   Transportation costs are a constant times the number of ton-miles[3] (that is, there are no terminal costs; cost per ton-mile is the same for input and output; and transportation is equally costly in all directions).
4   The firm is a price taker that has complete knowledge of all information necessary to accurately calculate transportation costs. Its goal is to choose the location that minimizes its transportation costs.

The first assumption defines the spatial context of the location problem, the second defines the firm's production technology, the third defines how transportation costs are calculated and the fourth gives as much behavioral information as is necessary to define the location problem.

Since there are only two points of reference in the plane, $S$ and $M$, we know at the outset that the cost-minimizing location $P$ must lie somewhere on the line segment connecting $S$ and $M$ in Figure 13.1. (You can verify for yourself that, for any point you might choose that is not on the line segment, it is possible to find a

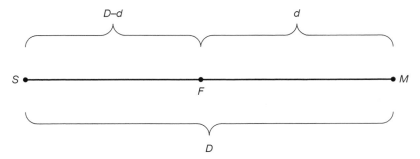

*Figure 13.1* Location on a line

point on the line segment that is either closer to $S$ without being farther away from $M$ or closer to $M$ without being farther away from $S$.)

The location of the production facility is designated as point $F$ (for "factory") and arbitrarily located in the middle of the line segment. We can define three distances: the distance $D$ from $S$ to $M$, the distance $d$ from $F$ to $M$ and the distance $D-d$ from $F$ to $S$. As we move the location of $F$ along the line the value of $d$ changes.

In order to find the location for $F$ that minimizes transportation costs, we need two further pieces of information: the weight $X$ of the localized input required to produce one unit of output and the weight $x$ of one unit of output. Defining $t$ as the transportation rate in dollars per ton-mile for both the input and output, the total transportation cost for one unit of output can be evaluated for any location of $F$ as

$$T = tX(D - d) + txd$$

(See Appendix to this chapter for a mathematical verification that in this simple case the location that minimized transportation cost is also the cost that maximizes profit.) The first term $tX(D - d)$ is the assembly cost, while the second term $txd$ is the distribution cost. Note that, since we have assumed constant returns to scale, we need only find the location where the transportation cost for producing one unit of output is lowest. (We will see in chapter 14 what happens when we change this assumption.)

As it turns out, the solution to the firm's location problem is simple. It just depends on the relative values of $X$ and $x$. If $X > x$ the solution that minimizes transportation cost is to locate the production facility $F$ at the source of the localized input $S$. (This means that $d = D$ so $D - d = 0$.) $X > x$ implies that for each unit of output produced the weight of the localized input is greater than the weight of the output. For this kind of "weight-losing" production process, it is cheaper to avoid the transportation of the input completely by locating at its source. This is illustrated in Figure 13.2, where the greater weight for the input than for output results in a steeper line for assembly cost ($AC$) than for distribution cost ($DC$). For this reason the total transportation cost ($TC = AC + DC$) is lowest at the material source $S$.

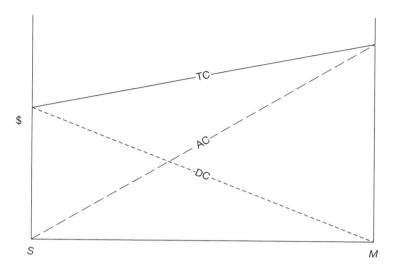

*Figure 13.2* Assembly, distribution and total transportation cost for $X>x$

An example of such a weight-losing production process is the smelting of metal from ores. Since most of the weight of the ore, which is a localized input, is lost in the process, it only makes sense to locate the smelter at the mine mouth rather than transport worthless waste products to the market.

The opposite situation is where $X < x$. Since the finished good is heavier than the input, it makes most sense to locate the production facility at the market $M$, as shown in Figure 13.3. (In this case $d = 0$ so $D - d = D$.) At first consideration

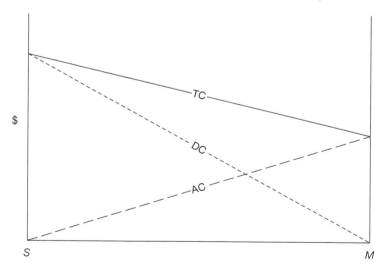

*Figure 13.3* Assembly, distribution and total transportation cost for $X<x$

this may not seem like a realistic situation. How can the output weigh more than the input? But remember, we have stipulated that there is only one *localized* input. Many products, such as soft-drink bottling, require the addition of water, which in some places can be treated as a ubiquitous input.

Given the assumptions of this simple model, the only situation where it would be efficient for $F$ to be located somewhere between $S$ and $M$ (as shown in Figure 13.1) is where $X = x$. Even in this case, a location of $F$ at either $S$ or $M$ would yield exactly the same transportation cost as an intermediate solution. (The reader should reproduce Figure 13.3 for the case of $X = x$ to verify that transportation costs are equal at all points.)

The general conclusion we can draw from our model of location on a line is that, other things being equal, weight-losing industries can minimize transportation cost by locating at the source of the localized input, thus they are "materials-oriented" industries. Weight-gaining industries can minimize transportation costs by locating at the market, thus they are "market-oriented" industries.

The alert reader may ask at this point: "If the firm has to pay the assembly costs, why shouldn't the consumer pay the distribution costs?" And this question suggests another: "If the firm can pass distribution costs onto the consumer, shouldn't it always locate where assembly costs are minimized?" In answer to the first question, it is true that for many goods the customer must pay a basic price (the mill price) plus a delivery charge – so the firm does not bear distribution costs directly. However, in answer to the second, distribution costs still affect the firm's profits because the demand for most goods is price sensitive (thus the downward sloping demand curve). A firm that chooses to locate a long distance from the market will have a high delivered price and will therefore sell less of its output. So a high distribution cost has a negative effect on the firm's profit either in terms of increased cost or reduced demand. (A version of the location-on-a-line problem in which consumers bear the distribution costs is provided in the Appendix to this chapter, equation A13.2.)

Even the simple location-on-a-line model sheds some light on Weber's question about why industry had shifted from the cities of eastern Germany to the Ruhr region. Until the middle of the nineteenth century, the main materials used in manufacturing were wood and textiles, which do not involve a very significant weight loss. Since industries using those inputs are neither weight-gaining nor weight-losing, their transportation costs do not vary over the interval from material source to market. Factors other than transportation cost, including access to labor, would therefore favor locations in eastern cities. These industries were gradually eclipsed by metals-based industries, especially iron and steel. Since manufacture of metals involves huge weight loss, transportation costs are much lower if they are produced close to the sources of ores. The Ruhr region was the location of mines for iron ore. It was also the location of coal mines – the use of coal in steel production further enhances its weight loss (see Box 13).

## Box 13 The Ruhr

"The Ruhr" generally refers to the industrial region that straddles the Ruhr River, from its confluence with the Rhine at Duisburg extending eastward to include the cities of Essen, Bochum and Dortmund as well as a number of smaller cities and towns (see Map B13.1). While none of the cities of the Ruhr has close to 1 million in population, together they constitute the largest urban agglomeration in Germany. Prior to the Industrial Revolution, this was a largely agrarian area with little urban population. But, by the late nineteenth and early twentieth centuries, it was to become the most important iron- and steel-producing region in the world.

In the nineteenth century, the Ruhr had local supplies of the two key ingredients of the iron and steel industry: iron and coal. But that is not the whole story. Both the inputs to and the outputs from this industry are heavy and bulky, requiring access to economical transportation. Since Roman times, the Rhine River was Europe's most important transportation corridor, extending from the heart of the continent in the Swiss Alps to the North Sea at Rotterdam. So being located along the Ruhr River was a bit like being located on the access road to a super-highway. This was not a purely "natural" advantage, however. Infrastructure projects by Frederick the Great in the eighteenth century were necessary to make the river navigable throughout the region.

The introduction of the steam engine to mining and technological innovations in iron production helped to promote a massive acceleration in urbanization and industrialization in the middle of the nineteenth century. While the Ruhr's coal reserves were vast, local reserves of iron ore were quickly depleted. This would have meant the demise of the industry were it not for the ability to move iron ore cheaply by water from Belgium. (Despite the weight-losing nature of iron ore, it can be moved very cheaply by water so location at the mine mouth is not always necessary.) By the twentieth century, most of the Ruhr's iron ore was actually coming from northern Sweden via a route that included the Norwegian port of Narwik, the North Sea and the Rhine. In 1899, a quicker route for Swedish iron to reach the western end of the Ruhr was created by a canal linking the Dortmund with the German seaport of Emden. A dense network of railways and later roads has developed over the years to support the distribution of steel and related industrial products throughout Europe.

As the core region of Germany's military-industrial complex, the cities of the Ruhr as well as key points on the iron ore route from Sweden became key strategic targets during the two World Wars of the twentieth century. The Ruhr maintained its industrial dominance throughout the post-war economic boom. But, by the 1970s, like many industrial regions in affluent countries, it entered a period of economic decline. In part, this was due to international competition from countries that could produce steel at lower cost. But it also reflected a transition in Germany to a more service-oriented, knowledge economy in which iron, coal and steel were less important.

Today, the Ruhr is a region in transition. While heavy industries are still important, they account for an ever dwindling share of employment. Economic growth in the region is based on technologically advanced manufacturing, services and cultural industries.

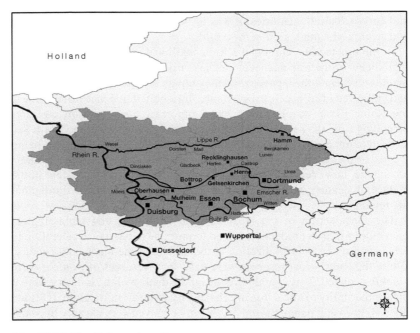

*Map B13.1*  The Ruhr region, Germany

There are many cases where the transportation cost per ton-mile of inputs and outputs differ. For example, the iron ore that is delivered to a steel mill generally comes either by water or rail, while a large proportion of the finished steel must be delivered by trucks. Since road transportation is more expensive than water or rail transportation, we can no longer apply the same rate $t$ to both inputs and outputs. Define $T$ as the transportation rate for inputs and $t$ as the rate for output. This means we must alter one of our assumptions; assumption 3 now becomes assumption 3a:

3a  Transportation costs are a constant $T$ times the number of ton-miles for inputs and $t$ times the number of ton-miles for output (that is, there are no terminal costs and transportation is equally costly in all directions).

In the case of the steel mill $T < t$. But this is not always the case. Consider a factory that cans tomatoes. Both the incoming fresh tomatoes and the outgoing canned tomatoes will generally go by truck. But, since perishable goods are generally more expensive to ship in trucks than are non-perishable goods, it will be more expensive per ton-miles to ship the fresh tomatoes. Thus, in the case of the tomato cannery, $T > t$.

This complicates our analysis a bit because the location rule is now locate at $S$ if $TX > tx$ and locate at $M$ if $TX < tx$. Now a weight-losing industry need not necessarily find its best location at input source $S$ – if $t/T > X/x$ it will minimize its total transportation costs by locating at the market $M$.

We can add a further twist by abandoning the assumption of linear transportation costs. Suppose there are some terminal costs. As discussed in chapter 2, this means that costs per mile go down as the length of trip increases. We might then change assumption 3 as follows:

3b  Transportation costs per ton-mile are declining with distance and transportation is equally costly in all directions.

Assume that $x = X$ and a marginally declining transportation rate is the same for both input and output. The resulting graph of assembly and distribution costs will now be as illustrated in Figure 13.4. The firm will be indifferent between locating at either $S$ or $M$. But recall that, under the assumption of linear transportation costs, the firm was indifferent between $S$, $M$ or any intermediate point. This is no longer the case because, by choosing an intermediate location, the firm has higher total transportation costs because it cannot take as much advantage of the marginally

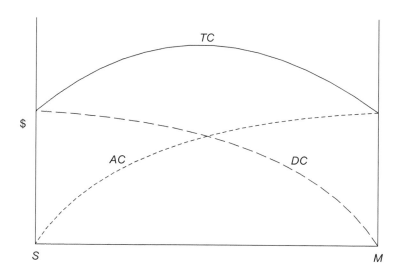

*Figure 13.4* Assembly, distribution and total transportation cost for $X = x$ and marginally decreasing transportation costs

decreasing transportation rates. Thus, under this realistic assumption about transportation rates, the firm would never choose an intermediate location.

## Location on a plane: Weber's Triangle

Our one-dimensional model of location on a line is easily extended to a two-dimensional model of location on a plane. Assumption 1 above is revised as follows:

1a    The firm uses two localized inputs, each of which is available at a single point ($S_1$ and $S_2$) on a featureless plane and sells all of its output in a single market located at point $M$ on the same plane (see Figure 13.4).

Unless the three points are aligned on a straight line, they form a triangle in space – thus, the two inputs/one market case is known as "Weber's Triangle." In order to find the location for $F$ that minimizes transportation costs, we must adjust our notation so that now $d_1$ is the distance from $S_1$ to $F$; $d_2$ is the distance from $S_2$ to $F$; and $d_m$ is the distance from $F$ to $M$. We also redefine the weights: $X_1$ is the weight of the first localized input per unit of output; $X_2$ is the weight of the second localized input per unit of output; and $x$ is the weight of one unit of output. To keep things simple, we return to the original version of assumption 3 – the constant transportation rate $t$ applies to all inputs and outputs. The problem is now to find the location that minimizes the total transportation cost

$$T = X_1 d_1 t + X_2 d_2 t + x d_m t$$

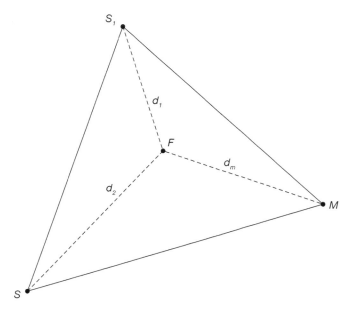

*Figure 13.5*
Weber's Triangle

This problem is a little bit harder to solve than the location-on-a-line problem. The mathematically inclined reader may want to consult the trigonometric solution found in Tellier (1972). But we can also find the solution by means of a mechanical device known as "Varignon's frame," which has the advantage of providing a great deal of intuition about how various sources act on the optimal location.

Imagine you are looking straight down on Figure 13.5 drawn on a flat table. At each corner there is a hole drilled through the table. Point $F$ represents a metal ring to which are tied three strings. Each string extends to one of the three holes and passes through it. Under the table, three weights are attached to the three strings, each of which is proportional to the weight ($X_1$, $X_2$ or $x$) associated with its corner. If the weights are allowed to fall freely, the point at which the ring rests at balance is the transportation cost minimizing location.

For example, imagine that $X_1 = X_2$ and $x > X_1$ (but $x < X_1 + X_2$). The point at which the ring will come to rest will be roughly as shown in Figure 13.6.

Now suppose that the weight of input 2 were greater than the weights of input 1 and one unit of output combined: $X_2 > X_1 + x$. The ring on our mechanical model would slide all the way over to the hole at $S2$, as shown in Figure 13.7. This means that if input 2 is sufficiently heavy, the best location is at its source where it need not be transported at all.

The intuition from this mechanical solution method is that each of the relevant points in space – each input source and each market – exerts a "pull" on the firm's location. The optimal location is the result of the pulls of all input sources and markets acting simultaneously. This analogy can be extended to more than three relevant points in space – say three input sources and two markets – and it still works.

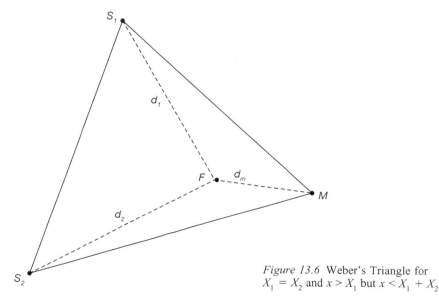

*Figure 13.6* Weber's Triangle for
$X_1 = X_2$ and $x > X_1$ but $x < X_1 + X_2$

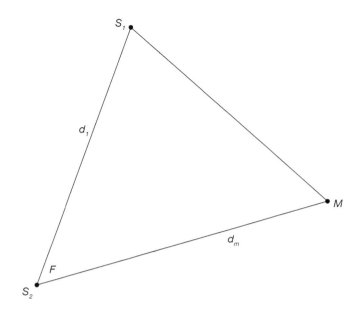

*Figure 13.7*
Weber's Triangle
for $X_2 > X_1 + x$

A shorthand way of characterizing the locational implications of the production technologies is to define a materials index $MI = (X_1 + X_2)/x$. The *MI* does not by itself tell us the exact location of the firm, but it allows us to make a simple generalization: the lower the value of *MI*, the closer the optimal location to the market. (This generalization will prove useful when we look at the effects of scale economies in chapter 14.)

## Location on a network

While location in a plane is intuitively more realistic than location on a line, it deviates from reality in assuming that travel between any two points is over a straight line. In reality, travel is most often over a network defined by infrastructure such as rail lines and highways. As a result, the actual travel distance between two points in space is often considerably longer than the straight-line distance. This has implications for location. Models of location on a network can involve some mathematics that are beyond the scope of this book, but we can use a simple example to demonstrate some basic principles. (You may want to review the basic definitions about networks that are found in the Appendix of chapter 2.)

Figure 13.8 recasts Weber's Triangle in the context of a grid pattern network. Such a network is typical of city street layouts, but can also be found at a larger scale where highway or rail infrastructure is laid out in east–west and north–south lines. Here the small squares represent nodes and the solid lines represent links. (The broken lines that form the triangle are just for illustration – it is not possible to travel along them.) This type of network is called "rectilinear." It is easy to

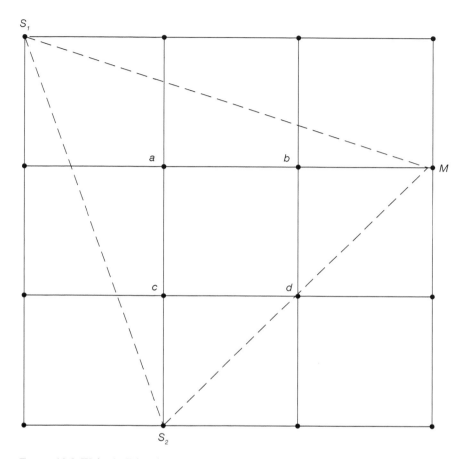

*Figure 13.8* Weber's Triangle on a network

calculate the network distance between any two nodes in such a network by summing of the north–south and east–west distances between them.

How do we find the optimal location $F$ for this case? Let's start by evaluating transportation costs only at the nodes of the network. We'll worry about locations between the nodes a bit later. It turns out that, in this simple example, only the nodes along or inside the triangle are potential cost-minimizing locations – although this is not necessarily true for all networks.[4] So we need only consider the possibility of locating $F$ at S1, S2, M or the nodes marked $a$, $b$, $c$ and $d$. Assume that the length of each link is exactly 1, so the distance between any pair of nodes is directly proportional to the number of links one must cross to get from one to the other. For simplicity, we'll assume that all weights and transport rates equal $1 (X_1 = X_2 = x = T = t = 1)$. It is easy to calculate all transportation costs associated with locating $F$ at different nodes, as shown in Table 13.1.

*Table 13.1* Transportation costs for alternative locations of F where $X_1 = X_2 = x = T = t = 1$; all nodes have length 1

| F location | from S1 | from S2 | to M | Total |
|---|---|---|---|---|
| a | 2 | 2 | 2 | 6 |
| b | 3 | 3 | 1 | 7 |
| c | 3 | 1 | 3 | 7 |
| d | 4 | 2 | 2 | 8 |
| S1 | 0 | 4 | 4 | 8 |
| S2 | 4 | 0 | 4 | 8 |
| M | 4 | 4 | 0 | 8 |

The results in the final column tell us that, of the nodes we have evaluated, *a* has the lowest transportation cost. But what about possible locations at points along the links between nodes? Under the assumptions of our model, it is only necessary to consider location at nodes because no off-node location will have transportation costs that are lower than the lowest cost node.[5] To understand this, notice that finding the cost-minimizing location along the link between, say, nodes *a* and *b* is basically the same as a location-on-a-line problem. If the transportation cost is lower at one end of the line segment (in this case the link) than the other, then that end (in this case node *a*) will have a lower cost than any intermediate point. If it were the case that transportation costs at *a* and *b* were identical, then the cost at all intermediate points along the link connecting them will also be identical. But it will never be the case that an off-node link will have lower transportation costs than the least-cost node.

This means we need only consider the network nodes as possible locations, rather than an infinite number of candidate points as in the case of location on a plane. This fact, along with the fact that movement along networks is more in tune with reality than movement across planes, explains why most applied location models are set in the context of "location on a network."

## Appendix: Mathematical equations

**A13.1** We can demonstrate that the location that minimizes transportation cost is also that location that maximizes profit in this case as follows. Define *c* as the on-site production cost of the firm and assume it does not vary across possible locations. Define the price of one unit of output as *p* and the price of one ton of the input as *P*. Define *q* as the quantity of output that will be produced at the factory once its location is chosen. The firm's profit can be defined as the market value of its output, minus the on-site production cost, the cost of the input and total transportation costs:

$$\Pi = pq - cq - PXq - (D - d)\,XTq - dxtq$$

We can decompose this expression into two parts: "basic" B which includes all elements of cost and revenue that *do not* depend on the value of d and "locational" L which includes all those that do:

$$\Pi = B + L$$
$$B = pq - cq - PXq$$
$$L = -(D - d)XTq - dxtq$$

The benefit of this decomposition is that in choosing the profit-maximizing location the firm need only pay attention to $L$. Given the assumptions we have made, $L$ includes only cost elements from the profit calculation – that is, revenue is independent of the chosen location. Furthermore, since we have assumed constant returns to scale, the location that maximizes the per unit value of $L$

$$\frac{L}{q} = -(D - d)XT - dxt$$

is also the location that maximizes total $L$. Finally, it is easy to show that maximizing the value $L/q$ is equivalent to minimizing $(D - d)XTq + dxtq$.

**A13.2** Assume that the distribution cost is borne by the consumers. At first blush, this might seem to suggest that the firm would always locate at the source $(S)$, but it's not quite that simple. In reality, if consumers must bear transport costs, they would buy less from a firm that is located further from the market. For this case we can define the delivered price paid on a product produced at distance $d$ as $\tilde{p} = p + txd$. Define a demand function

$$\tilde{q} = q - \beta txd$$

where $q$ is the level of the good demanded if $d = 0$ (that is, for a firm located at $M$). We now redefine profit as

$$\Pi = p\tilde{q} - c\tilde{q} - (D - d)XT\tilde{q}$$
$$\Pi = p(q - \beta txd) - c(q - \beta txd) - (D - d)XT(q - \beta txd)$$

Now there is no basic component because every factor contributing to revenue or cost depends on $q$, which in turn depends on $d$. (Remember, while consumers act on delivered price $\tilde{p}$, the firm gains revenue only at the rate $p$.)

The best location is at $S$ if

$$p(q - \beta txD) - c(q - \beta txD) > pq - cq - DXTq$$

After some substitution, this can be simplified to the following rule: locate at $S$ if

$$XTq > (p - c)\beta xt$$

$$XT > xt\left[\frac{(p - c)\beta}{q}\right]$$

$XTq$ is the assembly cost that is only incurred at $M$, $(p - c)\beta xt$ is the loss in revenue net of production cost due to the decline in output for locating at $S$ rather than $M$.
   General points:

- Higher price over cost margin $(p - c)$ favors location at $M$
- Higher price sensitivity $(\beta)$ favors location at $M$
- As usual, $x/X$ and $t/T$ favor locations at $M$

For what it is worth, if $[(p - c)\beta]/q = 1$, the fact that consumers bear the transportation costs is irrelevant.

# 14 Scale economies and input substitution

So far, we have treated the firm as if it had two separate types of decision to make in order to maximize its profit. The first type, which includes decisions about how to combine inputs to produce an optimal level of output, depends on the production technology. The second type is the location decision, which depends on the structure of transportation costs. In this chapter, we explore some interrelationships between these two types of decisions. More specifically, we consider how the production technology affects the location decision.

Internal scale economies and input substitution are two critical characteristics of the production technology. (Refer back to chapters 3 and 7 to review these concepts.) We will see that increasing returns to scale imply that the relative weight of inputs and output – and thereby the optimal location of the firm – depend on the scale of production. What is more, scale economies play a central role in the location decisions of firms that seek to sell their output in more than one market. We will also see that, in the presence of input substitution, the relative mill prices of inputs may influence the location decision.

## Scale economies and location on a line

In chapter 13, we defined four basic assumptions of the Weberian model of location on a line. Suppose we change assumption 2 to the following:

2a   The production technology of the firm is increasing return to scale and allows no input substitution.

Recall that our approach is to find the location that minimizes $TX(D - d) + txd$. If we retain the assumption that $T = t$, the firm should locate at the material source location $S$ if $X > x$ and at the market $M$ if $X < x$. If $X = x$, total transportation costs are equal at all points so the firm is indifferent among locations at $S$, $M$ and all points in between. How do scale economies come into play in our simple model?

First, recall that scale economies mean that the efficiency of the production technology improves as the scale of production increases. Define $q$ as the factory's planned level of output. Increasing returns to scale implies that $X$, defined as the weight of the localized input required to produce one unit of output with weight $x$,

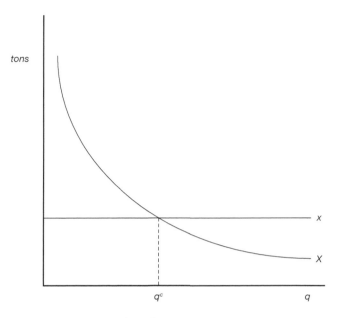

tons

$q^c$

$q$

$x$

$X$

*Figure 14.1* The
values of $X$ and $x$
with increasing
returns to scale

is lower for higher values of $q$, as illustrated in Figure 14.1. Since $x$ does not vary
with $q$, the effect of scale economies is to alter the value of $X$ relative to $x$, which
naturally has implications for location. Figure 14.1 illustrates a case where $X > x$
for production levels below a critical value $q^c$, and $X < x$ for levels above $q^c$. Thus,
whether the firm locates at $S$ or $M$ depends on the scale of production that is planned
for the factory. If the scale is below $q^c$ the cost-minimizing location is at $S$, while
if it is above $q^c$ it is at $M$.

This is a rather extreme case because it suggests that a weight-losing technology
is transformed into a weight-gaining technology with increasing scale – something
that can only happen if some ubiquitous input is included in the production process.
A more plausible scenario is that the technology continues to be weight losing, but
that the gap between $X$ and $x$ decreases with the scale of production, as shown in
the first half of Figure 14.2. If we combine this situation with a lower transportation
rate for the input than for output ($T < t$), we may still have a situation where the
best location switches from $S$ to $M$ once $q$ exceeds some critical value. As illustrated
in the second half of Figure 14.2, $TX > tx$ below $q^c$ but $TX < tx$ above $q^c$.

What are we to take from all this? First, it illustrates the basic principle that, as
we relax simplifying assumptions in an attempt to be more consistent with what
happens in the real world, location problems inevitably become more complicated.
When we assume constant returns to scale, we only need to know the values of $X$,
$x$, $T$ and $t$ to find the best location for the firm. Once we allow increasing (or
decreasing) returns, the best location also depends on the level of output $q$. Second,
it demonstrates that the scale of production affects the location problem with a
particular bias. In the presence of increasing returns to scale, big firms are more

likely to find their best location at the market than are small firms. (A discussion of how scale economies affect the location patterns of large and small steel producers is found in Box 14.)

---

## *Box 14* **Steel technology and location**

The steel industry is often used for case studies in location theory because it has two characteristics that strongly influence location choice. The first is a heavy dependence on weight-losing material and energy inputs: iron and coal respectively. We have already seen how this characteristic influenced industrial development in the Ruhr region of Germany. The second characteristic is the ability to achieve very significant scale economies in production. To understand this, we need to look at how an integrated steel production facility works. Steel does not come directly from iron ore. Rather, the ore is refined in a blast furnace to a relatively pure form of iron (called "pig iron" because early casting methods produced ingots that looked like a litter of suckling pigs), which is then passed to the steel-making stage, where the iron is subjected to chemical reactions that give it the malleable character of steel. The steel is cast into different shapes depending upon the ultimate product that is desired. Rods and billets are long shapes that are further refined in a rolling mill to make products ranging from concrete reinforcing bars and steel wire to the structural steel used in high-rise buildings. Slabs are flatter shapes that are rolled to produce "flat-rolled" products, including the sheet steel used in car bodies. An integrated steel-making facility is one where all three major processes – iron making, steel making and rolling – are combined on one site:

*Figure B14.1* Integrated steel production process

There are scale economies in all three processes, but they are especially pronounced in the blast furnace. In general, bigger blast furnaces have greater thermal efficiencies, making it possible to produce iron with less coal per ton. This reduces costs and also decreases the material index. There is some evidence that, as blast furnaces got bigger, the location of integrated steel production became more market oriented, just as Weberian theory would predict. For example, in Canada integrated production was established in three places: Nova Scotia, northern Ontario and southern Ontario. While both Nova Scotia and northern Ontario had superior access to coal and ore, it was the southern Ontario facilities that came to dominate Canadian steel production due, at least in part, to their superior market access (Anderson, 1987).

As steel became the most important industrial material of the late nine-teenth and early twentieth century, large quantities of scrap steel became available from worn-out or obsolete equipment and buildings. Fortunately, steel is highly recyclable. A variety of means were found to melt down old steel to produce new steel products. A certain amount of scrap can be introduced into the material stream in an integrated steel facility. But steel making based exclusively on scrap became possible when the electric arc furnace emerged as the core technology for a new type of steel plant known as the "mini-mill." Initially, mini-mills produced a limited range of products, beginning with concrete reinforcing bars and gradually expanding into other products based on steel bars and billets. More recently, mini-mills can even produce some flat-rolled steel products.

As the name suggests, mini-mills can produce efficiently at much smaller scales than integrated steel facilities. One reason for this is that the process with the greatest scale economy, the blast furnace, is eliminated because scrap rather than ore is used as a basic input. While mini-mills once represented only a tiny fraction of aggregate steel production, by the twenty-first century they accounted for more than half of the steel produced in the United States. The spatial pattern of mini-mill production is very different from that of integrated mills. Because they are less influenced by scale economies, they are more dispersed. Because there is little weight loss in their production technology, they are more market oriented. This is reinforced by the fact that the locations that demand the most steel are also the locations that tend to produce the most scrap. So mini-mills are found in many major urban areas that are remote from the traditional industrial regions where integrated mills are found. Because they are, in general, less dependent on transportation costs and scale economies, their locations are also influenced by a variety of non-Weberian location factors such as the advantages of locating in diverse industrial clusters (Giarratani *et al.*, 2007).

## Scale economies and Weber's Triangle

When we expand the model to include two inputs and shift the context of the model from location on a line to location on a plane, we find that the basic insights about the effect of scale economy on location are reinforced. Adopting assumption 2a for Weber's Triangle implies that the optimal location is now a function not only of the relative weights $x$, $X_1$ and $X_2$, but also of the level of output $q$. We can summarize the effect by using the material index ($MI$) introduced in chapter 13. Recall $MI = (X_1 + X_2)/x$. Since increasing returns do not affect the $x$, the $MI$ goes down as the scale of production goes up. As noted earlier, a decreasing $MI$ shifts the optimal location in the direction of the market. Figure 14.3 shows the effect of an increase in the scale of production from $q$ to $q'$ on the optimal location. As the scale increases, the optimal location gets closer to the market.

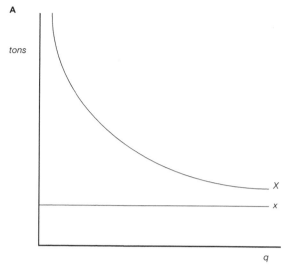

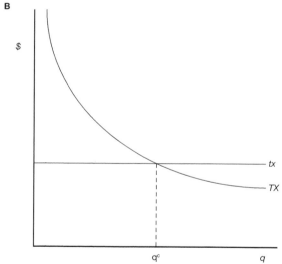

*Figure 14.2*
Relative values of *X*,
*x*, *TX* and *tx* with
increasing returns to
scale and *T<t*

## Scale economies and the multi-facility firm

So far, we have addressed the location problem of a firm that seeks to produce output to sell in a single spatial market. This is seldom the case in reality. A more typical situation is where the firm plans to sell into a number of markets that are scattered in space. Such a firm is always faced with a decision of whether to produce goods for all markets at a single centralized location or to locate a number of facilities in different locations, each of which will serve one or a few nearby markets.

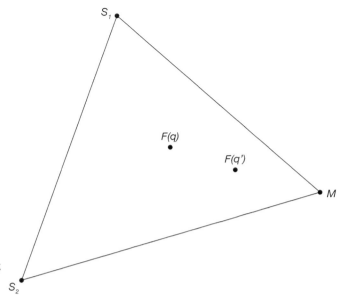

*Figure 14.3*
Effect of increasing
scale on optimal
location

An example is presented in Figure 14.4, where the firm wishes to sell its output in eight markets designated $M_1$, $M_2$, ... $M_8$. For simplicity, we assume that each market has the same level of demand so that no single market has a greater influence on the location decision than any other. We also assume that the firm produces a good that only uses ubiquitous inputs, so that the only transportation cost it has to worry about is the cost of transporting finished goods to the markets. So we have changed our initial assumption as follows:

1a   The firm uses only ubiquitous inputs and sells its output in eight markets located in a plane at points $M_1$, $M_2$, ... $M_8$.

Start with the assumption that the production technology is constant returns to scale. The best location option for the firm is obvious in this case: it should locate one factory at each of the eight markets, resulting in zero transportation costs. But what if the production technology has increasing returns? In this case, the firm would have lower production costs if it located just one facility to serve all markets. This illustrates a basic theme in location theory for firms serving multiple markets – that there is a trade-off between minimizing transportation costs and minimizing production costs.

How would such a firm determine its best strategy? First, it must know how much it expects to sell in each market. Let's say it expects to sell a constant amount $q$ in each of the eight markets. The cost of producing output $q$ in a single factory is $C(q)$. The cost of producing the output necessary to serve all eight markets in one factory is $C(8q)$. Increasing returns to scale implies $C(8q) < 8C(q)$. Before the

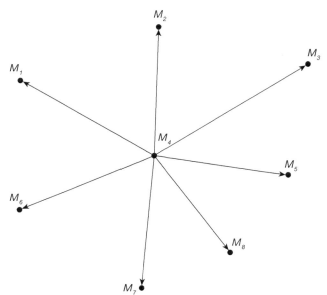

*Figure 14.4*
Location to serve
eight scattered
markets

firm can decide whether it would be more efficient to serve all markets from a single factory, it would need to know where that factory would be located. Clearly, the best location would be at one of the eight markets, but which one? Since there are only distribution costs in this example, the transportation cost incurred with a location at some market $M_i$ would be $\sum_{j=1}^{8} tqd_{ij}$ where $d_{ij}$ is the distance from $M_i$ to some other market $M_j$. Looking at Figure 14.4, it is obvious that this value would be minimized at the most centrally located market, which is $M_4$. So whether the firm chooses to locate eight factories, one at each market, or one factory at $M_4$ depends on the relative values of the extra production costs associated with the former strategy and the extra transportation cost associated with the latter. In other words, the firm will locate a single factory at $M_4$ if

$$8C(q) - C(8q) > \sum_{j=1}^{8} tqd_{4j}$$

Actually, the firm's location decision is a bit more complicated than this because it might also choose to locate two, three or as many as seven factories, each serving one or more markets. But the contrast between the two options described above is sufficient to illustrate an important principle about the location decisions of firms serving multiple markets: when there are scale economies in the production technology, the location option that minimizes transportation costs is not necessarily the one that minimizes total cost. In such cases centralized production is often more profitable than dispersed production. (This is illustrated by the difference in the spatial patterns of integrated steel mills and mini-mills described in Box 14.)

## Input substitution and Weber's Triangle

Input substitution means that there is flexibility in the production technology, allowing different combinations of input levels to produce a given level of output. (For example, a steel mill may be able to substitute between the levels of iron ore and scrap metal it uses in producing steel.) This will have an effect on optimal locations because it implies that the weight of input per unit of output is not constant. We can illustrate this using Weber's Triangle, which includes two localized inputs and a single market. To keep things simple, let's reinstate the constant returns assumption:

2b   The production technology of the firm yields constant return to scale and allows substitution between the two localized inputs.

Assuming a single transport rate, the optimal location depends on the relative weights of the two inputs $X_1$ and $X_2$ and of one unit of output $x$. With input substitution, there is a range of different values of $X_1$ and $X_2$, which implies there is a range of optimal locations. So which one is right?

Recall from chapter 7 that input substitution is induced by a change in the relative prices of inputs. The firm seeks to use more of any input that gets cheaper and less of any input that gets more expensive. Define $p_1$ and $p_2$ as the mill prices of the two inputs (that is, the prices net of transportation costs). Assuming the possibility of input substitution, Figure 14.5 shows a $Q = 1$ isoquant for the firm's output. At an initial ratio $p_2/p_1$ we get optimal input levels $X_1$ and $X_2$ ($p_2/p_1$ is the slope of the isoquant line). Now if the price of input 2 goes down relative to the price of input 1, we get a new optimal input combination $X_1'$ and $X_2'$ such that $X_1' < X_1$ and $X_2' > X_2$.

This outcome has implications for the optimal location, as shown in Figure 14.6. Since the value of $X_2$ goes up relative to the value of $X_1$, the "pull" of the *S2* corner goes up, resulting in a shift from $F$ to $F'$. (The mathematically inclined reader is referred to Miller and Jensen, 1978, who show how the optimal input combination and location may be determined simultaneously using trigonometry and calculus.)

Our example begs a question. Suppose the relative prices are at their initial values $p_2/p_1$ and the firm locates its factory at $F$. Then the relative prices change in such a way that the optimal location would be at $F'$. Would the firm relocate? The answer depends on two things. The first is whether the firm believes that the prices will stay at the new level or whether it expects them to revert to the initial level. The prices of many inputs (fuels, metal ores, wood, etc.) fluctuate considerably over time. The firm must make its location choice based on the average prices it expects to face over the life of the factory rather than those that it observes at a particular moment. The second is whether the change in relative prices is great enough to exceed the cost of relocation. In practice, the change in relative prices would have to be quite extreme to induce enough input substitution to cause a shift in transportation costs large enough to exceed the very substantial costs associated with relocation.

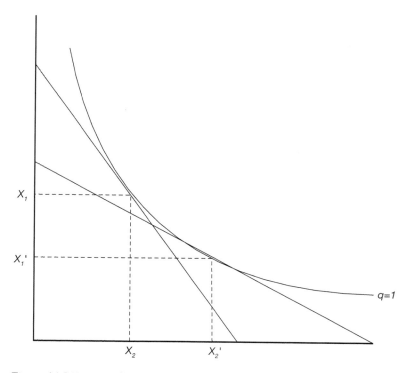

*Figure 14.5* Isoquant for two localized inputs

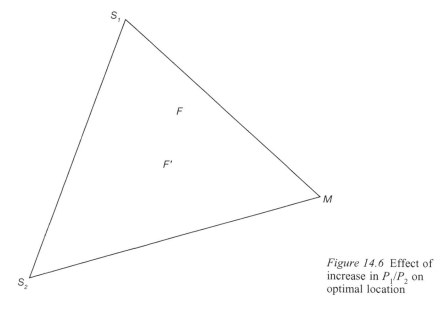

*Figure 14.6* Effect of increase in $P_1/P_2$ on optimal location

# 15  Labor, rent, taxes and subsidies

So far, our location theory has focused exclusively on transportation costs. But clearly there are other cost factors that affect the firm's location decision. In reality, any category of cost that varies over space must be taken into account in the firm's location decision. In this chapter, we will address two such categories: the cost of labor and the cost of land (rent). We will also consider how spatially varying payments to the government (taxes) and from the government (subsidies) affect location.

## Labor cost[1]

It is well known that the cost of labor varies over space. For example, one of the driving forces behind growth in international trade is the difference in labor costs between affluent countries and developing countries. Significant variations in labor costs exist within countries. For example, labor generally earns more in the southeast of England than in the north. We must be careful, however, that we do not confuse an apparent difference in labor cost per hour with a difference in effective labor cost. Labor productivity, defined as the amount of output produced per hour worked, may also vary over space. Table 15.1 provides a hypothetical example where labor costs and labor productivity both differ between two regions $A$ and $B$. Region $B$'s wage is 25 percent higher, but so is its productivity. Labor cost per unit of output is therefore the same in the two regions. Other things being equal, the firm would be indifferent between locating in $A$ and $B$. In what follows, we will only worry about the cost of labor per unit of output, designated as $w$.

Starting with the case of location on a line, it is easy to incorporate a difference in labor costs between the material source $S$ and the market $M$, which we indicate

*Table 15.1* Hypothetical two-region example of labor costs

|  | Region A | Region B |
| --- | --- | --- |
| Labor cost per hour | 8 | 10 |
| Units of output per hour (productivity) | 1 | 1.25 |
| Labor cost per unit of output | 8 | 8 |

as $w_S$ and $w_M$ respectively. (To keep things simple, we will assume constant returns to scale and no input substitution.) If we define total cost $C$ as comprising both labor and transportation costs

$$C_S = tX(D - d) + txd + w_S$$
$$C_M = tX(D - d) + txd + w_M$$

where $D$ is the distance from $S$ to $M$, $d$ is the distance from the chosen factory site to the market, $X$ is the weight of the single localized input per unit of output, $x$ is the weight of one unit of output and $t$ is the transport rate (see Figure 13.1). Recalling that a location at $S$ implies that $D = d$ and that a location at $M$ implies that $d = 0$,

$$C_S = tXD + w_S$$
$$C_M = tXD + w_M$$

so the firm chooses to locate at $M$ if $txD + w_S > txD + w_M$ or, rearranging terms, if

$$tD(x - X) > w_M - w_S$$

What does this condition mean? Assume for the moment that $x > X$, so the production technology is weight gaining. In our earlier model, this fact would be sufficient to determine that the best location is at the market $M$. Now, however, we have to take into account the possibility that labor cost might be higher at $M$ than at $S$ ($w_M > w_S$). In order for the cost-minimizing location to be at $M$, the left-hand side of the inequality, which measures the extra transport cost that would be incurred by locating at $S$ instead of $M$, must be greater than the right-hand side, which measures the extra labor cost that would be incurred by locating at $M$ instead of $S$. This means that a weight-gaining industry might be better off locating at the material source $S$ if labor costs are higher at the market $M$. Another important point is that in our original model, the best location was independent of the values of $t$ and $D$. Now they matter because the higher the transport rate and the longer the distance between $S$ and $M$, the greater is the effect of $(x - X)$ relative to the effect of $(w_M - w_S)$.

If we extend our analysis to the case of two localized inputs, we can use a simple graphical device that was first introduced by Weber himself to explain the effect of labor costs. In Figure 15.1, we have Weber's Triangle where it has been determined that the transportation cost-minimizing location is at point $F$. There are also a number of other lines called "isodopanes" that connect points of equal incremental transportation costs. If the firm locates at any point on the "+1" isodopane, its transportation costs per unit of output would be $1 higher than if it were located at $F$. If it locates on the "+2" isodopane, its transportation costs would be $2 higher, and so on.

Now suppose that the labor cost per unit of output is the same at all points except at point $L$, where it is lower. This might be because there is high unemployment at

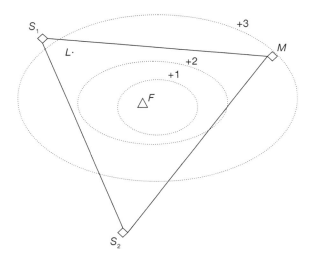

*Figure 15.1*
Weber's Triangle
with isodopanes

that point, inducing people to work more cheaply, or because the government is paying a wage subsidy to encourage firms to locate at $L$. Should the firm choose the low labor cost point $L$ instead of $F$? It depends on the magnitude of the labor cost savings. Looking at the isodopanes, we can see that, if the labor saving is $2, the firm is better off staying at $F$, while if it is $3 the firm is better off locating at $L$.

This basic logic can be used to explain the growth of Export Processing Zones in low-wage countries. International corporations often set up production facilities in these zones in order to save on labor costs, despite the fact that they are usually located far from both the sources of materials and the markets for the goods produced. Clearly, for the corporations that make this location choice, the labor cost savings outweigh the incremental transportation costs (see Box 15).

---

## *Box 15* **Export Processing Zones**

The International Labor Office defines export processing zones (EPZs) as "industrial zones with special incentives set up to attract foreign investors, in which imported materials undergo some degree of processing before being exported again" (McCallum, 2011). For example, suppose a garment factory producing denim jeans is set up in an EPZ. The company that manufactures the jeans is probably a foreign multinational. It brings in its own machinery, its own materials (denim, zippers, thread, rivets) and probably also its own management staff. Local employees work on the foreign machines, sewing the foreign denim into jeans that will then be sold into a foreign market. Aside from basic utilities like water and electricity, the only input provided by the host country is labor. The "zone" is defined by a set of specific regulatory concessions, including exemption from tariff and non-tariff barriers on imported materials and capital goods, and in some cases exemption from labor and environmental regulation. Naturally, the company incurs higher transportation costs than if it had located near either the source of the denim or one of its principal markets. But the labor cost saved by locating in the EPZ more than offset the incremental transportation costs.

EPZs have been established in many countries around the world. They occur not only in the poorest countries, but also in countries that can provide low wages relative to the markets for which the goods are intended. For example, one of the earliest EPZs was established in Shannon, Ireland in 1959. While Ireland was hardly a Third World country, its wages were substantially lower than elsewhere in western Europe at the time. Perhaps the most famous example is Mexico's *maquiladora* program, whereby factories located in Mexico employ Mexican workers to produce goods ranging from textiles to auto parts using American capital and materials and bound strictly for re-export to the United States. Since the daily minimum wage in Mexico is less than the hourly minimum wage in the U.S., substantial savings are achieved. (The *maquiladora* program is no longer limited to a small zone, however, as it is now possible to gain *maquiladora* status for factories located in most parts of Mexico.)

As countries with ever lower wages have established EPZs, production has shifted to locations that are increasingly far away from markets and material sources. This trend is reinforced by gradual reductions in transportation costs at the global scale over the past few decades. Thus, when China established EPZs in the 1980s, some (not all) American firms found them cheaper than the *maquiladoras*, leading to some loss in Mexican employment. For those firms, the reduction in labor cost of moving from Mexico to China was greater than the increase in transportation costs.

EPZs are controversial for a variety of reasons. In affluent countries, labor interests see them as unfair competition. Environmentalists note that the extra transportation used to exploit labor cost differences in this way leads to extra pollution and greenhouse gas emissions. Even for the countries that create EPZs within their territories, there is some question as to whether they are socially beneficial in the long run (McCallum, 2011). Because they do not use local inputs they have low multiplier effects and do little to encourage the development of local firms. In fact, they may retard local development by drawing away labor supplies. They do relatively little for skills development since higher-order functions such as marketing and R&D are all handled by foreigners. Also, since a low wage is their reason for being, they provide incentives for governments to make policies that retard, rather than boost, the earning power of workers.

> Still, for some countries, the EPZ model may provide a means of entry into the global economy. This was the case with China, where the EPZ program allowed the socialist state to experiment with new forms of labor relations and gauge the potential for export development. Today, China's ascendance as a global exporter depends less on EPZs and more on independent enterprises with strong domestic links and ever expanding technical capability.

## Rent

Another spatially variant cost, which is neglected in our initial definition of profit, is rent. If rent has the same value $R$ at all points along the line, then it only affects basic profit and therefore will not affect the profit-maximizing location. But suppose $M$ represents an urban market. Since rent often falls with distance from a city (a phenomenon that we will explore in chapter 17), we can define the rent at distance $d$ as $R_d = R_m - rd$ where $R_M$ is the rent at M and $r$ is a rate at which rent falls with distance from M.

How does the rent affect location? First, assume that the rent is defined on a per unit of output basis. The effect of rent is similar to the effect of difference in the wage: the firm locates at $M$ if $tD(x - X) > R_M - R_S$. Figure 15.2 shows how including rent in the analysis can result in a situation where the cost-minimizing location is at $S$, even though $x > X$.

In reality, however, comparing rent variations with variations in transportation costs may not be quite this simple because rent may not vary directly with the level of output. For example, it may be possible for a firm to increase its output

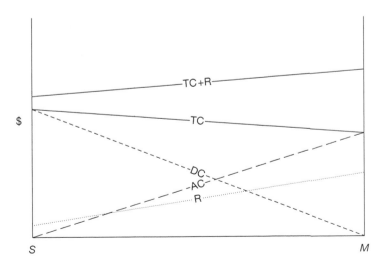

*Figure 15.2* Location on a line with $x > X$ and $R$ declining in $d$

without increasing the amount of land it occupies by making more efficient use of existing space or even building a second story on its factory building. If this is the case, then rent is a fixed cost rather than a variable (per unit) cost. This is an important distinction because if rent is a fixed cost it will have a more significant impact on the location decision of small factories than of big ones. (This is demonstrated algebraically in the Appendix to this chapter, equation A15.1.)

## Taxes, subsidies and location

Taxes come in a number of forms. Income taxes are charged as a percentage of the firm's profit level, while property taxes are charged against the value of the firm's assets, notably land. Some taxes are charged against specific inputs that the firm consumes, such as a payroll tax to support unemployment insurance or a tax on fuels. Consumption taxes such as sales or excise taxes are not charged directly to the firm, but since they increase the effective price of the firm's output, they may reduce sales, which in turn may reduce profit. Most taxes are spatially undifferentiated, which means that their levels are independent of the firm's location. That does not mean, however, that they have no impact on the firm's location choice.

Consider, for example, a spatially undifferentiated tax on diesel fuel. If most inputs are moved by trucks and trains, both of which use diesel, such a tax will create a general increase in transportation costs. Will this affect the firm's optimal location? For the simple situations described by the models in chapter 13, the answer is generally "no." So long as the effect of the tax is to increase the transportation rates for inputs ($T$) and for output ($t$) by the same proportion, the general results of the Weberian models will be unchanged. We can verify this for the simple case of location on a line. Assume that the diesel tax increases all transport rates by some constant proportion $\kappa$. Recall that our original location rule was: locate at the input source S if $t/T > X/x$. ($X$ is the weight of the single localized input in this model and $x$ is the weight of one unit of output.) After adjusting for the tax-induced increase in the transportation rates, the new location rule is: locate at the source S if $(1 + \kappa)t/(1 + \kappa)T > X/x$. Naturally, $(1 + \kappa)$ cancels out, so the location rule is unchanged.

The undifferentiated fuel tax may make a difference, however, where transportation costs must be balanced against some other spatial variant cost of production, such as labor cost. For example, look at what happens to the situation described in Figure 15.1 when the isodopanes are adjusted outward to reflect the effect of the fuel tax. Assume that at point $L$ labor costs are $3 lower than at all other points. Whether or not the firm will choose to shift its location from the transportation costs minimum point $F$ depends upon whether point $L$ lies inside the +3 isodopane. Figure 15.3 shows both the pre-tax and post-tax isodopanes – since transportation costs are higher post-tax, the distance away from $F$ at which the incremental cost of transportation is 3 declines. For the case illustrated here, the firm would prefer to locate at $L$ without the tax but it would prefer to locate at $F$ with the tax. So here is an example where a spatially undifferentiated tax has an effect on the firm's location decision.

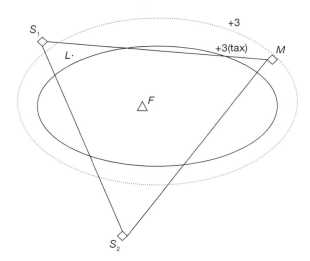

*Figure 15.3*
Weber's Triangle with
isodopanes and fuel tax

A spatially undifferentiated payroll tax may also affect location in a roundabout way. Because they make labor more expensive, payroll taxes provide incentives for firms to reduce the labor intensity of their production by substituting capital for labor. Reducing the labor intensity of production will reduce the attractiveness of low-wage locations.

A spatially undifferentiated income tax will not affect the results of any of the models we have considered so far. But, while it may not affect the firm's optimal location, it may affect a firm's *re*location decision. At the end of chapter 14, we considered whether a firm whose optimal location shifts because of a change in relative input prices will relocate to the new optimum. There are two reasons why it might not. The first is that it might be unsure as to whether the shift in relative prices is permanent and the second is that the costs of relocation may exceed the extra profit it would earn by moving to the new location. Focusing on the second of these reasons, the undifferentiated income tax will reduce the value of the profits earned by relocating. Therefore, a firm that chooses to relocate before the tax is imposed may choose not to after it is imposed. (The effect of income tax on the decision to relocate is explored in more detail in the Appendix to this chapter, equation A15.2.)

Of course, spatially differentiated taxes have the most direct influence on location. In countries that have federal political systems, such as the U.S. and Canada, income taxes can vary significantly from place to place. Property taxes are often set at the local level, so they can vary significantly even over rather short distances. We really don't need to develop new models to deal with the effect of these taxes because models that we have already seen will suffice. For example, spatial variations in the income tax function very much like spatial variations in labor costs and spatially variant property taxes function very much like spatial variations in rent. Whether firms choose low-tax locations depends on whether the tax saving is enough to offset lower transportation, labor and land costs that are found in higher-tax locations. Also, some taxes act like fixed costs, such as registration fees, inspection fees and taxes on assets. Since they do not vary with the level of output, they will have greater influence over smaller firms.

We can think of subsidies as negative taxes. Subsidies that are spatially undifferentiated may still have subtle effects on location. For example, subsidies that promote output growth in an industry may result in increased market orientation if the industry is subject to economies of scale. Spatially differentiated subsidies are sometimes used as instruments of regional policy to induce firms to locate in places that would not be chosen on the basis of transportation and production costs. (See chapter 12 for more on regional policy.) Here, as in the case of taxes, the effectiveness of subsidies will depend on how large they are compared with spatial variations in transportation, labor, land and other production costs.

# Appendix

## A15.1 Rent as a fixed cost

Assume that rent is a fixed cost. We can now rewrite our profit function

$$\Pi = pq - cq - (D - d)XTq - dxtq - (R - rd)$$

We can separate this equation into basic $(B)$ and locational $(L)$ components, where only the latter affect the location decision:

$$\Pi = B + L$$
$$B = pq - cq - R$$
$$L = -(D - d)XTq - dxtq + rd$$

Now if we compare the locational profits at $M$ and $S$, we find that the best location is at $S$ if

$$XT + \frac{r}{q} > xt$$

Now something interesting has happened. Because site rent is a fixed cost, its influence on unit profits declines with the scale of production. If $XT < xt$, it is still more profitable to locate at $S$ so long as $r/q > xt - XT$. Assuming $t = T$ this means that a weight-gaining good might still be better located at $S$. But notice that the rent savings benefit is inversely related to output $q$. So, for the same firm, location at the source $S$ might be more profitable for a low level of output, while location at the market $M$ is more profitable for a high level of output.

Alternatively, if we assume that rent is proportional to output,

$$\Pi = pq - cq - (D - d)XTq - dxtq - (R - rd)q$$

In this case it works out that the firm locates at $S$ if

$$r > xt - XT$$

so the result is independent of $q$.

Of course, the same framework can be used to show the effect of various types of subsidies.

### A15.2 Relocation and the income tax

Suppose a firm calculates that it can increase its annual profits by an amount $\Delta\Pi$ if it relocates. However, there is a cost of relocation $\mathbb{R}$. For the moment, suppose there is no income tax. The firm assumes that if it relocates it will be able to remain in the new location and reap the additional profit for a period of 20 years. This does not mean that it will be better off to relocate if $\mathbb{R} < 20\Delta\Pi$, however. Because the relocation cost must be paid up front, while the additional profit is a stream of revenues over 20 years, the correct rule is for the firm to relocate if the present value of the 20-year stream of extra profits exceeds the relocation cost (see the Appendix to chapter 6 for a discussion of present value):

$$\mathbb{R} > \sum_{t=1}^{20} \frac{\Delta\Pi}{(1 + r)^t}$$

where $r$ is a rate of return used for discounting. For example, suppose the expected incremental profit is 100, $r = .05$ and $\mathbb{R} = 1200$. The firm is better off relocating because the present value of the tax savings are 1,246.

Now suppose an income tax is instituted at a rate $\tau$. This means the extra income in any year will be $(1 - \tau)\Delta\Pi$. This means that the present value of extra income earned after relocating goes down. While this would appear to make relocation less desirable, bear in mind that the relocation cost will be a deduction from taxable income. Assuming that the entire relocation cost can be deducted up front, the new location rule becomes:

$$(1 - \tau)\mathbb{R} > \sum_{t=1}^{20} \frac{(1 - \tau)\Delta\Pi}{(1 + r)^t}$$

Dividing both sides by $(1 - \tau)$ reproduces the original location rule, so the income tax has no effect on the relocation decision. The situation would be different, however, if the firm is not able to write off the entire relocation cost up front. (Accounting rules usually require that capital costs be written off for tax over a number of years.) Suppose the firm can write off the relocation cost over ten years. Now the rule is to locate so long as:

$$\mathbb{R} - \sum_{t=1}^{5} \frac{\tau \frac{\mathbb{R}}{10}}{(1 + r)^t} < \sum_{t=1}^{20} \frac{(1 - \tau)\Delta\Pi}{(1 + r)^t}$$

Assuming all the values described above and a 20 percent tax rate ($\tau = .2$), the firm is now better off not to relocate because the relocation cost net of the tax benefit (1,015) is greater than the present value of extra after-tax profits (997).

# 16  Interrelated location choices

Up to this point, we have considered the decision of a single firm that chooses the location of one or more facilities under the assumption that the locations of all other firms and markets are fixed. The other firms whose locations are assumed to be fixed are those that either provide inputs to the firm's production process, in which case their locations constitute input sources, or purchase the firm's outputs, in which case they act as markets.

But, in reality, numerous firms make location choices on an ongoing basis. Since these firms are interconnected in various ways, the location choice of one firm may depend on contemporaneous or anticipated location choices by other firms. This makes the business of location theory more complicated, but at the same time more interesting. In this chapter, we look at two cases of how location choices are interrelated. The first considers how firms that are interrelated through the exchange of intermediate goods coordinate their location decisions to form *spatial industrial complexes*. The second, which addresses how competitors choose location to try to maximize market share, is called *strategic location*.

## The spatial industrial complex

A firm's location is interrelated with the locations of those firms with which it exchanges intermediate goods. Manufacturing firms produce output that falls into one of two categories: final goods, which are finished products sold to their ultimate consumers, and intermediate goods, which are semi-finished goods that are sold to other manufacturing firms for whom they become material inputs. Steel, for example, is almost always sold as an intermediate good to manufacturers of a variety of goods ranging from construction elements (girders, etc.) to cars and appliances. We refer to any pair of firms that exchange intermediate goods as economically linked.

Often, we can define a group of firms that are bound together by a series of pairwise economic linkages. For example, Figure 16.1 illustrates a group of firms involved in the production of automobiles. Here glass and electronics firms provide windshields and radios respectively to the automobile assembly plant. Some linkages are indirect. For example, a steel firm may sell flat-rolled steel in bulk to a fabricated metal firm, which forms the steel into body panels that are then sold to the assembly

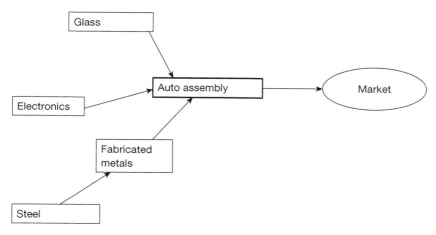

*Figure 16.1* Automotive industrial complex

plant. Only the assembly plant sells its output to final consumers in the market. (This diagram is just a simplified illustration – in reality, 100 or more firms may deliver components to a single automotive assembly plant.) We refer to such a group of firms connected by economic linkages as an *industrial complex*.

Since the linkages in the industrial complex require the movement of goods between plants, there is an incentive for all the firms to locate their plants relatively close together. This is important not only to save on the aggregate freight costs, but also to make it easy to deliver components in a timely fashion – that is to ensure that deliveries arrive within narrow "time windows." (You may remember that in chapter 2 we saw how timely deliveries allow the assembly plant to save money by maintaining smaller inventories of components on site.)

Timeliness is generally easier to achieve over short distances. For example, suppose a truck carrying components to an assembly plant covers each mile that it travels in an average time of 1.25 minutes. Because of randomly occurring congestion, traffic lights and possible mechanical failures, however, there is some variation around that average. Let's say the shipper is 90 percent sure that the truck will cover a mile in not less than 1 minute and not more than 1.5 minutes. If the truck has to travel 10 miles from the component plant to the assembly plant, the components will arrive in not less than 10 minutes and not more than 15 minutes 90 percent of the time. So we can define a 90 percent time window of 5 minutes for the shipment. Now suppose the truck has to travel 100 miles. The time window widens from 5 minutes to 50 minutes. Reality may be a bit more complicated than this simple example. For example, time variance per mile may be somewhat lower for long trips than for short trips. But the main point is that timeliness is more easily achieved over short distances than over long distances.

When the plants in an industrial complex locate close together, we call it a *spatial industrial complex*. As we have already noted in chapter 3, the spatial industrial complex is a kind of agglomeration phenomenon based on a specific type of agglomeration economy called juxtaposition economy. From the perspective of location theory, the observation that firms in an industrial complex will cluster tells only half the story. The obvious question that remains is: *where* will they cluster? To answer this question, it is useful to think of the spatial industrial complex as comprising two classes of industries: complex-serving industries and complex-forming industries. Complex-serving industries behave on that the assumption that location of the complex-forming industries is given. Thus, if the glass plant is complex serving, it will locate close to the automotive assembly plant if its optimal location from a Weberian perspective is market oriented. (In this context, the assembly plant represents the market to the glass plant.) On the other hand, complex-forming industries choose their locations based on factors outside the industrial complex, such as the location of localized raw materials, major markets and either high-skill or low-cost labor. The complex-forming industries choose their locations on the basis of those factors and the location of the spatial industrial complex is determined by the location of the complex-forming industries.

So which are the complex-forming industries in Figure 16.1? From a historical perspective, the steel industry was the key industry in the formation of most spatial industrial complexes. Since steel production depends upon the two localized inputs coal and iron ore, it can only be efficiently located where those inputs are accessible. As steel is the dominant material in automobiles (by weight), it made sense for auto plants to locate in steel-producing regions. This, in part, explains why the U.S. automobile industry eventually concentrated in the Great Lakes regions (specifically Detroit) rather than near the great markets of the East Coast. But it is not fair to label automobile assembly as complex serving. Access to appropriate labor forces and markets for cars also influence the location of assembly plants. Furthermore, as the automotive industry eventually became the primary customer of the steel industry, access to automotives became as important to steel plants as access to steel was to automotive plants. Thus, the steel and automotive industries are mutually dependent complex-forming industries in the spatial industrial complex. (See Box 16 for a discussion of the evolution of the spatial industrial complex around the U.S. automotive industry.)

---

### *Box 16* The evolution of Auto Alley[i]

Nothing is more essential to the American lifestyle than the automobile, so it is not surprising that nothing is more essential to America's economic history than the growth of the automotive industry. The industry has two distinct but tightly integrated types of production facilities: assembly plants and parts plants. Assembly plants are necessarily large (because of scale economies) and are operated by a handful of very large carmakers including the Detroit Three (General Motors, Ford and Chrysler) and the foreign-based manufacturers from Japan (Toyota, Honda, Nissan and Subaru), Germany

(Volkswagen, BMW and Mercedes Benz) and Korea (Hyundai and Kia). There are about 50 assembly plants in North America. Parts plants are a much more diverse group in terms of size, function and ownership. There are over 4,000 such plants in the U.S. and many more in Canada and Mexico. They range from small shops producing specialized parts and employing only a dozen people to very large plants with over 1,000 employees. At one time, a large proportion of the parts plants were owned by the carmakers, but by the 1990s nearly all parts facilities were owned and operated by separate firms – although some major parts such as engines and transmissions are still produced "in house" and some parts manufacturers are partially owned by carmakers. The parts plants actually create most of the value in finished cars and employ many more people than assembly plants. According to the U.S. Bureau of Labor Statistics, the automotive industry employed about 750,000 people in 2006, about 22 percent working in assembly plants and 78 percent working in parts plants. A single car may contain parts from 500 or more parts manufacturers, but that plant only buys directly from a smaller number of "tier 1" parts suppliers. The tier 1 suppliers build components from parts provided by tier 2 suppliers, who in turn buy parts from tier 3 suppliers, etc.

One implication of this highly dis-integrated production system is that a huge number of freight movements occur among parts plants in the different tiers and between the tier 1 suppliers and the assembly plants. Thus, the automotive industry constitutes an industrial complex *par excellence*. At the beginning of the twentieth century, this complex established a very compact spatial cluster around the city of Detroit, Michigan. There are a number of reasons for this focus. For one thing, Detroit has good access to steel, the basic material used in cars. Also, Detroit and some surrounding cities had already established firms in industries such as engine and carriage making that naturally evolved into automaking. It is also significant that it was a Detroit-based entrepreneur, Henry Ford, who did the most to develop the modern system of automotive production.

The spatial logic of the automotive industry as it developed through the twentieth century is interesting. Automotive assembly is not a weight-gaining process, since the finished car does not weigh more than the combined weight of the material inputs (parts), but it is a "bulk-gaining" process. Since the interior of the car is mostly air, the finished car takes up more space than the component parts would if they were neatly stacked. This makes the car more expensive to ship than the parts. So, as the demand for cars increased, new assembly plants were dispersed to the various centers of demand, especially on the east and west coasts. Parts production, however, remained concentrated in Michigan and the nearby Midwest states of Ohio, Indiana and Illinois. Since parts were cheaper to ship than cars, the most efficient pattern was to produce them in a narrow Midwest cluster and then ship them out to the market-oriented assembly plants.

By the 1960s, however, this logic ceased to work. The reason was that carmakers were producing an ever broader range of significantly different models. When Ford just made the Model T, it made sense to assign production to assembly plants on the basis of "one for the Midwest, one for New England, one for New York, one for California," etc. As the range of models increased, however, the carmakers found that economies of scale could be achieved by concentrating production of each model in a single plant. Thus, the assignment of production to assembly plants became "one for the Falcon, one for the Fairlane, one for the Galaxy 500, one for the Thunderbird," etc. Since it would not be efficient to locate plants for all models in all regions, assembly became re-concentrated in the Midwest and assembly plants on the two coasts were closed. (The last California assembly plant closed in 2010.) This is an excellent example of the trade-off between scale economies and transportation costs in location decisions. At the same time, the industry began to shift to a system of tightly integrated supply chains whereby parts are delivered "just-in-time" to reduce the need for large inventories of parts at assembly plants. Such a system is much more easily implemented if parts plants are located within a day's drive of the assembly plant. This further reinforced the benefits of concentrating both parts and assembly production in the Midwest.

The dominance of the American Midwest in the auto industry has been eroding over the past two decades for reasons that have less to do with transportation and scale economies and more to do with new competition and labor costs. In the 1970s, the Detroit Three began to lose their dominance of the U.S. auto market as imported cars from Japan and Europe increased their market shares. Given the scale of exports to the U.S., and the impending threat that the U.S. government would impose import quotas, the major Japanese producers began to set up production facilities in the U.S. In order to avoid the high wages and unionization found in the Midwest, they chose to locate some (but not all) of their plants further south, first in the mid-south states of Tennessee and Kentucky but eventually as far south as Texas. When German carmakers Volkswagen, BMW and Mercedes Benz set up production in the U.S., they followed a more explicitly southern strategy, establishing plants even in the "deep south" states of Alabama and Mississippi. None of these southern plants was unionized, so they gained considerable advantages in labor costs and work rules flexibility.

Of course, these new assembly plants still had the problem of access to parts suppliers. They addressed this problem in two ways. First, they encouraged parts suppliers to locate close to their southern plants. Second, they located their new plants along major north–south highways so that they could receive parts from plants in the Midwest reasonably quickly and cheaply. In a fascinating study of the evolution of the American auto industry, Klier and Rubenstein (2008) demonstrate that these strategies have given rise to a new spatial structure of automotive production along a corridor called

"Auto Alley." The corridor is defined by two major north–south interstate highways: I-65, which stretches from Gary, Indiana (near Chicago) to Mobile Alabama and I-75, which stretches from Sault Ste. Marie, Michigan, through Detroit and Toledo and on to near Miami, Florida. I-75 also connects to the major automotive centers in Ontario, Canada via Highway 401. Both roads pass through Tennessee and Kentucky and are crossed by a series of major east–west highways. The entire corridor now has a high density of automotive activity. Map B16.1 shows the spatial pattern of assembly plants. But this is just the tip of the iceberg, as there are roughly ten parts plants for every assembly plant. Furthermore, there is very little automotive activity in the United States outside of Auto Alley.

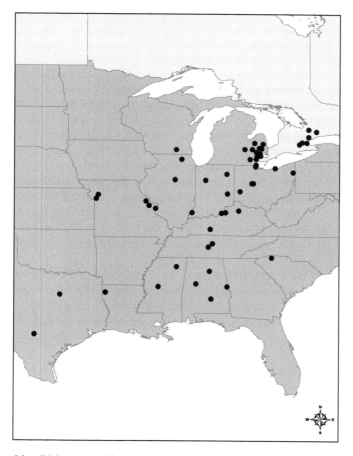

*Map B16.1* Assembly plants in "Auto Alley"

*Source*: Adapted from Klier and Rubenstein (2008).

Thus, while the tight concentration of the automotive complex in the Midwest is a thing of the past, an equally distinctive spatial pattern has emerged. The critical location factors – transportation costs, labor costs and scale economies – all played roles in creating this pattern. But it is important to note that a number of political factors such as favorable tax treatment and "right to work" laws that retard unionization in southern states are also important. Finally, the development of the cluster along a corridor rather than in a compact region illustrates the role of highway infrastructure in shaping economic space.

### Note

i   This example draws extensively from the information in Klier and Rubinstein (2008).

Are all industrial complexes spatial industrial complexes? In other words, do all groups of economically linked firms cluster in space? We can see that the answer is "no" by considering the industrial complex in Figure 16.2. Here we have a bakery providing fresh cakes and pastries to shops and restaurants in an urban market. Its main inputs are flour, which comes from a flour mill, and sugar from a sugar refinery. Do we expect to find the three plants clustered together in space?

First, it is obvious that the location of the bakery will be close to the urban market. Only extremely high-cost air freight would make it possible to deliver fresh pastries more than 100 miles or so. (The situation is different for mass-produced pastries that are laced with preservatives that give them a shelf life of more than a year!) The question is then whether a flour mill and sugar refinery will necessarily locate close to the bakery.

The answer is "no" for a couple of reasons. First, mills and refineries operate most efficiently at very large scales, while bakeries producing fresh products operate efficiently at relatively small scales. Each mill will provide enough flour for hundreds if not thousands of bakeries, so clearly they cannot collocate with every bakery. Second, both flour milling and sugar refining are weight-losing activities

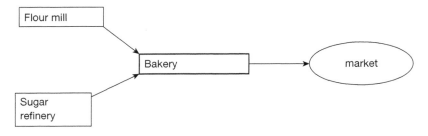

*Figure 16.2* Baked goods industrial complex

because their raw materials (wheat and cane) are heavier than their finished products. Sugar refineries tend to be located either in areas where sugar cane (or beets) are grown or at port locations where the raw cane can be delivered to the refinery by water.

This example demonstrates that the existence of an industrial complex is a necessary, but not sufficient, condition for the existence of a spatial industrial complex. Whether a spatial complex forms – and if so where it forms – can be largely explained by the principles of Weberian location theory. As we will see below, the interrelation between the location choices of firms that compete with one another don't fit the Weberian model well. Therefore, a new kind of analysis is needed.

## Strategic location

In conventional economic theory, producers of commodities (homogeneous goods) compete in terms of price. A process whereby firms undercut one another's price in order to gain market share continues until an equilibrium market price is determined. In economic geography, producers of commodities can also compete by means of their locations. As we have already seen, consumers only care about the delivered price (the sum of the mill price and transportation cost), so, if all firms have the same mill price, consumers will buy from the closest one. A firm that competes with one or more other firms for a finite market will choose its location in order to capture the largest possible share of the market. In doing so, however, it must anticipate the possibility that its competitors may shift their own locations to undermine its position in the market. Thus, location choice amounts to a game of strategy.

A very simple locational game is illustrated in Figure 16.3.[1] Assume that the horizontal line represents a bounded linear market over which consumers are evenly distributed. A and B are two firms that sell a homogeneous commodity. We assume that both firms charge the same mill price and that the delivered price is the mill price plus a transportation cost that is directly proportional to the distance between the firm and any potential consumer located along the line. This means that it is always cheapest to purchase the commodity from the closest firm. We assume further that each consumer purchases a fixed quantity of the commodity in each time period – in other words, the consumer's demand is independent of the delivered price.[2] However, given the choice, each consumer will purchase the commodity from the firm that offers the lowest delivered price – thus, each firm sells the commodity to all consumers who are closer to it than they are to the other firm. Both firms seek to choose their locations so as to maximize sales.

If these assumptions seem confusing (and a little bit contrived), we can think of a real-life example that fits them rather well. Imagine that the bounded linear market is a beach on which a large population of sunbathers is evenly distributed. There are two ice-cream vendors who simultaneously attempt to choose locations that will maximize their sales, based on the assumption that each sunbather buys one ice cream per day. Delivery costs are incurred not in monetary terms, but in terms of the effort expended by sunbathers walking from their spots on the beach to the location of one of the vendors. Since the vendors offer identical ice cream at the same price and sunbathers prefer to walk the shortest possible distance, each of them will buy from the closest vendor.

We can think of this locational game as playing out over a number of time periods, as shown in Figure 16.3. In each period, one firm shifts its location in such a way as to maximize its sales. In the first period, the market is evenly divided between A and B, with each firm located in the center of the part of the market it commands. (Here the sales of A will be proportional to the lightly shaded part of the linear market, while the sales of B will be proportional to the darkly shaded part.) In period 2, A has shifted its location to be very close to B. The result is that A now commands

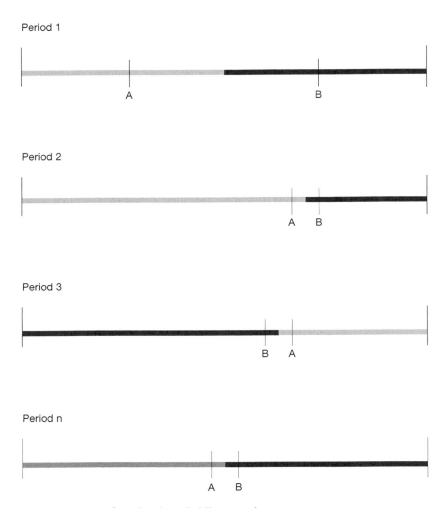

*Figure 16.3* Two firms in a bounded linear market

all of its original market, plus a substantial component of B's original market. In period 3, B responds in a predictable way: it "leapfrogs" A in order to command the greater share of the market. We can imagine how this process will play out over an arbitrary number $n$ of periods until both firms are located side by side in the center of the market. This is an equilibrium set of locations because neither firm can make itself better off by moving. For example, if A moves toward its own end of the market, its sales decline. If it leapfrogs B, its sales also decline. So, at the end of the locational game, both firms are best served by staying put.

The alert reader will have observed that there is a kind of futility to this process because the sales of both A and B are the same in period 1 as they are in period $n$. But the location of the two firms in period 1 is not a stable equilibrium because either firm could increases its sales by moving. Another peculiar aspect to this process is that the people in the market are better served by the locations of A and B in period 1 than in period $n$ because the average distance from consumers to the nearest firm is greater when both firms are concentrated in the center. This is illustrated graphically in Figure 16.4, where the upward sloping lines originating from the locations of A and B are the delivered costs at different locations in the bounded linear market. Since consumers will always buy from the firm that offers the lower delivered price, the lower envelope of the delivered price lines is the effective price of the goods for consumers at different points in the market. While consumers at the center of the market benefit when the firms locate close together, the average consumer gets a lower price when their locations spread out. Thus we have a case where the socially optimal location of the two firms does not coincide with the market equilibrium locations. Even in this simple example, when locational decisions interact, unexpected results sometimes come about.

How might this undesirable situation be avoided? One possibility is that public regulations are designed to maintain a separation between the competitors. As an example, a public highway agency might offer concessions by which private firms are allowed to provide food and fuel at certain points along a restricted access highway. In order to provide the most benefits to motorists, the agency will limit these concessions to designated locations that are evenly spaced along the road.

If we change our initial assumptions slightly, it is possible to see how the two firms might arrive at a different solution without government interference. Instead of assuming that each consumer purchases a fixed quantity of the commodity, assume that there is a downward sloping demand curve. The market is still split evenly whether the firms are separated as in period 1 or concentrated as in period $n$, but the size of the market is greater in period 1 because the average delivered price is lower. So both firms sell more in period 1 than in period $n$. Realizing this, the two firms may respond in one of two ways. First, they might agree to remain at the period 1 locations where they are both better off. Agreements whereby firms agree to avoid competitive actions in the market are called collusion and generally have negative consequences for consumers. But here is a situation where collusion can make both consumers and firms better off.

A second response is for the two firms to combine into one. If A and B are two facilities of a single firm, there will be no reason for their locations to deviate from

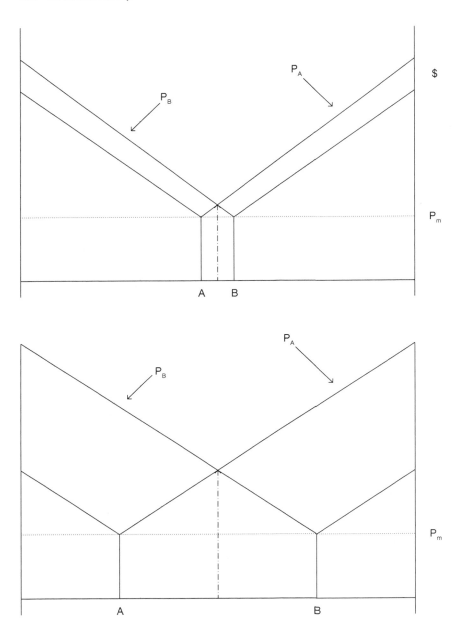

*Figure 16.4* Delivered prices for social and market optima

the period 1 locations. This explains, at least in part, why the business of supplying relatively undifferentiated services or products, such as convenience stores or donut shops, is often most profitable when a single firm controls a large number of facilities whose locations can be chosen jointly so as to maximize sales or profits.

## Other interrelationships

The concepts of the spatial industrial complex and strategic location address are just two of the many ways in which the location choices of firms are interrelated. There are a number of others, some of which we have already addressed and others of which we will address later in the book. They include:

- *Urbanization economies:* Even firms that have no relationship in terms of economic linkages or competition for the same market may have many of the same requirements: a large labor market; transportation, energy and water infrastructure; the services of firms in financial and other services; a secure environment maintained by police and fire services, etc. By clustering together, they make it possible for these services to be provided more efficiently.
- *Localization economies:* There is a variety of advantages that firms in the same industry gain from locating close together. The advantages, known collectively as localization economies, were introduced in chapter 3. Since localization economies often arise out of information spillovers, they will be discussed in more detail in Part VI on the global information economy.
- *External effects:* Positive and negative external effects refer to the benefits and costs that a firm confers on other firms by locating in a particular place. They were introduced in chapter 6 and will play throughout the remainder of the book.
- *Markets for space:* All economic activities consume space. If two firms want to use the same space, they must compete in a market where rents are bid up according to the willingness of potential users to pay for space. Thus, the location decisions of many different firms interact to give rise to spatial patterns of industrial and commercial rents. This is the central theme of Part IV.

Finally, the location decisions for firms constantly interact with the spatial decisions of households. Access to market is a key determinant of industrial location. For firms producing goods and services for final consumers, the location of the market depends on the location decisions of thousands of individual households. So does access to labor forces with appropriate skills. Firms and households sometimes compete for the same space, so the preferences of households may result in industrial and commercial rents being bid up. Many industries have negative external effects such as air, water and noise pollution, which encourage households to impose restrictions on industrial locations through their elected government officials. Many of these relationships will come to the fore in the coming chapters.

# Part IV

# Markets for space

# 17  Agricultural land use

This is the first of three chapters on how markets for space give rise to spatial patterns of *land use*. Unlike the models we have considered so far, land-use models recognize the fact that economic activities take up space – or, putting it differently, they consume land. This is rather obvious in the case of a farm, whose output depends in part on how much land is under cultivation, but it is equally true for any other economic activity. Factories, shopping malls, airports, public parks, roads, office buildings and private residences all require the exclusive use of some quantity of land. In other words, the economic agents who undertake these economic activities (firms, households, government agencies) are all *land users*. Since "exclusive use" implies that no two economic agents can occupy the same unit of land, a pattern of land use that can be plotted on a map emerges – but how?

Often, the distribution of land among various users is influenced by public policy. A great deal of land is state-owned and may be preserved as parkland or assigned to uses such as forestry on the basis of policy decisions. Zoning regulation in cities may also influence land-use patterns by restricting the use of private land, as when industrial land uses are restricted to some areas and residential land uses to others. In an economy where most land is privately owned, however, market forces determine the broader patterns of land use. Thus, understanding markets for space is one of the great challenges of economic geography.

Land-use models attempt to represent, at least partially, the workings of markets for space. Like location models, they are set in continuous space. But, unlike location models, their endogenous variables are areas rather than points. To some extent, competition for space is anticipated in the Hotelling model, where firms choose point locations so as to maximize market areas. But, in land-use models, each agent must purchase the right to have exclusive use of land. This implies a twofold decision: the agent must decide *where* to purchase that right and *how much* land to purchase. The purchase may be of a permanent right to use the land, in which case a purchase price is paid, or a temporary right to use the land, in which case a rent is paid. A basic characteristic of markets for space is that it is more expensive to use land in some places than in others. Spatial variations in land prices and rents can be attributed to spatial variations in site and situation attributes.

## Two views of agricultural land use

It should not be surprising that some of the earliest theorizing about markets for space was related to agricultural land use. Agriculture is an inherently land-intensive activity. Agricultural output is generally measured as yield per hectare and it is usual to describe a farm in terms of its specialization and spatial extent (for example, a 10,000-hectare wheat farm). Furthermore, until the Industrial Revolution was well established, agriculture was the most important economic activity in nearly all countries.

One of the first to introduce a systematic explanation for agricultural land-use markets was David Ricardo. (That is the same David Ricardo who devised the theory of comparative advantage.) He observed that there are significant differences in the productive capacity of different plots of land based on soil quality, elevation, availability of water, local climate, etc. He defined the rent of a particular plot of land as the difference between the market value of the crop that could be produced on it and the cost of producing that crop. This may run contrary to the common notion of rent as the amount one must pay for the exclusive use of the land. But, on some reflection, this economic return of revenue over costs is the amount one would be willing to pay to use the land. A recurring theme throughout land-use theory is that rent is directly tied to the economic benefit derived from the use of land.

In Ricardo's system, not only rents but also the prices of crops are determined by variations in land quality. He assumes that production takes place on the best-quality land first. As the demand for the crop increases, production is extended on to ever lower qualities of land. The price of the crop must be equal to the cost of producing it on the poorest land in cultivation. (If it were lower than that cost, no one would cultivate that land.) The rent of the poorest land in cultivation is zero by definition, because the difference between the cost of production and the price of the crop is zero. Rent for all superior plots of land depends on how much more cheaply the crop can be produced on them. As demand increases, production is extended to ever poorer land and therefore the price goes up. The person who owns the best plot of land reaps ever increasing rents as demand increases and production is extended onto ever poorer land.

Ricardo's rent model is based on site attributes. (Recall that site attributes are those physical characteristics of a particular location that make it advantageous for some economic activity.) Another nineteenth-century economist, Johann Heinrich von Thünen, devised an alternative theory of land rent based on situation attributes. (Recall that situation attributes refer to the accessibility of a place.) As a landowner himself, von Thünen observed that land rents varied significantly even within regions where the physical characteristic of the land varied little. Through careful observation, he discovered that these rent variations could be explained based on the accessibility of different plots of land to market towns. He extended this observation into a formal model not only of spatial variation in rents, but also of spatial patterns of different types of farming. Von Thünen's model is a foundation stone of economic geography. Not only is it one of the earliest economic models with an explicitly spatial expression, but its basic logic has been extended beyond agricultural land use to help explain urban land-use patterns, as we will see in chapter 18.

## Von Thünen's model

As always, the best way to start discussing a model is by listing its assumptions:

1 All agricultural activity takes place on an undifferentiated plain. That means there is no variation from place to place in soil quality, weather, slope or any other factor that might affect agricultural productivity.
2 At some point in the plain there is a single, isolated market town. All crops produced in the plain must be transported to this market town (hereafter "the market") for sale.
3 Market prices are assumed to be given (exogenous).
4 Transportation costs for crops produced at any point on the plain are a fixed rate times the distance to the market. The transportation rate may vary across crops.
5 The entire plain is under the ownership of landlords who rent their land to farmers. The landlords always rent to the farmer who is willing to pay the highest rent.
6 There are several categories of farmers, each associated with a type of crop and each with a large number of farmers. Different categories of farms face different market prices, yields and transportation rates, but there is no variation among farmers within a category.
7 There are no scale economies in production. Both the cost of cultivation and the crop yield per hectare are independent of number of hectares in cultivation.

The first three assumptions keep the model simple. We don't need to worry about which is the best land for agriculture, so Ricardo's theory of land rent does not come into play. Since there is only one market town, there is only one point around which spatial patterns of land use are defined. Exogenous market prices mean there are no local demand functions. This is a fairly extreme assumption, but the model would be more complicated if we had to determine the land rents and market prices simultaneously. One way to justify this assumption is to assume that farmers barter among themselves for crops for their own consumption, and the remainder is sent to the market town. From there, it is exported to some much larger market. Since the amount produced in our hypothetical region is small relative to the total amount consumed in that larger market, it has no measurable impact on the prices that are determined there.

Assumption 4 is critical for two reasons. First, it says that transportation costs for any given crop at any given point depend solely on the straight-line distance to the market. This assumes away the effect of any natural or man-made transportation network. Second, as we will see, the variation of transportation rates among crops is a critical factor in defining spatial land-use patterns.

Assumptions 5 and 6 define how the market for land works. Each landlord puts land up for bids and the different categories of farmers bid according to how much revenue they can generate on the land and how much it costs to generate it. The different categories of farmers bid against one another and ultimately the one that can generate the highest profit from the land will get to use it. So, clearly, in order to determine the land-use patterns, we must first determine the rent that farmers will bid. Assumption 7 implies that the size of the plots of land available for rent does not affect the cost or productivity of cultivation. This simplifies the model but, as we will see, relaxing assumption 7 has major implications.

To start with the simplest possible case, let's suppose that there is only one category of farmers. (To get a picture in your mind, you can think of them as mixed vegetable farmers.) It might seem that there is nothing to determine here – all the land will be cultivated by these farmers – but as we will see below that is not the case. We can define the rent bid by one of these farmers by the following equation:

$$R = E(p\text{-}a) - Efd$$

where $R$ is the rent, $E$ is the yield of the crop (measured, for example, in tonnes per hectare), $p$ is the market price of the crop per tonne and $a$ is the production cost per tonne. So $E(p\text{-}a)$ is the profit of growing the crop in the absence of transportation costs. (Note that, because of assumption 7, yield and production cost are independent of scale, so we can imagine the land as being offered for rent in 1-hectare plots.) The transportation cost $Efd$ depends on the transportation rate per kilometer $f$ and the distance $d$ from the market. Here is an important implication: farmers will bid higher rents for land closer to the market.[1]

This is illustrated in Figure 17.1, which graphs rent against distance from the market $d$. Here we see that, where $d = 0$, $R = E(p\text{-}a)$. The fact that the rent declines with $d$ means that landlords who own land closest to the market earn the highest rents, therefore, their lands are most valuable. The figure also illustrates that there is some distance $d = L$ beyond which the rent is zero or negative because $EfL = E(p\text{-}a)$. This distance is called the margin of cultivation because beyond it no farmer will pay to use the land. Thus, even in the simple one-crop case, the model defines a spatial land-use pattern: a circular zone of radius $L$ and centered on the market in which crops are grown. Outside this zone, the land is uncultivated.

We can now use the simple one-crop model to illustrate some interesting things about how variations in prices and costs affect agricultural land use and production. For example, Figure 17.2 illustrates what happens if the market price of the crop goes up to some level $p' > p$. Recall that $p$ is exogenous in this model, so the increase must be the outcome of some exogenous trend such as an increase in international demand for the crop.

As the figure illustrates, the rent at the market goes up because farmers' revenues increase, while their costs remain the same. Since transportation rates have not changed, the rent declines at the same rate as before, but from a higher initial value. As a result, the margin of cultivation shifts outward. This has a couple of implications. The first is that it is now economically feasible to grow crops further

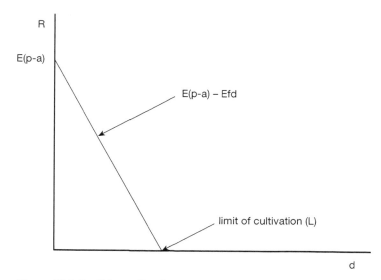

*Figure 17.1* Spatial rent function

away from the market. The second, which follows from the first, is that the total amount of the crop grown in the region increases. This is because the margin of cultivation is the radius of a circular region in which crops are grown. Total output $Q$ in the region is therefore equal to the area of that circle times the yield:

$$Q = E\pi L^2$$

So as $L$ increases, so does $Q$. This implies that there is an upward sloping supply function for the crop. What is interesting here is that the increasing relationship between price and output that defines the supply function now has a spatial basis. (The definition of supply functions in this model is taken up further in the Appendix to this chapter.)

It is worth pausing here to notice the parallels between the models of von Thünen and Ricardo. Ricardo defined a zero-rent plot of land as the least productive plot in cultivation. Von Thünen defined a similar plot as the most remote plot (located at $L$) in cultivation. In both cases, an increase in the price will drive cultivation onto more marginal plots and increase the rent of the best plots. It is just that in von Thünen, "marginal" and "best" are defined in terms of relative location rather than physical characteristics. Thus, while we may think of Ricardo and von Thünen as providing alternative views of agricultural land use, the economic mechanisms that drive their models are fundamentally the same.

Figure 17.3 illustrates the effect of an increase of production costs to $a' > a$, which might occur due to an increase in the price of fertilizer or seed. Because the maximum rent $E(p-a')$ is now lower, the limit of cultivation declines and so does

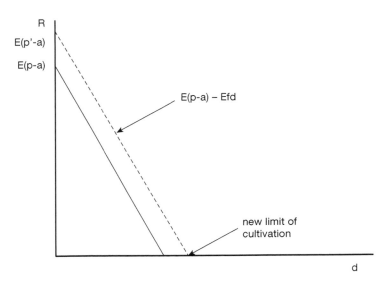

*Figure 17.2* Rent and price, *p'>p*

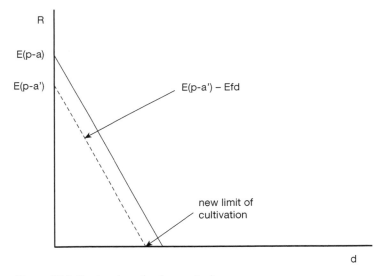

*Figure 17.3* Rent and production cost *a'>a*

the total output of the crop. Of course, if the production costs decline, the effect is exactly the opposite.

Transportation costs also have an effect on the limit of cultivation, but, as Figure 17.4 illustrates, the shift in the rent function is a bit different. Changes in both *p* and *a* produce parallel shifts in the rent function because they change the value of

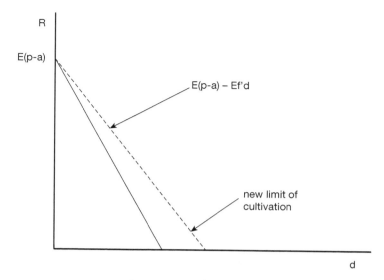

*Figure 17.4* Rent and transport cost $f' < f$

the maximum rent $E(p-a)$. However, since that rent occurs at $d = 0$, it is unaffected by a reduction in the transportation rate to $f' < f$. But, as $d$ becomes greater, the movement in the rent function becomes greater. Thus, the spatial rent function does not shift outward so much as rotate outward around the rent at $d = 0$. Nevertheless, the result is that a reduction in $f$ causes an increase in the limit of cultivation and in crop production. This is a very simple illustration of the way reductions in transportation costs tend to expand the economy by bringing previously inaccessible resources into use.

Von Thünen's model really gets interesting when we consider the case where there are two categories of farms in the region. To create an example, imagine that there are both vegetable farmers and wheat farmers in the region. Vegetables generally have a higher market value per tonne than does wheat so we can assume that $p_v > p_w$ (using the subscripts $v$ and $w$ to indicate vegetables and wheat respectively). However, vegetables, being more fragile and perishable, are generally more expensive to transport, so $f_v > f_w$. For the sake of illustration, we will assume that the constants $E$ (yield) and $a$ (production cost) are the same for vegetables and wheat. So now we define separate rent functions for the two crops:

$$R_v = E(p_v-a) - Ef_v d$$
$$R_w = E(p_w-a) - Ef_w d$$

This case is shown in Figure 17.5, where the spatial rent function of vegetables is shown as a solid line and the spatial rent function of wheat is shown as a broken line. Because $p_v > p_w$ the maximum rent is higher for vegetables, but because $f_v > f_w$ the rent of vegetables drops away much more quickly with distance from the market. At some distance $d^*$, the two spatial rent functions cross. For distances less than $d^*$, vegetable farmers are willing to pay a higher rent than wheat farmers, so the landlords rent to them. For distances greater than $d^*$ but less than $L$, wheat farmers are willing to pay more rent than vegetable farmers, so the landlords will rent to them. Thus, the distance $d^*$ at which $R_v = R_w$ defines a transition between a zone of vegetable cultivation and a zone of wheat cultivation in the agricultural landscape.

If you could fly in a helicopter over our hypothetical agricultural region, you would see something like Figure 17.6, which extends Figure 17.5 into three dimensions. Here a circular zone of vegetable cultivation of radius $d^*$ is centered on the market town. It is surrounded by a zone of wheat production and all cultivation ceases outside a circle of radius $L$.

The same kind of analysis is easily extended to a third crop, as shown in Figure 17.7a. The third category of farm here is "pasture," which refers to putting steers out to graze for the production of meat. Of course, meat has a high price per tonne, so we would expect $p_m > p_v > p_w$. However, since the biological process of transforming grass into meat is relatively inefficient, the yield of meat in tonnes per hectare is very low. Specifying yields for the individual farming categories (and recalling that we have assumed that the yields for vegetables and wheat are equal), we assume that $E_v = E_w > E_m$. If production cost $a$ is the same for all categories of farming, pasture will bid a lower rent than wheat at the market ($d = 0$) as long as the yield advantage of wheat outweighs the price advantage of pasture.[2]

Transportation costs for pasture are low because the animals can be herded to market, so no vehicles or transportation fuels are needed. Since pasture's rent

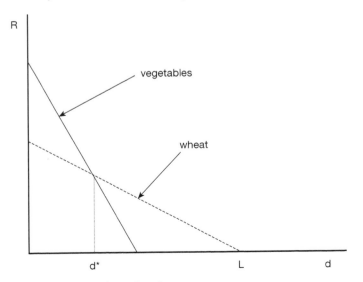

*Figure 17.5* Spatial rent function, two crops

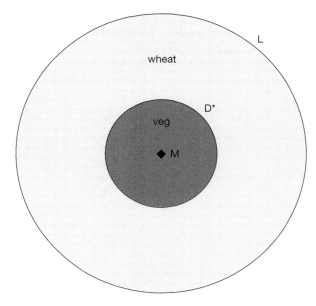

*Figure 17.6* Concentric agricultural zones

function has a very low slope (i.e. it is "flatter" than the other two), farmers in the pasture category are able to outbid farmers in the other two categories at longer distances away from the market.

Note that now there are two transition distances: $d^*$ where vegetable cultivation changes over to wheat cultivation and $d^{**}$ where wheat cultivation changes over to pasture. In comparing Figures 17.6 and 17.7a, it is clear that adding pasture to the mix reduces the amount of land that is devoted to wheat cultivation, which now extends as far as $d^{**}$ rather than $L$. With the addition of pasture, the limit of cultivation is now $L' > L$, so agricultural activity extends further from the market than was the case in the two-crop example.

Figure 17.7b illustrates how the rent functions of the different categories of farmers combine to make an overall rent function in the spatial market. Because we have assumed that transportation costs are a constant rate $f$ times the distance from market, the three rent functions are linear – that is, rent falls away with distance as a straight line. But each crop defines the rent paid in the market only over that range of distance in which it outbids the other two: $0-d^*$ for vegetables, $d^*-d^{**}$ for wheat and $d^{**}-L'$ for pasture. The overall rent pattern in the market (called the "rent gradient") is therefore defined by the upper envelope of the three rent functions as shown in Figure 17.7b. The interesting thing here is that the linear rent functions combine to create a non-linear market rent gradient in which rent falls off with distance from the market, but at a decreasing rate.

A natural reaction at this point might be to say, "This is a nice, logical model but why don't I see concentric patterns of agriculture when I fly over farming regions?" It is important to remember that models are simplified representations of reality, so real patterns are always more complex than the ones our models produce. At least this model generates a couple of basic propositions that can be borne out empirically. The first is that, after controlling for differences in physical characteristics, the value of agricultural land tends to decrease with distance away from spatial markets. The second is that perishable crops, which are more expensive to transport, are generally grown closer to centers of demand while bulk, non-

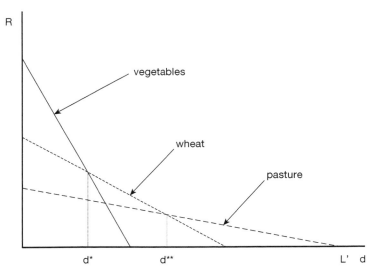

*Figure 17.7a* Spatial rent function, three crops

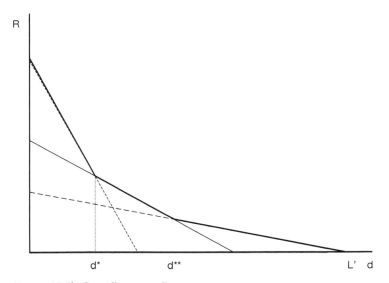

*Figure 17.7b* Overall rent gradient

perishable crops may be grown in remote areas. But there are a number of reasons why the simple, concentric patterns may not appear on the ground.

## Von Thünen and contemporary agricultural patterns

Despite his genius for abstract reasoning, von Thünen also applied a process of careful empirical observations in developing his model. But even in his day, the results of the model would not have matched reality precisely. For example, the concentric patterns depend on the assumption that transportation is equally costly in all directions. But most market towns would have been located along rivers, canals or improved roads. Figure 17.8 shows how the existence of a route for easy transportation would affect the crop pattern shown in Figure 17.6.

The pattern would be further complicated by variations in physical features. For example, in rolling terrain the valley bottoms might be planted with crops, while the higher places are devoted to forestry or grazing. But this does not mean the basic principles of the model cease to apply. In the valley bottoms, cultivators can pay the highest rent because they can generate the highest revenue per hectare, while, on the hillsides, cultivations costs are higher so pastoralists or foresters may bid the higher rents. The outcome is a complex pattern of agricultural activities that still fits within the simple logic of the model – but in this case the model would have to be extended to reflect the fact that production costs, as well as transportation costs, vary from place to place.

But the model would not seem able to explain the trend to monoculture in modern agriculture, whereby a large agricultural region is dominated by a single crop. The shift to monoculture is made possible by two powerful long-term trends: falling transportation costs and scale economies in agricultural production. We can think of existing agricultural patterns as being simultaneously driven by spatial variations in transportation costs (situation attributes) and in the physical characteristics of the land (site attributes). In the absence of transportation costs, all land would go

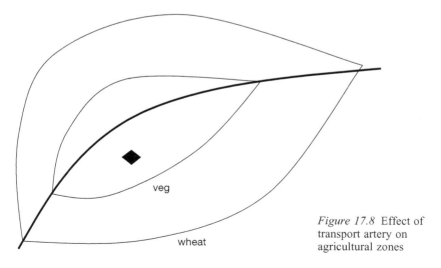

veg

wheat

*Figure 17.8* Effect of transport artery on agricultural zones

to the type of cultivation that could generate the highest net revenue $E$ $(p-a)$. If one crop had the highest price, presumably nothing else would be grown anywhere – that is unless production costs were crop specific and spatially variant. In North America, corn cultivation generally produces more revenue per hectare than wheat cultivation. In the most favorable soils and climates, the landscape is therefore dominated by corn. But in areas with less rainfall it is cheaper to grow wheat than corn. Where the gap in costs exceeds the gap in prices, wheat prevails. Thus, broad "belts" of corn and wheat monoculture have emerged.

Of course, transportation costs have not disappeared, but in some cases they have become so low that site attributes are now the dominant factor. Generally, this is due to more efficient engines, long-term reductions in the real price of energy and deregulation of the freight industries. In some specific cases, technological innovations have made previously unthinkable movements possible. It is now common for shoppers to find heads of lettuce in supermarkets in Boston and Montreal that come from the Central Valley of California, Mexico or beyond. Two types of innovation made this possible. One is refrigerated rail cars and trucks, which can keep lettuce in transit for several days without wilting. Refrigerated ground shipment is expensive, but it is much cheaper than shipment by air, the only other viable option. The second type of innovation has to do with the lettuce itself. The ubiquitous "iceberg" variety is an example of a vegetable that was developed to be more durable than traditional varieties. In recent years, there has been a popular backlash against long-distance transportation of food. Members of the "locavore" movement argue that the globalization of food markets leads to unnecessary long-distance transportation and therefore promotes greenhouse gas emissions. While this may be true in some instances, it is important to bear in mind that energy use in cultivation, as well as in transportation, may vary depending upon the location of a farm. If you live in a northern region, a tomato grown in the sunshine of a distant land with a warm climate will require less fossil energy to grow than a tomato grown locally in a heated greenhouse (see Box 17).

---

### *Box 17* **The locavore movement and greenhouse gas emissions**

Cheap transportation, refrigeration technologies and the opening up of global markets have led to the habit of consuming food from ever more distant places, especially in high-income countries. A shopper in the Boston area, with its short summers and poor soils, would have gradually seen the disappearance of locally produced foods in his supermarket over the past half-century. By the 1950s, nearly all the meat on display would have come from Chicago or points west. By the 1960s, an ever increasing share of fruits and vegetables were from Florida or California. By the 1990s, the produce and meat sections of the supermarket had gone global, with lamb and apples from New Zealand, grapes and other fruits from Latin America and citrus from Morocco.

In the twenty-first century, many people have rebelled against the globalization of food production and distribution. They call themselves "locavores" because they try to subsist on locally grown foods (a quick internet search will identify locavore organizations in a number of countries). Locavores eat local food for a number of reasons. In many cases they want to help preserve the farming culture in rural areas that are being squeezed by global competition. They also believe that big agribusiness firms will not act in the interest of human health and nutrition, so they seek to bypass them by purchasing directly from local producers. For those who prefer organic foods, it is much easier to observe the practices of local farmers than to trust the "organic" sticker on a piece of fruit from halfway around the world. But the most highly publicized argument of locavores is that by minimizing the number of "food-miles" in their diet (in other words, by minimizing the transportation requirement) they are reducing greenhouse gas emissions.

There is no doubt something silly about carting an apple from New Zealand to Boston when there are plenty of orchards in the Massachusetts countryside. (This practice is supported in part by consumers' love of variety as apples from different places have different flavors.) But the categorical claim that reducing food miles automatically reduces greenhouse gas emissions should be considered carefully. Production of the meat, fruit, vegetable or dairy product may generate more greenhouse gas than its transportation, and, since production methods vary over space, purchase of a remotely produced food may generate less than the purchase of a local food. To take an extreme example, Spanish tomatoes consumed by people in England produce less greenhouse gas than local English tomatoes grown in heated greenhouses, even when transportation emissions are included (Desrochers and Shimizu, 2010).

According to a life-cycle accounting conducted by researchers at Carnegie Mellon University, transportation is not the most critical factor affecting the rate of greenhouse gas emissions from agriculture (Weber and Matthews, 2008). Even though the average food item consumed by an American travels an amazing 1,640 km from the farm, total transportation (including the cost of transporting inputs to the farm) accounts for only 11 percent of greenhouse gas emissions. Transportation from the producer to the retailer contributes only 4 percent. Increasing imports increased the average distance that U.S. food is transported by 25 percent between 1997 and 2004, but this only translated into a 5 percent increase in transportation-related emissions because most of the extra food miles are in energy-efficient ocean shipping. Most of the emissions (well over 80 percent) come from food production rather than from transportation, so that is where the greatest potential for greenhouse gas emissions is found. For example, because beef production has extraordinarily high greenhouse gas emissions, consumers who want to reduce emissions can achieve far more by eating less beef than by focusing on local foods.

Falling transportation costs also eliminate the need for many market towns. Empty market towns with abandoned grain elevators are scattered across the North American prairies. They attest to a spatial transformation, whereby produce is now delivered to a smaller number of larger market centers. This spatial shift in itself leads to reduced complexity in the agricultural landscape and large zones of homogeneous cultivation.

A second explanation for the rise of monoculture has to do with the scale economies. Recall that in the von Thünen framework we assume them away (assumption 7 above). This may have been reasonable in von Thünen's time, when animals and humans provided all the energy and tools generally didn't get any bigger than a plow. But, by the end of the nineteenth century, the introduction of tractors and other machinery changed all that. A tractor can do in a few days what a horse and plow would do in a few weeks. But, in order to make efficient use of the tractor, you must have enough land to keep it busy for a substantial proportion of the year. Otherwise the tractor will mostly sit idle and not justify its cost. So mechanization leads to lower per hectare costs, but only on larger farms. This is an example of capital indivisibilities as a source of scale economies.

In principle, it is possible to incorporate scale economies into a von Thünen framework, but it gets complicated. Increasing returns means that production cost $a$, which helps determine the amount of land commanded by a particular crop, and therefore the output of that crop, is also a function of that output. This must lead to a model where a change in the value of one variable triggers a sequence of changes. Suppose the price of wheat goes up. Because this leads to more land in wheat, and therefore a greater scale of production, the production costs of wheat go down as well. So there is an additional increase in wheat cultivation. At the same time, the loss of land by vegetables and pasture leads to increasing costs, and thus to additional loss of land. This shows how scale economies tend to magnify any advantage that one crop gets over the other two. But will it lead to monoculture?

To answer this question, consider the simple (if somewhat contrived) example illustrated in Figure 17.8. We start with a three-crop example, where all crops are assumed to employ traditional technologies with constant returns to scale. Now suppose that a new technology called "large-scale wheat" makes it possible to produce wheat at much lower cost. As a crude way of representing scale economies in this technology, assume that large-scale wheat is only viable if it is able to command all of the land for which it can pay positive rents – in other words, it is only do-able if it can outbid all other crops at all distances. The justification for this assumption is that capital invisibilities dictate a minimum scale of production. In the figure, large-scale wheat is represented as a separate crop. Its bid rent function has the same slope as conventional wheat, but its rent is higher because its production costs are lower. In this example, its cost advantage is great enough to outbid vegetables at the market and to outbid pasture at the far margins of the region, so monoculture prevails.

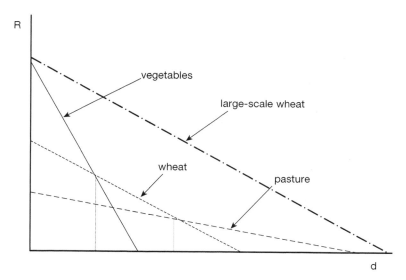

*Figure 17.9* Shift to monoculture

## Appendix: Generating agricultural supply functions from von Thünen's model

To start with the simplest case, suppose that there is a single crop (vegetables) with the following parameter values: $E = 10, p = 20, a = 10, f = .1$ Substituting these values into the basic rent equation and recalling that the limit of cultivation $L$ is defined as the value of $d$ where $(p - a)$, the reader can verify that $L = 100$. Recalling further that, in the single crop case, output $Q = E\pi L^2$. If we shift the value of $p_v$ we can now trace out a supply function by calculating:

$$p = 11 \rightarrow Q = 3,141$$
$$p = 15 \rightarrow Q = 78,549$$
$$p = 20 \rightarrow Q = 314,159$$
$$p = 25 \rightarrow Q = 706,858$$

and so on. The solid line in Figure A17.1 illustrates that this is a nonlinear supply function, where output increases at an increasing rate with price. This is because the area of a circle increases with square of the radius, which in this case is $L$. Notice that for $p_v \leq 10$ the supply is zero because rent is zero or negative, even at $d = 0$.

Finding the supply function becomes more complicated when we move to a situation of two crops: vegetables and wheat. Figure A17.2 shows that vegetables will be grown at all distances from 0 to $d^*$, while wheat will be grown at all distances from $d^*$ to $L$. So $Q_v = E\pi d^{*2}$.

To find $d^*$ set $R_v = R_w$. The reader can verify that, if $E_v = E_w = E$ and $a_v = a_w = a$, then $d^* = (p_v - p_w) / (f_v - f_w)$. So, if $p_v = 20, p_w = 17, f_v = .1, f_w = .03$, then

$d_* = 42.9$. Assuming once again that $E = 10$ and a $= 10$, then the output of vegetables is 57,702 – much lower than it would be in the absence of competition with wheat for the available farmland.

We can still draw out a supply function for vegetables, but now we must find the value of $d_*$ instead of $L$ to determine output levels. The broken line in Figure A17.1 defines the supply of vegetables given competition from wheat at $p_w = 17$. In this case no vegetable production below $p_v = 17$ and, for each value of $p_v$ up to about 26, the output of vegetables is lower than it would have been in the absence

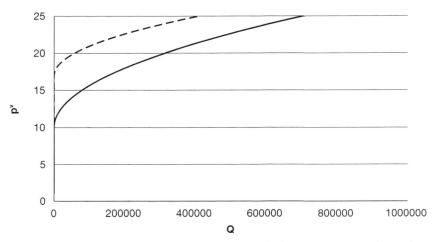

*Figure A17.1* Supply function of vegetables with and without competition from wheat

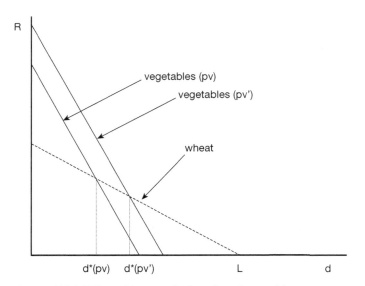

*Figure A17.2* Effect of increase in the price of vegetables

of wheat, as shown by the solid line. Note that the two supply functions converge at $p_v = 27$. Above this price vegetables outbid wheat at all distances.

Of course, it is also possible to define a supply function for wheat given a fixed price for vegetables. It's a bit trickier in this case because you need to calculate the area of the donut-shaped outer zone:

$$Q_w = E_w(\pi L^2 - \pi d^2)$$

Drawing out this supply function is left as an exercise for the reader.

# 18  Urban land use: the monocentric city

The von Thünen model provides a simple, logical framework that can be extended to patterns of land use outside the agricultural realm. The basic idea is that there are key points in space around which land-use patterns are arranged. Land users value access to those points so they are willing to pay more for space that is close to them. Near each key point, there is a market process whereby parcels of land go to the highest bidder, so those land users that place the highest value on access are able to secure the closest land. At greater distance from a key point, other land users may be willing to bid more. Thus, the land is distributed among different types of users based on their willingness to pay for access to the key point. This does not mean that every potential land user is able to secure land somewhere. If some potential land user is unable to make a positive bid that exceeds all other users at some distance, that user gets no land. This essentially means that the activity which user had in mind for the land is not economically viable.

In the agricultural case, the key point is the market town, but what about other land-use applications? Consider the distribution of seats to fans at a baseball game as a land-use pattern. Each fan seeks to use a small parcel of land just big enough to sit in (a seat). In this example the key point is obvious: home plate. If your seat is close to home plate, you have a good view of where most of the action takes place, and generally any seat close to home plate has a good view of the entire field. Excluding the "luxury boxes" and other vulgar marketing innovations, the most expensive seats are generally those that are closest to home plate. Thus, baseball-watching land users are stratified by how much they are willing to pay for seats closest to home plate.

You might object to this analogy on several grounds. For one thing, fans don't get to bid on seat tickets, they must accept the prices that the team owner offers. But these prices are set based on the owner's understanding, generally based on long experience, of what people are willing to pay. Also, many seats are purchased well in advance by third parties and auctioned on the Internet, so there is at least a secondary bidding market which tends to bear out the principle that people will pay more for seats close to home plate. A second objection is that willingness to pay in the agricultural case is based on objective criteria such as price, yield and transportation costs. In this case what are the objective criteria? The answer is that individual preferences are the main determinant of variation in fans' willingness to pay for proximity to home plate. The fact that preferences are subjective makes them no less important. (If you think about it, differences in agricultural commodity prices are partly driven by people's preference to eat vegetables vs. wheat.)

At this point, your objection may get personal. "The guy who is sitting in the most expensive seat doesn't value being close to home plate any more than I do – he's just richer than I am!" This may be true, and it brings up the important point that, in consumer decision making, willingness to pay depends not only on preferences but also on income. Thus, income must be considered in any analysis of the land-use behavior of individuals or households.

Finally, you might point out that there are factors other than nearness to home plate that affect where people prefer to sit. "My cousin sits as far away from home plate as possible because he wants to catch a home run." (Thus, the expression "hitting it into the cheap seats.") "My sister sits where she can get the best view of the third baseman, whom she loves." "My father sits where the television cameras are least likely to show him at the game while he is supposed to be at work." Naturally there are endless complications that affect the behavior of individuals. But recall that the modeling approach abstracts from such complications to create a simplified representation of reality. As long as proximity to home plate is the predominant driver of the market for parcels (seats) in the baseball stadium, and as long as the idiosyncrasies of individuals do not bias the aggregate patterns, a simple model can yield valuable insights.

## Urban land use

A model of urban land use extends the logic of von Thünen to define zones within the city devoted to different categories of land use such as financial, industrial, retailing, warehousing, high-income residential, low-income residential and others. The key point around which the patterns of these land uses are defined is called the *central business district* or CBD. Because it is the center of the urban pattern, it is sometimes referred to as the "nucleus" of the city.

How do we identify the CBD? As the name suggests, it is a point to which various economic actors come to conduct business and where a substantial proportion of the city's workforce is employed. It is generally known as "downtown" in most North American cities, and may be called the "city center" in the British Isles. The CBDs of many of the largest cities are known by familiar names: the Loop (Chicago), Lower Manhattan (New York) and La Défense (Paris).

Like the market town in the agricultural case, it is not really a point in the strict geometric sense, but rather an area. It is characterized by high buildings in which financial and other high-order services are located, with a high density of retail activity closer to ground level. One quantitative approach to identifying the CBD is as the point with the highest ratio of building floor space to actual land space. Another, and one that is especially relevant to the model we are about to develop, is as the point in the city with the highest land rent. (Here we make a distinction between rent defined per unit of land and per unit of floor space.)

As you will see, our model of urban land use defines the CBD as the sole point of reference in the urban area. In cities of the twenty-first century, this singular role is hard to justify. One can live and work a lifetime in a modern metropolitan area without even visiting the CBD. Shopping malls, suburban industrial parks and "edge cities" all provide adequate opportunities for commerce, recreation and employment. Certainly, this was not the case in the 1920s (Haig, 1926; Hurd, 1924), when the first descriptive analyses of the role of the CBD were written, nor even in the 1960s (Alonso, 1964; Muth, 1969), when the mathematical models we are about to discuss were introduced. Cities in those days were more nearly *monocentric*, while modern cities, especially in North America, are decidedly *polycentric*. It is therefore reasonable to ask whether models that describe a monocentric structure yield much insight about modern cities. We'll return to that question in the next chapter, but for the moment we'll start by defining a monocentric model.

## Stylized facts

Our purpose here is to develop a simple model of rents that can help explain some gross generalizations – or "stylized facts" – that characterize monocentric cities:

Urban land rents tend to decline with distance from the CBD.

This may seem counterintuitive, since the rent for apartments in fashionable suburbs is generally higher than in low-income urban neighborhoods. But remember that we are talking about the cost of land and not floor space. Suburban apartments are generally much larger. Also, they tend to be in buildings of three stories or less surrounded by parking lots and lawns. A suburban plot may have three renters each paying $500 per month, while an urban plot of the same size has ten renters each paying $250 per month. The rent for individual apartments is greater in the suburban plot, but the total rent per unit of land is higher in the urban plot. This leads us to a second stylized fact:

The density of residential areas tends to decline with distance from the CBD.

There are exceptions. For example, in recent years, we have seen the development of high-density nodes in suburban areas known as "edge cities." But, in general, land is less intensively settled as we move further into the urban periphery.

There are segregated zones of high- and low-income population.

Anyone who lives in a large metropolitan area will attest to this. People often attribute this segregation to exclusionary or "snob" zoning, which makes some places inaccessible to low-income residents. It is true that zoning has a profound influence on all urban land-use patterns (which we address in chapter 19), but, even in the absence of zoning, income segregation may develop because of differences in the needs and preferences of high- and low-income households.

Non-residential zones tend to be segregated according to different types of economic activity: manufacturing, warehousing, finance, retail, etc.

Again, this may come down to zoning, but market forces often come into play. Just as in the case of agricultural crops, some types of businesses will be able to outbid others for locations close to the CBD.

## A simple residential model

Both households and firms use land in the city. The land used by households is called residential land, while the land used by firms falls into categories defined by their lines of business: financial, retail, warehousing, etc. Since most of the urban area is taken up by residential land, it makes sense to begin with a model of residential land use, and then see how firms fit into the picture later. In developing the model, we assume that land is assigned to different uses via a market process very much like that of the agricultural land market in chapter 17. This means we are abstracting away from important institutional influences such as zoning, political fragmentation, rent control and housing standards, all of which will be addressed in later chapters.

Start with the following assumptions:

1   Each household is located at some distance $d$ from the CBD. All jobs are located in the CBD so each household incurs the cost of commuting its distance $d$.
2   Households derive utility from consumption of a quantity $z$ of a composite non-land good and a quantity $q$ of land. They derive no utility directly from their location relative to the CBD.
3   Each household has a fixed income $Y$ out of which it must pay for its purchases of $z$, its rent for space $q$ and commuting costs.
4   The household's consumption levels $z$ and $q$ are fixed and known.
5   Transportation costs are linear, so commuting costs are a constant times $d$.
6   The price of the composite good and the per kilometer cost of commuting are exogenous. Rent is endogenous.

The first assumption explains that the CBD is the key point of reference for households because working household members must commute there on a regular basis. The second assumption defines a simple rationale for household decisions, based on the concept of *utility*, which for our purposes is simply a measure of material well-being that households derive from consuming goods. To keep things simple, in this case we define two measures of goods consumed, a quantity $q$ of land and a quantity $z$ of a composite non-land good, which lumps together all other goods. Note that in our simple model utility *does not* depend on $d$, so, holding all other things equal, utility does not increase or decrease with distance from the CBD.[1] Assumption 3 explains that all households have the same fixed income $Y$ and that expenditures on commuting, land and the composite good must sum to $Y$.

Assumption 4 is highly restrictive because it suggests that households cannot substitute between land and all other goods. We will relax this assumption shortly. Assumption 5 keeps the mathematics simple by saying that commuting costs are directly proportional to distance. Finally, assumption 6 says that there are no pre-defined rents. Just as in the von Thünen model, they will be determined by a market process.

To develop the model, we first define the household's utility function as:

$$U = f(z,q)$$

Utility $U$ is an increasing function of the quantities $z$ of composite goods and $q$ land consumed. A useful way to think about the utility function is by analogy with the production function. (For a fuller discussion refer back to chapter 7.) Much as a firm consumes quantities of inputs to produce a quantity of output, the household consumes quantities of the two goods to produce a level of utility. Much as the firm is sometimes able to substitute between inputs, the household is sometimes able to substitute between goods. (While we have assumed away the possibility of substitution between $z$ and $q$ for the moment, we will relax that assumption shortly.)

There is a difference between the output-producing firm and the utility-producing household, however, in that the latter is faced with an income constraint that places a limit on how much it can consume in the way of goods. Furthermore, in our model the household's fixed income must also cover the cost of commuting. Defining $p$ as the price of the composite good, $r$ as the rent and $t$ as the per kilometer cost of commuting, the income constraint can be written

$$Y = pz + rq + td$$

We assume that $p$ and $t$ are exogenous, but the goal of our model is to determine the value of $r$. So what can we say about rent from what we have so far? We can easily find the rent that is consistent with the income constraint:

$$r = \frac{Y - pz - td}{q}$$

This is one of those mathematical statements that are easily put into words. The maximum rent that the household can bid is determined by dividing whatever is left of income after the costs of the composite good and commuting are deducted by the number of units of land the household consumes. Under our assumptions, the only variable on the right-hand side of our rent equation is $d$. So rent is a declining function of distance from the CBD, which matches the first of our stylized facts.

This is illustrated more clearly by Figure 18.1, where the income net of the cost of the composite good is divided into the cost of rent and the cost of commuting for different values of $d$. For households at greater distance from the CBD, commuting eats up a bigger share of income. Since $q$ is constant by assumption, $r$ must go down as $d$ goes up. At some distance $d_3$, commuting costs exhaust income so the rent falls to zero. (Note this is very much like the spatial margin of cultivation in the von Thünen model. No one will live beyond $d_3$.) This implies a linear bid rent function for households as shown by the solid line in Figure 18.2.

Clearly, the slope of the bid rent function depends on the transport rate $t$. A reduction in this rate would result in an outward rotation, as shown by the dotted line in Figure 18.2. The household would be willing to bid more rent at any distance because it would have more of its income after paying for commuting. (Note that this is parallel to the effect of reducing the transportation rate in the agricultural model.) As we will see, land users with steeper bid rent functions tend to command

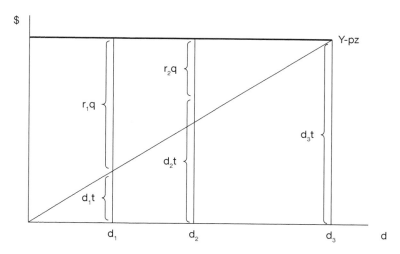

*Figure 18.1* Income breakdown and distance from CBD

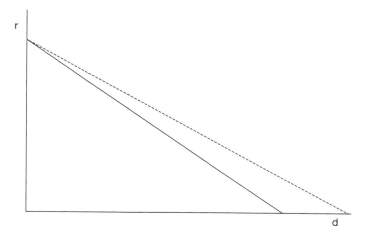

*Figure 18.2* Household bid rent function (utility fixed) with the effect of reduction in $t$

land parcels close to the CBD, irrespective of their incomes. So transportation costs play an important role in determining the spatial pattern of urban land use.

To stretch this model a little bit further, assume that there are two classes of household: high income ($H$) and low income ($L$). Since by definition $Y_H > Y_L$, a low-income household cannot consume the same quantities of land and the composite goods and incur the same commuting costs as a high-income household without violating the income constraint. One might think that the low-income household could achieve the same level of utility by living closer to the CBD and thereby incurring lower commuting costs than the high-income household. Unfortunately, it's not that simple since high-income households can outbid low-income households at any $d$.

Figure 18.3 shows the rent functions for high-income and low-income households when both consume the same quantities $q$ and $z$. Since at any value of $d$ the remaining income available for rent is lower for the low-income households, high-income households can outbid them everywhere. In order to have someplace to live, low-income households must reduce their levels of $q$, $z$ or both, allowing them to pay a rent that is higher than or equal to high-income households at some distance. Thus, to accommodate differences in income we must relax assumption 3 above. Of course, this means that low-income households must accept a lower level of utility.

Low-income households can just reduce their consumption of the composite good $z$ by an amount that is exactly sufficient to bring their rent function in line with that of high-income households. This would mean that low- and high-income households are able to pay the same rent at any distance, so there would be no residential segregation. In the more likely case where low-income people also decrease the consumption of land $q$, however, a spatial segregation results. Looking at the rent equation, it is easy to show that, for each kilometer the household moves away from the CBD, it must decrease its rent by an amount $t/q$. Comparing low- and high-income groups, we find that, since $q_H > q_L$,

$$\frac{t}{q_L} > \frac{t}{q_H}$$

This means that the rent function of low-income households is steeper, so they will outbid high-income households only at locations close to the CBD as shown in Figure 18.4. The fact that low-income households can outbid high-income households at some locations does not necessarily mean that they can command sufficient space to accommodate their numbers. In Figure 18.5, we see a situation where, in the first case, low-income households are still outbid at all locations, despite consuming less land. One solution would be for low-income households to also decrease their level $z_L$ of composite good consumption. This causes an upward shift in the bid rent curve. The more $z_L$ is dropped, the greater is the range of distances over which low-income households outbid high-income households. But this is achieved at the cost of lower utility.

The model can be extended in a couple of directions that reinforce the result that low-income people tend to live closer to the CBD. We won't go into the details

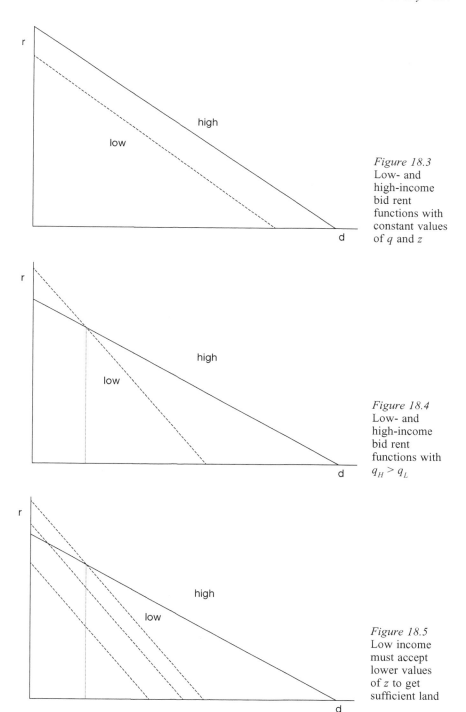

*Figure 18.3*
Low- and
high-income
bid rent
functions with
constant values
of $q$ and $z$

*Figure 18.4*
Low- and
high-income
bid rent
functions with
$q_H > q_L$

*Figure 18.5*
Low income
must accept
lower values
of $z$ to get
sufficient land

here,[2] but they are easily described in words. First, there is some evidence to suggest that land is an income-elastic good. This means that as a household's income increases it devotes an increasing share of it to land and a decreasing share to the composite good. This gives high-income households an added incentive to locate where land is relatively cheap, so they have flatter bid rent curves. Second, the cost of transportation may be more complicated than in our simple model. If high-income households have access to cars, while low-income households do not, the latter may have very high transportation costs beyond a narrow range of values $d$ where public transportation is available. This results in very steep bid rent functions for low-income households. It is possible, however, to define circumstances where the model predicts that high-income households live closer to the city, such as a case where affluent people have an inherent preference for a central location. (To build such a preference in the model, you need to add $d$ to the arguments in the utility function.) This helps to explain why the rich live closest to the CBD in Latin American cities such as Caracas, Venezuela.

A result that low-income households live closest to the CBD is consistent with two of our stylized facts. The first, naturally, is that there are segregated zones of high- and low-income population. It is also consistent with the fact that residential densities tend to decline with distance from the CBD, because it explains, first, why low-income people consume less land and, second, why they tend to live closer to the CBD. By extending the model, however, we can show that, even in a homogeneous population of households, residential densities are higher close to the CBD.

To do this, let's reinstate the assumption that all households have the same income and relax assumption 4 by allowing households to vary the quantities $z$ and $q$ that they consume. In general, land and non-land goods are substitutes, so households can enjoy the same level of utility with different combinations of $z$ and $q$. This point is illustrated in Figure 18.6, which shows three *indifference curves* for three levels of utility $U_3 > U_2 > U_1$. Each point on the indifference curve for $U_1$ defines a pair of quantities $z$, $q$ that produce exactly that much utility. The shape of the curve shows that if you decrease your consumption of land you can still maintain a consistent level of utility by increasing your consumption of the composite good and vice versa. Thus, the indifference curve is a graphical expression of the idea that $z$ and $q$ are substitutes. The indifference curve for $U_2$ defines the higher quantities of $z$ and $q$ that generate that higher level of utility and the indifference curve for $U_3$ does the same for an even higher level.

How does the household find its optimal levels of $z$ and $q$? In order to keep things simple, assume that the household knows the rent $r$ it must pay at any distance $d$ and that $r$ is a decreasing function of $d$. Thus, if $d' > d$ then $r(d) > r(d')$. (This is a bit like cheating because $r$ is supposed to be endogenous in this model. In the Appendix, we show how to determine the household's bid rent and optimal levels of $z$ and $q$ simultaneously.) At $d$ the household's budget constraint is

$$Y = pz + r(d)q + td$$

With a little algebra, we can get the equation

$$z = \frac{Y - td}{p} - \frac{r(d)}{p} q$$

which can be drawn as a straight line in the space of $z$ and $q$, as shown in Figure 18.7. Any combination of $z$ and $q$ on the budget constraint line exactly exhausts the household's income. The meaning of this line is simple. The intercept with the vertical axis, $(Y - td) / p$, is the amount of the composite good that the household could consume with its income, after deducting commuting costs, if the amount of land it consumes is zero. For each unit of land it consumes, it must reduce its consumption of the composite good by the price ratio $r(d)/p$, which is the slope of the line.

Referring back to Figure 18.6, we overlay the budget constraint line on the set of indifference curves. The household wants to be on the highest possible indifference curve, so it consumes the combination $z^*$, $q^*$, which is the point of tangency between the budget constraint line and the $U_2$ indifference curve.

This result is specific to a household living at distance $d$ from the CBD. If we consider a household at $d' > d$, the budget constraint line becomes

$$z = \frac{Y - td'}{p} - \frac{r(d')}{p} q$$

Comparing the budget constraints at $d$ and $d'$, as shown in Figure 18.7, reveals some important differences. First, the intercept with the vertical axis is lower for $d'$ because commuting costs are higher: $(Y - td') (p > Y - td/p)$. But the slope of the line is lower, because land is cheaper: $r(d')/p < r(d)/p$, so the household does not have to sacrifice as much of the composite good to consume an extra unit of land.

The effect of moving from $d$ to $d'$ on a household's consumption pattern is demonstrated in Figure 18.8, where the two budget constraints define different

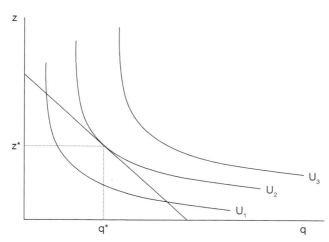

*Figure 18.6*
Household
indifference curves

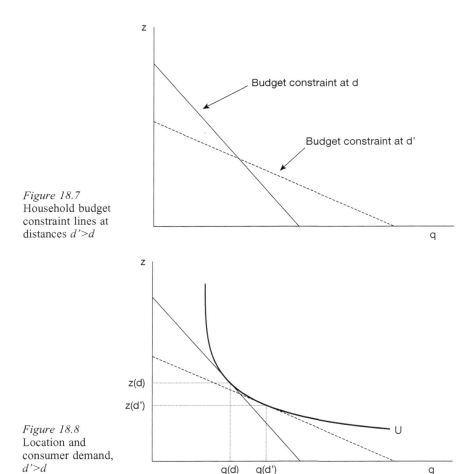

*Figure 18.7*
Household budget
constraint lines at
distances $d'>d$

*Figure 18.8*
Location and
consumer demand,
$d'>d$

points of tangency with the same indifference curve. The result is that the household at $d'$ consumes more land and less of the composite good than the household at $d$. (This means that households take advantage of lower land prices and live on large lots.) Since the typical household consumes more land at a higher $d$, we have explained why density decreases with distance from the CBD.

## Land use by firms

While residential land use accounts for most of the space in the city, land use by all types of firms is also important. Like the farmers in the von Thünen model and the households discussed above, firms are generally willing to pay a premium to be near the center of the region. As in the von Thünen model, those firms that are willing to pay the highest premiums outbid other firms to command the space closest to the CBD.

While households' bid rent functions define the rent that they are willing to pay at various distances while maintaining a constant level of utility, the bid rent functions of firms maintain a constant level of profit. We won't go into the mathematical details of how these functions are defined, but it is important to understand why some types of firms have steeper bid rent functions than others.

Consider three types of firms: financiers, bakers and junk yards. In a monocentric city, financiers are generally found close to the CBD. This is because their business depends on frequent exchanges of complex information that generally require face-to-face interaction. Since there are more people to interact with in the CBD than anywhere else, that is where they want to be. Bakeries also have a desire to be close to the CBD where their output will ultimately be sold – especially since baked goods are perishable. Junk yards, on the other hand, may have less need for a central location. Since financiers will lose revenue rapidly as they move to locations further from the CBD, they must be compensated by rapid reductions in rent, so their bid rent functions are steep. The junk yards' revenue is not much affected by moving further from the CBD, so their bid rent function is flatter. Bakeries' revenue declines less with $d$ than financiers' revenue, but more than that of junk yards, so the slope of their bid rent function lies somewhere in between.

There is another factor that comes into play that reinforces this ordering of bid rent slopes. The activities of financiers do not require much space, so their land requirement is lowest. Junk yards are by nature a land-intensive activity and bakeries lie somewhere in between. Recall from our earlier analysis that low-income households have steeper bid rent functions because their typical land consumption is lower than that of high-income households. By the same logic, the financiers' function should be steepest and the junk yards' should be flattest. Thus, we can say two things. First, financiers would bid the highest rent close to the CBD, with bakers a bit lower and junk yards lowest. Second, financiers have the steepest bid rent functions, while junk yards have the flattest functions and bakeries' functions are somewhere in between. The bid rent functions would look something like those shown in Figure 18.9.

Since households and firms must compete for the same land, we can overlay the residential and firm bid rent functions. Figure 18.10a demonstrates how the market would assign land in a city with five classes of users: high- and low-income residents, financiers, bakeries and junk yards. Viewed from above, the model produces a pattern of concentric zones much like those in the von Thünen model.

As Figure 18.7b demonstrates, we can also determine an overall rent gradient as the upper envelope of all bid rent functions. Note that, even though the bid rent functions are linear, the overall gradient is curved so that the rate of decline becomes more gradual as you move further from the CBD. Also, here we have defined an additional rent value $\bar{r}$, which for the moment we can think of as the rent paid by non-urban activities such as agriculture in the vicinity of the city. (More about this below.) The distance $\bar{d}$ defines the *urban frontier*, where the highest urban rent is just equal to the rural rent. Beyond this distance the city ends because rural activities provide higher rents to land owners.

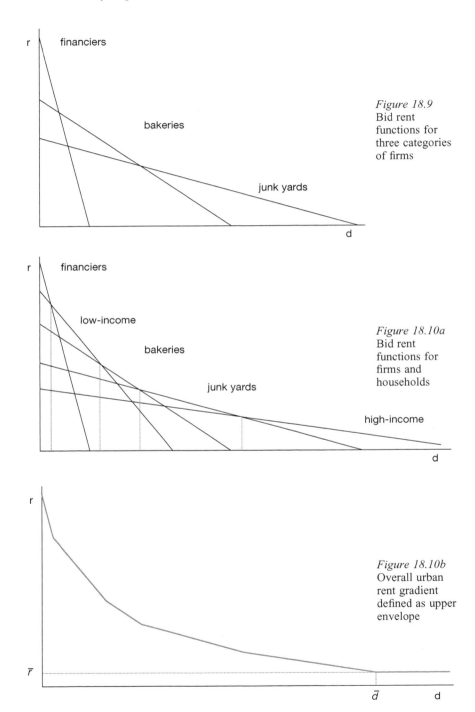

*Figure 18.9*
Bid rent
functions for
three categories
of firms

*Figure 18.10a*
Bid rent
functions for
firms and
households

*Figure 18.10b*
Overall urban
rent gradient
defined as upper
envelope

In the simple model described here, land is used as a proxy for the services provided by some sort of buildings: houses, factories, shops, apartment buildings, office towers, etc. Landlords who provide both land and buildings for sale or rent are therefore important players. To keep the math and graphs simple, we have ignored their role here except to assume that they provide land to the highest bidder. A more complete exposition of the monocentric model must include consideration of the rents that landowners are willing to accept, under the assumption that if rents are too low they may prefer to allow land to sit idle or return to rural uses.[3] *Developers* play an important role by purchasing land from rural owners, transforming it to urban uses (providing infrastructure and buildings) and adding to the urban space. Therefore, the minimum price at the urban periphery $\bar{r}$ must include not only the rent paid by farmers but also a mark-up to compensate developers for the cost of transforming the land from rural to urban use. Thus, the rent that urban land users are willing to pay at the urban frontier must be somewhat higher than the agricultural rent.

The monocentric model is appealing in its simplicity. But it predicts patterns of rent and land use that are unfamiliar to most modern readers – certainly to anyone less than 50 years of age. Urban land-use patterns have always been more complex than the model's predictions. This is not really a problem because the function of models is to represent simplified versions of reality. Over the past half century, however, the reality of cities dominated by strong CBDs has faded, especially in North America. Cities have become decidedly *polycentric* rather than *monocentric*. Why and how this has happened is the subject of the next chapter. As we will see, while the assumptions of the monocentric model are no longer valid, its results still yield insights to the analysis of modern urban land markets.

## Appendix: Simultaneous determination of residential rents and densities

This Appendix will illustrate two things about household bid rent functions. First, it will show how the household determines the rent that would maintain a constant level of utility as it moves to ever higher values of $d$ and how the changes in rent lead to changes in density. Second, it will explain why bid rent functions are not actually straight lines, but rather curves whose slopes decrease at increasing values of $d$.

Figure A18.1 illustrates the case of a household located at a distance $d_0$ from the CBD that achieves utility level $\bar{U}$ by bidding rent $r_0$ and consuming quantities $q_0$ and $z_0$ of land and the composite good respectively. This situation is defined by the point of tangency between the household's budget constraint:

$$z_0 = \frac{Y - td_0}{p} - \frac{r_0}{p} q_0$$

Note that the price of the composite good ($p$) and the transportation rate ($t$) are assumed to be constants, so they do not have the subscript 0. Now suppose the household is asked to define the bid rent at which it would be indifferent between staying at distance $d_0$ and moving to $d_1 > d_0$. If the household held its bid rent and consumption levels constant and moved to $d_1$, its budget constraint would become

$$z_0 = \frac{Y - td_1}{p} - \frac{r_0}{p} q_0$$

which is the dashed line shown in the figure. The original budget constraint has been shifted down by an amount $t(d_1 - d_0)$. Since there is no point of tangency between the new budget constraint and the indifference curve associated with utility level $\bar{U}$, the household is worse off at $d_1$ than at $d_0$. But it can find a rent $r_1$ that reduces the slope of the budget constraint just enough to create a new point of tangency at the combination $z_1$, $q_1$. Thus, in order to maintain its level of utility it must adjust not only its rent but also its consumption of land and the composite good.

Because the household bids a lower rent at $d_1$ than it did at $d_0$, it will also choose to consume more land and less of the composite good. Figure A18.2 shows the situation at an additional point $d_2 > d_1$, where the household's consumption of land will increase further ($q_1 > q_2$). The general pattern is that households will only move further away from the CBD if they can pay lower rents, which in turn leads them to consume ever higher quantities of land. As a result, residential density declines with distance from the CBD.

The fact that $q$ increases with distance from the CBD means that the household bid rent function cannot be a straight line. Recall that the budget constraint is

$$Y = pz + r(d)q + td$$

The slope of the bid rent function is the rate of change in the bid rent for a small increase in distance. Define the slope as $\Delta r/\Delta d$.[4] In order for the budget constraint

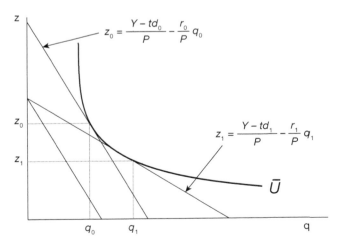

*Figure A18.1* Change in bid rent with increase in $d$

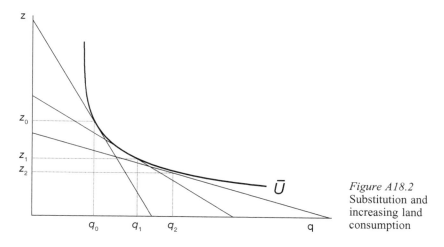

*Figure A18.2*
Substitution and
increasing land
consumption

to hold as the household moves further from the CBD, the change in rent payment
must exactly offset the change in commuting costs. In other words,

$$sq - t = 0$$

so

$$s = \frac{t}{q}$$

Since $q$ increases for higher values of $d$, the bid rent function is shaped as shown
in Figure A18.3.

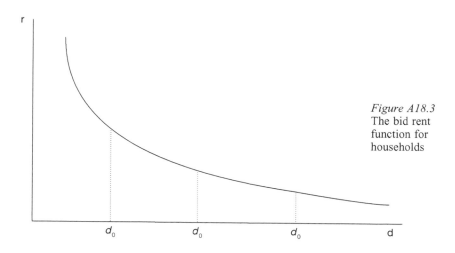

*Figure A18.3*
The bid rent
function for
households

# 19 Urban sprawl and the polycentric city

The monocentric model presented in the last chapter explains spatial patterns of urban rents and densities, along with the segregation of land among different classes of firms and households, in terms of a single variable: distance from the central business district (CBD). Real cities have always had other important reference points, such as port or rail terminals, churches, stadiums, parks and many more. To the extent that these things were located away from the CBD, they constituted secondary centers that might have significant impacts on spatial patterns in the city. Still, for most cities, the CBD was so clearly dominant in its influence on economic and social interaction that it was the only logical place to start in any explanation of the overall shape of the city.

In most cities, the CBD is still important, for a couple of reasons. First, it is still the largest single concentration of employment in all but a few cities. In North America, concentration of employment in the CBD is strongest for older, more service-oriented cities such as New York, Boston, Montreal, Toronto, Chicago and San Francisco. For those cities where the CBD has a much reduced share of employment, it remains important for historical reasons. Transportation infrastructure tends to be centered on the CBD and spatial patterns of land use, which are slow to change, still reflect the era of CBD dominance.

Despite all this, the notion of the CBD as the key point of reference for households and firms has steadily lost its relevance over the past 50 years. Teenagers, most of whom live in the suburbs, are apt to be more familiar with their regional shopping malls than with the downtown core. Their parents probably work at peripheral industrial parks, strip malls or the suburban "campuses" of giant corporations, to which they may commute in two opposite directions from their home. Since the dominant form of transportation is the private car, the CBD is often the *least* convenient place to go because of traffic congestion and the high cost of parking, which is generally free at malls and other peripheral facilities. If the CBD is the focal point of these kids' lives, they don't seem to know it.

Before dealing explicitly with the polycentric city, we need to consider the general trends whereby population and employment have become ever more dispersed away from the CBD. The general decentralization of the city is often called *urban sprawl*. This term has been used in such a variety of inconsistent ways that it has become almost meaningless. For some it refers to the incursion of

the city upon formerly quiet, rural areas. For others it refers to the uglier characteristics of low-density suburbs: garish strip malls, vast parking lots and undifferentiated housing subdivisions. It has become a standard joke among developers
and planners that there are two things that the public opposes: density and sprawl.
For a working definition, let us define urban sprawl as having the following four
characteristics: a rapid expansion of the urban frontier, low-density development,
segregation of land uses and a high-density transportation network providing easy
movement in all directions (Anderson *et al.*, 1996).

The implications of urban sprawl are well documented. Rapid expansion of the
urban frontier leads to the loss of agricultural land and rural landscapes. Low density
and segregation of land uses combine to preclude non-motorized transportation for
most trips and make it prohibitively expensive to provide public transportation. Thus,
the private car, supported by the high-density road network, is the dominant form
of transportation. Among other things, sprawl leads to a high rate of energy
consumption and a high cost for providing public services to the dispersed population. But it is not all bad. Rapid expansion onto peripheral land has made home
ownership more affordable for middle-class households. And, despite the admoni-
tions of environmental groups, households continue to crave the low-density lifestyle.

## Sprawl and the monocentric model

In explaining the trend to urban sprawl, most observers point to the mass production
and widespread adoption of the private car. While it is clear that sprawl would not
be possible without cars, it is less clear what mechanisms led from the adoption of
the car as the principal means of transportation to the decentralization of homes
and workplaces. Our monocentric model of urban land use is quite helpful in making
this link. Recall that a reduction in the transportation rate leads to a simultaneous
extension and flattening of bid rent functions as shown in Figure 19.1. Thus, by
making it economical to cover long commuting distances, the car shifted residential
bid rent functions in a way that leads to more households locating in peripheral
areas and an outward expansion of the urban frontier.

You might object to this conclusion by pointing out that traveling by car is not
cheaper than the traditional transit options. In fact, it is more expensive. But research
has shown that, when making transportation mode decisions, most people weigh not
only the out-of-pocket cost but also the implicit cost of travel time.[1] Faster commutes
mean more time to work or more time for leisure – either way, less time commuting
leads to higher utility. For locations more than a few miles from the CBD, travel by
car is generally faster than travel by other options. An important exception to this is
commuter rail transportation. In fact, it can be argued that rail transportation started
the process of urban decentralization long before car ownership became widespread.
(See Borchert, 1967, for a fascinating historical treatment of how changes in personal
transportation technology have affected urban form in North America.)

Other technological innovations have played roles in flattening bid rent functions.
After the car, the consumer durable that has contributed the most to suburbanization
is the refrigerator. Without home refrigeration, it is necessary for someone in the

household to make a trip to a central market on a daily basis to buy food. With a small refrigerator, perhaps one trip every other day is needed. With a large one, once-a-week grocery shopping is possible, assuming of course that the household has a car to haul a week's worth of groceries home. Even if all grocery shopping were located in the CBD, the household with a large refrigerator and a car would need to make fewer trips so the value of being close to the CBD would be diminished. As Figure 19.1 shows, this results in a change not only in the slope of the household bid rent function for a given level of utility but also in a reduction in its value at the CBD. (The argument here is that, because the household makes fewer purchases in the CBD, the utility value of locating at the CBD is reduced.)

Another more recent technological innovation – the Internet – has further weakened the appeal of the CBD, leading to flatter bid rent functions. By tele-commuting, some households are able to reduce or eliminate commuting trips to the CBD. Other central functions, such as organization meetings and social chats, can also be achieved at home. This does not mean that the Internet has made the CBD obsolete. Research shows that face-to-face communication is still necessary for the exchange of highly complex information. This explains in part why activities such as corporate law, advanced consulting and more complex financial activities remain oriented to the CBD (see Kobayashi *et al.*, 1998). (We will return to this theme in Part V, on the *information economy*.)

The flattening of bid rent curves may have nothing to do with transportation, but rather with a general preference for living near to or far from the CBD. Some people would like to live as close to the CBD as possible because they enjoy the urban ambience. Others see the CBD as the source of all sorts of negative externalities such as pollution, congestion and crime. To reflect these preferences, we must redefine the household utility function to include distance to the CBD:

$$U = f(z, q, d)$$

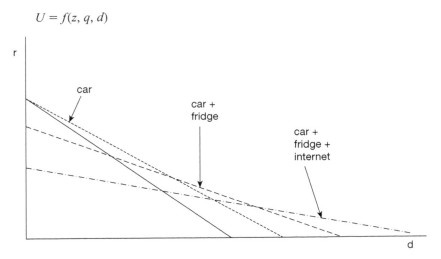

*Figure 19.1* Effect of consumer technologies on household bid rent function (utility constant)

For the former group of people described above (call them CBD lovers), utility declines with $d$, while for the second group (CBD haters) it increases with $d$. For CBD lovers, the attraction of urban living reinforces the effect of transportation cost, making their bid rent functions very steep. For the CBD haters, there are two counteracting effects: the direct positive utility effect of moving the residence away from the CBD and the negative transportation cost effect on bid rent. Even if the transportation effect exceeds the utility effect, the bid rent function at a given level of utility for the CBD haters will be much flatter than for the CBD lovers (Figure 19.2). An increasing proportion of CBD haters in the population over the past 50 years may account for a significant amount of decentralization and low-density development. In the past couple of decades, however, there appears to be a significant rebound in the share of CBD lovers, leading to the gentrification of some central city neighborhoods. The important point here is that, if we recognize differences in preferences across the population by including $d$ in the utility function, the monocentric model can show that households in the same income group may be found both near the CBD and in the periphery.

The foregoing discussion used the monocentric model of urban land use to provide some insights about modern decentralization trends in cities.[2] It falls short, however, in three key areas. First, it focuses on the utilities, profits and costs of the households and firms that use urban land, but says nothing about the providers of that land. In particular, developers, who are responsible for transforming land at the urban frontier from non-urban to urban uses, are often implicated as the agents of sprawl. Land-use segregation and low-density development come about in part because it is cheaper for developers to build very large numbers of similar houses in massive subdivisions. This argument has merit, but ultimately the successful developer's decisions regarding density are driven by the preferences of the home-buying public. Also, it is often the case that developers would like to build at higher densities but are prevented from doing so by zoning restrictions. In the next section, however, we will see how developers who undertake very large projects in the urban periphery can profoundly affect urban form.

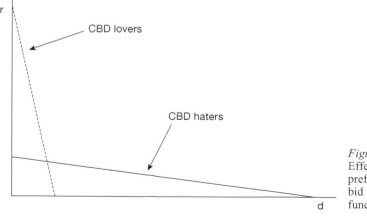

*Figure 19.2*
Effect of preferences on bid rent functions

That brings us to the second area of weakness in our discussion, which is that it ignores the role of the public sector in determining land-use patterns. Urban land markets are one of the most highly regulated components of the modern economy, so we can't assume that what we see on the ground is the effect of market forces alone. We will address the role of local government in shaping urban land-use patterns in the last section of this chapter.

Finally, explanations cast in the monocentric model are limited by the reality that most modern cities, especially in North America but increasingly in Europe as well, are essentially polycentric. We turn to that issue now.

## Polycentric cities

Analysts have always recognized that commercial centers exist outside the CBD. Convenience stores, branch banks, restaurants and shops have always dotted the landscapes of urban areas. As cities have expanded over time, previously distinct town centers in what had been a rural hinterland are absorbed as secondary concentrations of activity. Many urban areas comprise a significant number of municipalities, each with a town hall, a post office and a small "downtown." Still, none of these smaller centers detracted much from the dominance of the CBD.

By the 1960s in North America (a bit later in Europe), the picture began to change as new forms of development created peripheral centers that compete with the CBD in significant ways. Industrial parks allowed light manufacturing firms to locate in clusters along highways with relatively cheap land and good accessibility to a rapidly dispersing labor force. Suburban shopping malls provided the scale and variety of retail services previously found only in the CBD, usually including branches of the major downtown department stores. In a few cities, such as Detroit, competition from suburban centers resulted in near collapse of the CBD (see Box 19.1). Even in Boston, which has a thriving CBD from an employment perspective, downtown retail activity withered due to competition from suburban malls.

---

### *Box 19.1* Detroit: the case of the collapsing center

The trend in U.S. metropolitan areas has been for peripheral communities to grow more rapidly than central cities. In many cases, the central city populations have even declined during times of robust growth in metropolitan population. This does not necessarily indicate a serious economic decline, however, because older urban areas are often "built out," meaning there is no room for additional housing units. The average size of the American household has declined steadily since the 1960s, so a city with a fixed number of households is likely to experience gradual decline in population.

Detroit, however, is another matter. The City of Detroit has lost nearly one half of its population, declining from about 1.8 million in 1950 to less than

750,000 today. Even during the 1950s and 1960s when the Detroit-centered U.S. automotive industry was in its heyday and the population of the Detroit Metropolitan Area was expanding, the City's population was in decline. The first decade of the twenty-first century brought no relief as the U.S. Census reports a 25 percent reduction in City population between 2000 and 2010. In no other major U.S. metropolitan area did the central population collapse in this way.

Theories abound for why Detroit fared so much worse than other U.S. central cities. Some argue that the influence of the automotive industry prevented Detroit from developing the high-quality transit system necessary to promote central city growth. The land-intensive nature of the auto industry favored locations outside the city limits for new assembly plants. Certainly, the issue of race played a major part. During the middle of the twentieth century, millions of African Americans migrated from the rural south to the industrial cities of the north. In the City of Detroit, black people eventually became the majority. In the racial climate of America in the 1960s, this inevitably led to "white flight" to the suburbs, leaving Detroit with a relatively low-income population. Two of the "big three" automakers established their headquarters outside the city limits (General Motors' headquarters remain in downtown Detroit). Education, health care and other public services suffered from the inadequate tax base and the traditional disadvantages of minority people in labor markets led to high unemployment and the attendant problems of crime and substance abuse. Many African Americans who could afford to do so also left the City in hopes of finding better schools for their children in suburban communities. With ever more people leaving and very few moving in, the City of Detroit's population dwindled. This does not mean that the entire Detroit urban region declined. The other municipalities of the Detroit metropolitan area have experienced modest growth throughout the period of the City's decline. They now account for over 80 percent of the metropolitan population. (See Map B19.1.)

By the 1980s, peripheral centers in some of the largest cities evolved into something resembling the CBDs of medium-sized cities. Viewed from a distance, their concentrations of high-rise office and apartment buildings have the look of a city center. At street level, a rather "downtown" variety of shops and restaurants are found – although these areas lack the vibrant foot traffic of the traditional CBD. These "edge cities" (Garreau, 1992) account for an ever increasing share of urban economic activity in North America (see Box 19.2). Surely, these peripheral centers profoundly influence the overall patterns of rents, land uses and densities in urban areas.

Extending the basic mechanisms of the monocentric model to a city with multiple centers is not really that difficult.[3] To take a simple example, imagine that in addition

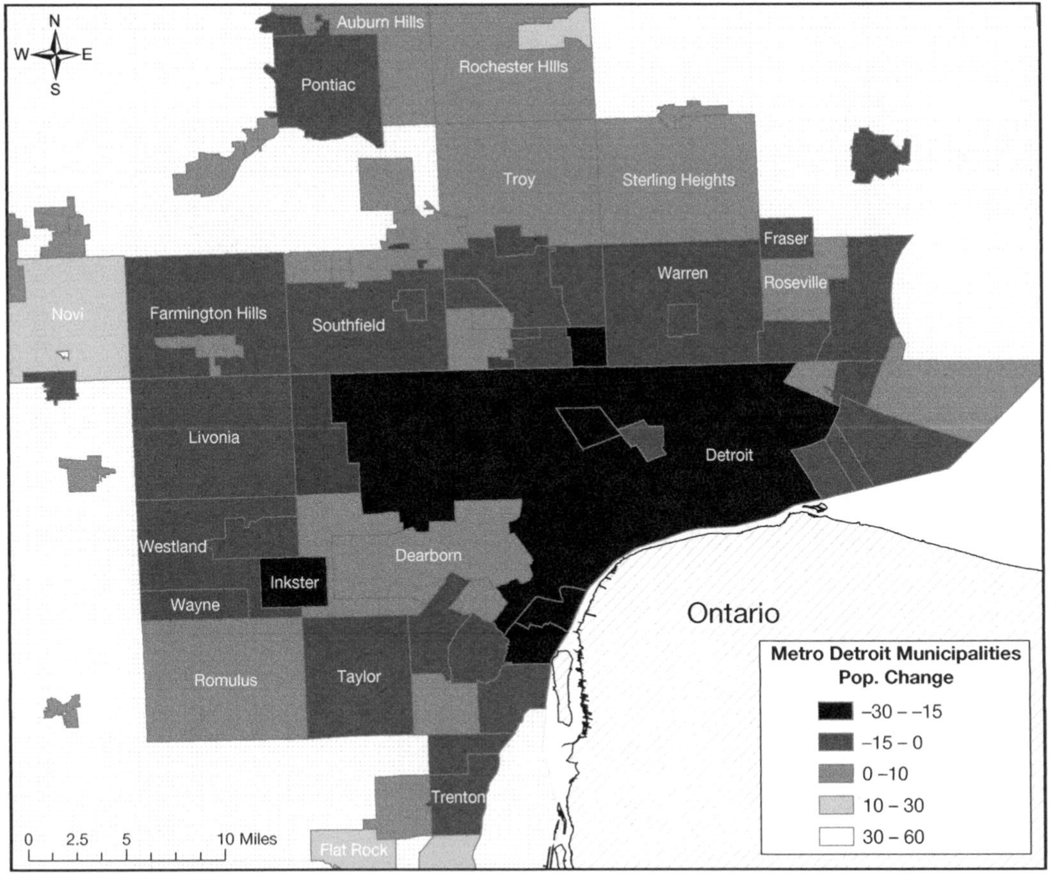

*Map B19.1* Population change by percentage, Detroit area municipalities, 2000–10

## Box 19.2 Edge cities

The term "edge city" as it was originally coined by Garreau (1992) should not be confused with more general terms such as "suburban development," "commercial cluster" or "regional mall." What Garreau had in mind were centers outside the traditional CBD that have many of the attributes of the CBD in terms of both scale and function. To qualify as an edge city, a place must meet a number of quantitative criteria, including over 5 million square feet of office space – enough to accommodate 20,000 or more employees – as well as over a half million square feet of retail space. The emphasis on office space over retail space reflects the CBD-like qualities of an edge city. It must be more than a mega-mall. More people must work in it than live in it, so peripheral clusters of condominium towers do not qualify. In general, edge cities develop at greenfield sites that may have been rural crossroads or even agricultural fields a few decades earlier. There is one important way in which they differ from traditional CBDs. Since most of them have little or no transit service at the early stage of development, most workers reach them by car. This means that massive parking facilities are required.

Three of the most "classic" edge cities are located on the periphery of fast-growing American cities. Tysons Corner in Fairfax County, Virginia near Washington DC has over 40 million square feet of commercial space and a daytime population of over 100,000 (as compared with only 20,000 residents). Uptown Houston, located a 15-minute drive from downtown Houston, has over 23 million square feet of office space and claims to be the seventeenth largest business district in the United States.[i] Perimeter Center in suburban Atlanta has over 28 million square feet of office space, which is more than downtown Atlanta. In fact, Atlanta's downtown accounts for only about 13 percent of the class A office space in the metropolitan area.[ii] All three edge cities are homes to headquarters of major U.S. corporations.

While edge cities provide a development structure that is inconsistent with our general definition of sprawl, they are still basically auto dependent. Unlike downtown CBDs where thousands arrive each morning by rail transit, the vast majority of those who come to edge cities use their cars. This means that massive investments in highway infrastructure are needed to support such developments and more environmentally benign transportation options are forgone. But the creation of such dense nodes provides opportunities to provide transit service that are not available for more dispersed development along highway corridors. For example, the Washington Metro is currently building a new "Silver Line" that will connect Tysons Corner and Dulles International Airport into the metropolitan rail network. It remains to be seen, however, how many Tysons Corner employees will give up their cars and use the transit service.

**Notes**

i   See http://www.uptown-houston.com/info/factSheets/UT_Fact_Office.pdf
    (accessed May, 2011).
ii  See http://dsg.colliers.com/document.aspx?report=1197.pdf (accessed May,
    2011).

to the CBD there is a peripheral business district (PBB) at which some proportion
of the urban population is employed. To keep things simple, assume that all
households, including those employed at the CBD and those employed at the PBD
must purchase the composite good at the CBD. Thus, people employed at the PBD
must also travel to the CBD to make those purchases, while everyone else travels
only to the CBD for both work and shopping. In Figure 19.3, there is one bid rent
curve for those who work at the CBD and one for those who work at the PBD,
with the latter extending in both directions. Note that maximum rent at the PBD is
lower than at the CBD because PBD workers still have to travel to the CBD for
shopping. The bid rent curve extending inward from the PBD is flatter than that of
the CBD workers because the extra commuting cost incurred from moving away
from the PBD is partially offset by reduced cost of travel to shop at the CBD. The
bid rent curve extending from the PBD and away from the CBD is steeper because
in this case both commuting and shopping transportation costs are increasing. The
result would be that along a straight line passing from the CBD and through the
PBD rent would no longer be monotonically decreasing. Instead, it would have a
local peak at the PBD.

Recall that households paying higher rents maximize utility by consuming less
land ($q$) and more of the composite good ($z$). This means that the local peak in

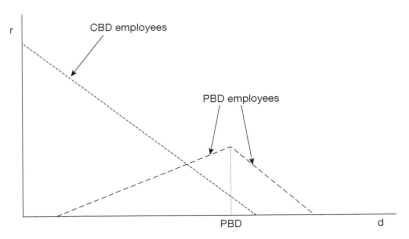

*Figure 19.3* Bid rent around CBD and PBD (peripheral business district)

rents around PBD would coincide with a local peak in residential density. The two-dimensional outcome is shown in Figure 19.4, where dark shading represents high density. Density is highest at the CBD but there is a secondary peak around the PBD. Also, the urban frontier is extended in the vicinity of the PBD. The point marked *a* is of particular interest. This point has higher rent and density than points close to it, including some points that are closer to the CBD. It also has higher rent and density than point *b* which is about the same distance from the PBD. This is because *a* is closer to the CBD than *b* is. There is an important implication here. In order to determine rent or density at point *a*, we have to consider its location relative to *both* the CBD and the PBD. More generally, in a polycentric city, the characteristics of land use at any point depend on its location relative to *all* centers. We'll return to this point below.

By adding more centers, we can generate ever more complex patterns of rent and density. However, this would not answer a couple of important questions. First, why do secondary centers emerge? And, second, where do they emerge?

## Highways, developers and urban form

To ask these questions begs the more fundamental questions: why is there a CBD and why is it where it is? The first question essentially asks why all transactions and production should occur at one point in space. Recalling our earlier discussions on agglomeration and markets (see chapters 3 and 4), production activities benefit from clustering by means of a variety of mechanisms, including urbanization economies, localization economies and juxtaposition economies. Markets function best when there is a high concentration of buyers and sellers. Obviously, not all

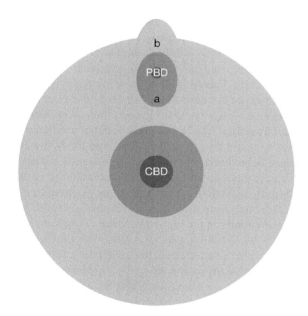

*Figure 19.4* Spatial density pattern with PBD

activities can occur in the same place, but in general the more compact the clustering of activities the better – at least in theory.

As for the second question, the monocentric model is mute. The implicit back story is that the CBD emerges at an arbitrary point in space and the city develops around it. But more historically minded geographers have been asking the question of why the city's core emerges and grows in a particular place for centuries. The complementary concepts of site and situation attributes, which were introduced in chapter 1, can be used to address this question. Recall that site attributes are physical characteristics of a place such as high ground that is easily defensible or location on a safe harbor or navigable river to facilitate trade. Situation attributes are the access characteristics of a place, defined in terms of how easily it can interact with other places that have some sort of economic potential, such as sources of inputs or markets for outputs. In terms of interactions within the city, the CBD has superior situation attributes to other nearby points because of its central location, which allows it to interact effectively with all parts of the urban area.

To envision how and why a secondary center might emerge, consider the case of an established CBD in an undifferentiated plane. Under the standard assumption that transportation costs at all points in the city are proportional to the distance from the CBD, we would expect to have a concentric urban form as shown in Figure 19.5a. Here the dark zone in the center represents an area of higher residential density and the outer ring is the urban frontier. (More correctly, there would be a gradual transition from high to low density as you move away from the CBD, but the idea of discrete high- and low-density zones is useful for this illustration.)

So far we have treated the city as if it were isolated from the rest of the world, but for commercial purposes it would have to be possible to move back and forth to other cities. Imagine that a regional or national government builds a series of highways to facilitate intercity movement and that two highways – one extending north to south (highway NS) and the other extending east to west (highway EW) – pass through the city as shown in Figure 19.5b. While the highways are intended for intercity travel, they could also be used for travel to and from the CBD ("intracity" travel) by residents of the city. Traveling along these highways is much easier and cheaper than traveling through other parts of the city. Households located along the highway therefore have much lower commuting costs than other households located at the same distance from the CBD. Households near, but not directly on, the highways find it cheaper to travel first from their homes to the highway and then along the highway to the CBD rather than travel directly to the CBD. Thus, a large number of households in the city benefit from reduced commuting costs after the highways are built. This affects both the shape and extent of urban land-use patterns. We have already seen that decreasing transportation costs result in increasing bid rents, so rents in the vicinity of the highway increase. Higher rents result in lower densities (as households substitute $z$ for $q$) so what was previously a circular zone of high density becomes a star-shaped zone extending along the highway corridors. The urban frontier also moves out along the corridors, creating a more extensive, star-shaped city. There are numerous examples of this type of development. For example, the Brooklyn–Queens Expressway promoted rapid urbanization eastward from New York City. Later, the Long Island Expressway promoted further eastward expansion.

As the urban form shifts from the pattern in Figure 19.5a to the pattern in Figure 19.5b, an increasing share of commuters will use either highway EW or highway NS to travel to the CBD. At some point, congestion may set in, especially in the vicinity of the CBD where the largest flow of traffic will occur. This detracts somewhat from the time savings that the highway provides for urban households. It will also slow down through traffic – that is, travelers headed for destinations outside the city who have to pass through the CBD. (This is a classic problem for transportation planners: roads envisioned for long-distance travel become clogged with local traffic.) A possible solution would be to build a *bypass* road around the CBD. In Figure 19.5c, we see the addition of a road that bypasses the CBD in the east–west direction. Travelers on highway EW who are not destined from the CBD will save time by taking the bypass at point *a*, crossing highway NS at point *b* and rejoining highway EW at point *c*. (Because roads of this type go around the urban core, they are sometimes called *circumferential highways*.)

Naturally, some of the city's households will take advantage of this new highway. Anyone living near it has a fast route to either highway EW or highway NS from which they have a fast route to the CBD. If this provides sufficient time savings, it will cause the urban frontier to expand in the northwest and northeast directions. Since the bypass does not affect commuters on the south side of the city, the urban frontier is now asymmetric.

The addition of the bypass also affects the accessibility pattern of the urban area. Prior to the addition of any highways, the CBD had superior accessibility to any other point because it was in the center of the city. The addition of highways EW and NS reinforced this accessibility by making the CBD the only point that could be reached using two highways. The addition of the bypass creates three points of high accessibility *a*, *b* and *c*, each of which can be reached by two highways. Of these, *b* has the best accessibility because, like the CBD, it can be reached by highway from four directions, while *a* and *c* can be reached by highway from only three directions. The CBD still has the best accessibility, since its location at the center gives it a lower overall average distance to points in the city, but, if a secondary center is to emerge, there is a logical place for it: point *b*.

But why would a secondary center emerge? Besides its superior accessibility, the CBD has the advantage of agglomeration economies, whereby economic activities are most efficient when they are spatially concentrated. As we pointed out in chapter 3, however, there are agglomeration costs such as congestion and pollution that limit the optimal size of economic clusters (see Figure 3.2). At some point, firms may see that it is in their interest to find a location outside the CBD. It is unlikely, however, that a small firm will independently make the move to point *b* because it would find itself with good accessibility, but a complete lack of agglomeration benefits. But a very large developer might be able to create its own agglomeration by locating a shopping mall, industrial park, high-density apartment complex or even all three at point *b*. This is a risky proposition, but one with a high potential payoff. As such, the initial establishment of the secondary center is an act of spatial entrepreneurship – something that is difficult to capture in models. Examples include major centers that developed around privately developed shopping malls (Buckhead, Atlanta) or mixed-use developments (Don Mills, Toronto). Once the center is established, however, the logic of the monocentric model kicks in.

Figure 19.5c portrays the situation after the creation of a PBD at point *b*. Because a lot of households are employed at the PBD, rents are bid up around it and a zone of high residential density emerges. The urban edge expands further to the north, driven not by reduced transportation costs but by the desire to locate close to the PBD. In this illustration, a corridor of high-density development connecting the

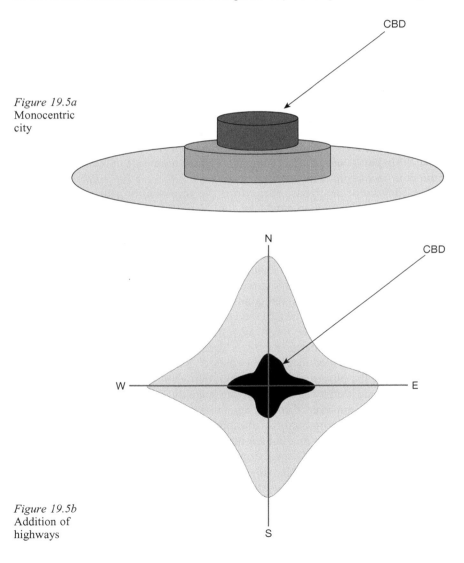

*Figure 19.5a*
Monocentric
city

*Figure 19.5b*
Addition of
highways

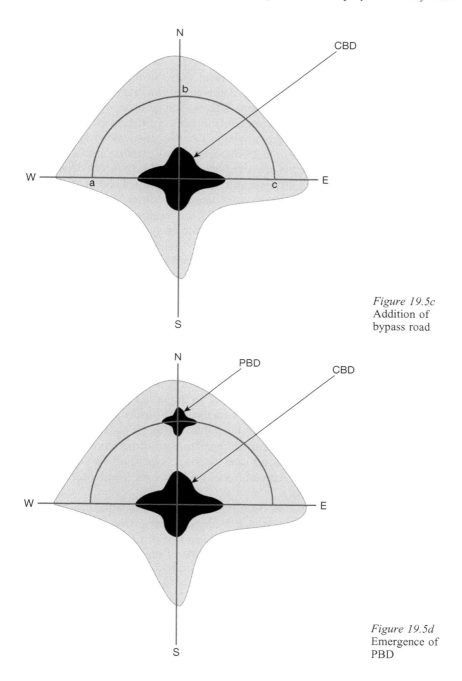

*Figure 19.5c*
Addition of
bypass road

*Figure 19.5d*
Emergence of
PBD

CBD and PBD is created. The initial concentric urban form is almost unrecognizable in the pattern that has emerged. Over time, especially if the city grows rapidly, new peripheral centers may emerge by means of similar mechanisms, creating an ever more complex urban pattern.

The foregoing discussion is just a hypothetical story, but it is at least consistent with the history of highway construction and land development that created – or at least promoted – polycentric urban forms. It shows that the economic mechanisms of the monocentric model still play a role. But this story is different from the classic model in two ways. First, it is largely driven by discrete, momentous decisions by actors who are exogenous to the model: national highway planners and large-scale developers. Second, the evolution of urban form described here is path dependent. If events had played out in a different order, if the highways had been aligned differently, if the developer had chosen point *a* instead of point *b* (perhaps because of a tax incentive from a suburban municipality), the resulting pattern might have been quite different. A clear implication is that the analytical tools of economic geography do not make it possible to predict the evolution of urban form in the long run. They do, however, make it possible to understand at least some of the mechanisms that drive that evolution. That is no small accomplishment.

## The role of the public sector

There are very few markets in which the intervention of the public sector is more pervasive or has greater impacts than markets for urban land. The notion that land-use patterns come about because land goes to the highest bidder must be tempered by the understanding that the public sector has veto power over many urban land transactions. Furthermore, the public sector is an important land user in its own right. Many of the functions we associate with the CBD – a city hall, a central post office, a public plaza – are properties of the public sector. Of equal importance is the fact that most transportation infrastructure and many transportation services are in the public domain. As we have just seen, decisions regarding the construction and alignment of major transportation arteries may have profound effects on the evolution of land-use patterns.

In most parts of the developed world, it is local governments rather than regional or national governments that have the greatest impact on urban land use. In assessing these impacts it is useful to distinguish between two different but interrelated functions of local government. The first is the role of planner and regulator and the second is the role of public service provider. It is beyond the scope of this text to provide a thorough analysis of these functions. Instead, what follows is a discussion of the most important ways in which local governments constrain the market mechanisms discussed thus far.

At the outset, it's important to consider an important contextual factor: *political fragmentation*. When geographers talk about "the city," they refer to the functional region of intense spatial interactions that surrounds a CBD. In the monocentric model, the city extends all the way to the point at which urban land uses give way to rural land uses. This is not the same thing as the "political city" which includes only the space inside a set of political boundaries over which a single local government has authority. To avoid confusion, the broader functional definition of the city is called the *metropolitan area*. Sometimes the political city and the metropolitan area are coterminous. But quite often the metropolitan area is much larger than the political city, with peripheral regions under the authority of a number of additional local governments.[4] *Political fragmentation* refers to the situation where there is a large number of separate local governments in the metropolitan area.

The presence and extent of political fragmentation is frequently the outcome of historical circumstances. For example, the city of Boston is one of the most politically fragmented cities in the world. In the seventeenth century, the political city of Boston was limited to a small peninsula extending into Massachusetts Bay. In the countryside surrounding Boston dozens of small farming towns – each with its own church, its own government charter and its own strong identity – were established by the beginning of the American Revolution (1775). The political city of Boston expanded by landfill throughout the nineteenth century and several bordering towns were annexed, but, as urbanization spread into the periphery, most towns remained independent. The result is that today the Boston metropolitan area is made up of over 100 local governments, most with their own school systems, police and fire departments, public works and land-use planning offices.

Some cities have little or no political fragmentation. In parts of the American west, city limits were expanded into unincorporated land or towns on the periphery were annexed into the political city. In Canada, the Province of Ontario has amalgamated local governments in an effort to reduce the level of fragmentation. Still, in most major cities there is more than one local government with substantial authority over land-use planning and public service provision. As we will see, political fragmentation has a big influence on how the public sector affects urban land markets.

## Planning and regulation

In chapter 6, we introduced the concepts of positive and negative externalities, defined as the positive or negative effect that the actions of one economic agent have on another for which no compensation is paid. Externalities among land users are common. Earlier, we suggested the extreme example of a piggery locating next to a health spa as a case of negative externality. In the jargon of planning, these are *incompatible land uses*. Many more realistic examples are possible. Suppose there is a residential development adjacent to some undeveloped land. Now suppose that, as the economy grows, industrial land users are able to outbid residential developers for the undeveloped land. The result will be residences in close proximity to the industrial land users. This situation occurs in many cities with no ill effect, so long as the industries in question do not create any negative outcomes. But, if the industry is noisy, smelly or creates pollution that has localized health impacts, the nearby residents will suffer a negative effect. If, as is often the case, the industries do not have to compensate the homeowners, a negative externality is created.[5]

There is no mechanism in the models we have discussed so far to deal with negative externalities. That does not mean that the market does not take externalities into account. If the situation described above occurs, the result will be that the rent of the properties close to the transition between residential and industrial users will decline. In essence, just as the rent at any location in a polycentric city is affected by location relative to a number of different centers, it is also affected by location relative to land uses with negative externalities. Households are willing to bid a higher rent to locate close to one or more centers, while they would bid a lower rent for a location close to one or more sources of negative externality. More complex models of rent can explain the externality problem, but they cannot solve it.

From social and political perspectives, the existence of externalities provides a rationale for public sector intervention in urban land markets. From the social perspective, the existence of externalities implies that the unregulated market cannot automatically create an optimal distribution of land uses. There is also a question of fairness: homeowners or landlords who purchase land before the industry locates nearby experience a loss on their investments if land values decline. From the political perspective, externalities generally pit the interests of firms against the interests of households, and it is household members who provide most of the votes in local government elections.

The main policy tool that local governments use to prevent incompatible land users from locating close together is *zoning*, defined as a code that restricts the range of acceptable land uses in different parts of the city. (The term *planning permission* is more commonly used in the United Kingdom.) An area may be zoned as residential, which means no industrial or commercial land user may be located there. On the other hand, another area may be zoned as industrial, meaning that no one can make a residence there. The effect is to keep incompatible land users away from each other. Zoning rules may restrict not only the type of land use that may occur, but also how it is used. For example, if the government decides that single-family detached homes and residential apartment buildings are incompatible land uses, it may designate some areas for the former and others for the latter. Sometimes, this type of zoning is specified in terms of minimum lot size or maximum building height restrictions.

Zoning can also be used to promote positive externalities. For example, the zoning code may limit retail activities to relatively small areas in order to encourage a compact retail center with agglomeration economies rather than a highly dispersed pattern of stores. Naturally, zoning may be used in ways that create economic distortions, as in the case where politically well-connected land developers are able to get changes in the zoning code that favor their planned projects at the expense of other potential land users.

In a politically fragmented city, towns on the periphery may use zoning as a way of preserving social homogeneity. Suppose a town on the outskirts of the city is initially settled by a high-income population. As the city grows, the range over which low-income households can outbid high-income households expands to include parts of this town. The local government may prevent low-income households from residing in their town by setting minimum lot size restrictions. Here the town is basically acting like a private club, using its authority over land-use planning to exclude undesirable members. Such practices are often called *snob zoning*. There may be economic incentives for the town to act in this way. For example, low-income people have less ability to pay taxes but will still require public services, so accommodating them may require an increase in tax burdens for the incumbent residents. But class barriers and racial prejudice are often equally at play.

There are a number of city-wide implications of such practices by local governments. First, since they rely on lot-size restrictions they lock in low-density development and thus accelerate urban sprawl. Also, because they effectively take a larger proportion of the land off the market for low-income households, they result in higher rents. As we explained in chapter 18, low-income households must sacrifice utility in order to compete for a limited supply of land. So when the supply is reduced, they become worse off. Finally, the segregation of income groups within the jurisdictions of different local governments effectively cuts off one of the routes by which wealthy people support the needs of poor people. Education, sanitation services and even some elements of health care are supported in whole or in part by local tax revenues. If low- and high-income people are segregated into different local revenue bases, some government services are likely to be inferior in those local jurisdictions with the highest proportion of poor people. Given that education is one of the principal vehicles for social mobility, inherited class distinctions are reinforced.

Despite the legacy of snob zoning, it is important to recognize that planning departments are often agents of economic and social change. For example, negative perceptions of urban sprawl and high auto dependence have spurred a movement toward planning regulations that promote higher densities and more use of public transport (see Calthorpe and Fulton, 2001). There has also been a move away from restrictive zoning approaches in favor of form-based design codes, which regulate design elements such as building dimensions, street layouts and public space rather than simply uses and lot sizes. Such codes can be used to create areas of mixed land use rather than promoting segregation.

## Public service provision

Local governments are responsible for a number of local services that affect the evolution of land-use patterns in the city. At a very basic level, they are responsible for "servicing" new land, which means providing infrastructure such as trunk lines for water and sewage as well as access roads. So, even in the absence of zoning, local governments can prevent the transformation of rural land on the periphery to residential, commercial or industrial uses by refusing to provide infrastructure. It is frequently the case that local governments are anxious to provide infrastructure because the tax revenue from developed land is much higher than from agricultural land. But, in some cases, incumbent residents may want to preserve a semi-rural environment, even if it means sacrificing tax revenues.

Development charges are fees that the local government requires from developers to offset the cost of providing infrastructure. So, by choosing whether or not to provide infrastructure and by setting development charges at rates lower than or higher than the actual cost of providing it, the local government can accelerate or retard the expansion of the urban frontier.

The quality of public services is also important. In many parts of the world, most notably in the United States, primary and secondary education is a responsibility of local government. With political fragmentation, the quality of schools often varies considerably across jurisdictions. To households with children, the quality of education may be the most important determinant in choosing a residential location. This is reflected in real estate values. A common remark heard from real estate agents in the U.S. is that the room that has the most impact on the price of a house is the school room. The quality of education services is therefore an additional item on the list of factors other than access to the CBD that affect rents.

So far, we have focused on negative aspects of political fragmentation. But there is an alternative view that says fragmentation provides better choice for households and healthy competition among governments. Think of the local government as a firm that provides services (schools, roads, water, sewage, garbage collection) to households at a price (property taxes or other local levies). In a heterogeneous population, different households prefer different combinations of services and tax. For example, households with children may be willing to pay higher taxes to have the best schools, while those without children prefer inferior schools if it means lower taxes. Some households are willing to pay for the convenience of curbside garbage collection, while others are happy to drive their garbage to a transfer station if it means lower taxes. There are also different views with regard to zoning. If a town imposes high minimum lot sizes, it can fit fewer households, so it forgoes tax revenue. Some households may be content paying higher taxes for lower density. Providing plenty of land zoned for commercial uses may attract a shopping mall that will pay a lot of taxes. Those taxes can be used either to improve local services or to cut taxes on households. Still, some households would rather not live in a town with a major mall because it generates traffic.

In a metropolitan area with a dozen or more local governments, a household has a wide range of tax/service/zoning combinations to choose from. It is therefore likely to find a combination that comes close to suiting its preference. This means that the average household will attain higher utility if there is political fragmentation than if there is a single metropolitan-wide government. It also creates a competitive pressure for local governments to spend efficiently and make options that reflect public preferences.[6]

Setting aside the pros and cons of political fragmentation, the argument above provides another way in which local government choices affect the pattern of densities and rents. Two areas at similar distances from the CBD or other centers may have different densities because their local governments have positioned themselves in order to attract households with different preferences for density. Also, since households weigh services against taxes, some towns may give better value for money. Since households will prefer to live in those towns, rents will be driven up. This is an additional mechanism acting on the spatial pattern of urban rents.

# Part V
# Systems of cities

# 20 Urbanization

These four chapters are on systems of cities. In modern economies, most people live in cities of various sizes and with various functions. The cities in which they live are not independent, self-sufficient economic units. Rather, each city contains a labor force and a set of firms that serve a set of specialized functions, and each city has a particular type of relationship with the rural area around it. Most importantly, each city has a set of economic interrelationships with other cities in the economy. These interrelationships give rise to a spatial pattern of cities.

In chapters 18 and 19, we addressed the spatial structure of a single city as defined by its land-use patterns. In the next few chapters, we are interested in defining the economic mechanisms that give rise to the spatial structure of a system of cities. Essentially, we will "zoom out" from the map of a single city to a map of much broader geographical scope, such as a regional, national or global map. At this scale, we cease to view any particular city as an area. Instead, we view each city as a point on the map. But these points are not homogeneous. They are differentiated to distinguish between cities in different size and functional classes. Our goal is to define the spatial patterns of cities in urban systems and to explain the economic mechanisms that give rise to those patterns. Thus, our subject matter is a particular type of differentiated point pattern.

Before we can start to analyze spatial patterns of cities, we need to know something about the process of *urbanization*, whereby the distribution of people shifts from a dispersed rural pattern to a clustered urban pattern. Naturally, this process is never complete. Even the most highly urbanized societies have some rural population. A gross illustration is provided by the data in Table 20.1, which shows the proportion of urban population for the years 1990 and 2005 in groups of countries in different income categories defined by the World Bank. Two things are clear. First, urbanization tends to increase with income and, second, even within income categories it tends to increase over time (although the rate of increase slows down as the proportion approaches a level of about 75 percent).

To understand the process of urbanization, we first need to ask some basic questions. Why are there cities in the first place? What are the functions of cities? What conditions make urbanization possible and what economic trends tend to favor growth in urban population over growth in rural population? How do cities grow and evolve over time? Where are they located? In the remainder of this

*Table 20.1* Percentage of urban population in total
            population of countries in different urban classes

|                     | 1990 | 2005 |
|---------------------|------|------|
| Low income          | 25   | 30   |
| Lower middle income | 38   | 50   |
| Upper middle income | 68   | 72   |
| High income         | 71   | 73   |

*Source*: World Bank (2007: 164).

chapter, we address these questions from a historical perspective. This, by necessity, will be a rather cursory treatment of what is a massive area of research. (See Knox and McCarthy, 2005, for an excellent overview.)

## Genesis of cities

The questions of when, why and where cities first appeared have engendered much academic debate. The practice of keeping historical records did not begin until long after the first cities were established, so we cannot appeal to history books for the answer to these questions. Instead, scholars have had to speculate based on the archeological record. As it is often possible to propose more than one explanation to fit a particular set of facts, competing theories of urban genesis have developed over the past 100 years or so. While we will never know which, if any, of these theories is correct, they all provide useful ideas about the origins and functions of cities.

Most anthropologists agree that human society was originally based on hunting and gathering. Eventually, there was a transition whereby cultivation of crops replaced gathering of plant food and herding activities replaced hunting. From a geographical perspective, this transition, known as the *agricultural revolution*, had two implications. First, it meant that much larger populations could be supported from a given amount of land, so the population could expand within a region. Second, it meant that people became more sedentary. While herding might still involve a good deal of seasonal wandering, cultivation required people to stay put – at least until the soil became exhausted. A dispersed but settled agricultural population is the context within which most theories of urban genesis are set.[1]

In an economy based on subsistence agriculture, each person produces just enough food to feed herself and her dependants. Urbanization implies that some proportion of the population is employed at something other than agriculture, which is not possible under subsistence agriculture because there would not be enough food to support urban residents. So an *agricultural surplus*, which means that the average farm family produces more food than it needs to consume, is an essential precondition for urbanization because the extra food can go to feed the city dwellers. But, even if urbanization is possible, why is it necessary? What will those city dwellers be doing?

Religious theories of urban genesis suggest that the existence of an agricultural surplus made it possible to release some people into a priestly class. These priests made offerings and performed ceremonies to the local gods in order to assure sufficient rainfall and protection from various natural and human threats. Once the priestly class was large enough to build temples, the sites of those temples became the earliest cities.

This explains why archeologists usually find religious buildings in the remains of the earliest cities. But it does not explain why cities emerged in some places and not in others. The earliest known cities were in Mesopotamia (modern Iraq) from about 3500 B.C.E., the Nile Valley (Egypt) from about 3100 B.C.E., the Indus Valley (India and Pakistan) from about 2500 B.C.E. and the plains of the Huang He River (northern China) from about 1800 B.C.E. Much later, but independently, cities also developed along rivers in Mesoamerica (Knox and McCarthy, 2005: 25–7). While the cities of all these regions appear to have served religious functions, they have something else in common: they all emerged in economies based on irrigated agriculture. According to the "hydraulic" theory of urban genesis, this is no coincidence. Irrigation requires the creation of a shared infrastructure of dykes and canals, an administrative bureaucracy to determine the allocation of water among farmers and a central authority to see that no one takes more than they are allocated. The earliest cities were the centers of a nascent public sector that served those functions.

An interesting wrinkle to this story is that the simple sequence from agricultural surplus to urbanization does not really apply. Suppose irrigation creates an increase in yields, making the agricultural surplus possible. So irrigation is necessary for a surplus, a surplus is necessary for urbanization and urbanization is necessary for irrigation. Since everything has to happen more or less simultaneously to make this work, urbanization and the agricultural surplus must be two aspects of the same social and economic transformation.

While irrigation may be the impetus for the earliest cities, the trade theory of urban genesis holds that by the first millennium B.C.E. the main economic function of cities had become trade. Early urban civilizations such as the Phoenicians and the Greeks were traders. While urbanization is not a precondition for small-scale, localized trade, the concentration of buyers and sellers at a common point makes the functioning of markets and the transition from barter to currency much easier. (A fuller discussion is found in chapter 4.) Trade at large scale and over long distances reinforces the usefulness of cities. As with the hydraulic theory, the trade theory of urban genesis sees the emergence of cities as part of a significant step forward in economic development: in this case the transition from regional autarky to specialization and trade (see chapter 8).

As a regional economy becomes richer through the creation of an agricultural surplus and through specialization and trade, there is an increasing incentive for outsiders to attack it and either seize its riches or control it as a vassal state. Even if cities did not exist for other purposes, it would be necessary to establish one or more cities for military purposes. A dispersed population is difficult to defend, so in time of war it makes sense to gather the population together at some fortified point. The existence of an external threat implies the need for a military establish-ment. According to military theories of urban genesis, the earliest cities served as defensive strong points (generally enclosed within walls) and as the permanent centers for the military establishment.

These four theories of urban genesis – religious, hydraulic, trade and military – are by no means mutually exclusive. But they all provide different perspectives on the functions of cities and have different implications for their locations.

## Function and location of cities

The various theories of urban genesis suggest a set of economic functions – ceremonial, administrative, mercantile, military – that have occurred in cities since ancient times. To some extent, the functions are complementary. For example, administrative and ceremonial functions are conveniently served in the same city because people who come to the city to make offerings at the temple may also want to register a birth or petition for a higher water allocation. Local trade is also a complementary function, as the concentration of people in the city makes it the natural place to establish a market.

But not all urban functions are complementary. Imagine a city that is meant to serve both as a center of long-distance trade and as a military strong point. Where should the city be located? As always in such cases, it is useful to think in terms of site and situation attributes. The classic site attribute for a military bastion is high ground where you are always in a superior position to your attackers. The fairy-tale cliché of a medieval castle on a hill reflects this defensive strategy. For the purpose of trade, however, a location by a navigable river or on a safe harbor has the right site attributes. In terms of situation attributes, a trading city would hope to be as accessible to potential markets as possible. But the folks who come to trade with you this year may come to invade you next year, so the military planner would like his city to be as inaccessible as possible. Locations on rivers or by seas, where your attackers can sail up to your doorstep, are to be avoided at all costs.

The relative advantages of trade-oriented and defense-oriented locations are reflected in patterns of urban development on the European continent. Veteran tourists will tell you that the most "unspoiled" cities are found on hilltops and set in rural regions, like Urbino and San Gimignano. But the condition of being unspoiled is often the outcome of arrested development as the spectacular period of trade-driven growth in the nineteenth and twentieth centuries largely passed these inaccessible bastions by.

The inexorable growth of trade at the regional and global scales from the seventeenth century up to the present day led to the emergence of great cities at points where site and situation attributes combine to provide ideal locations for the movement and exchange of goods. Where are such cities located? Recall that, until the middle of the nineteenth century, water transportation was preferred to overland transportation for nearly all forms of trade. Even today, water transportation is generally the cheapest option for long-distance shipments (see chapter 2). So a number of great trading centers are located at places where inland waterways (rivers and canals) meet up with the ocean, especially if the local terrain and coastline provide a good natural harbor. An example is Rotterdam, where the Rhine

River, Europe's great inland transportation artery, reaches the North Sea. Two great Chinese trading cities, Hong Kong and Shanghai, are located near the mouths of the Xi and Yangzi rivers (respectively). New York provides an excellent harbor where the Hudson River reaches the Atlantic. Three very important terms in the geographer's lexicon apply to these cities. First, each of these cities is an *entrepôt*, a point of entry from the ocean to the interior. They are all adjacent to a river that penetrates deep into the continental interior, establishing a *hinterland*, a German word that means "land behind." Because goods are moved from ocean-going ships to smaller inland vessels or barges at these cities, they are *trans-shipment points*.

Favorable locations for trading cities do not rely exclusively on natural features; transportation infrastructure can also play a role. For example, up until the nineteenth century, the hinterland of New York was limited to the Hudson River Valley. After the Erie Canal was built in 1825, connecting the Hudson with Lake Erie, it was possible to move goods by water all the way from northern Minnesota to the Port of New York. Because the Erie Canal massively expanded its hinterland, New York leapt ahead of the other East Coast ports of Boston and Philadelphia. Chicago became the American interior's trading hub in the nineteenth century and remains so today not because of the presence of any river but because a number of railroads serving vast agricultural regions came together there.

The fact that New York is still one of the largest ocean ports in the United States illustrates another important geographical concept: *locational inertia*. Except for a few preserved sections, the old Erie Canal is long gone and its replacement, known as the Barge Canal, is almost exclusively used by recreational boats. The all-water connection from New York to Lake Superior no longer functions. Yet the port of New York (most of which is actually located in New Jersey) is busier than ever – why? The answer is that, once a city is established as a dominant center of trade, inertia tends to preserve its dominance even after its initial advantages disappear. Water transportation was replaced by rail and truck transportation as a means of moving goods to and from the interior, although a few containers are barged up the Hudson to satellite distribution facilities.

The Industrial Revolution of the eighteenth and nineteenth centuries brought a new urban function to the fore: manufacturing. Before that time, the product of a national economy came mostly from agriculture, with contributions from mining, forestry and fishing – all of which are inherently non-urban activities. Manufacturing was relatively small scale and its output was of lesser value. The Industrial Revolution changed this picture in two ways. First, new technologies made the manufacture of familiar goods much cheaper and introduced a broad range of new manufactured goods, leading to an ever increasing share for manufacturing in national product. Second, the shift from traditional small-scale manufacturing to the factory system (remember Adam Smith's pin factory from chapter 3?) led to a spatial concentration of manufacturing into large facilities. The result was the emergence of the industrial cities, which would be the great centers of economic and population growth in Europe and North America until well into the twentieth century. These cities were not primarily centers of trade, ceremony, administration or defense. Rather, they were centers of production.

This new type of city called for new site and situation attributes. The site attributes of trading cities (harbors, rivers) were also needed for industrial cities, but the need to power manufacturing machinery using falling water became a critical attribute as well. (This explains why factories are still often called "mills.") Although water power was displaced by steam power in the second half of the nineteenth century, the influence of water power can still be seen on the industrial landscape as industrial cities such as Lowell, Massachusetts and Manchester, England, whose early development depended on fast-flowing water to power textile mills. As for situation attributes, accessibility of industrial inputs and markets for industrial outputs were key factors. Thus, the principles of Weberian location theory (chapters 13, 14 and 15) apply to the location of industrial cities as well as to individual production facilities.

As technological advances made the large-scale production of low-cost iron and steel possible, steel became the basic material of the industrial economy. As we saw in chapter 13, steel is a weight-losing and therefore materials-oriented industry. The location of steel production depends on access to two key inputs: iron ore and coal. Cities where these two inputs can be assembled easily, either because they are available locally or can be transported by water, became the new centers of economic growth. Pittsburgh, Pennsylvania and the cities of Germany's Ruhr region are examples.

While there are still lots of industrial cities, the largest cities of the twenty-first century are not manufacturing centers. Rather, cities like New York, Toronto, London, Paris and Tokyo are centers of higher-order services such as financial markets, design, research and range of consulting activities. (We will explain the meaning of "higher order" more clearly in chapter 22, but, for now, they are services that concentrate in the biggest cities.) They are also administrative centers, with concentrations of corporate headquarters and services such as corporate law that facilitate dealings among them.

You may have noticed that we used the example of New York as both an *entrepôt* city and a higher-order service center. In fact, New York over the course of its development has also been a major manufacturing city. Thus, the different city functions are not mutually exclusive and in many cases are complementary. For example, New York's function as a trade center meant that a variety of materials could be assembled there for use in the manufacture of many different goods. Also, the presence of the port made New York attractive to commodity traders and bankers, who also contributed to its emergence as one of the world's great financial centers. In the long run, however, some functions may be squeezed out by others. For example, competition from services ultimately drove up land values and wages, making New York an expensive place for manufacturing and eventually leading to its decline as an industrial center.

## The emergence of urban patterns

So far, we have considered the origin and growth of individual cities. We can conclude that, since cities serve different functions and have different histories, we might expect to see cities of different sizes scattered across the map. Since all cities must start out small, the presence of cities in different size categories raises the question of why some cities grow more than others.

Given the complexities and historical accidents that affect urban growth, it is perhaps unrealistic to devise a mathematical or graphical model to explain why some cities grow and others do not. But urban economic historians have proposed a number of *stage models*. The idea is that each city has its own peculiar history, but most cities that reach a particular size pass through a number of similar stages in getting there. Those cities that never progress beyond a certain stage do not grow as large as those that do. While this is a rather informal type of modeling, it can yield some insights both about the history of growth and about the functions of big cities *vs.* small cities.

First consider an "old world" stage model of urban growth,[2] so called because it applies best to Europe. The overwhelming majority of the cities in modern Europe were established as urban places by the late middle ages and at that time only a handful had reached any significant size. With the age of gunpowder, the function of cities as military strong points was somewhat diminished and the Industrial Revolution had not yet urbanized manufacturing, so the most important urban function was agricultural trade. Thus, it is somewhat reasonable to think of all cities as having the same starting point, as described in stage 1:

- *Stage 1: Independent market towns.* Each town essentially serves the function of the market town in the von Thünen model. Farmers bring their goods there for sale as do any small-scale manufacturers, such as brewers, located in the region. A few luxury goods or more sophisticated agricultural equipment are imported to the town and offered for sale.
- *Stage 2: Centers of interregional and international trade.* With the development of better transportation technologies, opportunities for trade over longer distances emerge. Commodities such as wheat, wool, cheese and flax that are produced in the agricultural hinterland are now carried by specialized traders to foreign lands and exchanged for goods that are not produced locally: perhaps spices, ceramics, fertilizers or exotic food crops. All of this trading will be carried on in a few towns that will grow larger with the introduction of more extensive trade activities. Locations at harbors or along navigable rivers will be especially advantageous for such towns.

At this point, let's pause to see what this implies for the pattern of cities. All towns start out in stage 1, serving an agricultural hinterland. Since each town needs its own hinterland, it cannot be too close to another town. Thus, in a world of only stage 1 towns, the urban pattern must be dispersed. Some, but not all, of the dispersed towns will advance to stage 2. The reason that not all towns will make the transition is that interregional and international trading activities require a greater scale of activities in order to be economically viable than do local trading activities. The outcome is that there will be a large number of small (stage 1) towns and a smaller number of large (stage 2) towns in the agricultural landscape. Thus, we have the beginnings of an *urban hierarchy*.

- *Stage 3: Manufacturing based on local or trade materials or energy resources.*
  Up to now we have described a world where everyone is either a farmer or a
  trader. Manufacturing emerges as an urban activity with the introduction of
  the factory system. Local resources such as wool and flax for textiles and
  apparel, coal and ore for metals or wood for machinery and furniture may be
  used. Alternatively, manufacturers may use goods that come in trade, such as
  cotton for textile mills. Local energy sources – particularly water power before
  the steam engine and coal thereafter – also provide a locational advantage for
  some places.

Again, only a few towns will make the transition to stage 3 because of the scale
economies inherent in the factory system. Those that had previously made the
transition from stage 1 to stage 2 are much more likely to move on to stage 3 for
a couple of reasons. First, manufacturing is often founded on imported inputs that
are available in trading centers. Second, large-scale manufacturing is never based
solely on local demand, so the capacity to export to broader markets is essential.
There may be circumstances where a stage 1 town becomes a stage 3 town because
of a local mineral deposit or an ideal water power site. In order to support manufacturing, however, the town would also need to develop a capacity in interregional
and international trade, so in making the jump from stage 1 to stage 3 it would also
develop the capacities of a stage 2 town. The result is a somewhat more complicated
urban hierarchy comprising a large number of small stage 1 towns, a smaller number
of larger stage 2 towns and an even smaller number of even larger stage 3 towns.

- *Stage 4: Emergence of dominant center(s).* Eventually, one or a small number
  of cities will emerge within a nation state as a center or centers of economic
  administration and control. The dominant center will be the focus of transportation network, the home of major banks and financial markets and the
  location of the headquarters of most of the largest firms. "Dominance" is
  defined here from an economic perspective – the economic and political centers
  may or may not coincide.

This old world stage model may not apply precisely to any of the national urban
systems in Europe. For one thing, it is focused on economic processes and ignores
the more political processes that have affected the observed patterns. But it provides
some insight into how a hierarchy of urban places evolves out of a dispersed pattern
of relatively small market towns. It is far less useful, however, in explaining the
process of urban development in North America. Unlike their counterparts in Meso-
America, the indigenous people of North America did not develop many permanent
cities. Thus, European colonists developed their urban system on a more or less
blank slate. Relatively few modern cities emerged from local agricultural market
towns. Most colonists in North America were not involved in agriculture for local
consumption, but rather in the production of staple commodities for export back
to Europe or on to other colonies. Thus, urban history evolved according to a
different set of stages:[3]

- *Stage 1: Centers for export of staple commodities*. Most European settlements were economically dependent on the export of commodities that could be sold into European markets. These include furs, salt fish, timber, tobacco, grain and cotton. The original function of cities and towns was to manage the production and export of these commodities.

The important point to notice here is that the independent agricultural market town never comes into the picture. For ease of export, nearly all cities were located where commodities could be transferred to water transportation: Montreal, New York and New Orleans all developed at the mouths of rivers leading to an interior with some valuable export commodity. Port cities such as Boston and Halifax were centers for the consolidation of goods moved by coastal shipping, such as salt fish and timber.

- *Stage 2: Diversification of the urban economy based on local demand*. As the export economy grew, incomes rose in the urban regions, leading to increased demand for a variety of goods and services. Initially, all but basic foodstuffs were imported from Europe, but eventually local industries developed to serve local demand.

Here we see that the order of economic development is reversed from the old world model. Instead of starting with production for local demand, cities are initially driven by export demand. Only after they are established does local demand become a major driver of growth. In some cases, it was not just consumer demand but the demands of the trade activities that produced growth. For example, the heavy reliance of the economies of New England and the Maritime region of Canada on shipping and fishing led to indigenous industries such as rope making and eventually ship building.

- *Stage 3: Manufacturing centers based around export commodities*. Eventually, instead of exporting goods as raw materials, manufacturing industries that use those goods as exports emerge. The process of adding value to the export commodity further increases income and employment levels.
- *Stage 4: Emergence of dominant centers*. This stage is much the same as in the "old world" stage model. A few cities become the centers of administration and the highest level markets.

Unlike in the old world model, where it is assumed that a city must pass through each stage of development before it can reach the next one, history has shown that some cities skipped stage 3. Manufacturing based around the export economy may be as elaborate as the fur clothing industry that developed in Montreal or as elementary as the sawmill industries that developed around all cities that exported timber. (In the latter case, manufacturing was principally based on the Weberian argument that weight-losing processes should be done close to the source to conserve on transportation costs.) Some cities never developed manufacturing industries based on export staples. For example, New Orleans became one of the great port cities of the world by exporting cotton, but never developed a major textile industry of its own.

Stage models are imprecise and contestable. The two models presented above are actually generalizations of more specific models introduced by various authors. Some would dispute their accuracy and others would question the underlying proposition that most cities go through similar stages of development. Despite these controversies, stage models are useful as ways to think about an empirical regularity that applies to almost all urbanized societies: the existence of an urban hierarchy. In the next chapter, we will begin to model urban hierarchies more formally.

## Primate cities

In some countries, a single city grows to be so large and influential that it dominates all others. The term *primate city*, first coined by geographer Mark Jefferson (1939), refers to a situation where the population of the largest city in a country is at least twice that of the second largest. According to Jefferson, such a city is typically more than twice as influential in political and economic matters as any other. The classic examples of primate cities are London, which has almost seven times the metropolitan population of second-place Birmingham, and Paris, with a metropolitan population of almost seven times those of Lyon and Marseille.[4] Other examples include Dublin, Vienna, Mexico City (see Box 20), Tokyo and Bangkok. Some of these cities fall into the category of *global cities*, which means that they serve important functions in the global economy, rather than just in their national economies. For example, London is a center of global finance. But the two terms are not synonymous; New York is surely a global city but it is not a primate city. Also, there are a number of poor countries with primate cities that have relatively poor international institutions. Examples include Kigali in Rwanda, Phnom Penh in Cambodia and Managua in Nicaragua.

---

### *Box 20* Mexico City: the classic primate

The Mexico City metropolitan area, which includes the core Federal District but also spills over to include over 40 municipalities in its periphery, has a population of over 21 million (almost 20 percent of the Mexican population), making it the largest urban agglomeration in the Western Hemisphere. It is almost four times as large as metropolitan Guadalajara, which holds the second place in Mexico's city size distribution. It is the classic example of a primate city. But how do we explain its dominance?

One thing is clear: the explanation does not lie in favorable site attributes. In fact, one might argue that it is in an extremely unfavorable spot. Mexico City sprawls over a valley at a very high elevation of 2,200 meters (for comparison, the "mile high" city of Denver, Colorado is at only about 1,600 meters). The mountains that surround it reach 5,000 meters. This has greatly increased the costs of the railroads and highways that serve it. Much of the city is built on landfill over the remnants of an old lake bed making it prone to flooding. Massive infrastructure is needed to drain storm water from the city. Yet there is a shortage of potable water, so that, while storm water flows down the mountain, fresh water must be pumped up. It lies in a seismically active zone. The combination of frequent earthquakes and construction on unstable landfill creates a dangerous situation, as the destruction wrought by the great 1985 earthquake demonstrated. Finally, its high valley location, coupled with its many industries and choking traffic congestion, have combined to distinguish it as the major world city with the worst air quality.

So why is there a megacity in such an unfavorable place? The answer lies deep in the pre-Columbian history of Middle America. By the time the first Europeans arrived, the Aztec Empire had already established itself as the most potent political and military force in what is now central Mexico. Its administrative and ceremonial center was at Tenochtitlan, on an island in the center of Lake Texcoco. The ruins of this city can still be seen at the very center of Mexico City. When the Aztecs were conquered by Cortes in 1521, the Spanish established their administrative center at Tenochtitlan. This made sense because the people controlled by the Aztec Empire, stretching from the Atlantic to Pacific oceans, would recognize those who conquered and controlled Tonochtitlan as their new overlords. Over the nearly three centuries of highly centralized Spanish administration that followed, the dominance of Mexico City increased. As the location of a ruling class that grew wealthy in the colonial period, it became the site of great churches, lavish homes and magnificent public buildings. Its dominance continued to increase through the post-independence period (after 1821) and throughout the political volatility of the nineteenth and early twentieth centuries. As Mexico industrialized, Mexico City became the largest industrial center. It is also the center of one of the most important financial sectors in Latin America.

Mexico City is an object lesson for economic geographers. It demonstrates that we cannot necessarily explain the spatial pattern of human activity strictly in terms of contemporary economic forces. The pattern of cities in particular is strongly affected by inertia – which means that once one or a few cities become very large the urban pattern changes only slowly. In part, this is because political and other institutional forces tend to defend the dominance of well-established places. But it is also the outcome of agglomeration economies. Once a city reaches a large enough size, agglomeration economies give it an advantage over smaller places, even if they have more favorable locations.

> Today, Mexico City is so congested and polluted that the Mexican government has taken some steps to discourage its further growth. For example, the *maquiladora* plants mentioned in chapter 15, which require government sanction to import components for assembly without duty, may not be established in Mexico City.

Why do some countries produce primate cities while others do not? We can usefully address the question by looking at some countries that do not have primate cities. Unlike France and England, Germany does not have a long history of political unity, so it did not develop a single dominant city (Hamburg has more than one half the population of Berlin). In general, countries with very strong central governments, such as France, the United Kingdom and many Latin American countries, have primate cities, while federal states where regional governments have substantial authority, such as Canada, the United States, India and Germany, do not. Sometimes, the absence of a primate city reflects the presence of geographically defined ethnic or religious differences. In Ukraine, for example, Kiev, with its population of 2.8 million dominated by ethnic Ukrainians, is balanced somewhat by the western cities of Karkhiv (1.4 million) and Dontsk (1 million), which have a significant Russian population. The existence of two large cities in the relatively small country of Ghana – Accra with 4 million population and Kumasi with 2.6 million – owes much to historical ethnic differences.

You are less likely to find a primate city in a very large country and more likely to find one in a compact country. For example, Canada has no primate city. But, if the movement to establish Quebec as a separate country had been successful, Montreal would easily qualify as its primate city. If the U.S. west of the Mississippi were an independent country, Los Angeles would be its primate city. The New York metropolitan area has almost 20 times the population of metropolitan Dublin, but Dublin is a primate city and New York is not. The point is that a city's "primacy" is not a measure of its independent status, but rather of its role in a national urban system. The distribution of city sizes within national systems will be a major topic of the next chapter.

# 21 City size distribution and urban hierarchies

In this chapter, we start to look at the structure of urban systems. An urban system is defined as a set of interrelated cities located within some defined region. For the most part, we will consider urban systems located within countries. For example, we can examine the U.S. urban system and compare it to the French urban system. But, given the high degree of economic integration among Canada, the U.S. and Mexico, it might be equally useful to look at the North American urban system. On the other hand, for a more detailed analysis we may want to focus in on the Californian urban system.

For the moment, we will not worry about the spatial distribution of cities in the urban system. (That will be the topic of chapter 22.) Instead, we will consider the *city size distribution*. The stage models of the last chapter indicate that as the urban system evolves some cities grow more quickly than others. Naturally, that means that at any point in time there will be cities of different sizes in the system. (For the purpose of this discussion, "size" refers to population, although it could also refer to total income, employment, value added, etc.)

To illustrate this, suppose there is a country with ten cities and a total urban population of 10 million. The city size distribution tells us how those 10 million people are distributed across the ten cities. Figure 21.1 shows three hypothetical distributions, labeled uniform, primate and intermediate. By the uniform distribution, all ten cities have the same population: 1 million. From the perspective of our stage model, this would seem an unlikely distribution since it implies that no city developed a national or global prominence. In contrast, the primate distribution has the vast majority of people (80 percent in our hypothetical example) in one city, while all the other cities are very small. By the intermediate distribution, there is a ratio of 19 to 1 between the population of the largest city (1,900,000) and the population of the smallest city (100,000) with a steady decline in population among the cities in between.

The hypothetical example suggests two questions. The first is: how are city sizes distributed in the real world? The second is: why should we care – what do we learn from studying city size distributions? The first question will be the subject of the next section, but the second deserves some sort of answer at the outset.

For one thing, a highly concentrated distribution such as the primate distribution in our example is consistent with a polarized economy as described in chapter 10.

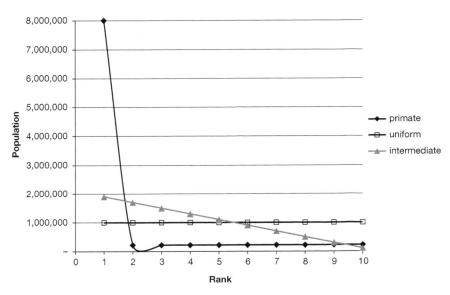

*Figure 21.1* Three hypothetical city size distributions

Observing such a distribution, one would suspect that the levels of affluence and economic opportunity were much greater in the largest city (although one would have to gather further data in order to confirm this). There is recent evidence (discussed below) that highly concentrated distributions are typical of authoritarian governments that concentrate all administrative functions in a single city. At the other extreme, a uniform distribution might suggest that no city has become large enough to develop infrastructure and institutions for international trade and economic innovation, which may bode ill for the country in the global economy. This is not to say, however, that there is an "ideal" city size distribution. There are both rich and poor countries with highly concentrated distributions.

Another reason for studying city size distributions is that they provide evidence for the existence of an urban hierarchy, which is a fundamental concept in models of the spatial distribution of cities that will be presented in chapter 22. While we tend to define the urban hierarchy simply in terms of population size, it is important to realize that there are differences in function and other qualitative differences between cities at different levels of the hierarchy. For example, recent research indicated that there are significant differences in human capital at different levels of the U.S. urban hierarchy (see Box 21).

## *Box 21*  Human capital and the U.S. urban hierarchy

As economic geographers, we are interested in patterns of economic activities and relations that are differentiated over space. The concept of an urban hierarchy is of limited utility if it is just about population size. The interesting question is whether cities at different levels in the hierarchy have different economic characteristics and play different roles in the spatial economy.

A recent study by Scott and Mantegna (2009) addresses this question by examining how human capital varies at different levels in the U.S. urban hierarchy. Recall from chapter 7 that human capital refers to the skills and capabilities that are embodied in the labor force. The term "capital" is appropriate here because human capital is a stock variable that is built up through time by investments of education, training and on-the-job experience.

Any serious economic geographer knows that human capital is one of the most important factors in determining the growth and prosperity of a region. The problem is that it is hard to measure, so it tends to be neglected in quantitative studies. Scott and Mantegna find a way to generate indicators of human capital based on two databases that are available from the U.S. government. The first of these breaks the labor force in each of 283 metropolitan areas into 471 occupations. The second rates each occupation on a large number of human capital and work characteristics.[i] For example, the occupation "computer programmer" would have a high rating on a characteristic called "analytical skills" and a low rating on "body strength and stamina," while the occupation "roofer" would have the opposite rating profile. Using the occupational shares as weights, the authors generate a rating for each of 26 human capital and work characteristics in each of the metropolitan areas.

The metropolitan areas are divided into a crude three-level hierarchy: level 1 contains 49 cities of more than 1 million population; level 2 contains 109 cities of between 250,000 and 1 million population; and level 3 contains 125 cities of less than 250,000 population. An average rating was calculated for each level on each of the 26 human capital and work characteristics. Table B21.1 provides a very rough summary of the results by identifying those characteristics for which ratings were highest for the top level of the hierarchy and lowest for the bottom level, and those for which ratings were highest for the bottom level and lowest for the top. Those characteristics in the data that did not show a clear pattern of change over the hierarchy are not listed.

The results clearly show that workers in cities at the top of the hierarchy are in occupations requiring analytical, managerial and relational skills, while workers in cities at the bottom of the hierarchy are in occupations requiring physical and manual skills. This is not to say that the human capital of people at the bottom of the hierarchy is clearly inferior – for example, they are stronger in aural and visual skills. But this dichotomy in human capital and work characteristics puts workers in the largest cities in a better position to succeed in the emerging information economy, which we will examine in chapter 26.

*Table B21.1*  Ratings of human capital characteristics at different levels of the urban hierarchy

| Characteristics rated highest for Level 1 and lowest for Level 3 | Self motivation vs. direction from others<br>Communication and information knowledge<br>Job stability and security<br>Business vs. practical interest<br>Analytical and independent work styles<br>Information processing<br>Cognitive vs. physical ability<br>Relational skills |
|---|---|
| Characteristics rated highest for Level 3 and lowest for Level 1 | Aural and visual activity<br>Physically hazardous work<br>Practical skills<br>Equipment and materials handling<br>Physical vs. mental work contexts<br>Body strength and stamina |

## Note

i  The occupational data for metropolitan areas was obtained from the Integrated Public Use Microdata Series (IPUMS) from the U.S. Bureau of the Census. The occupational characteristics data are from the U.S. Department of Labor's O\*NET database, which may be accessed at online.onetcenter.org. The latter provides ratings for each occupation on 261 dimensions. The authors reduced this to 26 characteristics using factor analysis.

## Zipf's law and the rank–size rule

Quantitative analysis of city size commenced with the work of George K. Zipf (1949), who proposed a simple relationship that does a surprisingly good job approximating city sizes in many urban systems. His method starts by sorting all the cities in the system by population from largest to smallest. Each city is assigned a rank $r$ such that $r = 1$ for the largest city, $r = 2$ for the second largest city and so on. An expression which has come to be known as *Zipf's law* is used to predict the population of any city in the system based on its rank and the population of the largest city:

$$P_r = \frac{P_1}{r}$$

where $P$ stands for population. By this rule the population of the second largest city $P_2$ is one half that of the largest $P_1$, so the largest city just barely meets the definition of a primate city. The population of the third largest city is one third that of the largest city, the population of the fourth largest is one fourth, etc. If Zipf's law holds exactly, you only need to know the population of the largest city to know the population of any other city of a given rank.

A couple of words of caution are needed here. First, the term "law" as it is used in this context is unfortunate. In the natural sciences, a law is a relationship that holds in all places and at all times. As we will see, Zipf's law doesn't even come close to meeting this criterion. But "Zipf's law" sounds more scientific than "Zipf's approximation" so the name stuck. Second, this relationship is best seen as a useful empirical regularity, rather than as a model because it *describes* the city size distribution but does not *explain* it. Knowing that city size follows a particular distribution is not the same thing as knowing why it follows that distribution.[1]

We can get a better understanding of Zipf's law by applying it to some real city size data. Table 21.1 lists the 2009 populations and ranks for the 30 largest metropolitan areas in the United States. Just looking at the first two entries, we see that the largest city (New York) is only about 1.5 times as large as the second largest city (Los Angeles), rather than twice as large as Zipf's law would predict. The size distribution for all 30 cities that would be predicted by Zipf's law, along with the observed distribution, is shown in Figure 21.2. Clearly, the actual distribution of city sizes in the U.S. is not as strongly polarized as Zipf's law would predict.

The fact that fit is not good does not necessarily mean that the rank–size relationship is not useful. We can generalize Zipf's law by adding a parameter to control the rate at which population declines with rank:

$$P_r = \frac{P_1}{r^\alpha}$$

This expression is called the *rank–size rule.* It is the same as Zipf's law if the parameter $\alpha = 1$. However, if $\alpha < 1$, the population will decline more slowly and the distribution will be less concentrated than Zipf's law would predict. If $\alpha > 1$, the distribution will be even more concentrated than under Zipf's law.

Figure 21.2 shows a third distribution that was generated using the rank–size rule by assuming that $\alpha = .65$. While the populations of a few cities are under-predicted or over-predicted, the under-predictions and over-predictions roughly cancel each other out. The correlation between the observed and estimated populations is greater than .99 and the sum of the predicted populations is within 1 percent of the observed sum. Thus, the rank–size rule does a remarkably good job of reproducing the city size distribution for the U.S. urban system. (You can easily reproduce these findings using a spreadsheet.)

Over the years, there have been many empirical tests of the rank–size relationship using rigorous statistical methods. (For a recent study, see Soo, 2005.) In general, they have found that it fits the data for the urban systems of most countries remarkably well, and that for many countries the special case of Zipf's law ($\alpha = 1$) is a good approximation.

Why does the rank–size relationship work so well? This is a question that still triggers debate 60 years after Zipf's work. In broad terms, the rank–size rule predicts

*Table 21.1* Populations of top 30 U.S. Metropolitan Statistical Areas 2009

| Metropolitan Statistical Areas | Rank | Population |
| --- | --- | --- |
| New York–Northern New Jersey–Long Island, NY–NJ–PA | 1 | 19,069,796 |
| Los Angeles–Long Beach–Santa Ana, CA | 2 | 12,874,797 |
| Chicago–Naperville–Joliet, IL–IN–WI | 3 | 9,580,567 |
| Dallas–Fort Worth–Arlington, TX | 4 | 6,447,615 |
| Philadelphia–Camden–Wilmington, PA–NJ–DE–MD | 5 | 5,968,252 |
| Houston–Sugar Land–Baytown, TX | 6 | 5,867,489 |
| Miami–Fort Lauderdale–Pompano Beach, FL | 7 | 5,547,051 |
| Washington–Arlington–Alexandria, DC–VA–MD–WV | 8 | 5,476,241 |
| Atlanta–Sandy Springs–Marietta, GA | 9 | 5,475,213 |
| Boston–Cambridge–Quincy, MA–NH | 10 | 4,588,680 |
| Detroit–Warren–Livonia, MI | 11 | 4,403,437 |
| Phoenix–Mesa–Scottsdale, AZ | 12 | 4,364,094 |
| San Francisco–Oakland–Fremont, CA | 13 | 4,317,853 |
| Riverside–San Bernardino–Ontario, CA | 14 | 4,143,113 |
| Seattle–Tacoma–Bellevue, WA | 15 | 3,407,848 |
| Minneapolis–St. Paul–Bloomington, MN–WI | 16 | 3,269,814 |
| San Diego–Carlsbad–San Marcos, CA | 17 | 3,053,793 |
| St. Louis, MO–IL | 18 | 2,828,990 |
| Tampa–St. Petersburg–Clearwater, FL | 19 | 2,747,272 |
| Baltimore–Towson, MD | 20 | 2,690,886 |
| Denver–Aurora–Broomfield, CO/1 | 21 | 2,552,195 |
| Pittsburgh, PA | 22 | 2,354,957 |
| Portland–Vancouver–Beaverton, OR–WA | 23 | 2,241,841 |
| Cincinnati–Middletown, OH–KY–IN | 24 | 2,171,896 |
| Sacramento–Arden–Arcade–Roseville, CA | 25 | 2,127,355 |
| Cleveland–Elyria–Mentor, OH | 26 | 2,091,286 |
| Orlando–Kissimmee, FL | 27 | 2,082,421 |
| San Antonio, TX | 28 | 2,072,128 |
| Kansas City, MO–KS | 29 | 2,067,585 |
| Las Vegas–Paradise, NV | 30 | 1,902,834 |

*Source*: U.S. Census Bureau (2009).

a distribution that is highly, but not completely polarized. This suggests that agglomeration forces are strong enough to attract a very large proportion of economic activity to the largest city, but not all of it. One factor that may come into play is congestion.[2] Suppose every household and every firm in a country perceives that it would be better off if it were to move to the largest city. Eventually, this influx would cause roads and other facilities to become so congested that the second and third largest cities would become more desirable destinations. As these cities become congested, the remnant population finds they are better off in much smaller places. The resulting distribution would resemble the rank–size rule.

Why are there differences across countries in the degree of polarization, as indicated by the value of $\alpha$? It could just be a matter of geographic scale – countries like the U.S., Australia and Canada are too big to be served by a single dominant center. Recent empirical analysis suggests that political factors are more effective for explaining variation in the level of polarization than economic factors (see Soo,

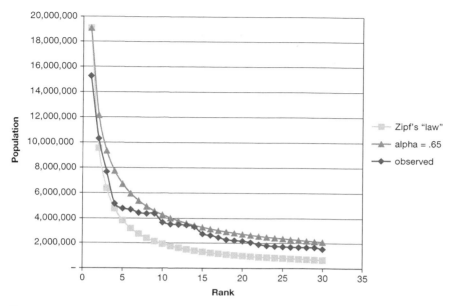

*Figure 21.2* Rank–size relationship for U.S. cities

2005: part 5). Dictatorial governments tend to concentrate administrative function and nationalized industries in the capital, where they are more easily controlled.

## Rank–size and the urban hierarchy

Another possible explanation for the ability of the rank–size rule to fit city size distributions is that it provides an approximation to what is really a hierarchical system of cities. Hierarchies exist in a lot of different systems. For example, the administration and faculty of a university forms a hierarchy of people with different functions and responsibilities. At the top is the president, at the next level down are deans, next are department heads and finally the base of the hierarchy is made up of professors. A characteristic of nearly all hierarchies is that, as you move from the top down, the number of elements (or in this case people) increases. Suppose the university has three faculties (natural science, social science and engineering), each faculty has three departments (for example, within natural science are physics, chemistry and biology) and each department has five faculty members. This means there is one president, three deans, nine department chairs and 45 professors.

In a hierarchical urban system, there would not be a smooth decline in the populations of cities with decreasing ranks. Instead, there would be clusters of cities in similar-size groups, or with the number of cities in each group getting bigger as the populations get smaller. This is not exactly consistent with the rank–size rule, but a rank–size distribution may provide a good approximation of a distribution that is actually hierarchical. Look again at Figure 21.2. As we already noted, the observed city sizes are very highly correlated with those predicted by the rank–size rule where $\alpha = .65$. If you look at the cities for which the fit is not good, you see that they are members of groups of cities with populations within relatively narrow bands: one just above and below 6 million and one just above 4 million. We can think of each of these groups as representing a level in the urban hierarchy. Also, the last dozen or so cities, which have populations within a fairly narrow band, may constitute a lower level of the hierarchy.

The U.S. urban population data are not completely consistent with the idea of an urban hierarchy because the number of cities in the 6 million range is one larger than the number of cities in the 4 million range. (In a hierarchy the number of elements should always be higher at lower levels.) But they provide some evidence of hierarchical structure in the urban system. Despite this hierarchical structure, the rank–size rule still predicts the city size distribution very well.

To build on this last point, Figure 21.3 shows a hypothetical distribution of city sizes arranged in a precise hierarchical structure. The largest city has a population of 1 million and there are five levels in the hierarchy, each of which has twice as many cities as the level above it. Thus, there are two cities in level 2, 4 in level 3, 8 in level 4 and 16 in level 5. Within each level all cities have exactly the same population. A distribution generated by the rank–size rule ($\alpha = .65$) is also shown, and it clearly provides a good approximation of the hierarchical distribution. In fact, the correlation between the city sizes in the hierarchical distribution and in the rank–size rule distribution is .98. Thus, one possible explanation for why the rank–size rule fits the data for city size distributions is that those distributions reflect underlying hierarchical structure. This is an important observation because, as we will see in the next chapter, models that seek to explain the spatial structure of urban systems make extensive use of the concept of urban hierarchy.

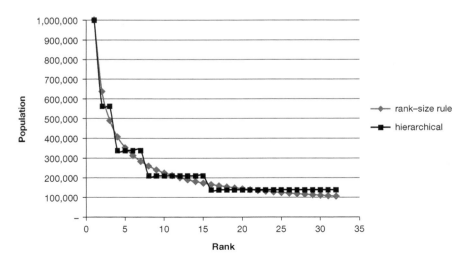

*Figure 21.3* Hierarchical and rank–size rule distributions

# Types of urban hierarchies

A natural question at this point is why we would expect to see the kind of hierarchical rank–size distribution shown in Figure 21.3. There is actually a variety of reasons why such a hierarchy might emerge. We will briefly describe three here: the transportation hierarchy, the administrative hierarchy and the service hierarchy.

- *Transportation hierarchy:* Cities often serve as nodes on transportation networks. Imagine a large area over which grain is grown for export to international markets. A fairly large number of towns might be established where, among other things, truck depots are located. The trucks are dispatched to pick up loads of grain from individual farmers. The grain is trucked to a smaller number of centers located along rail lines where grain is stored for eventual collection by trains. Ultimately, all grain is moved by train to a major port city from which it is exported. In this case the towns with the truck depots are the lowest level of the hierarchy, the rail centers where grain is stored and shipped are the next highest level and the port city is the highest level.
- *Administrative hierarchy:* Cities are also centers of public administration. A country may have a single capital where the organs of governance (legislature or parliament), the highest courts and the headquarters of various government agencies are located. There may also be a number of major regional administrative centers with regional courts and branches of government agencies. There may be an even lower level on the hierarchy with outposts for public safety and health services.
- *Service hierarchy:* Perhaps the most general way to think about cities is as locations where goods and services are provided. There are some services that can be supported by relatively small populations, so they will be located even at towns at the smallest level on the hierarchy. Gas stations and small markets are examples of such services. At the other end of the spectrum are services such as stock markets and operas that require a national market, so they are only located in cities of the highest level of the hierarchy. Intermediate levels of the hierarchy are defined by the range of services they supply.

In reality, observed city size distributions reflect the overlapping effect of all three types of hierarchies, as well as a variety of other complicating factors. But in order to develop coherent models it is necessary to look at the underlying mechanisms of the three types separately. In the next chapter, we will introduce a model that defines a spatial hierarchy according to the provision of services. That model will then be altered to incorporate transportation and administrative hierarchies.

# 22  Central place theory

In the last chapter, we saw evidence of hierarchical structure in city size distributions. As geographers, we are not much satisfied with size distributions; our main interest is in spatial distributions. We will see, however, that the idea of a hierarchical size distribution is a useful point of departure in developing models of the spatial distribution of cities.

The topic of this chapter is *central place theory*, which is a framework for explaining a spatial-hierarchical ordering of cities. This is one of the "classic" topics of research in economic geography, but in recent years it has fallen somewhat out of fashion. In fact, many recent texts don't even cover it, or if they do they focus on its outcomes – especially the peculiar hexagonal pattern of urban market areas that it predicts – rather than its underlying mechanisms. The main reason that central place theory has become *passé* is that its predicted patterns don't fit the urban systems of the twenty-first century very well. But it still yields some powerful insights when its underlying logic is understood.

As in the case of location "theory," central place "theory" would be more accurately defined as the central place model. (However, we will stick with convention and use the term "theory," albeit loosely.) Recall that models are simplified representations of reality that are constructed to explore and illustrate mechanisms that give rise to observed patterns. Models cannot reproduce the real world precisely, but they provide possible explanations as to what underlies the things we see in reality. The spatial patterns of urban systems are driven by an array of different and sometimes contradictory mechanisms. The most we can hope to get from any model is a better understanding of some of the most important of those mechanisms. Judged by that standard, central place theory still provides one of the most powerful models in economic geography.

Perhaps the most important thing to understand about central place theory is that it is meant to explain the spatial pattern of a particular class of cities known as central places. Roughly speaking, traditional classifications of cities define three functional types: transportation cities, production cities and central places. (In later chapters, we will propose some new types, including global cities and information cities.) Transportation cities are generally points of trans-shipment where different forms of transportation come together and the economy is dominated by industries such as trade, shipping, warehousing and distribution.

Production cities are manufacturing centers where a variety of inputs are assembled and transformed into goods of higher value. Central places are located in predominantly agricultural regions where they provide goods and services to a dispersed population. In the early stages of their development, transportation and production cities are located to take advantage of spatial variation in the natural landscape. Transportation cities are generally located on rivers or at natural harbors, or better yet where a river and a natural harbor come together. Production cities must locate where materials and energy resources are easily brought together. Central places, by contrast, are located in a relatively undifferentiated landscape with an evenly distributed population of potential customers. As such, their locations are not dictated by natural features. One might think, therefore, that they are "footloose" and that their location pattern could be more or less random. But because they compete for a finite market, their locations *relative to one another* affect their economic success.

Of course, few cities fit into any of these ideal types – nearly every city has elements of all three. But, since the locational forces acting on the three types differ, a model that addresses the locational pattern of just one type will be much easier to develop. This, in essence, is the modeling strategy of central place theory.

## Christaller's central place theory[1]

Central place theory was developed in the 1930s by the German geographer Walter Christaller. While most people think of central place theory as a highly theoretical exercise, Christaller's objectives were practical: he wanted to explain the spatial pattern of urban places in the agricultural region of southern Germany. In studying the region, he observed two spatial characteristics. First, the city size distribution was clearly hierarchical with few cities at the highest order and increasing numbers of cities at lower orders. (In central place theory, it is conventional to refer to levels of the hierarchy as "orders.") Second, he observed that within any order of cities the spatial pattern is dispersed. In other words, the highest-order cities are separated by long distances and the cities in each successively lower order are spread out as much as possible. Since there are more cities at the lower orders, the average distance between cities becomes progressively lower for lower orders of cities. He also observed something that is not explicitly spatial in nature, but which is a critical characteristic of the urban hierarchy: the number of goods and services on offer is higher at higher levels of the hierarchy. Christaller developed his model to describe economic mechanisms that would give rise to a spatial-hierarchical distribution with these three characteristics.

As we will see, central place theory produces some complex spatial patterns. But to get an understanding of its underlying mechanisms it's best to start with the simplest situation imaginable. To that end, make the following two simplifying assumptions:

1   The entire population of consumers is equally distributed in a bounded linear market at a density of $n$ per kilometer.

2   There is only one undifferentiated good (or service) that may be offered at central places.

We have used the first assumption before in the case of strategic location in chapter 16. For the moment, we adopt it because it makes graphical representation of the model simpler. We will eventually generalize the model to two-dimensional space. The second assumption means that any central place will be limited to offering just one good or service and that, if there is more than one central place, each will offer exactly the same thing. (To be general, we will refer to any good or service offered at a central place as a *central function*.) In a real agricultural landscape, the most typical central function might be a general store, but, since such an establishment offers a variety of goods and services, it is simpler to think of the central function as offering a single good (for example, an ice-cream stand) or a single service (for example, a barber shop). We now need a couple of assumptions about consumers.

3   Consumers have downward sloping demand functions such that above some price they purchase nothing from the central function (see Figure 22.1).
4   The effective price for a consumer is the sum of a fixed purchase price $P_c$ and a travel cost that is proportional to their distance from the central place.

To make assumption 4 more explicit, the effective price of the central function to a consumer located at distance $d_i$ from a central place is

$$P_i = P_c + td_i$$

where $t$ is a constant transportation cost per unit of distance. The fact that $P_c$ is constant means that firms at central places do not compete with one another on price – an important limitation of central place theory to which we will return later.

Assumptions 3 and 4 together imply that we can define a spatial demand curve around the location of a central place as shown in Figure 22.2. The height of this graph shows the amount that someone located at any distance from the central place will consumer per unit of time (say a year). The slope of the curve depends both on the slope of the demand function (Figure 22.1) and on the transportation rate $t$. The distance defines the point in the linear market where demand goes to zero. This implies that

$$P_0 = P_c + td_R$$

and therefore

$$d_R = \frac{P_0 - P_c}{t}$$

Consumers located at a distance greater than $d_R$ consume nothing from the central place.

We can use this diagram to determine the total sales of the central function. Recalling that $n$ is the density of consumers, total sales are equal to the area under the spatial demand curve times the density times the average revenue:[2]

$$S_R = nd_R Q_c P_c$$

From this we can observe two things. First, sales are increasing in the density $n$ of consumers. Second, since $d_R$ is decreasing in $t$ and $S_R$ is increasing in $d_R$, a decrease in the transportation rate will bring about an increase in sales.

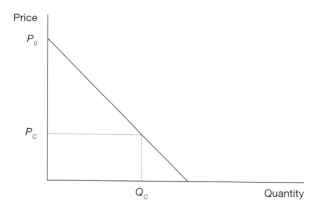

*Figure 22.1* Demand curve

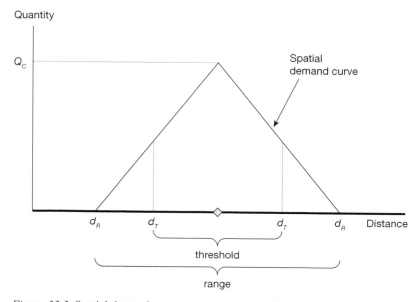

*Figure 22.2* Spatial demand curve, range and threshold

A second critical distance $d_T$ is called the *threshold distance*. Because of fixed cost, a firm that wants to provide the central function must have a certain minimum sales level $S_T$ in order to break even. The threshold distance defines the length of the linear market necessary to provide this minimum sales level. In the figure, the threshold distance is smaller than the range, which means that the firm earns revenues that are greater than the break-even level. If $d_T > d_R$ then the central function is not economically viable because the length of market that it must command to break even is greater than the maximum distance that people would travel to consume it.

Figure 22.3a shows what happens if there are two firms at different locations offering the central function. If they locate well apart as shown, they will not affect each other's sales because no part of the line (and therefore no consumers) will be within the range of both. In fact, a number of consumers will be within the range of neither, so the market is not completely covered. In Figure 22.3b, we see what happens if a third firm enters the market. In this case the other two shift their locations to become evenly spaced at a distance $2d_R$, so once again their ranges do not cross. This means that each of the three firms would have sales $S_R$ – in other words, their sales are unaffected by the presence of the other firms. But things get more interesting if a fourth firm enters the market. Assuming once again that the firms space themselves equally, the *minimum* feasible spacing is $2d_R$ where each firm is able to get its threshold sales level $S_T$. If they were spaced closer, none of the firms would be economically viable. Thus, the threshold sales level and its related threshold distance determine the number of firms that can "fit" in this market.

In our simple example, there is only one central function, so the location of each firm offering that function represents the establishment of a central place. In other words, the pattern of firm locations determines the pattern and density of urban locations in this very simple system of cities. The density of cities is determined by the threshold, which is essentially a reflection of scale economies. The pattern of cities is dispersed as a result of an implied assumption that cities space themselves evenly so that a maximum number can fit in the market. This has been a point of much criticism of central place theory, since the mechanisms underlying this dispersed pattern are not defined.[3] In fact, the Hotelling model of chapter 16 suggests that competing firms left to their own devices may cluster rather than disperse. Because there is a limited range, however, a clustered pattern would miss potential sales to much of the dispersed population. Thus, the range provides at least a rationale, if not a precise mechanism, for the dispersed pattern.

We can extend the model to two-dimensional space by changing assumption 1 as follows:

1a   The entire population of consumers is equally distributed in an undifferentiated plane at a density of $n$ per square kilometer.

(Note that the density $n$ has a different meaning now because it is defined per square kilometer instead of per meter.) Figure 22.4 shows the two-dimensional versions of the range and the threshold distance as the radii of concentric circles around the

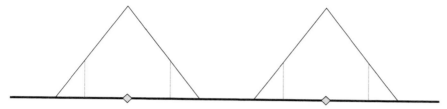

*Figure 22.3a* Two firms with uncovered market

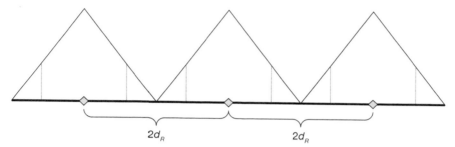

*Figure 22.3b* Three firms, fully covered market

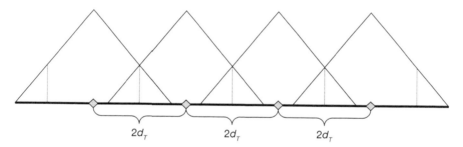

*Figure 22.3c* Four firms, minimum spacing

central place. Here the "hats" over the distance variables $\hat{d}_R$ and $\hat{d}_T$ are there to indicate that the distance variables are defined in two-dimensional space rather than one-dimensional space as before. The range distance $\hat{d}_R$ still has the same basic meaning as the maximum distance that anyone would travel to consume the central function. The threshold distance $\hat{d}_T$, however, has a slightly different meaning from before. In the two-dimensional case, it is the radius of a circle that encloses a population large enough to provide the threshold level of sales $S_T$. Thus, with a given population density and demand curve, the threshold is defined in terms of a minimum market area that the central place must command.

If we arrange central places spaced at $2\hat{d}_R$ (analogous to Figure 23.3b) we get the pattern in Figure 22.5. In this case the market is not completely covered by the

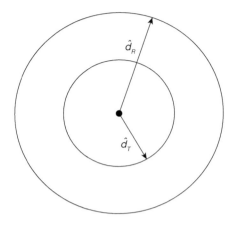

*Figure 22.4* The range and threshold in two dimensions

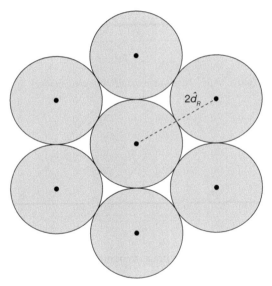

*Figure 22.5* Central places spaced at the range distance

circles defined by the range, so some people in the plane will have zero demand. Extending the results of our one-dimensional model, we should be able to space the central places at $2\hat{d}_T$ as shown in Figure 22.6a. Now all the parts of the plane are within the range distance of at least one central place. But the circles defined by the range distance overlap. So how do we define a distinct market area around each central place? This is where the hexagons come in.

The hexagonal market areas diagrams produced by central place theory are perhaps the most iconic image associated with economic geography. Sadly, if you ask a sample of students who have completed an introductory course in economic geography to define central place theory, a fair number will probably tell you that it's the theory that market areas are shaped like hexagons. In fact, the hexagon is just a geometric convenience with no intrinsic meaning in the theory. Certain geometric shapes – including triangles, squares and hexagons – are space filling, which means that they can be arranged to cover an entire space with no gaps or overlaps. The figures above indicate that circles are not space-filling shapes; if they do not overlap they leave gaps (Figure 22.5) and if they do not leave gaps they overlap (Figure 22.6a).

Figure 22.6b shows that hexagons can provide a space-filling approximation to circles. Note that a straight line between the central place in the middle of the figure and any other central place is exactly bisected by one side of the hexagon at a distance $\hat{d}_T$. This pattern can be extended to define exclusive market areas – each sufficiently large to generate the threshold sales level $S_T$ – around evenly spaced central places as shown in Figure 22.7. The market areas make it possible to know where a person at any point in the plane will go to consume the central function. Since central functions are undifferentiated, one always consumes from the closest center. A person located within a given market area will always consume from the central place at its center.

## Central place hierarchy

So far, the idea of an urban hierarchy has been absent from our model development. Christaller's theory explains the hierarchy as arising out of variability of the thresholds for different central functions on offer. To explain this, first alter assumption 2 as follows:

2a   There are two undifferentiated goods (or services) with different thresholds that may be offered at central places.

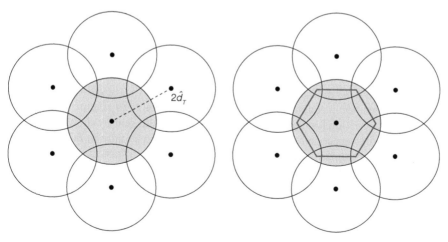

*Figure 22.6a* Central places spaced at the threshold distance

*Figure 22.6b* The hexagonal market area

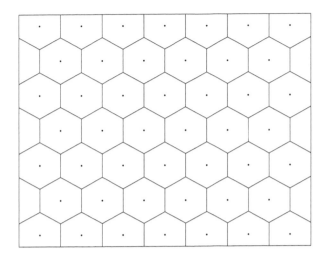

*Figure 22.7* Region of
hexagonal market areas

For example, suppose the central function with the lower threshold is barber shops. The function with the higher threshold may be doctors. Since a doctor must make a higher investment in education and equipment than a barber, she needs a larger market area to make her practice economically viable.

We have demonstrated that the spacing, and therefore the number, of central places depends on the required threshold distance $\hat{d}_T$, which in turn depends on the required threshold sales $S_T$. Let's say that Figure 22.7 represents the spacing of the central places defined by the central function with the lower threshold. What can we say about the locations of the central function with the higher threshold? Clearly, with a higher threshold they must be spaced further apart, and therefore there must be fewer of them. But how will the patterns of the two types of central places relate to one another?

Define the central function with the lower threshold as the first-order central function and all the places at which it is offered as first-order central places. Now define the function with the higher threshold as the second-order central function. If a pattern of first-order central places already existed and the second-order function were an innovation just getting established, it is reasonable to assume that anyone looking for a location for the second-order function would start by choosing among the existing first-order central places. Such places would already be familiar to the population of consumers and would have some elementary infrastructure that would not be found at other points in the plane. In this case a second-order place would be defined as a place offering *both* the second-order service and the first-order service. In fact, this is a fundamental assumption of Christaller's central place theory:

1   If a higher-order service is offered at a central place, all lower-order services will also be offered at that central place.

The number of first-order centers that become second-order centers will depend on the relative size of the ranges of the two central functions. Define $k$ as the ratio of the second-order market areas to the first-order market areas. For example, if $k = 3$ and the market area for the first-order central places is 10 square kilometers, the market area for the second-order central places must be 30 square kilometers. Figure 22.8 illustrates the spatial pattern of central places and market areas for two orders of central function and $k = 3$.

It is easy to verify that the market areas for the second-order central places are three times the size of those for the first-order central places. Each second-order market area includes one first-order market area at its center and one-third of each of the first-order market areas surrounding it. This also indicates that there are three times as many first-order centers as second order-centers.

We can extend this system to include a third-order central place function. Once again, we will use the $k = 3$ rule and assume that the market area for each third-order central place will be three times the market area for the second-order central places and therefore nine times as big as the market areas for the first-order central places. For example, assume once again that the first-order function is barber shops and the second-order function is doctors. We now add ballroom dance instructor as the third-order function. This example may not make sense to you at first. After all, we said earlier that doctors are a higher-order function than barber shops because of their greater investment in education and equipment. Certainly, a ballroom dance instructor does not need as much education as a doctor and his equipment is not as expensive. So why does he provide a higher-order service? Consider that nearly all men (so half the population) use barber shops and just about everyone uses the services of the doctor, although not as often. A very small proportion of the population, however, will use the services of a ballroom dance instructor. (In economic terms, he faces a demand function that is lower than those for barbers and doctors.) It is therefore necessary to serve a market with a large population in

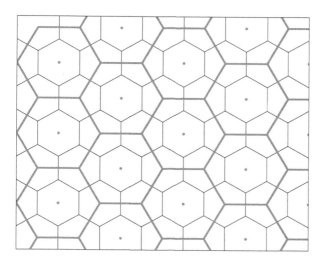

*Figure 22.8* Two-level central place system ($k = 3$)

order to have enough customers to make a ballroom dance studio viable. The point of this example is that a higher-order central function is simply one that requires a large market area, which may be the case for a variety of reasons.

Figure 22.9 shows the central place system for three orders. Note that the relationship between the third-order centers and the second-order centers is exactly the same as the relationship between the second-order centers and the third-order centers. We could easily expand this to include a fourth, fifth or even higher order of center. The pattern will become more complex, but the relationship between orders will remain the same as long as $k = 3$.

This is an extremely stylized pattern generated by a model with strong assumptions, but it offers an explanation for the three empirical regularities that Christaller observed in southern Germany: the hierarchical structure of city sizes, the dispersed patterns of cities within a particular order, and the provision of all lower-order functions at higher-order central places (although, to be honest, the third is an assumption rather than a result of the model).

## The significance of $k$

The choice of $k = 3$ for the development of the central place systems illustrated in Figures 22.8 and 22.9 was not arbitrary. A ratio of three between central places of

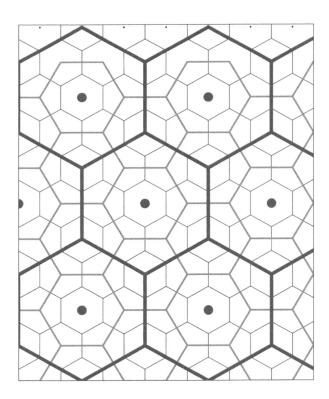

*Figure 22.9*
Three-level central
place system ($k = 3$)

different orders provides a neat, repeatable pattern of nesting of market areas. By contrast, there is no way to draw the spatial pattern of a $k = 2$ system. You can draw a hexagonal market area that is around a particular central place that is twice as large as that of the next lowest order, but it does not yield a pattern such that, for example, all the second-order centers fall at the locations of first-order centers.

It is, however, possible to devise central place systems for a number of other values of $k$ including 4, 7, 9 and 12.[4] We will not go into these in detail – if you are interested you can consult an advanced book on central place such as Berry (1967). But it is worth noting that systems based on values of $k$ other than 3 produce systems that are different from the $k = 3$ system in interesting ways. The relative placement of first- and second-order central places for $k = 4$ and $k = 7$ are shown in Figure 22.10.

Recall that, in the $k = 3$ system, first-order central places are located at the vertices of the hexagonal market area of a second-order central place. In the $k = 4$ system, the first-order places are located on the sides of the octagon. This arrangement actually makes more sense from a transportation perspective because it means that each first-order place is located on a straight line connecting two second-order places, so a much more efficient road network could be set up to connect all central places. For this reason, the $k = 4$ is known as the *transport principle*. In the $k = 7$ system, six first-order centers are located inside the triangular market area of the second-order center. In contrast to the $k = 3$ and $k = 4$ systems, where the first-order places are located equidistant to three and two second-order places respectively, all first-order places are clearly in the "orbit" of one and only one second-order place. This makes sense in an administrative system where the first-order places are under the jurisdiction of the second-order places. Thus, $k = 7$ is known as the administrative principle.

## Contemporary relevance of central place theory

For a number of reasons, central place theory does not lend itself easily to application in real urban systems. For one thing, its assumption of an undifferentiated plane seldom applies in practice because variations in the natural landscape and the structure of transportation networks tend to disconnect transportation costs from

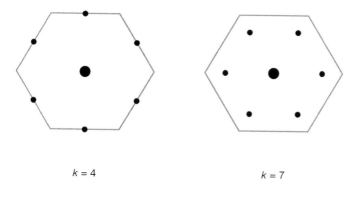

$k = 4$

$k = 7$

*Figure 22.10*
The transportation
and administrative
principles

straight-line distance. Also, it applies only to central places, whereas most urban systems are hybrids of central place, transportation, production and other functional types. It was designed to address a settlement pattern where most people live in rural areas and cities exist to serve them. In fact, the great majority of people in the twenty-first century live in cities. Finally, it assumes that central functions are undifferentiated, so distance is the main concern in consumers' spatial choices. As pointed out in earlier chapters, the modern economy is increasingly characterized by differentiated goods and services.

Despite these problems, there have been a number of empirical studies applying principles from central place theory to real urban systems. Generally, they focus on places that come close to meeting the assumptions of the model: agricultural regions in relatively undifferentiated terrain. Of course, the most famous of these is Christaller's own application of his theory to the pattern of cities and towns in southern Germany at the beginning of the twentieth century. Perhaps the best known of more recent applications is Berry's (1967) study of southwestern Iowa, which used modern statistical methods to define urban hierarchies based on the variety of goods and services offered and traced spatial patterns of consumer travel to make purchases of various types. Various principles from the theory were confirmed, such as the tendency of people to travel long distances only for higher-order functions and to shop in the closest place where the needed goods were available. It also observed trends that can be explained using the underlying logic of central place theory, such as the disappearance of some of the lowest-order centers due to declining rural population densities.[5]

Despite the strong assumptions of central place theory, recent authors still find it useful in modified version for the analysis of modern retail systems (Dennis *et al.*, 2002). Also, providing a set of rather stark results, central place theory generates a number of testable hypotheses that can be addressed by statistical analysis (Mushinski and Weiler, 2002).

Some of the most interesting applications of central place theory are by archeologists (see Box 22). Since they often turn up evidence of settlement patterns from societies for which there is no written history, central place theory provides a useful framework for understanding the relationships between settlements of different sizes in societies with dispersed agricultural populations and small urban populations (Kosso and Kosso, 1995).

---

### *Box 22* Central place theory and ancient Mayan settlement patterns

In 1973, archeologist Joyce Marcus published a paper with the title "Territorial Organization of the Lowland Classic Maya," in which she drew strong parallels between the spatial patterns of excavated Mayan settlements and the settlement pattern envisioned by central place theory. The classic Mayan civilization flourished in what is now the tropical rainforest of the Yucatan

Peninsula between 600 and 900 C.E. In the nineteenth and twentieth centuries archeologists turned up numerous "lost cities" of the Mayas, with large stone structures, regular urban patterns and carved hieroglyphs. As more and more cities were uncovered, a regular pattern began to emerge. Marcus borrowed some regularities from central place theory to explain the pattern.

The Mayan view of the universe helped create a spatial structure within which a hierarchical urban pattern could exist. They believed that heaven and earth were divided into four segments, and so they established four primary ceremonial and administrative cities broadly spaced across their lowland realm, which at the time was deforested and planted in corn and other crops. Each primary center had an acropolis, large plazas and numerous monuments. A large set of secondary centers each had a pyramid and some monuments. A third order of centers, which controlled shifting agricultural hamlets, could also be identified from the archeological findings. Particularly noteworthy was the fact that the major sites (primary and secondary centers) were quite evenly spaced at an average distance of 10.33 kilometers with a standard deviation of only 1.9. Furthermore, the hierarchy of centers was structured according to a hexagonal lattice very similar to that of central place theory. Figure B22.1 shows Marcus's idealized representation of the spatial

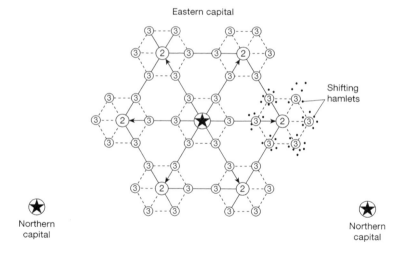

*Figure B22.1* Idealized spatial structure of classic Mayan settlements
*Source*: Marcus, 1973: Figure 8.

system of cities. Here the points marked with a star represent the four primary centers, while those marked 2 and 3 represent secondary and tertiary centers respectively. A similar lattice would have surrounded each of the four primary centers, although it is only shown for one in the diagram.

We should take care not to draw too strong an analogy from the ancient Mayan lowlands to the central places of southern Germany. After all, the relationships among centers were more ceremonial than economic, although a large agricultural surplus must have flowed up the hierarchy from the hamlets to the urban nobility. But the interesting thing is that socioeconomic processes appear to have given rise to a regularly spaced and hierarchical settlement pattern. It is tempting to think that the pattern simply reflects a grand design imposed by a powerful centralized authority, but Marcus doubts whether the Maya either planned or recognized the pattern. Rather, it emerged out of dependency relationships between settlements with different functions and different levels of importance.

In a sense, the utility of central place theory does not rest solely in its ability to reproduce, predict or explain contemporary urban patterns. It has provided many insights that are useful even in contexts that are very different from the world of undifferentiated geography and goods. For example, Christaller's work introduced the notion that a city's place in the hierarchy may be defined by the variety of goods and services that it provides rather than simply by its population. Also, by defining a fundamental logic for the development of a spatial urban hierarchy and a concise set of results, central place theory established a point of departure for the study of systems of cities. When the observed reality doesn't fit the results of the model, the logic must be adjusted to generate new results that can be tested against reality. The result of this process has been the development of new models of urban systems, some of which will be introduced in the next chapter.

# 23  Network urban systems

Christaller's central place theory has limited application to contemporary urban systems for a variety of reasons. Perhaps the most obvious reason is that it envisions an economy where most people are scattered across the landscape in a dispersed pattern and cities exist primarily to serve the needs of those people. The current reality – certainly in the developed world but even in an increasing share of the developing world – is that most people live in cities. Thus, most goods and services provided in cities must be intended for an urban market; either they are sold to people within the city in which they are provided or they are sold to people in other cities. This means that it is necessary to think about two things that central place theory does not address: first, flows of goods and services among economic agents within the city and, second, flows of goods and services between cities. In this chapter, we focus on the latter.

If you think about it, central place theory does not view cities as entities that interact with one another. It represents a kind of interaction in the sense that people living in the market area of a particular first-order central place will go to a specific second-order central place to buy higher-threshold goods. But this is an indirect kind of interaction. The first-order place does not play any explicit role in the purchases by people in its market area of higher-order goods. And it is limited to interaction up the hierarchy. People living sufficiently close to a second-order place will never travel to a first-order place for any reason, and people in the market area of any central place never travel to other places of the same order. Clearly, this is at odds with a large volume of traffic data that show goods and people moving in all directions among cities in an urban hierarchy.

Even in a region that fits the basic assumptions of central place theory (dispersed population, cities as centers of distribution), we might expect this limited pattern of interaction to change over time because of two nearly universal trends: the reduction in transportation costs and the increasing role of differentiated goods. Suppose a system of central places in a region has evolved over a long period of time. What happens when transportation costs fall? The range of the central functions of any order will expand. This in itself will not induce a person living in the market area of one central place to travel to another place of the same order because it is still most advantageous to consume the function at the closest place. But suppose the function becomes differentiated. Returning to our example of the barber shop, suppose there are two first-order central places A and B. The barber shop at A provides a traditional haircut for a moderate price. The barber shop at B bills itself as a "salon" where a man can be made to look like his favorite celebrity, at a somewhat higher price. Some men in the market area of A will incur the extra transport cost and pay the extra price to get the more luxurious service offered at B. At the same time, some men from the market area of B will travel to the shop at A in order to avoid the effeminizing influence of hair spray and at the same time save a little money. In general, falling transportation costs and increased product differentiation open up possibilities for interaction across the hierarchy rather than just up it.

The potential for cross-hierarchy interaction becomes much greater when we consider cities as points of production, rather than just distribution. Production of most things, whether goods or services, involves scale economies. In central place theory, scale economies figure only in the limited sense that there is some minimum efficient level of operation (the threshold sales level). In reality, scale economies may be so extensive in production technologies that local specialization becomes inevitable. For example, a dairy operating in a relatively small city may find that it can reduce its production costs through scale economies to offset the transportation cost necessary for it to sell into other markets of about the same size. By doing this it may displace dairies in those markets, but other specializations may develop in those places. Product differentiation such as introducing organically produced milk or delivering milk in plastic bags rather than cartons may reinforce the ability of the dairy to sell into non-local markets.

Both the example of the barber shop and the dairy illustrate that there are mechanisms that lead to increasing specialization at the local level. (This is at odds with the assumptions of central place theory, where each city of the same order serves exactly the same functions.) Specialization gives rise to complementarities among cities, which in turn give rise to economic interconnections. We can think of this in terms of the bases of spatial interaction: complementarity, transferability and intervening opportunity (chapter 5). According to the assumption of central place theory, there is no complementarity among places of the same order so there is spatial interaction among them. Once we allow for specialization, complementarities emerge.

The recognition that urban systems involve complex patterns of interrelationships among cities has led in recent years to a shifting perspective among economic geographers and other analysts. Instead of viewing urban systems as hierarchies, the more recent literature prefers to view them as *networks* (see Batten, 1995; Camagni and Salone, 1993; Meijers, 2005; Rozenblat and Pumain, 2007). This new perspective has not given rise to elegant mathematical/geometric models in the tradition of central place theory, but it provides a framework for identifying more realistic mechanisms and classifications for systems of cities.

## Networks versus hierarchies

The word "network" is commonly used in two ways. The first refers to a physical infrastructure such as a highway network or a network for the transmission and distribution of electric power. The second is in the context of interactions among businesses (as in a "supplier network"), institutions ("research network") or individuals ("social network"). When we speak of networks of cities, we invoke both meanings. Transportation networks are especially important to facilitate movement of goods and people, but communication networks are increasingly important as the transfer of information becomes as important as the transfer of goods. Infrastructure only permits interaction to happen, however. Corporate, institutional and personal relationships are necessary to make it happen.

Studying a system of cities as a network rather than as a hierarchy opens up a wealth of new insight and information, but it also involves a lot more work. To analyze a hierarchy, it is only necessary to have information on each city, such as its population size or the range of services it provides. To analyze the same cities as a network, it will be necessary to measure not only characteristics of the cities but also of the interactions among them. In a system of 10 cities, there are 90 possible intercity relationships, so the volume of data required for a network-based analysis is much greater.

At this point, we need to make a distinction between two related but different concepts: a *network of cities* and a *network city*. A network of cities refers to a group of cities that are highly accessible to one another via transportation and communications infrastructure and among which high levels of spatial interaction are observed. The fact that spatial interaction is used as the defining characteristic means that this is a *functional region* as defined in chapter 1. However, it is not necessarily a compact region. For example, a network of cities may include an ocean port city and one or more inland distribution centers, which may be separated by hundreds or even thousands of kilometers but which are strongly linked by rail infrastructure along which huge volumes of freight are moved. A network city is a group of cities, generally without a single dominant city, that are located close together and that are so highly interdependent that they function as a single economic entity.[1] The term *polycentric urban region* (PUR) is synonymous with network city. We'll return to this phenomenon later, but for the moment we will focus on networks *of* cities.

One can envision many types of networks of cities. At one extreme, two cities with a complementary trading relationship may constitute a network in themselves. At the other, all the cities in the world that are involved in any type of trade might be described as a global network of cities. It is useful, however, to identify characteristic types that can be identified in terms of their city size distributions and their geographical configurations. We will consider two such types here: monocentric networks of cities and corridor networks of cities.

## Monocentric networks

As the name suggests, a monocentric network of cities includes a single dominant city that commands a large share of intercity interactions. (Note, this is not to be confused with a monocentric city. The monocentric network of cities includes several distinct cities, each with a separate CBD, which are separated by some non-urban space.) There is likely to be some hierarchy in city size, but not a strict functional hierarchy in the central place sense. Typically, the large dominant city will be a center for high-order services. Some of the other cities in the network will be specialized centers for manufacturing or specific kinds of services such as insurance or research and development. Other smaller cities may be limited to local retail and other consumer service. Cities of all sizes are distributed around the dominant city, although not necessarily with a simple hierarchical pattern (see Figure 23.1).

Economic activities tend to be distributed among cities by means of market mechanisms similar to those in the urban land-use model. Activities with the greatest agglomeration economies will locate in the dominant city. Over the past century, high-order services, rather than manufacturing, have come to dominate very large cities. Stock markets and other financial institutions, corporate headquarters and creative activities such as design and the arts bid up the value of land throughout the largest city and tend to "squeeze out" manufacturing (Baldwin *et al.*, 2001), which is a land-intensive activity. In a monocentric network of cities, manufacturing can shift its location to smaller cities, where it can take advantage of lower rents. The smaller city will also generally have less congestion, which reduces transportation costs, and perhaps even lower wages. But locating in a small or medium city within a network of cities is more advantageous than locating in an isolated city of the same size. Because the city is located within a relatively short distance of a very large market and has access to a large labor force, it can achieve scale

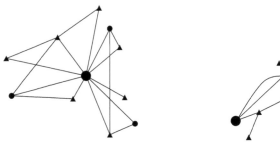

**Monocentric network of cities**          **Corridor network of cities**

●   Large city
•   Medium city
▲   Small city

*Figure 23.1* Two types of networks of cities

economies. It can also exchange intermediate goods with a large number of producers located among the cities in the network.

The region of southern Ontario, Canada around the city of Toronto (Map 23.1) provides a good example of a monocentric network of cities. With a metropolitan population of over 5 million, Toronto is Canada's economic (although not political) capital and a global city in every sense. It is home to Canada's largest stock exchange, the headquarters of the largest banks and most major corporations. It has Canada's largest airport for both passengers and freight, three large universities and a vibrant arts scene. It also has world-class property rental rates and traffic delays.

Within 100 kilometers of Toronto are a large number of medium and small cities, ranging from Hamilton, which at over 500,000 is the ninth largest municipality in Canada, to small rural towns with a post office, a small supermarket and an agricultural supply store.

Many of the cities surrounding Toronto are specialized manufacturing centers. Hamilton is Toronto's steel capital. Oshawa, St Catherines, Cambridge and Woodstock are centers of automotive production, while Guelph is an important center for agribusiness. The twin cities of Kitchener-Waterloo, home to two major universities and the BlackBerry smartphone, is known around the world as a center for communications and information technology.

Thanks to location within this city-rich region, even relatively small places can serve functions that we would normally expect to see only in large cities. For example, Magna International, one of the world's largest manufacturers of auto parts, chose to locate its headquarters in Aurora, Ontario, a town of about 50,000 population within commuting range of Toronto. Perhaps more remarkable is the decision by Toyota to open an assembly plant with capacity for up to 150,000 vehicles per year at Woodstock, Ontario, a town of about 40,000 located in a predominantly agricultural area. This seemingly remote site is less than two hours from Toronto and located on the major highway to the U.S. industrial heartland. Thus, Toyota is able to enjoy the cost benefits of a semi-rural location, while maintaining good accessibility to suppliers and markets.

A good way to think of a monocentric network of cities is as a system that can accommodate a variety of different types of agglomeration economies. (See chapter 3 for a review of agglomeration concepts.) Manufacturing firms benefit from localization economies, which induce them to locate in clusters, and juxtaposition economies, which require them to be within easy reach of suppliers and markets. Artists and designers benefit from the kind of economies of variety described by Jane Jacobs (1969) as only occurring in large cities. All sorts of firms benefit from urbanization economies in the form of major infrastructure such as an international airport. Agglomeration economies play out over different geographical scales. Manufacturing facilities in just-in-time supply chains benefit from being within two to three hours of one another. Corporate lawyers, corporate officers, artists and designers need to get in the same room on a regular basis. The advantage of the network of cities that surrounds Toronto is that it offers all types of firms a range of location options within which they can balance the benefits of agglomeration against a variety of costs.

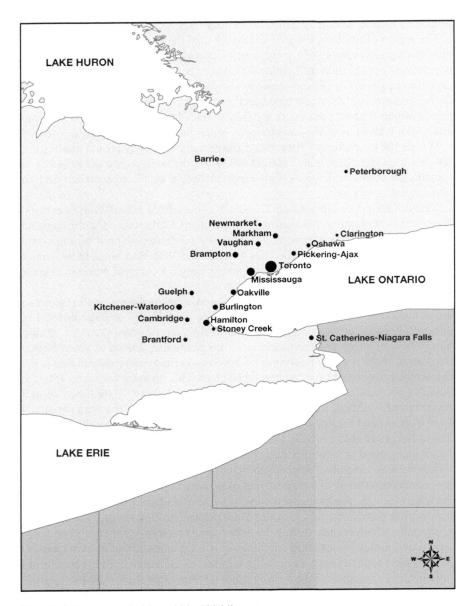

*Map 23.1* Toronto and cities within 100 kilometers

## Networks of cities defined at different scales

One problem in studying networks of cities is that it is never quite clear how far they extend. For example, does the polycentric network of cities centered on Toronto extend as far as London, Ontario, which is about 180 kilometers to the southwest on a major highway? Does the Northeast Corridor include rapidly growing cities in Maine and Virginia (see Box 23)? These questions can only be answered by choosing cut-off points for distances and levels of interaction that may be somewhat arbitrary.

---

### *Box 23* Corridor networks in the U.S.

A number of well-known networks of cities are not centered on a dominant city but rather strung out along a corridor defined by a major transportation route, as illustrated in Map B23.1. A famous example is the network of coastal cities along the northeast coast of the United States. First identified as "megalopolis" by Gottmann (1961), the corridor comprises an almost uninterrupted region of urbanization extending from Boston at the northern end to Washington DC at the southern end. It includes the largest northeastern U.S. cities (Boston, New York, Philadelphia and Washington), a number of mid-sized cities (Hartford CT, Newark NY, Wilmington DE, Baltimore MD) and a number of smaller centers. While it is sometimes portrayed as "one big city," anyone who is familiar with this region knows that the cities have distinct identities, economic specializations labor forces and market characteristics. Also, while New York is by far the largest city, Boston, Philadelphia and Washington are all easily large enough to act as centers to their own urban networks.

The genesis of the corridor is the coastal shipping that once constituted both the major mode of transportation among the cities in the corridor and the main connection to the European markets. By the twentieth century, shipping had become inconsequential for movements among these cities, but new rail, highway and airport infrastructure was created so as to reinforce the high level of integration within what is now known as the "Northeast Corridor." (The name "Bosnywash" is also popular.) The combination of the economic (New York) and political (Washington) capitals of the United States, along with its greatest concentration of universities and life science industries (Boston) and some of its most important manufacturing centers (Philadelphia and midsized metropolitan areas) create an array of com-plementarities resulting in perhaps the highest density of intercity economic linkages found anywhere in the world. The Northeast Corridor is also well connected to global markets via major airports at the largest cities and the giant ocean port of New York and New Jersey, with its extensive rail and road linkages.

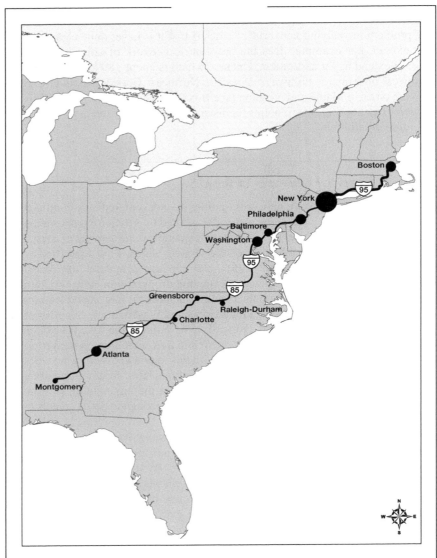

*Map B23.1* Corridor networks of cities: Northeast Corridor and U.S. Interstate I-85

The Northeast Corridor developed into an economic mega-region over a period of more than a century. A question of interest to policy makers is whether the benefits of complementarity, specialization and agglomeration can be induced to occur by the construction of a new highway or other infra-structure connecting free-standing cities. A recent study of ten economic regions defined around highway corridors in the United States produced a mixed answer to this question (Lakshmanan *et al.*, 2009). Some corridors failed to grow any faster than the broader regions within which they are set, while others showed signs of developing into functional regions with increasing integration among member cities and better than average economic growth. Since not all corridor regions experienced exceptional growth, the "if you build it, they will come" mentality that believes that infrastructure investments necessarily spur economic growth, was not confirmed by this study.

One successful corridor identified in the study stretches over 400 miles along Interstate Highway 85 (I-85) between two fast-growing metropolitan areas: Raleigh–Durham, North Carolina, which is a center for university-driven research and development, and Atlanta, Georgia, which has been the economic engine of the American southeast for several decades. Unlike some other corridors, the I-85 corridor contains a number of emerging metropolitan areas along its length, including Greensboro, North Carolina and Charlotte, North Carolina. It will be interesting to see whether this corridor network of cities continues to outperform the region in which it is located.

Moreover, since networks are defined in terms of levels of interactions, shouldn't they be much more broadly defined in a global economy? How can Montreal be excluded from Toronto's network of cities? Don't Toronto and New York both belong to a global network of prominent cities?

The best way to address this type of problem is to recognize that networks of cities exist at different geographical scales. Toronto is the center of a relatively compact network of cities located in southern Ontario, but it is also part of a much broader corridor-type network extending from Quebec City, 800 kilometers to the northeast, and Windsor, Ontario, about 250 kilometers to the southwest. This vast, predominantly urban, corridor includes more than half of Canada's population.[2] New York and Toronto are part of a network that includes the financial capitals and headquarters locations of all the world's major economies.

Figure 23.2 illustrates that networks exist at different scales and are interconnected. At the global scale, there is a network of very large cities. Any one of these global cities may be a member of a national network of cities, any one of which might be a member of a more locally defined network of cities. Through this hierarchy of networks, even relatively small cities are economically interconnected with other cities all over the world. However, connections across this hierarchy, whereby firms in small cities in different parts of the world interact directly, are increasingly possible due in part to the availability of communications technology.

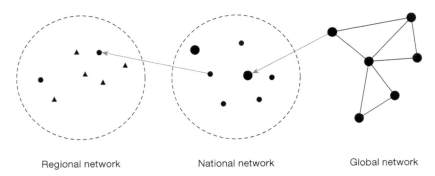

*Figure 23.2* Relationships among networks defined at different scales

## Polycentric urban regions

Network cities, also known as polycentric urban regions (PUR), occur where a number of large but not "world-class" cities located in close proximity with excellent infrastructure linkages act as a single functional region with sufficient economic weight to be competitive at the global scale. In some ways, the PUR may have advantages over regions based around the very largest cities. Because none of the cities reaches the size where negative externalities such as traffic congestion and high levels of pollution come into play, the PUR may achieve a high level of economic efficiency with a better quality of life.

Two prominent examples of PURs are found in the literature: Randstad, Holland and the Kansai region of Japan (Batten, 1995). The Randstad region includes four cities – Amsterdam, Rotterdam, The Hague and Utrecht – which are large, but significantly smaller than Europe's largest cities, such as Paris and London. There are also a number of smaller but highly productive cities located nearby. (See Map 23.2.) People and goods can move easily around the region by rail or car. There is significant specialization among the individual cities and a good deal of policy coordination at all levels of government. The outcome is a region that can compete effectively at the global scale despite the absence of a single "global city."

The Kansai region of Japan includes the major cities of Osaka, Kyoto and Kobe as well as the smaller cities of Himeji, Nara, Ohtsu and Wakayama. All of these cities are dwarfed in size by Tokyo. However, the combined urban core of the Kansai region has a population greater than the combined populations of Tokyo and Yokahama. The Kansai region has been noted as a center of innovation, education and advanced technology (Kobayashi and Takebayashi, 2001). Also, the location in this region of Japan's two previous imperial capitals (Nara and Kyoto) makes it one of the world's top tourist destinations. As in the case of Randstad in Holland, cooperation by regional and local governments in recent decades has sought to advance the level of integration among the cities.

There are many other regions around the world with a high density of cities that may or may not qualify as PURs. Noting a lack of consistency in the way the concept is applied, Parr (2004) has suggested the following seven criteria for identifying PURs:

*Map 23.2*
Randstad
polycentric
urban region

1 There is a cluster of cities separated by open land.
2 There is a defined maximum separation between them, such as one hour's drive.
3 There is a defined minimum separation to exclude situations where cities have effectively "grown together."
4 The spacing of cities of similar size is closer than in other parts of the same country or region. (This is to distinguish the PUR from hierarchically structured urban systems.)
5 Among the largest cities, there is no single one that dominates all others in terms of population or level of economic activity.
6 There is a higher level of spatial interaction among cities in the PUR than would be observed among comparably sized cities outside it.

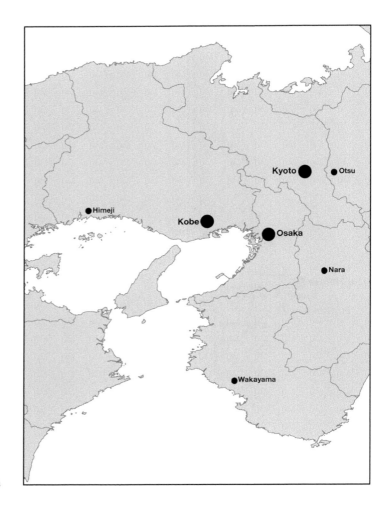

*Map 23.3*
Kansai
polycentric
urban region

7    There is significant specialization in economic activities among the cities that make up the PUR.

The concept of the PUR has taken on strong policy dimension. There are many cases where, for historical reasons, a cluster of cities exists but where high levels of specialization and spatial interaction are not found. On the evidence that PURs appear to show exceptional economic performance, governments are taking steps to turn potential PURs into actual ones. This is especially the case in the European Union, where the PUR has been established as planning strategy. Existing PURs, however, have evolved over long periods of time through a variety of economic and social mechanisms, so it remains to be seen whether government policy can effectively create new ones.

# Part VI

# Globalization and the knowledge economy

# 24 International trade and foreign direct investment

This is the first of three chapters on *globalization* and the *knowledge economy*. These two topics address profound changes in the spatial patterns of production, distribution and consumption that are rapidly altering the economic landscape. While neither topic is really new – both refer to processes that have been under way for centuries – political, institutional and technological changes in the second half of the twentieth century have led to ever faster and more obvious economic transformation.

A number of books have been written that seek to explain how the global knowledge economy of the twenty-first century came to be, how it works, who benefits, who suffers and what implications it has for global politics.[1] Our objective here is more modest. Essentially, the next three chapters address the following question: how does the transition to a global knowledge economy affect the principles of economic geography as set forth in the first five sections of this book? Some observers argue that globalization and the proliferation of information and communications technology means that space is becoming irrelevant, distance is disappearing, so economic geography as we know it is out the window. But the fact that distance is getting easier to overcome does not mean it no longer matters. As we have already seen, reductions in the friction of distance lead to predictable changes such as increased scale of production and more spatial interaction. Perhaps most importantly, cheaper transportation and better communication make it easier for firms to exploit spatial differentiation at a global scale.

These issues will be addressed in detail later, but at the outset some basic definitions are needed. The term "globalization" seems to have as many definitions as there are books and articles written about it. For the moment, let's settle for a very simple definition of globalization as the integration of economic activity at a global scale. Of course, this begs the question: what do we mean by integration? International trade and foreign direct investment are both forms of economic integration that can be measured in terms of flows of goods or funds between nations. In these cases, production is still conducted within national borders. At a deeper level of integration, the production process itself involves tasks performed by different actors at different locations around the globe who are closely coordinated via information and communications networks. As we will see, people from a dozen or more countries may have been involved in the design, production, distribution and marketing of the shirt you are wearing right now. It is this more complex type of integration that most people have in mind when they speak of globalization. To make this distinction clear, we will use the term *internationalization* to refer to integration across national borders that involves goods that are produced in a single country but sold in to an international market. Internationalization is not distinct from globalization; rather, it is a limited form of globalization.

The knowledge economy is not quite so easily defined. A precise definition, including an explanation of the distinction between information and knowledge, is deferred until chapter 26. For now, we can explain the difference between the knowledge economy and the traditional economy as follows: when you buy a good or service in the knowledge economy you pay more for information and knowledge inputs and less for physical inputs. For example, compare paying $50 for a pile of bricks and $50 for a video game. In the case of the bricks, a large proportion of the purchase price will go to the materials (clay and sand) from which they are made. Only a tiny proportion of the cost of the video game goes toward the plastic and other materials in the game cartridge (if you download the game, there are no materials). The labor that goes into production is also different. Brick manufacturing requires hard physical labor, while the video game programmer barely has to get out of his chair – but he must have a wealth of accumulated knowledge to do his job. The capital used in brick making plays the traditional role of transforming materials into new, more valuable forms. By contrast, the production of video games relies on capital that embodies information and communications technologies.

The transition to the knowledge economy is progressing in two ways. First, of the total goods and services produced in the global economy, the share of goods that are similar to the bricks is declining, while the share of goods that are similar to the video game is growing. Second, most goods lie somewhere between the two extremes, but they are changing through time in ways that make them less like bricks and more like video games. Cars provide the best example. If you compare a car from the 1960s to a 2010 model, most of the differences you find will be the result of technical refinements driven by the application of science and engineering.

Globalization and the emergence of the knowledge economy are not trends that just happen to be occurring at the same time. Rather, they are complementary trends. The kind of deep integration described above is only possible if production activities can be coordinated on a global scale – something that would not be possible were it not for communications and information technologies. At the same time, the trend for production to be less material intensive means that there is less to move per dollar of output, so longer shipments are more economically viable. A product like software requires no physical transportation, but rather is transmitted electronically. This means that the cost of buying software from a programmer on the other side of the globe may be no higher than buying it from a programmer located in your building. Does this mean transportation is becoming unnecessary? As we will see, electronic communication tends to stimulate the demand for face-to-face interaction, so passenger transportation continues to grow. Also, while the weight of materials per dollar of output is decreasing, the average distances that goods move are increasing even faster, so freight transportation continues to grow.

The remainder of this chapter lays a foundation for what is to come with a review of the simpler forms of globalization that we have already defined as internationalization. Chapter 25 examines the more fully developed process of globalization and its implications for the spatial configuration of economic activities. Chapter 26 turns to the knowledge economy and the evolving meaning of economic geography in a rapidly changing global economy.

## Trade barriers and international trade

Chapter 8 introduced the theory of comparative advantage in the context of two regions that are part of the same national economy but which have different endowments. To quickly summarize, the notion of absolute advantage is illustrated by two regions, one of which (The Hills) is more efficient than the other in producing wine and the other (The Plains) is more efficient in producing wheat. (Efficiency was defined in terms of labor requirements.) It is easy to see in this case why the residents of both regions are better off if they specialize in the good in which they have absolute advantage and trade for the other good. The example is then extended to a case where The Plains is more efficient in the production of both wheat and wine. But, because The Hills has a lower opportunity cost for wine, specialization and trade is still beneficial to both regions. In this case, The Plains has absolute advantage in wine but The Hills has comparative advantage in wine. (Go back and review chapter 8 if you are unclear on the theory of comparative advantage.)

The same economic logic applies to trade between independent nations as to trade between regions within a nation. However, a complicating institutional factor comes into play. For a variety of reasons, national governments may impose trade barriers to make it more difficult for international goods to cross its borders. The most common type of trade barrier is a tariff, which is a tax charged either per unit or as a percentage of the value of the imported goods. (The former is called a *specific* tariff, while the latter is called an *ad valorum* tariff.) The effect of the tariff is to reduce the level of imports, which may be beneficial to domestic producers of the good in question, but which generally makes consumers of the good worse off.

To illustrate, first imagine a situation of autarky in which all domestic demand must be met by domestic supply. For the sake of illustration, consider some homogeneous good such as wheat. Figure 24.1 shows how the levels of domestic output and the price are determined by the intersection of supply and demand functions. Unlike the simple example in chapter 8 where production costs are constant, in this case there is an upward sloping supply function. This means that, in order to produce greater quantities, producers must be enticed with higher prices. In the case of wheat, this might occur because farmers have to move onto progressively lower-yielding land in order to increase the supply. Adopting the assumptions of perfect competition from chapter 4, the price $P_a$ and quantity $Q_a$ are determined at the point where the supply and demand functions intersect.

Now suppose we move from a situation of autarky to one of free trade as shown in Figure 24.2. Assume further that the nation in question does not have comparative advantage in wheat, so there is an import price $P_i < P_a$ at which wheat can be purchased from abroad.[2] (This implies that transportation costs are included in $P_i$.) Assuming that domestic wheat and imported wheat are perfect substitutes, the import price will prevail in the domestic market. Because there is an upward sloping supply curve, domestic production will not fall to zero. Rather, it will fall to a level $Q_d$ at which the import price coincides with the domestic supply function. Because the prevailing price is lower than the price under autarky, total domestic

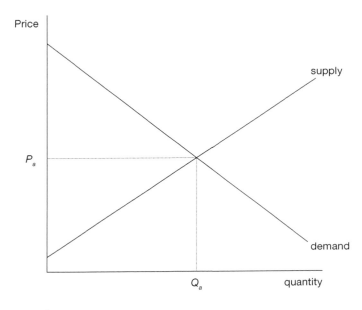

*Figure 24.1*
Price and
quantity under
autarky

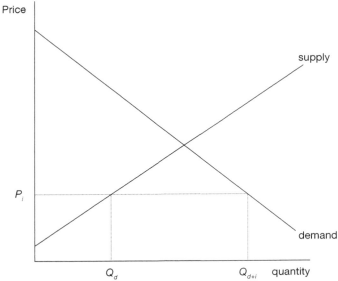

*Figure 24.2*
Price and
quantity in the
absence of trade
barriers

consumption shifts up to a level $Q_{d+i} = Q_d + Q_i$, where $Q_i$ is the amount of imported wheat. Domestic consumers are better off than they were under autarky, but domestic producers are worse off.

An intermediate situation occurs when a specific (per unit) tariff is imposed on imported wheat, as shown in Figure 24.3. $P_i + T$ is the effective price in the market, as long as it does not exceed $P_a$. (If $P_i + T > P_a$ there will be no imports.) With this higher price, total consumption declines to $Q_{d+i}$ but domestic production increases to $Q_d'$. This means consumers are worse off but domestic producers are better off.

It would seem therefore that whether or not to impose tariffs is a question of whether the government wants to help producers and consumers. Of course, this distinction is somewhat artificial because, as Abraham Lincoln once noted, there is not one class of people with hands (producers) and another with mouths (consumers). We are all in some sense both producers and consumers. The theory of comparative advantage tells us that all trading partners are better off under free trade than under autarky. If the country in our example loses domestic wheat production to foreign competition, capital and labor resources will be transferred to the production of goods in which it has comparative advantage, thereby increasing overall productivity. Since tariffs interfere with this efficient allocation of resources, their overall effect on welfare is negative. (In the Appendix to this chapter, it is demonstrated that the benefit to producers resulting from a tariff is lower than the loss to consumers.)

So why do countries impose tariffs? To some extent, this is a political rather than economic question. In a pluralist society, where various interest groups compete for political influence, producer groups may be better at promoting their interests

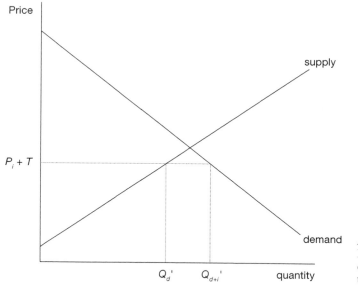

Figure 24.3
Price and quantity with tariff *T*

than consumer groups. Also, the benefits of free trade tend to be broadly spread across consumers, while the costs tend to be more concentrated. For example, liberalization of the global trade in apparel has made clothing much cheaper for nearly everyone in North America, while eliminating jobs for a much smaller number of garment workers. In the long run, transferring U.S. and Canadian labor resources from apparel to more productive sectors is beneficial – but that is little consolation for the 50-year-old garment worker with no transferable skills. It is not surprising, therefore, that the fear of job loss outweighs the desire for lower prices in the political calculus of many middle-income households who support tariffs and other trade barriers.

Not all arguments in favor of trade barriers are based on narrow interests, however. Consider the case of a country that has comparative advantage only in rice. The theory tells us that this country should concentrate on rice production for export and trade for other goods. But the prices of agricultural commodities in global markets tend to fluctuate more broadly than prices of other goods, leaving the country's economy vulnerable to boom and bust cycles. Also, rice is not an income-elastic good, so in the long run global rice demand will grow more slowly than the demand for other goods, dooming the country to relatively slow economic growth. In short, comparative advantage has dealt this country a bad hand.

The theory of comparative advantage as explained in chapter 8 is static in the sense that it views the variations in endowments across nations that lead to a particular pattern of comparative advantage as given and fixed. Some endowments, such as the natural resource base and the weather, are in fact relatively fixed. But other endowments, such as the skills of the labor force, the stock of productive capital and the quality of public infrastructure, can change over time. Political leaders in the country described above, therefore, have the option of trying to develop endowments that create comparative advantage for goods other than rice. In order to do this, they target certain industries that they believe have the potential for rapid development and provide protection from foreign competition by means of tariffs or other trade barriers for a limited period of time. During that time, firms in the targeted industries can achieve scale economies via sales to the domestic market, invest in capital embodying the newest technologies and upgrade the skills of its labor force. At the same time, the government can invest in public infrastructure that supports those industries. Since the idea here is to protect industries during the early stages of their development, this strategy has become known as the *infant industry* argument for limited application of trade barriers.

While the infant industry argument is generally heard in the context of developing countries, the strategy was used by advanced countries including the United States, Japan and Canada at some point in their economic development. In fact, Alexander Hamilton, the first U.S. Treasury Secretary, used this argument in favor of tariffs in 1790.[3] Today, low-income countries often use the infant industry argument to counter pressure to open their economies to competition from the developed world.

The weakness of the infant industry strategy is that it depends on the government, rather than on market forces, to make decisions about which industries to protect and for how long. Ideally, the government should choose industries for which the country has some natural advantage and only needs development of capital and labor resources to be competitive globally. However, protection may go to the industry with the most political clout or to goods such as cars and computers that convey the most prestige in the world economy. Also, the economic rationale for this argument implies that trade barriers should be temporary, but industries that have enjoyed protection for decades are likely to use their political influence to make it permanent. Countries such as Japan and South Korea that have used the strategy successfully are still reluctant to open up their domestic markets long after their industries have achieved high levels of global competitiveness.

## The liberalization of global markets

The explosive growth in international trade that has occurred in recent decades is not a completely new phenomenon. The late nineteenth and early twentieth centuries were periods of rapid growth in trade, but much of that growth fell off with the coming of the Great Depression in 1929. In response to that economic crisis, many countries increased tariffs in a vain attempt to stop rapid industrial decline by cutting off imports. Since all countries did the same thing, the result was to make things worse by stifling international trade.

In the aftermath of World War II, western countries that wanted to avoid another round of destructive protectionism created the General Agreement on Tariffs and Trade (GATT). The GATT was essentially a series of negotiations at which participants agreed to reduce tariffs. Starting in 1948 with just 9 countries, the more recent rounds of negotiations involved over 150 countries accounting for virtually all of the world's trade. In 1995, the relatively informal GATT structure was transformed to create the World Trade Organization (WTO) with powers to oversee dispute resolution.

In addition to the global effort to reduce trade barriers by the GATT/WTO, a number of regional trade organizations with limited memberships have emerged. The best known of these is the European Union (EU), which was founded in 1957 with 6 member states and has since expanded to 27 member countries stretching from the British Isles in the west to the Black Sea in the east. The second largest (by GDP) regional trade organization is the North American Free Trade Agreement (NAFTA), which has only three members: the United States, Canada and Mexico. The Mercado Común del Sur (Mercosur), which includes the Latin American giants Argentina and Brazil along with Uruguay and Paraguay, is the most highly developed regional trade organization in the developing world. The level of economic integration within these organizations varies. The EU allows free movement of labor and capital, has a common parliament and court system, and has virtually eliminated borders between most member states. Both the EU and Mercosur are customs unions, which means that they agree to a common tariff schedule on goods from non-member countries. NAFTA has none of these characteristics, but like the other two it has almost completely eliminated tariffs among member states.

The combination of the GATT/WTO process, the creation of regional free trade organizations and numerous bilateral agreements between trading nations has led to extensive trade liberalization at the global scale. The term "liberalization" is used instead of "free trade" because some tariffs remain and a variety of "non-tariff barriers," such as technical standards that make it hard to sell certain goods internationally, are still significant barriers. Nevertheless, international trade has never been cheaper or easier than it has been in the first decade of the twenty-first century.

A good indicator of the growing role of international trade in national economies is the "openness" measure defined as total trade (imports + exports) as a percentage of GDP. For a completely closed economy, this measure is zero, while for a completely open economy it can be higher than 100 percent – for example, if there were a country that exported everything it produced and imported everything it consumed, its openness measure would be around 200 percent. Table 24.1 shows this measure for some of the world's largest economies for the years 1950, 1970, 1990 and 2004.

By this measure, Canada and Germany are the most open economies, but all of the rich countries became more trade intensive over this period by a factor of at least 2. The three largest economies in the world – the U.S., Japan and China – all increased by factors greater than 4. In the developing world, the increases were not continuous. The decline for Brazil and India reflects economic policies in those countries that stressed domestic production for domestic consumption, but even they became more highly trade oriented by the twenty-first century. The only country whose openness measure declined over this period was South Africa. This probably reflects economic sanctions during the Apartheid era and a return to previous high levels is evident by 2004. The most striking trend in this table is the increasing openness of China, which went from a relatively closed economy in 1970 to one of the most trade-dependent countries in the world. By the end of the 2000s, China was neck-and-neck with Germany as the world's leading exporter.

## Foreign direct investment

The flows of trade in goods and services across borders are the most obvious indicator of the internationalization of the economy. But trade is not the only way

*Table 24.1* Openness measure (total trade/GDP) 1950–2004

| Country | 1950 | 1970 | 1990 | 2004 |
|---|---|---|---|---|
| United States | 6.26 | 10.23 | 12.67 | 26.60 |
| United Kingdom | 22.13 | 28.45 | 41.25 | 59.90 |
| Canada | 31.72 | 43.56 | 56.63 | 81.80 |
| Germany | – | 26.34 | 43.32 | 76.56 |
| Brazil | 17.93 | 11.15 | 13.01 | 33.30* |
| South Africa | 55.16 | 63.66 | 37.58 | 54.36 |
| India | 26.19 | 14.81 | 14.00 | 28.18* |
| Japan | 3.37 | 9.96 | 15.58 | 23.41 |
| China | 8.58** | 8.21 | 39.86 | 54.38 |

* 2003 data, **1952 data, – no data
*Source*: Heston *et al.* (n.d.); calculated at constant 2000 prices.

that firms engage in an international marketplace. Suppose a firm based in England has a product that it thinks would sell well in Mexico. There are three ways that the firm can exploit this opportunity. The first is to manufacture the product in England and export it to Mexico. Naturally, this is an example of international trade. If the firm wants to avoid the costs of shipping, tariffs and all the paperwork that goes with moving goods across borders, it can simply license the product to a Mexican manufacturer and profit through a royalty on each unit that the licensee sells. But this is not always a practical alternative. The product may require manufacturing expertise that only the English firm has or there may be trade secrets that the English firm does not want to share with a foreign producer. The third alternative is for the English firm to set up its own production facilities in Mexico, which would be an example of *foreign direct investment* (FDI).

To be specific, FDI is defined as an investment in physical facilities in a foreign country by which the investor takes principal control of those facilities and their operations. There is an important distinction between investing in facilities and operations in a foreign country and investing in that same country by buying shares in its existing firms. The latter is called *foreign portfolio investment* and does not imply that the investor takes control of foreign operations – that is unless it buys enough stock to have a controlling interest.

The discussion thus far implies that FDI is done for the purpose of selling manufactured goods into foreign markets. But some of the most conspicuous FDI is done for selling services. For example, McDonald's and Starbucks are now found in a host of cities outside North America and retail giants like Walmart and Tesco are now truly global operations. Also, firms may enter into FDI for reasons that have nothing to do with selling into the markets where they invest. For example, *maquiladora* plants located along the U.S.–Mexico border are often the result of U.S. and other foreign investment, but are producing goods principally intended for the U.S. market. In this case it is not the Mexican market that attracts attention, but rather cheap Mexican labor. (We'll expand on this theme in the next chapter.) Also, firms in resource sectors such as mining and forestry make FDI in those countries where mineral and forest resources are found with the intent of marketing to a global market.

Growth in FDI in recent decades has been as spectacular as growth in trade. According to the United Nations, world FDI increased from about \$13 billion in 1970 to \$2.1 trillion in 2007 – a more than 150-fold increase.[4] In large part, this is the result of the relaxation of restrictions on foreign investment that are imposed by national governments. For example, before the 1990s, India placed a variety of restrictions on FDI in terms of percentage of foreign ownership, transfer of technology, etc. These restrictions reflect the legacy of colonialism, as many people feared that India would become independent of a foreign nation only to become equally dependent on foreign firms. Reforms instituted in 1991 made India much more open to foreign investors, resulting in a more than tenfold increase in FDI inflows between 1991–2 and 2001–2.[5] Many other countries have adopted similar liberalization of investment rules, although restrictions are still common, especially in sectors such as natural resources, railroads and utilities.

While a full-blown formal model of the spatial distribution of FDI does not exist, a framework introduced by Dunning (1981, 1988) is useful for understanding why a particular firm makes an investment in a particular foreign country. Dunning defines three critical factors: firm-specific advantage, impediments to export and licensing, and location-specific advantages. Firm-specific advantage explains why the firm will have a competitive advantage over domestic firms in producing or marketing the intended good or service in a foreign country. While there may be many such advantages, we can identify two major categories. The first is a technological, managerial or other advantage that the firm has gained from its experience in a particular type of business. For example, a Canadian gold mining company may be able to transfer its know-how to mining gold in a foreign country, and would thus be more efficient than the domestic firms in that country. The second is some marketing advantage due to brand recognition. Because of communications technologies such as satellite television and the Internet, brand names from wealthy countries are seen all over the world. Someone in Indonesia may therefore be willing to pay a higher price for a genuine McDonald's hamburger than for a domestic imitation.

Impediments to licensing and export include anything that makes those two options impractical. With respect to licensing, the firm may not want to share its technological and managerial expertise as that would amount to giving up its firm-specific advantage. Also, for international brands there is a danger in licensing to foreign partners who may not uphold standards and thereby reduce the value of the brand. As for exports, Weber's location theory tells us that weight-gaining goods such as beer or Coca-Cola are much more efficiently produced close to the intended market. (See Box 24 on Coca-Cola's FDI in India.) Also, export may not be practical because of high tariff or other trade barriers. When the firm's advantage is in the production of a service that is "non-tradeable," exports are not an option. For example, it is not possible for McDonald's to make fresh-cooked hamburgers in the U.S. and sell them to consumers in other countries. As we will see, when the location-specific advantage is something other than the market, production in the firm's home country is not a practical option.

---

### *Box 24* Coca-Cola in India

Coca-Cola, which was invented by a pharmacist in 1886, has been the world's most popular soft drink for decades. While the precise formula for "Coke" remains a closely guarded secret, numerous other firms (including arch-rival Pepsi) are able to produce very similar drinks. What sets Coke apart is the Coca-Cola brand, which is instantly recognized all over the world as a symbol of American culture. In 2010, the world's largest brand consulting firm declared it the best global brand, ahead of IBM, Microsoft, Google, General Electric and McDonald's.[i] Thus, Coca-Cola owns one of the world's most valuable firm-specific advantages, which it exploits by selling its products in over 200 countries.

Location theory tells us that FDI is a better strategy than direct export for Coca-Cola. Beverages are the classic weight-gaining product. While direct export can work for high-margin beverages that are difficult to reproduce abroad, such as wine, liquor and sometimes beer, the best strategy for soft drinks is to produce close to the consumer using local bottles and water. Coca-Cola was already doing this in seven foreign countries including Canada, France and several in Latin America by 1918, creating one of the first truly global brands. (If you can find a copy, you may enjoy the 1961 Hollywood movie *One, Two, Three*, starring James Cagney as a Coca-Cola executive attempting to break into the Soviet market at the height of the Cold War.)

With its rapidly growing middle class, broad use of the English language and a history of adopting elements of Western culture, it is not surprising that India has been one of Coca-Cola's most important FDI targets. By the early 1970s, the brand was well established and wildly popular, but in 1977 an unprecedented event took place: Coke withdrew from India. The most publicized reason was an insistence by the Indian government that Coca-Cola reveal its secret formula to them, but probably more important were laws requiring a high level of domestic ownership for foreign enterprises operating in India. Those laws were a legacy of India's long colonial domination, which left a deep distrust of foreign economic interests. They didn't fit Coca-Cola's FDI model, however, which stresses strong central control in order to maintain the quality and distinctive flavor of the product.

Starting in 1991, India implemented a program of economic reforms that eliminated many regulations, including those that had led to the departure of Coca-Cola. Spurred by the fact that rival Pepsi was already active in India, Coke jumped back in by purchasing the largest domestic producer of soft drinks in 1992. A range of Coca-Cola brands such as Fanta, Minute Maid juices and a number of domestic brand names are now produced out of 56 bottling plants. Coca-Cola India is number one in sparkling drinks, juice drinks and bottled water.[ii] Thus, by economic measures, Coca-Cola has been enormously successful in India, but its recent tenure has not been without controversy.

Coke's success has been accompanied by a growing anti-Coke movement in India, which is now publicized around the world via the Internet. Both Coke and Pepsi have been accused of selling products with high levels of pesticide contamination – a charge they hotly deny. More frequently, bottling plants are seen as a threat because of their use of water, which is hardly a ubiquitous input in India. Some bottling plants are located close to rural villages and draw water from aquifers that have been used for centuries by local farmers. A number of these plants have been accused of causing severe water shortages and discharging polluted waste water. Coca-Cola counters that it uses the best environmental practices and that claims of excess water use are without grounds. In fact, the corporation claims to be a leader in water conservation, and has set a global goal of replacing as much water as it withdraws by 2020.[iii]

Whatever the merits of the environmental case against Coca-Cola in India, it illustrates something important. Brands have value, but they may also carry baggage. While the Indian government has abandoned its policies of restricting foreign direct investment, the distrust of foreign interests lives on among a large proportion of the population. Especially in rural areas, where most Indians still live, there is a strong devotion to the idea of *swadeshi* (self-reliance), which was promoted by Mahatma Gandhi in the struggle leading up to independence. This idea is rooted not only in economics but also in culture, as it aims to protect traditional arts, foods and social practices from replacement by foreign substitutes. To many people in India, a brand like Coca-Cola is emblematic of such cultural invasion from abroad and therefore acts as a symbol to rally against (Varmin and Belk, 2009).

**Notes**

i    InterBrand Best Global Brands, 2010: http://www.interbrand.com/en/best-global-brands/best-global-brands-2008/best-global-brands-2010.aspx, accessed October 2, 2011.
ii   http://www.coca-colaindia.com/ourcompany/company.html, accessed October 2, 2011.
iii  http://www.thecoca-colacompany.com/citizenship/index.html, accessed October 2, 2011.

A location-specific advantage is something about a foreign country that is conducive to production there. In many of the examples we have used so far, the location-specific advantage is the market. For example, Starbucks coffee shops made a major investment in Japan during the 1990s. The huge population of affluent urbanites with a taste for up-scale coffee was an ideal market for them. In many developing countries, large middle classes are emerging who make an excellent market for firms from affluent countries with long experience in catering to a middle-class clientele. Another category of location-specific advantage is natural resources. A Scandinavian forestry firm may apply its experience to operations in other countries, but only where there are forests.

Probably the most important location-specific advantage for FDI in manufactured goods is inexpensive labor. We avoid the term "cheap" here because a low wage is not in itself an economic advantage. Low-wage workers with low skills and therefore low productivity are not necessarily inexpensive. If the foreign wage is one half of the firm's domestic wage, while the foreign productivity is one third of the domestic productivity, then the "cheap" foreign labor is actually more expensive. However, with adequate literacy and basic skills and a moderate investment in training, firms located in high-income countries can often reduce overall production costs by transferring the most labor-intensive functions to low-income countries. In most cases, the key to reducing labor costs by means of FDI is the ability to geographically separate high-skilled functions from low-skilled functions in the production process. (This will be a major theme of the next chapter.)

Tariff barriers are one of the impediments to exports that make FDI an attractive option for many firms. Thus, one might think of FDI as a substitute for international trade. For example, in the latter part of the nineteenth century, Canada instituted a program of high tariffs against U.S. manufactured goods, with the goal of protecting its own nascent manufacturing sector. The outcome was that many U.S. manufacturers that had previously exported to Canada made investments across the border so that their goods could be treated as domestic production rather than as imports to Canada. In other words, FDI was the way around the tariff barrier. This type of substitution relationship may have dominated FDI in the nineteenth century and the early part of the twentieth, and it still plays a role today. But, more often, FDI and exports are complementary and interrelated strategies that firms use in international business. For example, an American firm may build an assembly factory in Mexico, export components to it and then re-import the finished good. Thus, FDI, exports and imports are all part of an effort to reduce labor costs.

FDI is not the only mechanism by which firms can reduce costs by assigning functions to different parts of the world. In fact, firms may prefer to avoid the risks of holding foreign assets while still benefiting from international production. The multinational enterprise, whose expertise lies in coordinating production among global networks of firms, is among the topics of the next chapter.

## Appendix: Effect of tariff on welfare

This Appendix provides a graphical demonstration that, under the assumptions used in the standard model of trade with perfect competition, free trade yields greater economic welfare than either autarky or trade subject to a tariff. The demonstration depends on the concepts of *consumer surplus* and *producer surplus*, which are measures of economic welfare. Consumer surplus is the benefit that consumers get from being able to buy a particular quantity of output at a particular price, while producer surplus is the benefit that producers get from being able to sell the same quantity at the same price. The sum of consumer and producer surplus, which is called *economic surplus*, is a measure of the aggregate benefit derived from the production and consumption of a commodity in the market.

This is illustrated in Figure A24.1 which shows the price and quantity determination under autarky. The labels *CS* and *PS* represent the consumer and producer surplus as being equal to the areas of the polygons in which the labels are located. To understand why this is the case, remember that the demand function is downward sloping, which means that, for the first unit, consumers would be willing to pay a much higher price than the price they must pay, which is $P_a$. So, for that unit, the consumer surplus is equal to the difference between $P_a$ and the price indicated by the demand function. For the second unit, the gap would be a bit smaller so the

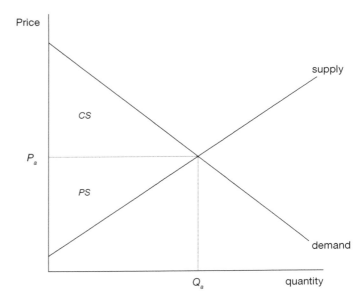

*Figure A24.1*
Consumer and
producer
surplus under
autarky

surplus would be a bit smaller. We can do a similar calculation for every unit consumed up to $Q_a$ where the gap becomes zero. Summing all these surplus values up, we get a total equivalent to the area of the triangle labeled $CS$. As for producer surplus, producers are willing to offer the first unit of output at a much lower price than the price they receive, which is $P_a$. Applying the same procedure as before, the total producer surplus is equal to the area of the triangle labeled $PS$. With this graphical device, we can look at the impact of various changes on economic welfare as indicated by the value of $CS + PS$. For example, you can demonstrate for yourself that a technological improvement that shifts the supply function to the right causes an increase in welfare.

Figure A24.2 shows the effect of opening up the economy to trade on total welfare. Not surprisingly, since the price goes down the value of consumer surplus, which is now $CS_1 + CS_2$, goes up, while the producer surplus, which is now $PS_1$, goes down. However, the change in the total surplus is positive:

$$CS_1 + CS_2 + PS_1 > CS + PS$$

To verify this, note that $CS_1 + PS_1 = CS + PS$, so the total surplus increases by $CS_2$.

We can now see what happens with the imposition of the tariff as shown in Figure A24.3. Producer surplus increases relative to the free trade case by the amount $PS_2$. But note that this increase is part of a reduction in consumer surplus equal to $PS_2 + L_1 + R + L_2$. Here $R$ represents government revenue from the tariff, defined as the product of $T$ and the quantity of imports. This should not be counted as a loss in surplus because it can be used to provide public services or reduce taxes. However, the total surplus declines by the value $L_1 + L_2$.

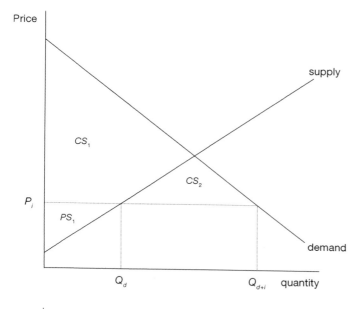

*Figure A24.2*
The effect of
opening up
economy to
trade on total
welfare

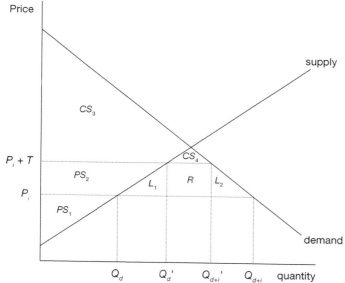

*Figure A24.3*
The effects of
tariff imposition

# 25 The globalization of production systems

What do we mean by globalization? Wolf (2004: 14) defines it as "The integration of economic activities, across borders, through markets." But the word "integration" can mean a great many things. Any form of international trade constitutes economic integration, but a more profound type of integration occurs when production systems, transportation networks or even economic policies from different countries are combined into one.

When a word ends in "-ation" it describes either a process or the end state of that process. The following definition is of the end state of globalization:

> The free movement of goods, services, labor and capital, thereby creating a single market in inputs and outputs; and full national treatment for foreign investors (and nationals working abroad) so that, economically speaking, there are no foreigners.[1]

Even in the European Union, where the specifics of this definition are met in a legal sense, it is not realistic to say that there are "no foreigners" since differences in language, culture and history still influence the patterns of economic interaction. But the countries of the European Union are much closer to complete integration than are the countries of NAFTA, which in turn are closer than the countries of the African Union.

We may define the process of globalization as the gradual movement from a condition of complete autarky to a condition of complete integration. Some regions and countries are much further along in this process than others, but with a very few exceptions all have been moving in the same direction. This is not to say that process is irreversible. During the protectionist era of the Great Depression, the general movement shifted back in the direction of autarky. Given the economic tumult in which we enter the second decade of the twenty-first century, the process of globalization may lose momentum and possibly even shift into reverse. But trends in technology, communications, the nature of the business enterprise and the role of the state all suggest that globalization will continue in the long term, although the end state of "no foreigners" may never be met.

How does the process of globalization play out? To answer this question, we must start by defining increasing levels of integration in production systems. We must also look at some institutional trends, including the changing nature of borders, the changing shape of the business enterprise.

## The integration of production systems

Consider two countries, each of which has automotive production exclusively for domestic demand and strict trade barriers preventing automotive imports. The nature of automotive production is for components to be manufactured in separate plants and then shipped to large assembly plants, where the final car is produced and shipped to final demand. Figure 25.1a represents this situation for two hypothetical countries A and B. Arrows represent physical shipments of components from any of three plants to a single large assembly plant and shipment of cars to final demand. Under the state of autarky, none of these arrows crosses the border between the two countries because there is no trade in either cars or components.[2] To make this simple example a bit more interesting, assume that A is a higher-income country than B.

Now suppose trade restrictions are reduced, allowing for the sale of cars across the A–B border, as shown in Figure 25.1b. Since B has lower income, it would probably produce a relatively small economical car, while A would produce a larger more luxurious car. Even in high-income A, there may be some thrifty people who would prefer to own the more economical model from B, while political and business elites in A might be able to afford the model from B and would be willing to pay for the prestige of owning one. Thus, product differentiation and heterogeneity in the population of car buyers would be sufficient to stimulate a significant trade in cars.

Note that this does not constitute an integration of the production system, since each car is completely manufactured in one country or the other. This situation is consistent with internationalization as defined in chapter 24. It is also quite similar to the situation in the 1960s when there was rapid growth in the global trade in finished vehicles.

In Figure 25.1c, trade flows are added to account for shipments from component plants in one country to assembly plants in the other. Why would this happen? One reason is that, even though the cars being produced in the two countries are different, they will have components in common. For example, instead of separate plants producing windshields for the assembly plants in the two countries, a single plant located in B might provide windshields for both. Similarly, a single plant located in A might produce radios for both assembly plants. While the components required by the two plants may be somewhat different, their production will require common equipment and expertise allowing component producers to achieve scale economies. In this case we see true integration of the production system because every car produced in A will include some components made in B and every car produced in B will include some components made in A.

Integration of the production system may take an asymmetric form. Once we allow for trade in components, the notion of comparative advantage can apply to components as well as to finished goods. Since B has lower income, it would not

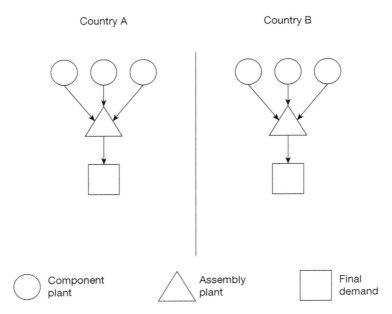

*Figure 25.1a* Automotive industries under autarky

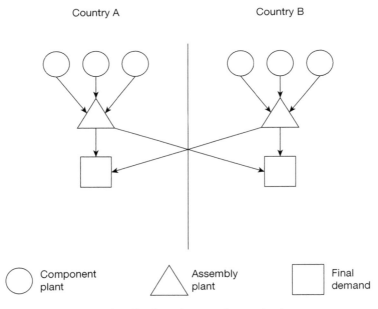

*Figure 25.1b* Internationalization of automotive production

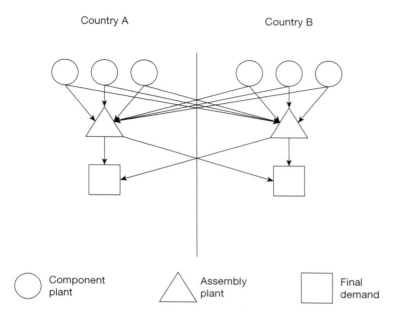

*Figure 25.1c* Full integration of automotive production

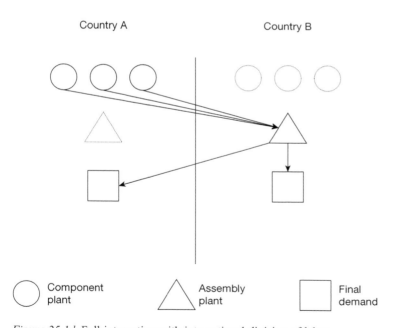

*Figure 25.1d* Full integration with international division of labor

be surprising to find that B has comparative advantage in labor-intensive production, while A has comparative advantage in capital-intensive production. Suppose that (as is often the case) assembly is more labor intensive than component manufacturing. If the comparative advantages are large enough, we might eventually see a shift of all assembly to A and a shift of all component production to B. This *international division of labor*, whereby the most labor-intensive activities are shifted to the lower-wage countries, is a typical outcome of globalization.

The kind of integration described in this hypothetical example has actually occurred in the automotive industries of Canada and the U.S. Up until the 1960s, the two countries were served by separate automotive production systems, despite the fact that both markets were dominated by the same producers: Ford, General Motors and Chrysler. In 1965, an agreement between Canada and the U.S. allowed for the tariff-free movement of finished cars and trucks as well as components (Anastakis, 2005). (Strictly speaking, this was a "managed trade" agreement since Canada's market share was protected.)

Within a few years, Canada–U.S. trade in cars, trucks and components exploded, becoming the most important sector in Canada–U.S. trade, which became the largest bilateral trade relationship in the world. Total labor costs were significantly lower in Canada, not only because of somewhat lower incomes but also because of a publicly funded health system that reduces the labor benefit costs of manufacturers operating in Canada. Because assembly is more labor intensive, automotive exports from Canada to the U.S. are mostly finished vehicles, while automotive exports from the U.S. to Canada are mostly components.

More than just Canada and the U.S. are involved in the production of North American cars. Especially since the implementation of NAFTA, Mexico has played a growing role in both parts production and assembly. Many auto parts for U.S. and Canadian assembled vehicles are produced in *maquiladora* plants, and some popular "American" cars are actually produced south of the border. Furthermore, many North American cars are now truly global, with an increasing share of components from China and other countries (see Box 25).

---

## *Box 25* **The globalization of the "American" car**

Prior to the 1970s, the "big three" Detroit-based companies General Motors, Ford and Chrysler dominated the U.S. market. The few imported cars seen on American roads filled market niches, such as Italian sports cars for rich playboys and Volkswagen Beetles for poor students. But, after about 1973, Japanese manufacturers Toyota, Honda and Nissan (then called Datsun) began to make significant market inroads. There were a number of reasons for this. Cheaper Japanese labor made it possible to undercut the prices of both American and European competitors. The Arab oil embargo of 1973 led to rapid price rises and absolute shortages of gasoline, giving a further advantage to more fuel-efficient Japanese models. Furthermore, the North

American manufacturers had come to compete more in terms of style than quality, while Japanese firms stressed dependability. Japanese brands quickly surpassed the sales of European imports and made a serious dent in the once invincible market dominance of the big three.

By the 1980s, Japanese wages had risen close to North American levels, but the reputation of Japanese brands for quality and fuel efficiency allowed them to increase their market shares by moving upscale into larger models and even luxury brands like Lexus and Infiniti. The U.S. government came under pressure from the domestic industry and labor to limit import competition through high tariffs or quotas. In an attempt to head off the imposition of trade barriers, the government of Japan agreed to impose voluntary export restraints, under which its automakers were forbidden to sell beyond a prescribed number of cars into the U.S. market. Rather than forgo continued growth based on North American demand, Honda and Toyota opened assembly plants (popularly known as "transplants") in the U.S. and Canada for popular models such as the Toyota Corolla and Camry, and the Honda Civic and Accord, all of which have consistently ranked among the top North American sellers for the past two decades. Other Japanese companies soon followed, including Nissan, Subaru, Suzuki and Mitsubishi, as did a number of European automobile manufacturers.

The success of Japanese cars in the North American and other global markets has required that the "big three" be renamed the "Detroit three," since Toyota now builds more cars than Ford or Chrysler and earns far more profit than General Motors. In both the U.S. and Canada, employment by the Detroit three has been declining, while the transplant employment has been growing. Still, many people still view Detroit three cars as "American" and all others as "foreign," even if they are assembled in the U.S. or Canada. Their impression is that, even if a Honda is assembled in Ohio, it is probably made largely of Japanese parts and therefore fails to generate as much spin-off employment as a Chevrolet or a Ford. Largely in order to make buyers aware of such a possibility, the U.S. Congress enacted the American Automotive Labeling Act in 1992, requiring a sticker on each new car saying what proportion of the components in the car by value were produced in either the U.S. or Canada and where the car was assembled.

Information gleaned from these stickers is shown in Table B25.1 for some of the most popular models. The numbers are rather surprising. It does not appear that a Japanese nameplate indicates a high proportion of Japanese parts, as Honda's compact Civic is assembled from 70 percent U.S./Canada parts and the comparable number for Toyota's mid-sized Camry is 80 percent. Of the cars on this list, only Chrysler's new mid-size 200 exceeds the Camry for U.S./Canada parts content, but its affordable Dodge Journey SUV is assembled in Mexico and contains only 38 percent U.S./Canada parts. The Ford Fusion, which is often touted as the Detroit three's top contender to take on the Honda Accord and Toyota Camry, which have long divided the lion's share of the lucrative mid-size class between them, is assembled in Mexico and uses only 20 percent U.S./Canada parts. (The Cars.com website has a "Made in America index" in which the Camry and Accord rank 1 and 2.) This is not to say that all Japanese cars are North American made. Toyota's famous Prius hybrid is made in Japan and contains no U.S./Canada parts. The same is true for all but one of its luxury Lexus models. The main point here is that those who wish to remain loyal to the "American car" will need to do a little research before they buy.

*Table B25.1*  North American content and assembly locations for models popular in North America

| Manufacturer | Model | % U.S./Canada content | Assembly plant location |
| --- | --- | --- | --- |
| Honda | Civic | 70 | Canada (Ontario) and U.S. (Indiana) |
| Chrysler | 200 | 81 | U.S. (Michigan) |
| Chrysler | Dodge Journey | 38 | Mexico |
| Ford | Focus | 60 | U.S. (Michigan) |
| Ford | Fusion | 20 | Mexico |
| General Motors | Buick Lucerne | 76 | U.S. (Michigan) |
| General Motors | Buick Regal | 21 | Germany |
| General Motors | Chevrolet Cruze | 45 | U.S. (Ohio) |
| General Motors | Chevrolet Malibu | 75 | U.S. (Michigan) |
| Mercedes | C-class | 0 | Mexico |
| Mercedes | GL-class | 62 | U.S. (Alabama) |
| Toyota | Camry | 80 | Kentucky |
| Toyota | Prius | 0 | Japan |

*Source*: National Highway Traffic Safety Administration, U.S. Department of Transportation (2011); state location of U.S. plant obtained from various industry and media sources.

An especially interesting case here is the Chevrolet Cruze, which was introduced into the U.S. market in 2010, but which had been produced earlier in a number of countries including Australia, India, Brazil, China and South Korea. Despite the fact that the Cruze is assembled in Lordstown Ohio, its North American version contains only 45 percent U.S./Canada parts. This is not surprising for a truly global car, because parts manufacturers who are already serving assembly plants in Asia, Australia and Latin America have a head start in providing parts to the new American plant. But there is another side to this. Those American and Canadian firms that provide parts to the Cruze plant in Ohio will be able to compete to supply nine other Cruze plants around the world, thus increasing exports. The Cruze probably provides a good model for how the automotive industry will work in the future. In a world of global cars, the idea of an American car may have little meaning.

The most successful new player in the North American automotive market is Hyundai Motor Company of South Korea. Hyundai has actually been selling cars in the U.S. since 1986, but it started with a very low-cost model with a poor reputation for quality. Over time, however, Hyundai improved its quality and expanded its product line. It now even offers a luxury model called the Equus with a list price over U.S.\$60,000. It originally was an import-only company, but it has recently set up assembly plants for two popular models in Montgomery, Alabama, proving that it can compete without the benefit of low-cost Korean assembly labor.

Many Americans and Canadians are surprised that such stylish and sophisticated cars can come from what they think of as a "Third World" country. The fact is that, after decades of spectacular growth, South Korea has joined the club of affluent countries, and in many ways is more similar to Japan than it is to China. Low-income countries are making inroads into the North American automotive market, however, not through assembled vehicles but through parts. Figure B25.1 shows the trend in China–U.S. trade in auto parts. With the exception of the recession year 2009, China's exports to the U.S. rose every year from 2000 to 2010, increasing by a factor of more than 5 over the decade, to reach about 11 percent of U.S. imports and over 20 percent of imports from outside the NAFTA area. This share will probably continue to grow, making China one of the most important contributors to value in cars produced in North America.

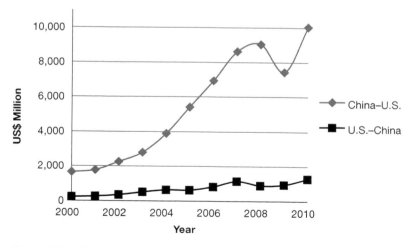

*Figure B25.1* China–U.S. trade in auto parts, 2000–10

*Source*: International Trade Administration (2011: Chart 12).

Integration of production systems occurs not only between neighboring countries like Canada, the U.S. and Mexico. In fact, for electronic goods, whose high ratio of value to weight makes them relatively insensitive to transportation costs, production systems can span much of the globe. A recent study of the third-generation Apple iPod music player provides some interesting insights into the nature of globalized production (Linden *et al.*, 2009). The iPod, which at the time of the study sold for U.S.$299, was assembled in China from components produced in the United States, Japan, Korea and Taiwan. Although the iPod was marked "made in China," the cost of Chinese assembly was only a few dollars – the components produced in other countries represented much larger shares of total production costs. Still, the cost of the device to Apple, which did not manufacture any part of the product, was estimated by the study to be only about $145 – less than half the final retail cost. Of the remaining $150, about $75 went to distribution costs and retail margins, while Apple retained an estimated margin of $80. This does not mean that Apple made an outrageous profit, since out of that margin it must recoup the costs of technological development, product design, a great deal of advertising and product support.

The iPod example provides a couple of important lessons regarding globally integrated production. First, the "made in China" label is highly misleading because, of all the countries involved in the production of the device, China actually added the least to its value. Assembly tends to occur in the lowest-income location because it is labor intensive, but in this case assembly contributed little to the final price. Second, the location and cost of manufacturing activities tell only part of the story when it comes to technology- and marketing-intensive products such as the iPod. We will return to this theme in chapter 26, which is on the *knowledge economy*.

Some might take the case of the iPod as evidence that space and distance, which are the hallmarks of economic geography, no longer have much bearing on the global economy. After all, producing components in the United States, shipping them to an assembly plant in China, and then effectively shipping them back to the United States as part of the assembled iPod does not make much sense from a transportation perspective. But, in fact, it is an excellent example of the trade-off between transportation and labor costs described in Weber's location model, only at a much broader scale than Weber could ever have imagined. (Return to chapter 15, Table 15.1 and Figure 15.1 to review this model.) Shifting assembly to China only makes sense because the transportation costs of the tiny devices are so low relative to the labor cost gap between China and the United States. For a product that is more expensive to transport, such as a car or a piece of industrial machinery, shifting assembly to low-wage locations is a less viable option.

## Borders

A common way to describe globalization is as the creation of a "borderless world" (Ohmae, 1999). Once again, this is an end-state definition, as borders still play an important role in the global economy. Changes in borders over the past couple of decades can tell us a lot about the prospects and limitations of globalization.

First, it's important to make a distinction between *boundaries* and *borders*. A boundary is a legal concept: an abstract line separating the territories over which two adjacent states have sovereignty. A border, on the other hand, is a more concrete geographical entity, comprising elements of the natural and built environment that define the boundary and facilitate (highways, bridges, ferries), prevent (fences, military installations), monitor (cameras, motion detectors) and control (border-crossing facilities) movement of goods and people across the boundary. While in history borders existed primarily for the defense of national territory, in modern times a number of other functions including customs (collection of tariffs and general control of goods movement), immigration (control of people movements) and security (detecting goods or people entering the national territory with criminal intent) have become the dominant border functions.

Borders vary greatly in terms of *permeability*, defined as the ease of movement across them. Borders act as barriers to integration, but, as they become more permeable, more integration becomes possible. This is true not only for integration in the form of trade, but also for the integration of infrastructure systems that support economic activity. This is illustrated by Figure 25.2, which shows how road networks in two sovereign states can become more integrated as the border becomes more permeable. In Figure 25.2a, the border is completely impermeable, so the networks are unconnected and cross-border movement is impossible. In Figure 25.2b, movement is possible through a couple of border crossings, so movement across the border is possible, but it is still more difficult than movement within either of the national networks. At this level of network integration, economic integration can occur but with significant friction across the border. In Figure 25.2c, the two networks are completely connected and border crossings with their typical delays and other costs have been eliminated.

These days, most of the world's borders are of the type shown in Figure 25.2b. Movement is possible but the border constitutes a significant bottleneck. Cross-border movements are retarded due to inspections and paperwork required by the government agencies responsible for border functions and because of the congestion that typically arises at bottlenecks in networks. Of course, if the movement between two countries involves crossing an ocean the picture is somewhat different as goods and people must cross some international space between crossing marine borders and entering territorial waters, but the basic idea is still the same as entry is possible only through a limited number of ports managed by government officials. Similarly, movement of goods and people by air occurs only through a small number of international airports with border inspection facilities. In all cases there are costs to crossing the border that would not be incurred on a trip or shipment of the same distance that did not cross a border. These costs include direct monetary costs, such as the payments of customs duties and visa charges, and costs of delays at border crossings, which can be translated into equivalent monetary value. Border costs place limits on integration among countries.

To illustrate, return to the example shown in Figure 25.1 and suppose that the managers of an assembly plant in either of the two countries is deciding whether

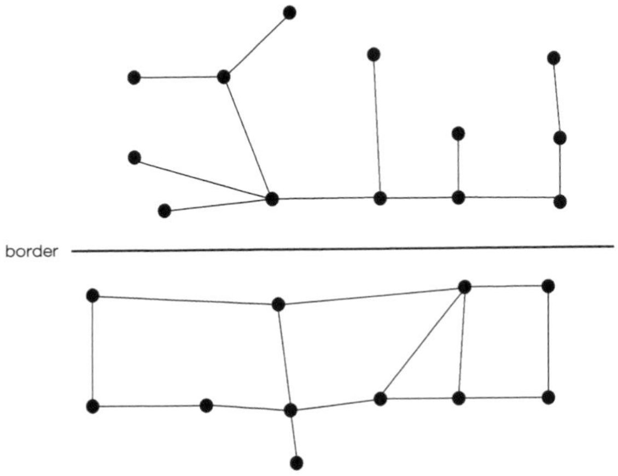

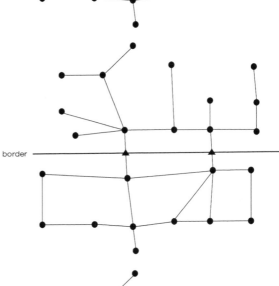

*Figure 25.2a*
Impermeable border

*Figure 25.2b*
Partially permeable border

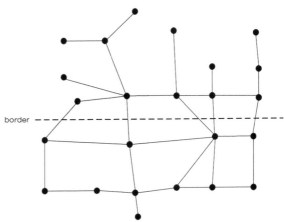

*Figure 25.2c*
Fully permeable border

to purchase a particular component from a domestic supplier or a cross-border supplier. We can define the delivered price of the domestic supplier as

$$P_d = \bar{P}_d + t_d$$

where $\bar{P}_d$ is the mill price of the domestic supplier and $t_d$ is its transportation cost. The comparable delivered price for the cross-border supplier must also include the cost of crossing the border, so it is

$$P_c = \bar{P}_c + t_c + b_c$$

where $b_c$ is the cost of crossing the border. If the two suppliers provide perfectly interchangeable goods and if $t_d = t_c$, then the factory will only source from the cross-border supplier if

$$\bar{P}_d - \bar{P}_c + b_c$$

The cross-border supplier can only compete if it is willing to accept a lower per unit revenue than the domestic supplier. It also implies a potential cost to the assembly plant because in those cases where $\bar{P}_d - \bar{P}_c > 0$ but $\bar{P}_d - \bar{P}_c < b_c$ it is not able to take advantage of whatever cost or efficiency advantages allow the cross-border supplier to sell the input at a lower price.

We can express the border costs as a tariff rate equivalent $r_c$, such that

$$P_c = (\bar{P}_c + t_c)(1 + r_c)$$

$$r_c = \frac{b_c}{(\bar{P}_c + t_c)}$$

While there is little empirical evidence on the magnitude of $r_c$, a detailed study of the Canada–U.S. border (Taylor *et al.*, 2004) found that for goods moved by trucks it is about 4 percent, which is roughly equal to the tariff rates that the two countries charge on imports from non-NAFTA countries.[3] If the border cost is this high for two countries with such good trade relations as the United States and Canada, they are undoubtedly even higher elsewhere.

The end state of complete integration can only be achieved when borders and their costs are eliminated completely, as illustrated in Figure 25.2c. In this case, not only are the costs of border crossings eliminated, but transportation networks are integrated to allow more efficient movement. But is the complete elimination of borders even possible?

In fact, the elimination of borders has been achieved in what is called the Schengen Area, which includes most of the states in the European Union, plus Norway, Iceland and Switzerland. (The name comes from a town in Luxembourg where a treaty to eliminate borders was signed in 1985.) Within the area, goods and people can move across national boundaries without stopping for inspections or paperwork. The key to eliminating borders in the Schengen Area was the complete harmonization of policies such as external tariffs and visa requirements. Since the requirements for a good or a person to be in one Schengen member is the same as the requirements to be in any other, there is no need to check people and goods as they cross borders within the area. Stringent customs, immigration and security checks are still applied at the borders that define the perimeter of the Area. For this reason, the Schengen model is often called the *perimeter* approach to border management.

So far, the Schengen example has not spread to other parts of the world. For example, there have been calls for a perimeter approach that would virtually eliminate the border between the United States and Canada, but there has been little progress toward achieving it (Noble, 2005), largely because of the difficulties of harmonizing what are now very different policies on things like external tariffs, visas and firearms. For the foreseeable future, the world's largest bilateral trade relationship will continue to contend with border costs.

The terrorist attacks of September 11, 2001 and subsequent attacks in London, Madrid and elsewhere have further retarded progress toward eliminating borders. To a great extent, the elimination of tariffs and other barriers to travel and trade across borders has been offset by an increased concern on the part of border officials with a class of *clandestine transnational actors*, that includes terrorists, drug smugglers, human smugglers, illegal aliens and others with criminal intent (Andreas, 2003). Especially for movements into the United States, these concerns led to more stringent security inspections and additional identification requirements at borders, resulting in substantially less permeable borders. Thus, the borderless world is still a long way off.

## The multinational enterprise

In principle, the kind of cross-border integration shown in Figure 25.1c could be accomplished via sales of final and intermediate goods by and among individual firms, each of which operates in only one country. In practice, however, some firms operate in more than one country and are therefore called multinational enterprises (MNEs). MNEs come into being through the mechanism of foreign direct investment (FDI), which was discussed in the previous chapter. Under some circumstances, FDI may be an alternative to trade, but just as often it gives rise to trade as goods are sold between affiliates of the same firm in different countries – a phenomenon known as *intra-firm trade*.

We generally think of MNEs as gigantic corporations based in North America, Europe or Japan and operating in a dozen or more countries. But much smaller firms based all over the globe meet the definition of operating in more than one country. Still, the few multinational giants account for a very large share of global production. Since they are so diverse, there is probably no such thing as a typical MNE, but we can usefully classify them as operating according to two broad strategies: multidomestic and global.

A *multidomestic* firm is one that locates a full range of corporate functions in each of the markets in which it operates. For example, suppose a company produces a range of consumer goods such as household cleaning products in a large affluent country. It may want to exploit its accumulated experience and brand recognition by entering a number of other markets. A possible strategy would be to look at the corporate structures and practices that have worked in its home market and try to transfer them to each of the new markets it enters. It would manufacture all of its products and have separate marketing and distribution systems in each new market. Given the variety of functions it will be managing, it would also make sense to have a central administration in each market. Since it is recreating something very much like its domestic operations in each country, the name multidomestic fits well.

A *global* firm takes a very different approach. Instead of producing a product in a particular location, it finds the best location for every step in the production process and scatters production activities across those locations. Global firms generally produce complex goods such as aircraft and electronics that include a variety of components and production processes.[4] For each component or process it tries to find the best location based on cost, quality and reliability of production. It also makes a decision whether to produce in-house or subcontract production of each component and process to other firms. A number of factors go into this decision, including the availability of reliable subcontractors with sufficient expertise, the cost of contracting complex functions and the long-term risk of making investments in foreign countries.

Naturally, the benefits of distributing production to different locations have to be weighed against the extra costs of transportation and crossing borders. The types of goods produced by global firms generally have complex supply chains comprising the movement of components among facilities around the globe. One of the principles of supply chain managements is that inventories of components should be kept low to avoid carrying costs, which leaves little buffer for missed or late shipments. A high degree of sophistication in logistics functions is therefore *sine qua non* for an MNE pursuing the global strategy.

The global firm essentially takes comparative advantage to a new level by distributing not just the production of goods, but all the intermediate steps in the production of goods to their most efficient locations. By so doing, it generates a great deal of trade. As a result of globally integrated production, intermediate goods now represent more than 50 percent of international trade in goods and intra-firm transfers account for substantial shares of the imports and exports of many countries (OECD, 2010). The Apple iPod case is an excellent example of global production. Recall that in that case components were exported from the United States, Taiwan, Korea and Japan to China. After assembly, the complete device was exported from China to the United States or other market. Since trade statistics are based on the value of goods shipped rather than value added, the value of each component actually gets counted twice!

The multidomestic and global firms represent two ends of a spectrum. While the global strategy is superior from a cost perspective, a multidomestic strategy has the advantage of allowing firms to cater production to the varying tastes and expectations of different markets. Firms in many industries exhibit elements of both strategies. For example, in the automotive industry, General Motors and Ford have recently shown global tendencies by transferring models designed for Europe to the North American market, while Toyota has moved in a multidomestic direction by shifting its production closer to its main markets. Some industries, such as production of commercial airplanes, are global by nature, while others, such as fast-food restaurants, are multidomestic.

The impact of MNEs on host countries has been the subject of much debate over the years. Multidomestic MNEs have technological advantages that help them to out-compete domestic competitors. On the positive side, this leads to higher productivity and per capita income. On the negative side, the loss of domestic producers may reduce industry employment and eliminate certain functions such as research and development that even multidomestic producers conduct only in their home countries. The presence of global MNEs allows host countries to rapidly boost exports, but also makes them vulnerable to fluctuations in the demand over which they have no control. All MNEs act as vehicles for technology transfer, but sometimes technological advances that reduce labor requirements have negative impacts on some segments of society. (For a detailed exploration of these issues, see Dicken, 2007.)

## Globalization and economic geography

This brief chapter only scratches the surface by describing a few of the many aspects of the process of globalization. Issues such as the rise of globalized cities and the growth of global finance networks are not addressed, and the interaction between information and communications technology and patterns of global production are left to the next chapter. But even this brief treatment should be sufficient to illustrate that the transition from a local world to a global world does not undermine the study and methods of economic geography.

For example, the strategy of the global firm arises in large part from two classic themes in economic geography: differentiated space and the trade-off between scale economies and transportation costs. Differentiated space means that a variety of factors that vary across the map – labor costs, skills, natural resources, energy prices, infrastructure, political stability and many more – make some places more advantageous than others for a given production step. But there may not be a single best place for every step in the production process. Since the different steps have different requirements, they will have different best locations. From the perspective of production efficiency, the best thing is for every step to take place in its best location, not only because this strategy exploits spatial differentiation but also because it maximizes any scale economies that can be achieved at the level of a single step. However, since goods in process must pass from one step to the next, such a dispersed configuration of production will have high transportation costs, which at the global scale include the costs of crossing borders. Thus, the global firm faces a problem of balancing locational advantages, scale economies and transportation costs. This is a much more complex problem than the simple location models presented in Part III, but it involves many of the same principles.

An effect of globalization is to increase the geographical scope of economic decision making. Firms routinely make decisions between sourcing inputs from factories located 10,000 km apart. It may be impossible to attribute more than about 30 percent of the value of a complex electronic device to any single country. In a way, we are all making global decisions on a daily basis without even thinking about it, as when we choose a garment made in Indonesia over one made in Britain because the former is cheaper.

Recall from chapter 1 that economic geographers study and attempt to explain the spatial configuration of economic activities. As spatial configurations become more complex and far-flung, the challenge of economic geography has never been greater.

# 26  The knowledge economy

Before we can define the knowledge economy, we need first to explain what we mean by knowledge. Conventional definitions of the word tend to be complex and highly variable, so an easier way is to appeal to the *DIKW hierarchy* (referring to data, information, knowledge and wisdom). Data are isolated pieces of information with no meaning or practical application in their own right. Data can be the binomial bits in a computer, a table of numbers or the names of a set of unrelated objects. Information is data that is organized in such a way as to make it meaningful or useful. In particular, information is useful for decision making. For example, the latitudes and longitudes of a list of cities are data, but when they are organized into a map that makes it possible to plan a trip, they convey information.

The distinction between information and knowledge is controversial,[1] but by most definitions knowledge combines information in such a way as to achieve understanding or "know-how." Another important distinction is that things can have information, but only people have knowledge (although the science of artificial intelligence makes it possible to endow machines with knowledge). A map has information, but a person with access to maps and an understanding of how to interpret them has the knowledge necessary to find her way around a complex landscape. Knowledge can be described as either explicit or tacit. Explicit knowledge can be passed from one person to another by means of a set of instructions. For example, a bicycle that arrives broken down in a packing crate may come with a set of assembly instructions. Each instruction is information, but by reading those instructions the person gains the knowledge of how to assemble the bike. Tacit knowledge cannot be conveyed so simply because it involves concepts in the mind that are not easy to specify. Aesthetic capabilities such as the ability to judge wines or appreciate jazz music are often used as examples of tacit knowledge. In general, tacit knowledge can only be conveyed from one person to another by means of personal contact and it usually takes a good deal of time to "sink in" to the person receiving the knowledge. As we will see, the distinction between explicit and tacit knowledge has some implications for economic geography.

Wisdom, which is the pinnacle of the DIKW hierarchy, is beyond the scope of this book (and perhaps beyond the ken of its author). It is the member of the hierarchy with the greatest variety of definitions, including the ability to transfer knowledge from one domain to another, the power of foresight, and the integration of ethics and beliefs into knowledge systems.

So what is the knowledge economy? Strictly speaking, a knowledge economy refers to markets for the sale or transfer of expertise, know-how or other assets that fall under the heading of knowledge. More generally, the term "knowledge economy" refers to a *knowledge-based* economy, in which knowledge-intensive goods and services are prominent. (In what follows, we use the term "knowledge economy" in this more general sense.) A knowledge-intensive good is one whose value arises predominantly from the knowledge of the people who produce it, rather than from physical labor, energy or material inputs. Of course, every type of production requires knowledge, but some are more knowledge intensive than others (refer back to the comparison of a video game and a load of bricks in chapter 24). When we hear "knowledge intensive," we tend to think of high-tech gadgets, but knowledge intensity often occurs in ways that are not immediately visible. For example, a genetically engineered seed is clearly a knowledge-intensive good. Also, it is not only "new" things that are knowledge intensive. Musicians, teachers and wood carvers provide knowledge-intensive services and have done so for centuries.

As in the case of globalization, when we study the knowledge economy we are more interested in a process than an end state. The end state of a pure knowledge economy – one in which the value of every good and service arises exclusively from the knowledge applied in its production – will never be reached. But, over time, the knowledge content of the economy increases. In chapter 24, we noted that this happens via two simultaneous processes: first, the growth of more knowledge-poor goods at the expense of fewer knowledge-intensive goods (more video games and fewer bricks) and, second, through the increasing knowledge intensity of existing goods, such as the addition of more information technologies and advanced materials to cars.

The terms "information economy" and "knowledge economy" are often used interchangeably, but they are not quite the same thing. For one thing, a product can "be" information (as in the case of the map) but it can only be an outcome of knowledge, which is an attribute of people rather than things. At a more practical level, the information economy generally refers to the class of information and communications technologies (ICT) – either products of those technologies, such as computers and global positioning system (GPS) devices, or activities and services that make intensive use of those technologies, such as e-commerce and distance education. The information economy is therefore a narrower concept, but it is a core component of the knowledge economy.

The growth of knowledge-intensive goods and services is not easy to measure since there is some subjectivity involved in deciding what is knowledge intensive and what is not. For the U.S., industries typically regarded as "high-tech," including aerospace, pharmaceuticals, computers, communication equipment and medical instruments, grew from a bit over one-tenth of total manufacturing value-added in the mid-1990s to about a third of the total by the mid-2000s, and services classified as knowledge intensive experienced similar growth.[2] This is typical of many countries, where the most rapidly growing part of the economy is also the most knowledge-intensive part.

The focus of this chapter is how the transition to the knowledge economy affects the spatial configuration of economic activity (recall that configuration refers to both spatial patterns of things and spatial interaction within those patterns). It starts by considering the impacts of ICT, looking specifically at the geographical implications of e-commerce and the relationship between communications technologies and transportation. It then considers geographical aspects of knowledge-intensive industries, especially the tendency of firms in those industries to cluster in space, and the implications for regional economic convergence. Finally, it explores the relationship between globalization and the knowledge economy.

## ICT and economic geography

ICT refers to hardware and software used to record, store, process, display and transfer information. Until about the 1990s, it was common to refer to information technologies and communications technologies independently. Most early computers were either free-standing or consisted of a central processor with a number of terminals hard-wired in within a relatively compact space. When personal computers were introduced they were also free-standing and data could only be transferred between them by means of magnetic disks. Gradually, computers of all types became interconnected, first via telephone-based modems and eventually by a variety of much faster wired and wireless technologies. At the same time, communications technologies were shifting to digital technologies, making them more compatible with computers. The Internet was the key integrating infrastructure that merged information and communication into a common system called ICT. Today, technologies such as laptop computers, smartphones, GPS systems, etc. are neither information nor communications technologies, but rather both.

The pervasiveness of ICT in daily life has profound implications for economic geography. It does not, however, mean that distance is disappearing or that spatial decisions no longer matter. Rather, it alters patterns of accessibility and thereby changes locational decisions. One of the most pervasive manifestations of ICT is e-commerce, defined as the buying and selling of goods and services using the Internet or other electronic networks. E-commerce can be divided into two sectors: business-to-business (B2B) and business-to-consumer (B2C). We focus first on B2C, which is also sometimes called e-retailing.

There are some consumer goods that can be purchased online and downloaded to the customer's computer or other electronic device. The most famous example would be the purchase of music files from iTunes and other music e-retailers or the purchase of an e-book from Amazon.com. We might call this "pure" e-retail because goods are both purchased and delivered by electronic means. But most B2C transactions involve the purchase of some good that is transferred physically rather than digitally, such as the purchase of a paper book from Amazon.com or the purchase of shoes from Zappos.com.

Figure 26.1 compares the spatial interactions that occur when goods are purchased from a traditional "brick and mortar" (B&M) retailer to those that occur when the purchase is from an e-retailer. In Figure 26.1a, goods are shipped via freight transportation from their manufacturers to a distribution center. There goods from different manufacturers are combined into freight shipments to the B&M stores. Consumers travel to the store by some form of personal transportation (public transportation or private car), select the goods to purchase and then carry them back home, again by personal transportation. Now consider the e-retailer shown in Figure 26.1b. The goods still start out at the manufacturer and are shipped to the e-retailer's fulfillment center. ("Fulfillment center" sounds like a place for spiritual development, but it simply refers to the fulfillment of customer orders.) At this point, things start to look different. The B&M stores have been eliminated and people no longer leave their homes to make the transaction, so there is no personal transportation involved. Instead, a communications link via the Internet is used to place the order and the goods are delivered by freight transportation directly to the consumer's home. The elimination of a link in the relationship between the buyer and the seller – in this case the elimination of the stores – is an example of *disintermediation*, which is a common outcome of e-commerce.

An obvious outcome of switching from B&M retail to e-retail is a change in the structure of transportation. The actual quantity of transportation service required does not change because the same goods must go from the same manufacturers to the same households. But, now, deliveries are made by firms providing small-parcel services such as UPS, Fedex and DHL. (Naturally, these firms have benefited enormously from the growth of e-retail.) This has implications for transportation planning because it means fewer car trips and more truck trips, although the time saved by consumers may be applied to leisure activities that also require personal transportation.

There are other implications to the growth of e-retail that become evident when viewed through the lens of economic geography. Urban land-use theory is based on the idea that the location preferences of households are driven by accessibility. Accessibility to workplaces is emphasized in the theory but accessibility to shopping activities is also important. If the consumer is no longer traveling to stores, however, an important advantage of living relatively close to urban centers is eliminated. Thus, the growth of e-retail may contribute to land-use dispersion by making locations far from shopping centers more attractive relative to central locations. Of course, the delivery of goods direct to the consumer's door is not free; the consumer has to pay a delivery charge. But most e-retailers use a uniform delivery charge that does not vary according to the customer's home location. It costs more to deliver goods to people living in remote locations, so by charging a uniform rate the e-retailer is essentially asking more centrally located customers to subsidize the more remotely located ones. This pricing policy only reinforces the tendency of e-retail to make remote living more attractive.

On top of this, e-retailing detracts from one of the key advantages to living in cities, which is the great variety of goods and services on offer because the web

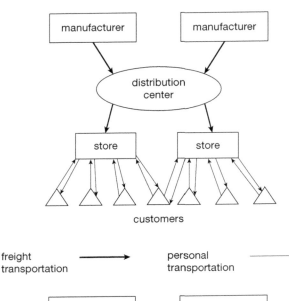

*Figure 26.1a*
Brick and mortar
retail (adapted
from Anderson
*et al.*, 2003)

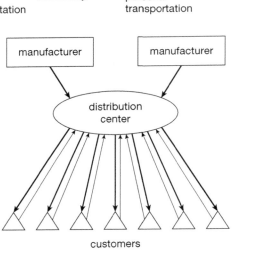

*Figure 26.1b*
E-retail (adapted
from Anderson
*et al.*, 2003)

site offers a variety that not even the largest B&M retailers can match. So, all told, the growth of e-retailing appears to promote more dispersed living patterns (Anderson, Chatterjee and Lakshmanan, 2003). Of course, there are limits to this effect. Most people enjoy traditional shopping, and e-retailing is a poor option for goods that require close tactile inspection such as fresh produce or cashmere sweaters. Also, as we will discuss below, there are other aspects of the knowledge economy that favor urban living.

The case of pure e-retail such as downloading music or software is of particular interest because it essentially eliminates transportation of all types by delivering the goods digitally. This type of transaction is expanding into publishing, as an ever greater share of sales from Amazon.com are of e-books for its Kindle reader and new devices like the iPad seek to take the place of paper books, magazines and newspapers. This trend is not limited to B2C but also extends to B2B when, for example, custom software and associated manuals are delivered exclusively in digital form. This type of transaction virtually frees certain types of transactions from the friction of distance, as in the case where programming services are sold by Indian firms to customers in Europe and North America. Borders are still an issue, however. For example, iTunes must maintain separate operations in the U.S. and Canada because of differences in intellectual property laws.

In examples like these, communications technologies are able to substitute for transportation, which leads some to suggest that transportation will become less important in the knowledge economy. This is a fascinating possibility from the perspective of economic geography since transportation is the main cause of the friction of distance, which has such a great influence on the spatial configuration of economic activities. But caution is in order. The examples above are not of goods that have information content; they are of goods that *are* information. Since ICT makes it possible to transfer virtually any information electronically, the distribution of such goods can be done without transportation. Information goods are a growing share of the total economy, but they are still a small share. Most goods embody not just bytes of information but also molecules of matter, so they require physical transportation.

Personal communications technologies have an even greater scope for replacing personal transportation. Old forms of long-distance information, such as the telephone, telegraph and mail, were inefficient and ineffective compared with face-to-face communication. New technologies for teleconferencing and virtual conferencing, and applications that allow people in different locations to work collaboratively on complex plans and documents can take the place of many personal trips. Telecommuting (working from home with the help of ICT) can even replace the journey to work. But, as we will explore below, some aspects of the knowledge economy increase the need for people to be close together, especially when there is a need to transfer complex information or share tacit knowledge.

When viewed from the narrow perspective of specific tasks, communication and transportation may be viewed as substitutes, which means that you can reduce your use of one by increasing your use of the other. But, from a broader perspective, communications and transportation may be complements, which means that consuming more of one leads to consuming more of the other (Mokhtarian, 1990). To give a simple example, suppose two people register with an online dating web site, one from Baltimore and one from Seattle. If they are matched up as compatible they will begin to communicate, and if their online relationship develops sufficiently one or the other of them will have to make a long flight. Neither of these people would have met a potential mate from so far away were it not for the communications technology, nor would they have made a 5,000-km flight to go on a date. So, in this case, more communication led to more transportation.

To give a more economically oriented example, suppose a manager in a Spanish telecommunications firm begins to contract software online from a firm in India. If this transaction proves successful, she will have gained a new appreciation of the technical capability of Indian firms and she will have personal contacts in India, so she will be far more likely to source electronic equipment from India, which will result in long-distance freight service. Essentially, communications technologies expand the range of locations over which we have personal contacts. While those contacts may only involve communication in the beginning, they are likely to involve transportation in the long run – and that transportation may be over very long distances. More communication often leads to more, rather than less, transportation.

## Agglomeration in the knowledge economy

Agglomeration, defined as the concentration of people and their activities in space, is the subject of chapter 3. To recap briefly, agglomeration occurs because spatial concentration yields economic benefits called agglomeration economies. Agglomeration economies are of two types: urbanization economies, which are the benefits arising when a variety of economic activities are located together; and localization economies, which arise when firms in the same industry locate together. One might expect that knowledge-intensive firms would be less inclined to agglomerate, since many of the factors driving agglomeration – internal scale economies, infrastructure and transportation of material inputs among firms – are relatively unimportant to them. Yet empirical research indicates a strong tendency for clustering among firms in the knowledge economy (Porter, 1998). Prominent examples are the clustering of computer industries in California's Silicon Valley (Box 26) and the clustering of biotechnology firms in San Diego, California and Cambridge, Massachusetts. So why do knowledge-intensive firms cluster? There are a number of different explanations, all of which have some validity.

### *Box 26* Silicon Valley

In the early part of the twentieth century, the Santa Clara Valley, located just south of San Francisco Bay, was a largely agricultural region with an ideal climate for fruit orchards. By the end of the century, it had emerged as the undisputed center of the global ICT industry, home to the headquarters of Apple, Intel, Hewlett-Packard, Oracle, AMD, Sun Microsystems, Cisco Systems, Adobe Systems and many others. In the 1970s, it came to be known as "Silicon Valley," after the silicon chips that were then produced there. Most of the chip manufacturers eventually moved elsewhere, but the name stuck. Today, San Jose, which is the urban center of Silicon Valley is the third largest metropolitan area in California. The proportion of high-tech and science and engineering occupations in the labor force is almost three times the overall U.S. average.[i] Unlike other centers of ICT concentration – such as the 128 Highway region around Boston, which had a boom in the 1970s but later declined – Silicon Valley's leadership has proved highly durable. The same region that pioneered the integrated circuit in the 1950s is the most important center for smartphone technology in 2011.

As economic geographers, we should be asking two questions. First, why did a cluster of high-tech firms get established in the Santa Clara Valley? Second, why did that cluster expand and endure to a greater extent than any other cluster? On the first question, there is a temptation to attribute the location to an accident of history. In 1955, a company called Beckman Instruments hired William Shockley, a Nobel laureate and co-inventor of the transistor, to establish a laboratory for the commercialization of silicon semiconductor devices. Shockley asked that the lab be located in the Valley at Palo Alto, California, close to the home of his aging mother. Shockley assembled some of the best young technical minds in America at his lab, but he lacked the management skills to make a commercial success. Soon, eight of his brightest engineers left him in frustration. This group, which came to be known as the "traitorous eight," went on to found Fairchild Semiconductor, the first firm to successfully manufacture silicon-based integrated circuits on a massive scale. Within a few years, a number of Fairchild employees left to start their own firms, including two of the original eight who founded the global chip giant Intel. These spin-off firms, nearly all of which were located near Palo Alto, became known as "Fairchildren." They became the foundation of Silicon Valley (Adams, 2011; Berlin, 2010).

It is probably naïve, however, to attribute too much to the coincidence involving Shockley's mother. As a former Caltech professor, he was very familiar with engineering expertise in California's universities, so he realized that Stanford University, also in Palo Alto, would be a source of technical consultation and its graduates would provide the skilled manpower that is the most precious input for any technology firm. In fact, the original Shockley lab was located in an industrial park operated by the university. Also, the commercialization of technology was already well established in the Valley. Successful firms in radio and aeronautics had already demonstrated that environmental amenities and access to San Francisco made it easy to attract talented people from outside the region, and made them tend to stay once they were there. By the time Shockley came to Palo Alto, industrial giants like IBM, Westinghouse and Lockheed were already present nearby (Adams, 2011). Hewlett-Packard had already established the model for high-tech start-ups, beginning in a garage in 1939. By the 1950s, it was well established as a maker of sophisticated testing equipment.

Stanford was by no means a passive player in the history of Silicon Valley. After World War II, it faced increasing demands to admit the brightest of a huge cohort of veterans, and needed to look for financial resources in unconventional places to fund its growth. Professors were encouraged to seek partnerships with private-sector firms and even to create their own commercial spin-offs. The Stanford Research Park, which was created to allow professors, students and firms to work together on commercializing technology, provided a model that has been duplicated in universities around the world. The University of California at Berkeley was another nearby source of people with knowledge of the most advanced technologies. In response to the growing demand for engineers, the California government funded a major expansion of engineering education at San Jose State University, providing yet another source of youthful expertise. By the 1960s, the Valley could rival Boston and New York in terms of the reservoir of skills available, at least in electrical engineering and related fields.

Once Silicon Valley was established in the early 1970s as the leading ICT cluster, it continued to solidify that position through the constant creation of new firms producing new and better products. Intel co-founder Robert Noyce described the business model that has been repeated time and again through a simple analogy. He said that making integrated circuits is a lot like publishing books. It is very expensive to produce one book because of the volume of information that goes into it, but the marginal cost of printing additional books is low. Producing a circuit is very expensive because of the research and development that goes into it, but the marginal costs of additional chips is fairly low. Thus, in order to sell a lot of chips, you may need to set your price so low that you will initially lose money (Berlin, 2010). But, if the price is low enough to stimulate significant demand, eventually the average cost will dip below the sales price. So, if you are to make money you can't be afraid to lose money, at least for a while. Noyce's Intel partner Gordon E. Moore is responsible for Moore's law, which states that the number of transistors that can be manufactured into an integrated circuit doubles about every two years. This means that a cutting-edge product today is likely to be obsolete in a year or so. These two ideas taken together mean that in the fastest-moving technology sectors it is necessary to constantly expand markets by aggressive pricing and improve product performance by continuous technological innovation.

Saxenian (1994) has argued that, in addition to its skilled people and successful business model, Silicon Valley developed a culture and institutional structure that made it more successful than other regions. Unlike the vertically integrated and hierarchical firms of the East Coast, Silicon Valley firms tend to have "flat" hierarchies and be relatively open to interaction with other firms. Keeping technological secrets was not stressed as much, and start-ups were encouraged rather than viewed as the acts of renegades. Interaction among firms comes in the form of contracting out services, participating in joint ventures, movement of employees among firms or simply sharing information on the latest development via the casual interaction of employees.

Steven Klepper (2010) has another way of explaining the growth and success of Silicon Valley, in which the process by which new firms are created as spin-offs of existing firms is of central importance. Bigger and better firms are more likely to have employees with the ability to leave and create their own firms. Furthermore, Klepper's empirical research shows that the most effective firms tend to spawn the most successful spin-offs (he calls this process *reproduction and heredity*). Thus, the process that began with Fairchild Semiconductor has produced successive generations of new firms with strong pedigrees. While he is able to demonstrate this process over the history of Silicon Valley, he notes that the rate at which new firms spin off from old firms is five times higher there than in the U.S. overall. This rapid rate of reproduction could be due to the unique culture described by Saxenian (1994).

It could also have to do with the availability of finance for start-up firms. No other region in the U.S. and perhaps no other region in the world, including other high-tech clusters, has as much active participation by venture capitalist (VC) firms (Ferrary and Granovetter, 2009). Start-up firms in rapidly changing technologies have a high probability of failure, so commercial banks are generally unwilling to lend them money. VC firms are willing to provide loans to such firms in return for an equity stake. If the firm fails the VC firm loses its entire investment, but if it succeeds, the VC firm is part owner and may recover many times its initial investment. The great majority of successful firms in Silicon Valley had support from VC firms at the early stages of development.

While the firms that created Silicon Valley catered to a narrow market of electronics, aerospace and defense companies, the newer firms have become gradually more consumer oriented. Internet icons like eBay, Google, Yahoo, YouTube and Facebook are located there, along with Apple, the largest consumer electronics company in the world. Any thought that the Valley has lost its prominence in the world of ITC is dispelled by its position as the global hub of the smartphone and tablet computer industry. Apple's iPhone and iPad, along with Google's Android operating system, dominate this sector. While none of these devices is manufactured there, design, product development, software development, marketing and distribution – which together account for most of the value of mobile devices – are controlled from Silicon Valley. Furthermore, service providers now feel the need to be close to the action, with AT&T, Verizon and Vodaphone all opening research, testing and incubation centers in either the Valley or San Francisco in 2011.

The fame of Silicon Valley has led governments in other parts of the U.S. and around the world to try to recreate its success in a long succession of "Silicon Somethings," including Silicon Snowbank (Minnesota), Silicon Desert (Arizona), Silicon Prairie (Illinois), Silicon Glen (Scotland), Silicon Polder (The Netherlands), Silicon Plateau (Bangalore, India), and many others.[ii] While some, like Bangalore, have succeeded, most have not come close to reproducing the self-sustaining economic dynamism of the real thing. The growth of Silicon Valley was a complex process that involved countless ground-level interactions between people and firms. While military and other government procurement played a role, market forces and technological innovation were the key drivers. Attempts to reproduce such a process through policy are unlikely to succeed (Hospers *et al.*, 2009). But there are many lessons – such as the positive role of universities and the importance of private funding for risky venture – that can be applied in policy making.

There is, however, a mechanism by which Silicon Valley's model has spread to other parts of the world. One of the most visible characteristics of the region is its multiculturalism. The best and brightest from many countries have come, often with a stop at a U.S. university, to Silicon Valley to be where their talents can be best applied. Many of these people – from countries as diverse as India, Israel and Ireland – eventually return to their home lands to start new companies, some of which have become world-class ICT firms. Saxenian (2006) calls these people "The New Argonauts." In this way, the business culture of Silicon Valley is spreading throughout the global economy.

**Notes**

i    Joint Venture Silicon Valley Network, Silicon Valley Index 2011, available at http://www.jointventure.org/images/stories/pdf/The%20Index%20of%20Silicon%20Valley%202011.pdf (accessed October 7, 2011).

ii   A much longer list may be found in Hospers *et al.* (2009).

The English economist Alfred Marshall (1890), who pioneered the study of agglomeration economies, dealt principally with localization economies. He argued that if many firms in the same industry are clustered in the same location the resulting proximity offers three types of advantages: access to a specialized labor pool, efficient provision of some specialist inputs and services to a concentration of firms with similar needs, and knowledge spillovers, which means the ability of firms to gain knowledge by closely observing other firms around them. Clearly the first and third of these advantages are especially relevant for knowledge-intensive firms. For example, the most pressing need for a firm in the medical biotechnology industry is to hire people with expertise in molecular biology, so it needs to be where those people are available. Also, by being close to other biotech firms, it will pick up information about new trends and technologies.

Knowledge spillovers have played a central role in geographers' ideas about both localization and urbanization economies in the knowledge economy. The diffusion of tacit knowledge, which is sometimes called "sticky knowledge" because it doesn't flow easily from place to place, requires face-to-face frequent contact and observation (Gertler, 2003; von Hippel, 1994). Spatial proximity enhances this process, and so firms in innovative and knowledge-intensive industries benefit from clustering.

Jane Jacobs (1969) emphasized urbanization economies – also described as "economies of variety" (Quigley, 1998). Her thesis is that diversity fosters cross-fertilization of knowledge. In a diversified urban environment, information and knowledge about new ideas, techniques and organizational models spills over among different industries promoting innovation. This innovative atmosphere may derive from factors beyond the normal industrial location factors, including the presence of artistic communities and tolerance among people of different socio-economic, ethnic and sexual orientation groups (Florida, 2003).

Some have argued that clustering reflects the development of social networks based on cooperation. Knowledge-intensive economic clusters are characterized by many interconnections among small, medium and large firms, government agencies and civil society institutions such as charities. In some cases geographical proximity and social proximity (shared attitudes, trust, sense of community) go together, making it easier for firms to cooperate and overcome some of the uncertainties of innovation (Camagni, 2004; Scott, 1988; Storper, 1997). Porter (1990) provides a related, but quite different, view of agglomeration economies based on local rivalry rather than cooperation. He argues that firms in a cluster are able to gain knowledge by observing their rivals and are driven by them to greater competitiveness in global markets. This is particularly true for small firms, with the consequence that localization enhances the overall competitiveness of the entire economic cluster.

Another interesting way to explain clustering starts with two observations about knowledge industries: first, highly qualified people are their most important resource and, second, they are high-risk and high-reward industries. For example, medical biotechnology firms need to hire lab-trained specialists in molecular biology, generally with doctorates or other advanced degrees. Nothing is more important to their success than attracting these people either from university research labs or from other firms. But the nature of biotech innovations is that, while the successes reap huge profits, the great majority of them fail to reach the market, usually because they cannot prove their effectiveness in expensive and time-consuming trials. So anyone who goes to work for a new firm knows that there is a high probability that the firm will go bankrupt within a few years. Since a large share of the income earned in knowledge industries is dependent upon the success of the firm (for example, the ability to cash in on stock options), each highly qualified person must balance risk against potential reward in choosing an employer. To mitigate risk, the best strategy is to go to work for someone you trust. Trust is most likely to develop through the frequent face-to-face relationships that occur in a geographically compact research/business community, so even if people change jobs they are likely to remain within the same region (Stuart and Sorenson, 2003).

The presence of a university with research strengths that can feed directly into the research and development activities of innovative firms is one of the most important factors explaining why knowledge-intensive clusters arise in certain places and not in others. The synergy between a university and a firm can arise in two ways. First, university researchers are good at invention and innovation but generally not at commercialization. So, in many cases, things that are invented in university labs are licensed to firms that carry through the later stages of commercial development. Second, universities generate the talent pools from which knowledge-intensive firms recruit highly qualified people. Being close to and having regular interactions with a university laboratory gives a firm an inside track in recruiting the graduate researchers being trained there. In a survey of biotech firms in Cambridge, Massachusetts, most firms rated the importance of interacting with universities more highly than interacting with other firms in their industry (Breznitz and Anderson, 2005).

## Regional convergence in the knowledge economy

Recall from chapter 9 that the interregional movement of labor and capital leads to convergence of wages and productivity levels in multiregional economies. It is common for one or more regions to have higher wages and higher ratios of capital to labor than others. But, as workers move in the direction of high-wage regions and capital moves in the direction of low-wage regions, these differences can be expected to decline and, at least in theory, disappear in the long run. Empirical research suggests that this has been a slow, but steady, process in many multiregional economies over the past 50 years or so.

The forces that drive clustering in the knowledge economy, however, are more consistent with the model of a self-reinforcing group described in chapter 10, whereby regions that gain initial advantages tend to maintain their edge indefinitely, leading to polarization rather than convergence of regional economies in the long run. As we have seen, there are a number of frictions acting on the movement of capital and labor in knowledge-intensive industries. The importance of tacit knowledge, which is geographically "sticky," is one such friction. The importance of trust for highly qualified employees making risky employment decisions is another. Furthermore, the location of a small number of leading research universities is likely to carry more weight than the possibility of paying lower wages in a knowledge-intensive firm's location decision. This raises the question of whether the transition to a knowledge economy will lead to rapid economic growth in a few, already affluent places, while many other regions are left behind.

Preliminary evidence on this question is found in a statistical analysis of economic convergence among the 50 U.S. states over the period from 1983 to 2004 (Ó hUallacháin, 2007). The process of economic convergence which had been observed in many studies was still evident during this period, but it slowed down significantly after about 1993, which is about the time that economic growth in the U.S. became dominated by knowledge-intensive industries. Based on the assumption that a highly educated population and a high rate of innovations are hallmarks of the knowledge economy, the proportion of population with a college degree and the number of patents registered in the state were entered into the analysis as independent variables. The results showed that the upward convergence of low-income states was significantly retarded by low values for those variables. States with a large share of employment in primary activities such as mining, forestry, agriculture and fishing also fared poorly. While the study does not indicate a reversal of trends in the direction of polarization, it suggests that the process of regional convergence may be stalling in the knowledge economy.

## Globalization and the knowledge economy

Globalization and the transition to the knowledge economy do not just happen to be going on at the same time. They are interrelated and self-reinforcing processes. The most obvious common thread is ICT. The development of computers and their application in all aspects of economic activity created a demand for people with training in mathematics and the abstract, step-by-step logic of algorithms. Faster and better computers unlocked the computational constraints on a huge range of research areas with business applications, extending from inventory management to gene sequencing. But it was the complete integration of communications and information technologies through the institution of the Internet that has done the most to accelerate the process of globalization.

The great challenge of the global firm is to coordinate people, processes and goods around the world. Databases that are instantaneously updated via GPS devices, bar-code readers and a variety of other technologies provide the managers of global supply chains with more detailed information on where things are, where they are going and when they will get there than managers of logistics systems spanning no more than 100 km had a couple of decades ago.

Technology is only part of the story. Institutional and cultural changes may be just as important. The elimination of tariff and non-tariff barriers means that every new product idea coming out of a research lab can be positioned for a global market. Borders are still an impediment but some, as in the Schengen Area, have been eliminated and new technologies are making others work better. The terrorist threat is a challenge to globalization, but the economic stakes are high enough to overcome the cost of enhanced security, especially as the resources of knowledge-intensive industries are directed toward surveillance and identification technologies.

The elimination of cultural barriers reinforces both globalization and the knowledge economy. The near-universal acceptance of English as the language of international business has eliminated one of the greatest sources of friction. It has also contributed to the free movement of highly qualified people at the global scale. The notion of knowledge-intensive clusters should not be misunderstood to mean that only "local people" work together. A characteristic of every cluster is the presence of knowledge workers born in other parts of the world. Neither an Indian analyst in Silicon Valley nor an American analyst in Bangalore looks or feels out of place.

In a sense, the knowledge economy provides an answer to the question of what will happen to workers in affluent countries as low-wage labor in the developing world is ever more accessible to global firms. The comparative advantage of the rich countries will be in knowledge-intensive industries and functions, so young people are well advised to prepare themselves through formal education before entering the labor force and to upgrade their skills regularly once they are there. This is little comfort to those working in manufacturing industries whose hard-won, non-transferable skills are undermined by globalization. But the next generation of workers may be able to avoid finding themselves in similar positions.

A challenge for economic geographers is how to reconcile the idea of knowledge workers interacting in local clusters with the globalizing economy. In fact, this contradiction is more apparent than real. Nearly all knowledge-intensive industries produce for the global market, so they must function through local networks within global networks. Local networks of knowledge workers interacting via urban transportation and face-to-face communication are connected into global networks of industry players interacting via ICT as well as air, ground and marine transportation. The notion that direct, interpersonal communication will ultimately be supplanted by electronic communications over long distances is much too simple. As production of goods and services becomes more knowledge intensive, interactions among people become more complex and tacit knowledge becomes more important, so face-to-face communication is indispensable. At the same time, as markets and supply chains expand to the global scale, long-distance communication via ICT is indispensable. This complementary relationship between the local and the global is a fascinating frontier in economic geography research.

# Notes

## 1 Introduction

1   The reader should understand that the hypothesis-testing approach is not universally accepted by economic geographers. For an alternative perspective, see Barnes (1996).

2   As an example of one of these rare cases, we may consider the State of Hawaii as a study area comprising the Hawaiian Islands. As the boundaries of each island are defined by its shoreline, the analyst need not provide a set of boundaries.

3   This is called Weber's Triangle because it was introduced by Alfred Weber (1909) in his seminal book on industrial location.

4   The field of spatial economic theory is currently in a period of rapid development. Two recent books providing mathematical treatments are by Fujita *et al.* (1999) and Brakman *et al.* (2001).

5   This important distinction between economics and economic geography was made by Butler (1980).

## 2 The friction of distance

1   These rates were obtained from the UPS web site (http://wwwapps.ups.com/calTimeCost?loc=en_US) on September 6, 2006.

2   Derived from Bureau of Transportation Statistics (2005) *Pocket Guide to Transportation*, Washington: US Department of Transportation, Table 11.

3   In formal network theory, nodes and links are sometimes referred to as vertices and edges respectively.

4   The distance term is usually raised to some power $\beta$ to indicate whether the effect of distance is marginally increasing ($\beta > 1$) or marginally decreasing ($\beta < 1$). To keep things simple, we assume here that $\beta = 1$.

## 3 Agglomeration

1   The terms "urbanization economies" and "localization economies" are generally attributed to Hoover (1948).

2   This type of agglomeration economy was recognized by one of the giants of economic science, Alfred Marshall (1890), when he observed the benefits accruing to cutlery firms locating in Sheffield, England at the dawn of the twentieth century.

3   For those with a background in econometrics, Rosenthal and Strange (2004) provide an excellent review, covering most of the results listed below.

4   A number of studies are reviewed in Rosenthal and Strange (2004).

**4 Markets**

1 The price is always expressed in terms of units of money per unit of the good. For our purposes, the units are not that important because you can always express the price as a given value by adjusting the units. For example, suppose the price of wheat is $10 per kilogram. You can also express that price as 1 cent per gram. In general, you can always adjust the units in the price to define a base price of 1. Then, if you keep the units consistent, you can define increases or decreases around that base level.

2 The expression "demand function" is preferred to "demand curve" here to stress the notion that the quantity demanded is a function of the price. The same goes for "supply function." However, "function" and "curve" can be used interchangeably in this context.

3 This way of thinking about individual demand makes the most sense when we are talking about some major good that one buys or doesn't buy, depending upon the price. A car might be an example. Each person has a maximum price in mind. If the price is below that maximum he buys one car, if it is above it he buys no car and uses public transportation.

4 In the railroad and airline industries, competition has at times led to instability as new firms keep entering the markets only to exit via bankruptcy. The "ruinous competition" argument has been used, however, by firms hoping to protect their monopolies.

5 This example is adapted from Berry *et al.* (1996).

**5 Spatial interaction**

1 The movement of invasion troops from one country to another fits the definition of spatial interaction. There may be a rationale for this movement, but the destination country hardly derives a benefit from it.

2 Three types of symbols appear in equations: operators (+, -, =, etc.), variables and parameters (constants). This book follows the convention that all parameters are represented by Greek letters, while all variables are represented by Latin letters.

3 A concise review of gravity model specifications is found in Haynes and Fotheringham (1984).

4 There have been a number of demonstrations that the gravity model can be derived from microeconomic theory. For example, see Niedercorn and Bechdolt (1969).

**6 Resources and the environment**

1 Sir Thomas More (1478–1535) was an early critic of the enclosure movement. (See quote from More's *Utopia* in Boyle, 2003: 34.)

2 Differences in the discount rate are greatly magnified over such long time horizons. Using a 5 percent rate, a million dollars discounted over a period of 100 years becomes $7,604.

**7 The production technology**

1 The term "factors of production" is sometimes used in place of "productive inputs." Some texts, however, apply the term "factor" only to capital and labor. To avoid confusion, we don't use the term.

2 This is why statistical agencies refer to the combined contribution to value of capital and labor inputs as "value added." Value added is also sometimes calculated as a residual by subtracting the cost of all inputs other than capital and labor from the value of the finished good or service. It is important to remember, however, that both environmental services and public infrastructure services are often unpriced or priced far below their true market values. In such cases, the true value added may be less than the reported one.

3   Technological progress as it is shown here in both the production function and the isoquant diagram is neutral, in the sense that it affects the productivity of all inputs equally. Technological progress can also be biased, meaning that it improves the productivity of one or a few inputs, while leaving others the same.
4   A household is one or more people who participate jointly in consumption and share a common income.

## 8 Specialization and trade

1   Canada also includes two more political subdivisions: the Northwest Territories and Nunavut. Lying largely above the Arctic Circle, they are huge in area and in cultural significance because of the Indian and Inuit aboriginal people who make up most of their populations. The discovery of diamonds has recently increased the economic significant of the far north. Still, the two territories account for tiny shares of the Canadian population and national product.

## 9 Interregional movements of labor and capital

1   To name two examples, Barro and Sala-i-Martin (1991); Anderson and Papageorgiou (1994).
2   This is called the "human capital" theory of migration because it represents the decision to migrate as an investment decision (Sjastaad, 1962.)

## 10 Polarization in the multiregional economy

1   The U.S. also has pockets of abject poverty within some of its wealthiest metropolitan areas. We return to that issue in chapters 19 and 20.
2   Myrdal (1957) was principally concerned with economic polarization across nations, but his logic is equally applicable to regions within a multiregional economy.
3   The assertion here that regional growth is "self-reinforcing" has essentially the same meaning as the assertion in earlier texts that regional growth is "cumulative." (See, for example, Lloyd and Dicken, 1977.)
4   In practice, the fact that a region specializes in a particular activity does not prove that it has comparative advantage, as the location of an activity may reflect government subsidies and regulations or may be the outcome of imperfect competition.
5   In some texts, these residentiary activities are called "non-basic" activities.
6   A classic study by Alan Pred (1966) identified numerous mechanisms. While this work is over 40 years old, it still provides many useful insights.
7   The important distinction between intermediate sales and final demand sales in the input–output model is that sales to final demand are treated as exogenous, while intermediate sales are treated as endogenous.
8   This need not be true if regional disposable income included things other than total regional wage payments, such as expenditures from savings, income from transfer payments or employment income earned outside the region.

## 11 Scale economies and imperfect competition in the multiregional economy

1   While the idea of monopolistic competition is attributed to Edward Chamberlin and Joan Robinson, the model presented in this chapter is based on the general equilibrium framework introduced in Dixit and Stiglitz (1977).
2   As with most commodities that are sold to consumers rather than firms, the producers make an attempt through advertising to present their brand as different from their competitors' brands using claims about additives or other features. For the purposes of our discussion, let us assume that consumers are not taken in by such claims.

3 In reality, the firm might be able to sell some gasoline at a higher price if its stations are more conveniently located than those of its competitors. In this case location would be a form of product differentiation. (We return to this case in Part III.) For our purposes, however, let us assume that all customers have equal access to the stations of all producers.

4 In principle, another firm could produce a "knock-off" version that is nearly identical. This sort of behavior sometimes works for high-fashion dresses and handbags, which are produced at relatively small scale. For a good that is mass produced, however, the original manufacturer would have a large initial advantage in terms of scale economies that would make such an imitation strategy impractical.

5 Furthermore, general equilibrium under perfect competition requires the assumption of constant returns to scale. Early applications of monopolistic competition to models of multiregional economies stress the pragmatic advantages of that assumption, rather than whether it is more or less realistic than perfect competition (see Krugman, 1991).

## 12 Unemployment and regional policy

1 In this case a person is not making a choice between working and not working, but rather between working for cash outside the home or working without formal wages in the home.

2 With notable exceptions – petroleum is a commodity that is income elastic.

3 For a review, see Lakshmanan and Anderson (2007).

4 The rental cost of capital is the cost to maintain one dollar's worth of capital for a period of time (usually a year).

## 13 Transportation and location

1 As discussed in chapter 1, the term "theory" is used rather informally here. Based on our working definitions of theories and models, Weberian location "theory" is best described as a set of models with similar structure and purpose.

2 The notion of input substitution may seem not to apply in the case of only one localized input, but the assumptions do not rule out the existence of one or more ubiquitous inputs.

3 Ton-miles are defined as the product of the weight that is transported times the distance it is moved. Moving 1 ton 10 miles implies 10 ton-miles, as does moving 10 tons 1 mile.

4 For example, in a branching network (as defined in the Appendix to chapter 2), a "root" location is almost certain to be the cost-minimizing point, even if it lies outside the triangle.

5 "Haikimi's Theorem" proves that the optimal location on a network is always at a node. See Handler and Mirchandani (1979: ch. 2).

## 15 Labor, rent, taxes and subsidies

1 I prefer "labor cost" to "wages" because it is a more general term. In affluent countries, a worker's wages seldom cover more than about 75 percent of her compensation, with the remainder going to benefits such as health insurance and pension contributions. From the perspective of the firm, a dollar spent on labor compensation has the same impact on profit whether it is for wages or benefits. Also, a distinction is often made between wages and salaries, depending upon the type of work in question.

## 16 Interrelated location choices

1 This example is based on a classic 1929 paper by Harold Hotelling, so it is often called the "Hotelling Problem."

2    This assumption is equivalent to saying that the consumer's demand function is a straight, vertical line such that the amount demand is the same at every price.

## 17 Agricultural land use

1    The rent defined here is equal to the profit that could be earned if the land were free. So it is reasonable to ask why farmers are willing to grow crops if all their profits go to the landlord. First, if there were only one farmer she would bid a much lower rent and retain some of the profits. But we have assumed that there are numerous farmers, even within categories, so competitive bidding will tend to squeeze out all profits. So why do the farmers bother to grow crops at all? The best way to think about this is to assume that the production cost $a$ includes some minimum profit (sometimes called "normal profit") below which farmers would not cultivate.
2    With a little algebra, you can demonstrate that $E_w(p_w-a)>E_m(p_m-a)$ as long as $E_w/E_m> (p_m-a)/(p_w-a)$.

## 18 Urban land use: the monocentric city

1    In reality, this may not be true because some people may have a preference for urban lifestyles, while others have a preference for being close to the rural edge of the city. Like all other assumptions, we make this one to keep the model simple.
2    A mathematically rigorous treatment of the relationship between income and bid rent functions can be found in Pines (1975).
3    Papageorgiou and Pines (1999) include a good discussion of the role of land users in the monocentric model.
4    This is the derivative of the bid rent function. We use the $\Delta$ instead of the conventional $d$ to avoid confusion since $d$ represents distance in this model.

## 19 Urban sprawl and the polycentric city

1    Mackie *et al.* (2003) provide a review of studies using travel time in the UK.
2    See chapter 8 of Papageorgiou and Pines (1999) for a defense of the enduring relevance of the monocentric model.
3    See Miron (1978) for a full mathematical treatment of the example presented here.
4    The general term "local governments" is used here to represent municipalities (cities and towns) and other levels of government that are subsets of or coterminous with the metropolitan area. Depending upon the context, this may include counties and a variety of special service jurisdictions such as regional school boards or transit commissions.
5    It happens that I (W. Anderson) live within about 100 meters of a facility where a famous Canadian whiskey is aged via a process that requires charcoal. The production of the charcoal results in a black ash which is too dispersed to be visible and has no known health effect. Over the course of two or three years, however, the ash results in discoloration of the brick homes in my neighborhood. In the interest of avoiding conflict, the whiskey maker pays to clean all the buildings in the neighborhood. This is an example of how a negative externality can be resolved by means of compensation.
6    The argument that political fragmentation leads to economic efficiency is known as the Tiebout hypothesis, after the economist who first expressed these ideas in the 1950s. See Tiebout (1956).

## 20 Urbanization

1    There is some disagreement even on this point. Jacobs (1969) argues that, since cities are the source of technological innovations, they would have predated systematic agriculture.

2    What follows is a simplified version of class stage models. For a complete review see Hoover (1937).
3    North (1955) observed that stage models based on the European experience were not transferable to North America. The "new world" stages described below embody some of his observations about urban development in North America.
4    Because of the issue of political fragmentation discussed in chapter 19, metropolitan populations are always more appropriate than the populations of political jurisdictions when comparing city sizes.

## 21 City size distribution and urban hierarchies

1    To be fair, explanation was not Zipf's objective. He was not a geographer, but rather a brilliant linguist and statistician who found that similar rank–size relationships could be used to describe a wide variety of phenomena, including the frequency of word use in a language, the distribution of particle sizes in sand, the lengths of rivers and the distribution of city sizes.
2    Brakman *et al.* (2001: ch. 7) discuss the effects of congestion on city size distributions in the context of New Economic Geography models.

## 22 Central place theory

1    The exposition below draws extensively from King (1984), which differs from other pedagogical treatments by emphasizing underlying principles rather than the geometric results of Christaller's model.
2    Note that the length of the base of the triangle that constitutes the spatial demand curve is twice the range and the area of the triangle is one half the area of a rectangle formed by the length of the base and the demand at the central place.
3    According to Preston (1983), the criticism that Christaller's theory is exclusively static and therefore cannot explain the evolution of observed patterns is unfair. While his more formal theory is static, much of the more historical and empirical part of his work is focused on how systems of cities change through time.
4    The extension of market area definitions to *k* values other than 3 is part of the contribution of August Lösch, a German economist who extended Christaller's models in a variety of ways (Lösch, 1954).
5    An excellent review of empirical studies related to central place theory is found in Yeates and Garner (1976).

## 23 Network urban systems

1    See Batten (1995) for an introduction to the concept of network cities.
2    This corridor is often referred to as "Main Street Canada." See Yeates (1975).

## 24 International trade and foreign direct investment

1    For an optimistic view see Wolf (2004). For a more critical view see Dicken (2007) and Grant (2003). Hill and McKaig (2006) provide a practical overview from a business perspective.
2    We assume that this is a "world price" at which wheat is trading internationally and that it is constant, which means that the nation's demand is not large enough to shift the world price.
3    For a recent reprint see Hamilton (2007).
4    United Nations Conference on Trade and Development, FDIStat database: http://stats.unctad.org/FDI/TableViewer/tableView.aspx?ReportId=4031 (values in current dollars).

5    Data from Indian Department of Industrial Policy and Promotion, Ministry of Commerce and Industry, obtained from //dipp.nic.in/fdi_statistics/India_yearwise.pdf.

## 25 The globalization of production systems

1    Martin Wolf (2004: 14) quoting David Henderson, former chief economist of the Organisation for Economic Co-operation and Development.
2    Of course, this is a gross simplification of real automotive production systems. In reality, there are several "tiers" of component manufacturers producing everything from cheap plastic connectors to major modules such as transmissions and engines. For any given vehicle, there are hundreds of movements of intermediate goods among component plants before the major modules are shipped to the assembly plant.
3    According to the World Trade Organization (2009), the simple average of tariffs charged against most favored nations in 2008 was 4.7 percent for Canada and 3.5 percent for the United States.
4    Porter (1986), who is most closely associated with the multidomestic/global dichotomy, uses these terms not to describe firm strategies but rather the competitive characteristics of different industries. Multidomestic industries generally have lower scale economies and can benefit from goods catering to the demands of different markets, while global industries produce complex goods with scale economies that can be marketed without much differentiation in many different markets.

## 26 The knowledge economy

1    Rowly (2007) provides an excellent review of definitions and controversies concerning the DIKW hierarchy.
2    Based on Figure 1 of Ò hUallacháin (2007), which is derived from U.S. National Science Foundation data.

# References

Adams, Stephen B. (2011) "Growing Where You Are Planted: Exogenous Firms and the Seeding of Silicon Valley," *Research Policy* 40(3):368–379.

Alonso, William (1964) *Location and Land Use: Towards a General Theory of Land Rent.* Cambridge MA: Harvard University Press.

Anastakis, Dimitry (2005) *Auto Pact: Creating a Borderless North American Auto Industry, 1960 – 1971.* Toronto: University of Toronto Press.

Anderson, William P. (1987) "The Changing Competitive Position of Hamilton's Steel Industry," in M.J. Dear, J.J. Drake and L.G. Reeds (eds.) *Steel City: Hamilton and Region.* Toronto: University of Toronto Press.

Anderson, William P. and Yorgos Y. Papageorgiou (1994) "An Analysis of Migration Streams for the Canadian Regional System, 1952–1983: 1. Migration Probabilities," *Geographical Analysis* 26(1):15–36.

Anderson, William P., Pavlos S. Kanaroglou and Eric Miller (1996) "Urban Form, Energy, and the Environment: A Review of Issues, Evidence, and Policy," *Urban Studies* 33:7–35.

Anderson, William P., Lata Chatterjee and T.R. Lakshmanan (2003) "E-commerce, Transportation and Economic Geography," *Growth and Change* 34(4):415–432.

Andreas, P. (2003) "Redrawing the Line: Borders and Security in the 21st Century," *International Security* 28(2):78–111.

Armstrong, Harvey and Jim Taylor (2000) *Regional Economics and Policy*, 3rd edn. Oxford: Blackwell.

Baldwin, John R., W. Mark Brown and Tara Vinodrai (2001) *Dynamics of the Canadian Manufacturing Sector in Metropolitan and Rural Regions.* Analytical Studies Branch Research Paper 2001169e. Ottawa: Statistics Canada.

Barca, Fabrizio (2001) "New Trends and the Policy Shift in the Italian Mezzogiorno," *Daedalus* 130(2):93–113.

Barnes, Trevor (1996) *Logics of Dislocation: Models, Metaphors and Meanings in Economic Space.* New York: Guilford.

Barro, Robert J. and Xavier Sala-i-Martin (1991) "Convergence across States and Regions," *Brookings Papers on Economic Activity* 1991(1):107–158.

Batten, David F. (1995) "Network Cities: Creative Urban Agglomeration for the 21st Century," *Urban Studies* 32(2):313–327.

Begg, Iain (2010) "Cohesion or Confusion: A Policy Searching for Objectives," *European Integration* 32(1):77–96.

Berlin, Leslie (2010) "Robert Noyce, Silicon Valley, and the Teamwork behind the High-tech Revolution," *OAH Magazine of History* 24(1):33–36.

Berry, Brian J.L. (1967) *Geography of Market Centers and Retail Distribution*. Englewood Cliffs, NJ: Prentice Hall.

Berry, Brian J.L., Edgar C. Conkling and D. Michael Ray (1996) *The World Economy in Transition*, 2nd edn. Englewood Cliffs, NJ: Prentice Hall.

Borchert, John R. (1967) "American Metropolitan Evolution," *Geographical Review* 57(3):301–332.

Boyle, James (2003) "The Second Enclosure Movement and the Construction of the Public Domain," *Law and Contemporary Problems* 66:33–74.

Brakman, Steven, Harry Garretsen and Charles van Marrewijk (2001) *An Introduction to Geographical Economics*. Cambridge: Cambridge University Press.

Breznitz, Shiri M. and William P. Anderson (2005) "Boston Metropolitan Area Biotechnology Cluster," *Canadian Journal of Regional Science* 28(2):249–267.

Buenstorf, Guido and Steven Keppler (2009) "Heritage and Agglomeration: The Akron Tyre Cluster Revisited," *Economic Journal* 119:705–733.

Bureau of Transportation Statistics (2005) *Pocket Guide to Transportation*. Washington, DC: U.S. Department of Transportation.

Bureau of Transportation Statistics (2006) *National Transportation Statistics*. Washington, DC: U.S. Department of Transportation.

Butler, Joseph H. (1980) *Economic Geography: Spatial and Environmental Aspects of Economic Activity*. New York: Wiley.

Cairncross, Frances C. (2001) *The Death of Distance: How the Communications Revolution is Changing Our Lives*. Cambridge, MA: Harvard Business School Press.

Calthorpe, Peter and William Fulton (2001) *The Regional City: Planning for the End of Sprawl*. Washington, DC: Island Press.

Camagni, R. (2004) "Uncertainty, Social Capital, and Community Governance," pp. 121–150 in R. Capello and P. Nijkamp (eds.) *Urban Dynamics and Growth*. Amsterdam: Elsevier.

Camagni, Roberto P. and Carlo Salone (1993) "Network Urban Structures in Northern Italy: Elements for a Theoretical Framework," *Urban Studies* 30(6):1053–1064.

Caselli, Francesco and Wilbur John Coleman II (2001) "The U.S. Structural Transformation and Regional Convergence: A Reinterpretation," *Journal of Political Economy* 109(3):585–616.

Charles, Anthony T. (1997) "Fisheries Management in Atlantic Canada," *Ocean and Coastal Management* 35(2–3):101–119.

Christaller, Walter (1933) *Die zentralen Orte in Suddeutschland*. Jena: Gustav Fischer. (English Translation: Carlisle W. Baskin (1966) *Central Places in Southern Germany*, Englewood Cliffs, N.J.: Prentice Hall.)

Ciccone, Antonio and Robert E. Hall (1996) "Productivity and Density of Economic Activity," *American Economic Review* 86:54–70.

Commission of the European Communities (2008) *Green Paper on Territorial Cohesion: Turning Territorial Diversity into Strength*. Brussels: CEC.

Courchene, Thomas J. (1974) *Migration, Income and Employment: Canada 1965–1968*. Montreal: C.D. Howe Research Institute.

Cowan, Rick and Douglas Century (2002) *Takedown: The Fall of the Last Mafia Empire*. New York: Berkley.

Dennis, Charles, David Marsland and Tony Cockett (2002) "Central Place Practice: Shopping Centre Attractiveness Measures, Hinterland Boundaries and the UK Retailing Hierarchy," *Journal of Retailing and Consumer Services* 9(4):185–199.

Desrochers, Pierre and Hiroku Shimizu (2010) *Will Buying Food Locally Save the Planet?* Economic Note, Montreal Economic Institute.

Dicken, Peter (2007) *Global Shift*, 5th edn. New York: Guilford Press.

Dixit, A.K. and J.E. Stiglitz (1977) "Monopolistic Competition and Optimum Product Diversity," *American Economic Review* 67(3):297–308.

Dunning, John H. (1981) *International Production and the Multinational Enterprise*. London: Allen and Unwin.

Dunning, John H. (1988) "The Eclectic Paradigm of International Production: A Restatement and Some Possible Extensions," *Journal of International Business* 19(1):1–31.

Erbetta, Fabrizio and Carmelo Petraglia (2011) "Drivers of Regional Efficiency Differentials in Italy: Technical Inefficiency or Allocative Distortions," *Growth and Change* 42(3):351–375.

Farole, Thomas, Andrea Rodriguez-Pose and Michael Storper (2011) "Cohesion Policy in the European Union: Growth, Geography and Institutions," *Journal of Common Market Studies* 49(5):1089–1111.

Ferrary, Michel and Mark Granovetter (2009) "The Role of Venture Capital Firms in Silicon Valley's Complex Innovation Network," *Economy and Society* 38(2):326–359.

Florida, Richard (2003) *The Rise of the Creative Class*. Cambridge, MA: Basic Books.

Florida, Richard and Gary Gates (2001) *Technology and Tolerance: The Importance of Diversity to High Technology Growth*. Washington DC: Center for Urban and Metropolitan Policy, The Brookings Institution.

Fujita, Masahisa, Paul Krugman and Anthony J. Venables (1999) *The Spatial Economy: Cities Regions and International Trade*. Cambridge, MA: MIT Press.

Garreau, Joel (1992) *Edge City: Life on the New Frontier*. Grantham: Anchor Books.

Gertler, Meric (2003) "Tacit Knowledge and the Economic Geography of Context, or the Undefined Tacitness of Being (There)," *Journal of Economic Geography* 3(1):75–99.

Giarratani, Frank, Gene Gruver and Randall Jackson (2007) "Clusters, Agglomeration and Economic Development Potential: Empirical Evidence Based on the Advent of Slab Casting by U.S. Steel Minimills," *Economic Development Quarterly* 21(2):148–164.

Gottmann, Jean (1961) *Megalopolis: The Urbanized Northeast Seaboard of the United States*. Cambridge, MA: MIT Press.

Grant, Richard (2003) "The Economic Geography of Global Trade," in Eric Sheppard and Trevor J. Barnes (eds.) *A Companion to Economic Geography*. Oxford: Blackwell.

Haig, R.M. (1926) "Towards an Understanding of the Metropolis," *Quarterly Journal of Economics* 40:421–433.

Hamilton, Alexander (2007) *Report on the Subject of Manufactures*, Cosimo Classics Economics, 6th edn. New York: Cosimo.

Handler, Gabriel Y. and Pitu B. Mirchandani (1979) *Location on Networks: Theory and Algorithms*. Cambridge, MA: MIT Press.

Hardin, Garrett (1968) "The Tragedy of the Commons," *Science* 162:1243–1248.

Haynes, Kingsley E. and A. Stewart Fotheringham (1984) *Gravity and Spatial Interaction Models*. Beverley Hills, CA: Sage Publications.

Heston, Alan, Robert Summers and Bettina Hetton (n.d.) *Penn World Tables*, retrieved from University of Toronto, http://datacenter2.chass.utoronto.ca/pwt/

Hill, Charles W.L. and Thomas McKaig (2006) *Global Business Today: Canadian Edition*. Toronto: McGraw-Hill Ryerson.

Hoover, Edgar M. (1937) *Location Theory and the Shoe and Leather Industry*. Cambridge, MA: Harvard University Press.

Hoover, Edgar M. (1948) *The Location of Economic Activity*. New York: McGraw-Hill.

Hospers, Gert-Jan, Pierre Desrochers and Frédéric Sautet (2009) "The Next Silicon Valley? On the Relationship between Geographical Clustering and Public Policy," *International Entrepreneurship and Management Journal* 5(3):285–299.

Hurd, R.M. (1924) *Principles of City Land Values*. New York: Record and Guide.

International Trade Administration (2011) *On the Road: U.S. Automotive Parts Industry Annual Assessment*. Washington, DC: Office of Transportation and Machinery, U.S. Department of Commerce.

Jacobs, Jane (1969) *The Economy of Cities*. New York: Random House.

Jefferson, Mark (1939) "The Law of the Primate City," *Geographical Review* 29:226–232.

King, Leslie J. (1984) *Central Place Theory*. Beverly Hills, CA: Sage Publications.

Klepper, Steven (2010) "The Origin and Growth of Industry Clusters: The Making of Silicon Valley and Detroit," *Journal of Urban Economics* 67(1):15–32.

Klier, Thomas and James Rubenstein (2008) *Who Really Made Your Car? Restructuring and Geographic Change in the Auto Industry*. Kalamazoo, MI: Upjohn Institute for Employment Research.

Knox, Paul and Linda McCarthy (2005) *Urbanization*. Upper Saddle River, NJ: Pearson.

Kobayashi, Kiyoshi and Mikio Takebayashi (2001) "Exploring Gateway Externalities: The Future of Osaka/Kansai," pp. 235–253 in Ake E. Andersson and David E. Andersson (eds.) *Gateways to Global Economies*. Cheltenham: Edward Elgar.

Kobayashi, Kiyoshi, John R. Roy and Kei Fukuyam (1998) "Contracts with Agreements: Towards Face-to-face Communications Modeling," *Annals of Regional Science* 32:389–406.

Kosso, Peter and Cynthia Kosso (1995) "Central Place Theory and the Reciprocity between Theory and Evidence," *Philosophy of Science* 9(4):185–199.

Krugman, Paul (1991) *Geography and Trade*. Cambridge, MA: MIT Press.

Kujovich, Mary Yeager (1970) "The Refrigerated Car and the Growth of the American Dressed Beef Industry," *Business History Review* 44(4):460–482.

Kurlansky, Mark (1998) *Cod: A Biography of the Fish that Changed the World*. New York: Penguin.

Lakshmanan, T.R. and W. Anderson (2002) A White Paper on "Transportation Infrastructure, Freight Services Sector, and Economic Growth," prepared for the U.S. Department of Transportation, Federal Highway Administration, http://www.bu.edu/transportation/WPSeries.html

Lakshmanan, T.R. and William P. Anderson (2007) "Contextual Determinants of Transport Infrastructure Productivity: The Need for Model Reformulation," in Charlie Karlsson, William P. Anderson, Börje Johansson and Kiyoshi Kobayashi (eds.) *The Management and Measurement of Infrastructure: Performance, Efficiency and Innovation*. Cheltenham: Edward Elgar.

Lakshmanan, T.R., William P. Anderson, Yena Song and Dan Li (2009) *Broader Economic Consequences of Transport Infrastructure: The Case of Economic Evolution in Dynamic Transport Corridors*. Report by the Boston University Center for Transportation Studies to the Federal Highway Administration, US Department of Transportation.

Levinson, Marc (2005) *The Box*. Princeton, NJ: Princeton University Press.

Linden, Greg, Kenneth L. Kraemer and Jason Dedrick (2009) "Who Captures Value in a Global Innovation Network: The Case of Apple's iPod," *Communications of the ACM* 53(3):140–144.

Lloyd, Peter E. and Peter Dicken (1977) *Location in Space*, 2nd edn. London: Harper and Row.

Lösch, August (1954) *The Economics of Location*, trans. W.H. Woglom. New Haven, CT: Yale University Press.

Mackie, P.J., M. Wardman, A.S. Fowkes, G. Whelan and J. Nellthorp (2003) *Value of Travel Time Savings in the UK: Report to Department of Transport*. Leeds: Institute for Transport Studies, University of Leeds.

Marcus, Joyce (1973) "Territorial Organization of the Lowland Classic Maya," *Science* 180(4089):911–916.

Marshall, Alfred (1890) *Principles of Economics*. London: Macmillan.

McCallum, Jamie K. (2011) *Export Processing Zones: Comparative Data from China, Honduras, Nicaragua and South Africa*, Working Paper No. 21. Geneva: International Labor Office.

Meadows, Donella H. (1974) *Limits to Growth: A Report for the Club of Rome's Project on the Predicament of Mankind*. New York: Universe Books.

Meijers, Evert (2005) "Polycentric Urban Regions and the Quest for Synergy: Is a Network of Cities More than the Sum of the Parts?" *Urban Studies* 42(4):765–781.

Miller, Ronald E. and Peter D. Blair (1985) *Input–Output Analysis: Foundations and Extensions*. Englewood Cliffs, NJ: Prentice Hall.

Miller, Stephen M. and Oscar W. Jensen (1978) "Location and the Theory of Production: A Review, Summary and Critique of Recent Contributions," *Regional Science and Urban Economics* 8(2):117–128.

Miron, John (1978) "Nucleated Suburbanization in a Competitive Market Economy," *Urban Studies* 15:223–229.

Mokhtarian, Patricia L. (1990) "A Typology of Relations between Telecommunications and Transportation," *Transportation Research, A* 24A(3):231–242.

Mushinski, David and Steven Weiler (2002) "A Note on the Geographic Interdependencies of Retail Areas," *Journal of Regional Science* 48(1):75–86.

Muth, Richard F. (1969) *Cities and Housing*. Chicago: University of Chicago Press.

Myrdal, Gunnar (1957) *Rich Lands and Poor*. New York: Harper and Row.

National Highway Traffic Safety Administration, U.S. Department of Transportation (2011) "AALA Listed by Percentages," http://www.nhtsa.gov/staticfiles/rulemaking/pdf/AALA/2011_AALA_Percent2.pdf

Niedercorn, John H. and B.V. Bechdolt Jr. (1969) "An Economic Derivation of the 'Gravity Law' of Spatial Interaction," *Journal of Regional Science* 9(2):273–282.

Noble, J. (2005) "Fortress America or Fortress North America?" *Law and Business Review of the Americas* 13(3):619–642.

North, Douglas C. (1955) "Location Theory and Regional Economic Growth," *Journal of Political Geography* 63(3):243–258.

Ó hUallacháin, Breandán (2007) "Regional Growth in a Knowledge-based Economy," *International Regional Science Review* 30(3):221–248.

Office of Management and Budget (2000) "Standards for Defining Metropolitan and Micropolitan Statistical Areas; Notice," *Federal Register* 65(249):82228–82238.

Ohmae, Kenichi (1999) *The Borderless World*. New York: HarperCollins.

Organisation for Economic Co-operation and Development (2010) *Measuring Globalization: OECD Economic Globalization Indicators 2010*. Paris: OECD.

Papageorgiou, Yorgos Y. and David Pines (1999) *An Essay on Urban Economic Theory*. Boston, MA: Kluwer.

Parr, John B. (2004) "The Polycentric Urban Region: A Closer Inspection," *Regional Studies* 38(3):231–240.

Pines, David (1975) "On the Spatial Distribution of Households According to Income," *Economic Geography* 51:142–149.

Porter, Michael (1986) *Competition in Global Industries*. Cambridge, MA: Harvard Business Press.

Porter, Michael E. (1990) *The Competitive Advantage of Nations*. New York: Free Press.

Porter, Michael E. (1998) "Clusters and the New Economics of Competition," *Harvard Business Review* 76(6):77–90.

Pred, Alan (1966) *The Spatial Dynamics of U.S. Urban-Industrial Growth: 1800–1924.* Cambridge, MA: MIT Press.

Preston, Richard E. (1983) "The Dynamic Components of Christaller's Central Place Theory and the Theme of Change in his Research," *Canadian Geographer* 27(1):4–16.

Quigley, John M. (1998) "Urban Diversity and Economic Growth," *Journal of Economic Perspectives* 12(2):127–138.

Ravenstein, Ernest George (1889) "The Laws of Migration," *Journal of the Royal Statistical Society* 52(2):241–305.

Rozenblat, Céline and Denise Pumain (2007) "Firm Linkages, Innovation and the Evolution of the Urban System," in Peter Taylor, Ben Derudder, Pieter Saey and Frank Witlox (eds.), *Cities in Globalization.* Oxford: Routledge.

Rosenthal, Stuart S. and William C. Strange (2004) "Evidence on the Nature and Source of Agglomeration Economies," ch. 49 in J.V. Henderson and J.F. Thisse (eds.) *Handbook of Regional and Urban Economics.* Amsterdam: Elsevier.

Rowly, Jennifer (2007) "The Wisdom Hierarchy: Representations of the DIKW Hierarchy," *Journal of Information Science* 33(2):163–180.

Saxenian, A. (1994) *Regional Advantage: Culture and Competition in Silicon Valley and Route 128.* Cambridge, MA: Harvard University Press.

Saxenian, A. (2006) *The New Argonauts: Regional Advantage in a Global Economy.* Cambridge MA: Harvard University Press.

Scott, Allen J. (1988) *New Industrial Spaces.* London: Pion.

Scott, Allen J. and Agostino Mantegna (2009) "Human Capital Assets and Structures of Work in the US Metropolitan Hierarchy," *International Regional Science Review* 32(2):173–194.

Sjastaad, L.A. (1962) "The Costs and Returns of Human Migration," *Journal of Political Economy* Supplement, 70:80–93.

Smith, Adam (1776) *An Inquiry into the Nature and Causes of the Wealth of Nations.* London: W. Strahan and T. Cadell.

Sobel, Irvin (1954) "Collective Bargaining and Decentralization in the Rubber-tire Industry," *Journal of Political Economy* 62(1):12–25.

Soo, Kwok Tong (2005) "Zipf's Law for Cities: A Cross-country Investigation," *Regional Science and Urban Economics* 35:239–263.

Storper, Michael (1997) *The Regional World: Territorial Development in the Global Economy.* New York: Guilford Press.

Stuart, Toby and Olav Sorenson (2003) "The Geography of Opportunity: Spatial Heterogeneity in Founding Rates and Performance in Biotechnology Firms," *Research Policy* 32(2):229–253.

Sull, Donald N. (2003) "The Co-evolution of Technology and Industrial Clusters: The Rise and Fall of the Akron Tire Cluster," London Business School, unpublished paper available at: http://www.donsull.com/downloads/cluster_inertia.pdf (accessed August 17, 2011).

Tabuchi, T. and A. Yoshida (2000) "Separating Agglomeration Economies in Production and Consumption," *Journal of Urban Economics* 20:211–228.

Taylor, J., D.R. Robideaux and G.C. Jackson (2004) "U.S.–Canada Transportation and Logistics: Border Impacts and Costs, Causes and Possible Solutions," *Transportation Journal* 43(4):5–21.

Tellier, Luc-Normand (1972) "The Weber Problem: Solution and Interpretation," *Geographical Analysis* 4(3):215–233.

Thünen, J.H. von (1966) *Isolated State: An English Edition of Der Isolierte Staat*, trans. P. Hall. London: Pergamon. (Original German edition published in 1826.)

Tiebout, Charles (1956) "A Pure Theory of Local Expenditures," *Journal of Political Economy* 64(5):416–424

Ullman, Edward L. (1956) "The Role of Transportation and the Bases for Interaction," pp. 862–880 in W.L. Thomas (ed.) *Man's Role in Changing the Face of the Earth*. Chicago: University of Chicago Press.

U.S. Bureau of Economic Analysis (n.d. a) "Fixed Asset Table, Table 3.2ES Chain-Type Quantity Indexes for Net Stock of Private Fixed Assets by Industry," http://192.149.12.20/national/FA2004/TablePrint.asp?FirstYear=1948&LastYear=1948&Freq=Year&SelectedTable=23&ViewSeries=Yes&Java=Yes&MaxValue=144.562&MaxChars=7&Request3Place=N&3Place=N&FromView=YES&Legal=&Land=

U.S. Bureau of Economic Analysis (n.d. b) "National Income and Product Accounts, Table 6.5 (A-D) Full Time Equivalent Employees by Industry," http://www.bea.gov/national/FA2004/TableView.asp?SelectedTable=23&FirstYear=2005&LastYear=2010&Freq=Year&JavaBox=Y

U.S. Census Bureau (2009) *Annual Estimates of the Population of Metropolitan and Micropolitan Statistical Areas: April 1, 2000 to July 1, 2009 (CBSA-EST-2009-2)*. Washington, DC: U.S. Department of Commerce.

U.S. Office of Management and Budget (2000) "Standards for Defining Metropolitan and Micropolitan Statistical Areas: Notice," *Federal Register* 65(249):82228–82238.

Varian, Hal R. (1992) *Microeconomic Analysis*, 3rd edn. New York: Norton.

Varmin, Rohit and Russell W. Belk (2009) "Nationalism and Ideology in an Anticonsumption Movement," *Journal of Consumer Research* 36(4):686–700.

Von Hippel, E. (1994) "Sticky Information and the Locus of Problem Solving: Implications for Innovation," *Management Science* 40:429–439.

Weber, Alfred (1929) *Theory of the Location of Industries*, translated from the 1909 German edition by Carl J. Friedrich, Chicago: University of Chicago Press.

Weber, Christopher L. and H. Scott Matthews (2008) "Food-miles and the Relative Climate Impacts of Food Choices in the United States," *Environmental Science and Technology* 42(10):3508–3513.

Wolf, Martin (2004) *Why Globalization Works*. New Haven, CT: Yale University Press.

World Bank (2006) *2006 World Development Indicators*. Washington, DC: The World Bank.

World Bank (2007) *2007 World Development Indicators*. Washington, DC: The World Bank.

World Bank (2009) *World Development Report 2009*. Washington, DC: The World Bank.

World Resources Institute (n.d.) Earth Trends: The Environmental Information Portal, http://earthtrends.wri.org/searchable_db/index.php?action=select_theme&theme=8

World Trade Organization (2009) *World Tariff Profiles*. Geneva: WTO.

Yeates, Maurice (1975) *Main Street: Windsor to Quebec City*. Toronto: Macmillan Canada.

Yeates, Maurice and Barry Garner (1976) *The North American City*, 3rd edn. New York: Harper and Row.

Zipf, George K. (1949) *Human Behavior and the Principle of Least Effort*. New York: Addison-Wesley.

# Index